The Independent Filmmaker's
Law and Business Guide

—— **THIRD EDITION** ——

Financing, Shooting, and Distributing
Independent Films and Series

JON M. GARON

Published by Chicago Review Press Incorporated
814 North Franklin Street
Chicago, IL 60610
ISBN 978-1-64160-424-6

Library of Congress Cataloging-in-Publication Data
Names: Garon, Jon M., author.
Title: The independent filmmaker's law and business guide : financing,
    shooting, and distributing independent films and series / Jon M. Garon.
Description: Third edition. | Chicago, IL : Chicago Review Press, [2021] |
    Includes bibliographical references. | Summary: "Preparing independent
    or guerrilla filmmakers for the legal, financial, and organizational
    questions that can doom a project if unanswered, this guide demystifies
    issues such as developing a concept, founding a film company, obtaining
    financing, securing locations, casting, shooting, granting screen
    credits, and distributing, exhibiting, and marketing a film. Updated to
    include digital marketing and distribution strategies through YouTube or
    webisodes, online streaming, crowdfunding, and the importance of
    diversity, inclusion, and compensation equity"— Provided by publisher.
Identifiers: LCCN 2021011039 (print) | LCCN 2021011040 (ebook) | ISBN
    9781641604246 (trade paperback) | ISBN 9781641604253 (adobe pdf) | ISBN
    9781641604277 (epub) | ISBN 9781641604260 (kindle edition)
Subjects: LCSH: Motion picture industry—United States—Finance. | Motion
    pictures—United States—Distribution. | Motion picture
    industry—Finance—Law and legislation—United States. | Motion
    pictures—Distribution—Law and legislation—United States. | Motion
    picture industry—Law and legislation—United States. | Independent
    filmmakers.
Classification: LCC PN1993.5.U6 G34 2021 (print) | LCC PN1993.5.U6
    (ebook) | DDC 384/.830973—dc23
LC record available at https://lccn.loc.gov/2021011039
LC ebook record available at https://lccn.loc.gov/2021011040

Cover design: Sadie Teper
Cover photo: Chris Murray/Unsplash
Interior design: Jonathan Hahn

Printed in the United States of America
5 4 3 2 1

To my mother, Lorraine Garon,
the creative artist who inspired us above all others.

Contents

PART ① MAKING A FILM COMPANY TO MAKE A MOVIE

Preface

With a video camera and an Internet connection, anyone can shoot a movie. Advancements in film and digital video camera technology have made it easier than ever to access quality equipment. But as independent film companies have proliferated, competing for funding and audiences has become more challenging than ever before. Professional filmmaking requires much more than just access to equipment; it also requires a deep understanding of the laws, contracts, and business practices that shape the production and distribution of motion pictures. Whether a filmmaker is interested in creating documentaries, fictional films, or docudramas, the filmmaker must understand the rules to bring a story to life on film, the techniques to sell that film, and the strategies to promote the film to audiences.

The Independent Filmmaker's Law and Business Guide provides a distillation of the best practical advice available for independent filmmakers today. It answers the legal, financial, and organizational questions that an independent or guerrilla filmmaker must face, problems that will doom a project if left unanswered. In chronological order, it demystifies issues such as developing a concept, founding a film company, obtaining financing, casting, securing locations, shooting, granting screen credits, distributing, exhibiting, and marketing a film. It even anticipates the "problems" generated by a blockbuster hit: soundtrack albums, merchandizing, and licensing.

This third edition includes new chapters that deal with the unique concerns of documentary filmmaking and unfinanced productions. Other chapters have been expanded to provide guidance on the use of film clips, soundtracks, background artwork, and commercial products. The new edition also provides comprehensive coverage of domestic and international distribution and addresses new possibilities for digital distribution through Internet retailers and online digital media outlets. Expanded appendixes offer sample contracts, copyright circulars, a guide to writing credits, studio contact information, and a host of other resources that provide the filmmaker with all the tools necessary to make a successful film.

Introduction

Technology has transformed the way the entertainment industry does business. Netflix, Amazon Prime Video, Disney+, and myriad streaming platforms have entered into a crowded field once dominated by YouTube. For film distributors, new technologies are transforming the system of print distribution that has existed since the end of the 19th century. Internet video sites provide direct distribution opportunities for short films and episodic content that will only increase as technology prices continue dropping and bandwidth continues to improve on mobile devices.

Technology is also changing the medium itself. Film, the standard medium of the feature motion picture since its inception, has been replaced with digital recording devices. Digital technologies have made low-cost filmmaking possible for everyone while adding editorial technologies that have blurred the distinction between live action and animation. Since today's special effects rely heavily on digital manipulation of the image, capturing that image directly in the digital medium eliminates one step of the process, adding greater speed and flexibility. And with digital equipment, feature-length and short films can be made for hundreds rather than hundreds of thousands or millions of dollars. The Internet has opened new distribution methods for these low-budget projects that expand the potential audience well beyond the traditional college campus and film festival circuit. At a minimum, they are creating new opportunities for rookie filmmakers to showcase their skills to the traditional industry. At the same time, as the amount of content has exploded in recent years, the challenge to find an audience has become harder than ever.

Despite the increased opportunities to make and distribute a movie, many artistic, business, and legal barriers continue to frustrate filmmakers and stop movies from being completed or distributed. This book was written to provide guidance through the rocky waters of independent motion picture production for low-budget feature films, shorts, and serialized productions.

Making a movie, even a small-budget, backyard production, is a long process of negotiating and signing contracts; complying with labor, health, safety, and revenue codes; recognizing and protecting the rights of artists, writers, musicians, performers, bystanders, and others; and becoming a specialist in dozens of areas of business and law in a matter of weeks. This book will serve as your guide.

About This Book

This book is a guide, not a blueprint. At some point in the process, the filmmaker must build a team that includes not only a cast and crew but also a lawyer and an accountant. But the book should save the filmmaker legal fees, eliminating hours an attorney would have to spend explaining the items discussed in the book.

The book does not constitute the practice of law or provide legal advice that can be relied upon as authoritative. This information is general in nature, and should only be used in conjunction with a licensed attorney properly familiar with the issues presented in the specific legal matter in question.

This book identifies particular individuals, firms, and companies. Nothing herein constitutes an endorsement of these entities or of their services, and the book cannot be relied upon as the legal basis for engaging such services.

Although many of the companies listed are the largest or most visible in the respective fields, the names are used either for illustrative purposes or to provide a starting point for the reader's own research. Conversely, the failure to appear in the book should not be deemed a negative assessment of any particular product, service, or organization.

The book uses some terms that might not seem appropriate. The most striking is to call the digital creation of a motion picture *filmmaking* and the creators *filmmakers*. The choice reflects the history of the craft rather than the current state of the medium. Historically based terms evolve new meanings. Americans still use the term *album* for a collection of songs recorded and sold together as a compilation, although the cardboard album that held a collection of 78 RPM records has been long abandoned as the distribution mechanism for music. Motion pictures that run longer than an hour will remain *feature films* long after the celluloid and optical processes that originally characterized them have faded into distant memory like cardboard albums.

A Chronology: From Idea to Academy Awards

Independent filmmaking generally begins with a single idea, an original concept that will serve as the core of the film project. The owner of that idea may be a writer who can shape the idea into a written script, a director who can visualize how to tell that story, a performer who knows how to portray a character central to the story, or a producer who knows where to find the elements for telling the story. Using the areas of expertise of the filmmaker, the originator of the idea shares the concept with the other creative people necessary to translate the idea into a story, and the story into a screenplay. Even at this early stage, many legal and business choices must be made. One individual becomes the "owner" and others become employees of that owner—or the parties agree to work as partners, or choose a more complex legal relationship. The idea is translated from something not protected by copyright into an expressive work that cannot be copied without the owner's consent (although the ideas and general plot concept will not be protected by copyright). Rights to the story must be acquired, the production entity formed, budgets penciled in, and some employment commitments initiated.

Once the organizational approach has been selected and the script developed, the creative process moves into high gear. A script can be shared with potential investors, shown to actors, entered into contests, and used to introduce the project to the public. Fundraising can range from simple loans from the filmmaker's family to very sophisticated financial transactions. Crowdfunding campaigns can build an audience as well as help pay for the project. Financial decisions must be made carefully to protect the growth and success of the filmmaker's vision.

A successful script will gain momentum for the project. If the filmmaker is not the director, then a director will be selected. With a working script, the director and producer can agree on a budget for the film that can range from the cost of buying (or even borrowing) the cheapest of cameras to a budget in excess of $250 million for an effects-laden film with well-known stars. The budget—not the screenplay—may also dictate where filming will take place. Locations are selected or rejected based on availability, the cost of filming in those locations, and the locations' ability to further the story.

The director, having accepted a working script and projected budget, can begin to make casting choices. Actors are auditioned or interviewed for parts. Since casting is often about chemistry and the interaction of actors with each other, it becomes a logistical puzzle: the director must make offers so the right combination of people will accept. At the same time, the director needs to assemble the creative crew behind the camera. A cinematographer and set, lighting, and costume designers are hired to refine the decisions tentatively made by the producer and director.

Throughout the preproduction process, money is needed. The director, writer, and producer may require payments. Expenses begin to mount for the budgeting, casting, and design work. As the money is found, so are the additional people necessary to build the project. Additional writers, producers, directors, designers, and cameramen are hired and added to the team. The script will undergo changes to accommodate the locations available, the cast assembled, and the suggestions of the growing production team. With efforts underway to finalize script revisions, select locations, rent equipment, secure financing, and finish casting, production can begin.

Preproduction ends and principal photography begins with the first day of filming. Each day, a few more minutes of film footage are captured. Filming is often done out of sequence, based on weather; availability of locations, sets, or cast; and other script requirements. Typically, the day's work is reviewed each evening. The rough footage from the day's shooting is typically described using historical terms *dailies* or *rushes*. Each day's work is reviewed to be sure the production is ready to move on to the next scene. As the footage accumulates, rough editing of the film may be taking place. Finally, after weeks or months of filming, principal photography ends.

With the filming completed, the filmmaker is halfway home. The next stage of the process is postproduction. The footage is edited into a cohesive, linear film that hopefully translates the filmmaker's original idea into a visual narrative form. A composer creates a musical score to highlight the story and enhance the effectiveness of the film. Sound effects, songs, and special effects are added. The finished film, complete with sound, is finally ready for marketing and distribution.

If the film is an independent production, then often no prior arrangements exist for its marketing and distribution. If the filmmaker is not also marketing the film directly online, the filmmaker will present the film to potential distributors and negotiate for payments based on an advance and a portion of the royalties. Distributors are often exposed to independent films through film festivals or film markets, but independent filmmakers can also send a copy of the film to potential distributors without waiting for entry into competitions.

Once a distributor buys the rights to a motion picture, it takes over, creating or changing the marketing of the film. If the film runs in movie theaters in the United States, it becomes eligible for a number of award competitions. If the film remains as potent on the screen as it was in the original concept, the filmmaker's peers in the industry may vote to nominate the film for an Oscar from the Academy of Motion Picture Arts and Sciences. Following exhibition in US movie theaters, the film may be distributed in movie theaters throughout the rest of the world. After theatrical distribution comes distribution on streaming platforms or through DVD sales and through pay-per-view cable television. Although the DVD sales market has declined significantly, certain titles still sell well in retail stores. Approximately a year after theatrical distribution come showings on premium cable (e.g., HBO or Showtime), then broadcast television, then finally basic cable. If successful, the movie could be shown for decades, or even centuries, to come.

At each stage in this process, the filmmaking team must make hundreds of artistic, business, and legal decisions. Some of those choices are truly unique to the particular film. Other choices, however, have been faced by many filmmakers before.

Most important, filmmaking is a long, complicated, and complex process, involving thousands of choices, strong personalities, and emotional decisions. Given the pressures of too little time and money, even small mistakes can be exacerbated by poor communication or haphazard planning and escalate into disaster. To reduce that risk, the filmmaker must be proactive; the producer and director together must anticipate and plan for future crises and fully understand the consequences of every choice they make. That's where *The Independent Filmmaker's Law and Business Guide* comes in. It analyzes each stage in the process in detail, outlines the common choices available to the film production team, and provides information for making the most appropriate decision under the circumstances.

Please remember this book when you thank the Academy for your Oscar.

Making a Film Company to Make a Movie

Preparing to Make a Film or Media Project

Only one thing separates great films from the thousands of finished films that go undistributed each year: great storytelling. A powerful story featuring engaging characters, dramatic tension, and a well-crafted plot helps make a successful movie. What went on behind the camera or in the cutting room rarely influences the audience's experience watching the film. Most viewers will never know whether the filmmaker was delighted with the completed film or devastated that the first choice of cast rejected the script. The audience pays the same price for the theater seat and popcorn whether the film's budget was $250,000 or $250 million.

But at each stage in the filmmaking process, business and financial decisions will affect the story being told as much or more than the artistic decisions. Without the business structure, casts will not be paid, locations will not be available, and the film cannot be exhibited. The filmmaker's job is to manage the tremendous amount of time, funds, talent, and energy expended offscreen to ensure the best possible result onscreen. During the feverish pace of principal photography, a director has little opportunity for reflection. Effective preparation and thoughtful contingency planning made in advance of the filming can save a movie from ruin. The more thoroughly the filmmaker has prepared every step in the filmmaking process, the better chance there is for creating a finished film that captures the original vision.

A. Who Is the Filmmaker?

Filmmaking is a communal process. The filmmaker becomes a parent, artistic mentor, instructor, boss, and police officer to the small army that join together to bring the filmmaker's vision to the screen. Although each project requires a strong writer, producer, and director to shape the process, each one has a very different set of responsibilities and priorities. As a result, there is a constant tension among the three. Ultimately, the filmmaker will dictate how those tensions are resolved and bring together the creative and business aspects of the film. The filmmaker stands at the center of every production, serving as its spine and brain.

It is important that the filmmaker on the team be recognized early. Productions vary, but generally the filmmaker will be the producer or director, or occasionally the writer. Typically, a single individual holds the role, but a collaborative team may share the duties.

1. Independent vs. Guerrilla Filmmaking

Guerrilla filmmaking is a special subspecies of independent filmmaking. The guerrilla filmmaker is generally a storyteller with a vision. Sources for guerrilla films come from the stage, from life experience, or from literature that transfixes the filmmaker and makes the production the only reason for being. Spike Lee, producer/director/writer/actor of *Do the Right Thing*; Jim Jarmusch, producer/director/writer of *Night on Earth*; Robert Rodriguez, writer/director of *El Mariachi*; and John Sayles, writer/director of *Eight Men Out* and *Matewan*, are a few of the more prominent guerrilla artists, but many established filmmakers, including Michael Apted, Joel and Ethan Coen, Keenen Ivory Wayans, David Zucker, Jerry Zucker, Jim Abrahams, and Taika Waititi created their first films as guerrilla filmmakers. The great Orson Welles ended his career as a guerrilla filmmaker, having divorced from Hollywood.

The essence of the guerrilla filmmaker is twofold. First, the filmmaker must need, desire, and crave to bring a project of particular passion and vision—not just any movie—to the screen. Second, the filmmaker must have this craving despite the fact that no money, social network, business connections, studio interest, or external support exists to make this possible. This contrasts guerrilla filmmakers with famous low-budget filmmakers like Ed Wood and Roger Corman. Both Wood and Corman were low-budget, B-film powerhouses, but their primary drive was not passion for a particular project but a desire to get in and out of a film as quickly as possible.

Another way to describe the guerrilla filmmaker is to characterize the director/producer like any other filmmaker—only more so. The guerrilla filmmaker is an entrepreneur with the desire to make a film rather than start a business. Like the typical entrepreneur, the guerrilla filmmaker is an extreme risk taker. By contrast, the traditional independent filmmaker described in this book is a more cautious businessperson, typically more willing to make reasonable compromises to make a film. Both the traditional independent filmmaker and the guerrilla filmmaker will use loans to make their films, but only the guerrilla would be willing to mortgage the film-maker's house—or the houses of friends and family. This book will outline the path for the independent filmmaker, but wherever possible it will also note those few guideposts available to help the guerrilla filmmaker cut a new trail.

2. Independent vs. Studio Filmmaking

Independent filmmaking, whether traditional or guerrilla, is different from a studio production because, unlike with many commercial films, an independent film dictates the package. Producers of studio films often describe their preproduction development as "creating a package." They create line-ups of stars, bestsellers, merchandizing tie-ins, audience demographics, locations, directors, and writers that, if executed properly, will inevitably result in blockbusters.

Independent and guerrilla filmmakers, on the other hand, focus on a personal vision instead of working to accommodate stars, investors, prior contractual commitments, or audience response cards. Unlike carefully packaged studio films, movies by smart independent filmmakers tend to be highly opportunistic, using available locations, actors, situations, or other organic elements that can enhance or even redirect the story. As a result, many of the steps in the independent filmmaking process are different than with studio productions. Still, when everything works, the resulting films are the best the industry can create.

Given the tremendous consolidation in the entertainment industry, independent moviemaking has become increasingly difficult to define. Technically, an independent feature is any film not made at one of the major studios—Sony (home to Columbia Pictures, MGM, and United Artists), Warner Bros., Universal, Disney, or Paramount. Twentieth Century Fox, long a leading studio, sold its film divisions to Disney and ended over a century of filmmaking.

For a 10-year period beginning in 1996, independent films were considered a very profitable market. All the major studios acquired independent production companies or developed their own indie houses, creating a group of production entities that were small and somewhat autonomous but still within the influence of the studio system. A decade later, the independent studios largely retreated. Lionsgate became the exception; it has eclipsed its role as an independent producer by acquiring many other independents to become a major studio.

Beginning in 2018, a new production race emerged among the growing list of online streaming services. Competition between Netflix and Amazon Prime Video has initiated a revolution in the distribution of film and series content that most broadcasters are struggling to keep up with. These companies are increasingly using theatrical distribution to bolster their catalogs, upending the traditional distribution windows and film acquisition models. Netflix and Amazon have essentially redefined the role of the studio. Disney has been the most aggressive of the traditional studios to follow their lead, giving Disney a leadership position among both the original studios and the new online streamers.

For first-time filmmakers, the largest practical difference between studio and independent filmmaking is the amount of authority and control they retain over artistic and budgetary decisions. With an independent film, the filmmaker possesses substantial autonomy in these decisions— usually accompanied by significant financial risk. If the film has studio distribution, each major decision is usually subject to approval by the studio, and such approvals generally transform the project from an independent film into studio product.

3. The Filmmaker's Team

Filmmaking is an intensely collaborative, communal process. While there are exceptional guerrilla filmmakers who can successfully walk around with a handheld camera, capture content, edit it themselves, and compose their own score to accompany their film, most films require a large company of specialists to bring the project to completion. Composed initially of a director, writer, and producer, the production team should quickly grow to include members of the business and artistic teams. In the beginning, the prospective team members may simply be consulted for their availability and interest in the project. But once a decision to go forward with a film is made, there is often limited opportunity to deal with logistical concerns before principal photography must begin. If the filmmaker lines up the team in advance, launch of the film company will go much more smoothly, and the team behind the film will have the time needed to build a common vision.

The artistic team includes the location manager, the director of photography, and designers for sets, costumes, and lighting. Collaboration between the director and this group of professionals will help clarify the vision of the film and establish the look and feel of the project. The artistic team should also include the principal actors. The leading actors will champion their characters, and the filmmaker will need them to display their enthusiasm for the script during the struggles for financing and distribution. An independent film with committed actors is far more likely to succeed than one with a cast that treats it like just another job.

The business team should include a line producer, a law firm, accountants, and key investors. Inexperienced filmmakers often wait too long to seek the assistance of lawyers and accountants. Since many of the critical decisions regarding financing, production, and distribution are made quite early in development, filmmakers should not try to avoid the costs of experienced legal and financial counsel. Mistakes in structuring the financing can close down a production or lead to criminal violations of securities laws.

Filmmakers should also consider their lead investors to be part of the filmmaking process. For projects that require more funding than is available from a family member or a credit card, the investors' opinions on the business structure and financing strategy will be critical to success. Moreover, few investors are willing to tie up their funds unless they know the funding will be completed, so first investors are harder to lure into a project than later investors. But film investors are generally willing to invest because of their interest in the project. Allowing them to contribute to the business strategy can help solidify their support and encourage them to help raise the necessary additional funds.

4. Integrating Online and Social Media

One of the greatest cultural changes in the 21st century has been the growth of social media as a wholly new medium of social engagement. Social media has had the same revolutionary cultural influence as radio and television had when each of those platforms was introduced. And unlike radio and television, the open content model allows anyone to go online and develop an audience. Not since the earliest days of unregulated radio has the public been presented with such a chaotic and expansive set of media choices.

For the purposes of independent and guerrilla filmmaking, social media has become an essential element of the production mix. While a filmmaker could choose to ignore all social media and hope that the sale of the film to a large distributor will relieve the filmmaker of social media engagement, most independent films find success by embracing social media opportunities.

Social media is both an audiovisual arts platform and a marketing platform for more traditional films and series. YouTube dominates video sharing for both amateur and professional content, but mobile apps such as TikTok, Cheez, Funimate, and Likee make short-form videos and video editing easy for anyone with a smartphone. Many of these apps are also social media platforms, enabling content creators to build audiences and popularity. Filmmakers can use these platforms to create video storyboards, test material, and gain a following to help sell their films.

Social media is also important for sharing text and images in order to develop an audience for a project, build a community around the filmmaker, and potentially finance the project. As such, today's independent productions should involve a senior production team member and additional staff to engage the audience from the earliest stages of the production.

The filmmakers will also want senior leadership on the team to be sure that any private or confidential information does not leak onto social media. Every outdoor location will risk being filmed by casual observers. Cast and crew will often share clips and stories online. To the extent that a production does not want plotlines or locations to leak, the use of social media must be carefully managed. As a result, whether the filmmaker views social media as a blessing or a curse, it must still be managed throughout the production process.

B. Selecting the Scale

By choosing to make an independent film, the filmmaker has already begun to make the first critical decision regarding the film: determining the scale of the production. The scale determines the size of the cast and crew and how much they are paid, the cost of the locations, the nature of the equipment to be used, the extent of any special effects, and the length of the shoot. These aspects of a production need not be proportional to each other, but they usually are.

It is commonly assumed that the subject matter dictates scale, but this is a misconception. A two-person love story can be told in exotic locales with expensive panoramic shots, requiring a budget of well over $150 million. A story about Alexander the Great or Napoleon can distill the conflict into a personal tragedy that can be shot for far less than $1 million.

1. Talent, Location, and FX

The scale is primarily based on the three components of a production that account for the greatest range of costs: above-the-line talent, locations, and special effects and/or visual effects. A Marvel superhero movie will feature famous actors, exotic locations, and very expensive special effects and visual (digital) effects. The production costs for such a movie now exceed $250 million.

The scale of the production will dictate every subsequent choice. It shapes the vision of the filmmaker. For example, Francis Ford Coppola tells of his original concept for *Apocalypse Now:* he hoped to sneak his independent production company into Vietnam to shoot the film surreptitiously against the backdrop of the actual "police action." Instead, the movie was shot in the Philippines after Coppola had become a Hollywood success. The production became a bloated Hollywood extravaganza that required well over a year of principal photography. The scale of the movie had changed in the filmmaker's mind, reshaping every decision regarding the production.

Independent filmmakers often back into the scale of their projects based on the financial resources available. If they choose to avoid most unions, they will have a lower budget but may face unanticipated costs caused by a relatively inexperienced talent and crew. If they choose to acquire the film rights to a particular novel, short story, or comic book, the rights holders may require them to adopt a higher budget and a higher-profile cast as a condition of selling the rights. In each case, the key decision sets the scale against which all other budgetary decisions will be made.

Setting the overall scale of the film production may not be a conscious choice, but the individual decisions that determine scale are usually carefully considered. Most filmmakers have definite opinions about available financing, locations, visual effects, and Screen Actors Guild member actors. Together, these preferences set the scale of the production. Being aware of them and the scale they imply will help the filmmaker prepare for the many choices that will flow from this first step in the filmmaking process.

2. Realities of the New Normal for Media Distribution

Since the introduction of Napster in 1999, media distribution has never been the same. The ability to get music, television, and film for free (even if illegally) has reshaped consumer expectations and practices. Publishing always faced the pressure of lending libraries, so the transition has been more gradual. For music, the change was catastrophic, with the industry losing two thirds of its revenue from its peak in 1999 to its low in 2015. While streaming has reversed the trend, the total music industry revenue remains less than half what it was in inflation-adjusted dollars.

Film and television are following the model established by the music industry, though the transition is more gradual. Since broadcast and basic cable are largely advertiser-funded and therefore free to the consumer, the pressure for uncompensated free content was less dramatic. At the same time, the new technologies created billions of hours of additional content with which film and television companies needed to compete.

The lessons from the interactive streaming service model have pervaded the film and television markets. Led by Netflix and Amazon Prime Video, more and more artists are looking to streaming services as their first choice in high-quality, commercial distribution. Some of these deals include short theatrical releases. However, given the challenges for the filmmaker to see a profit at the box office from anything other than blockbusters produced with $200+ million budgets, the freedom and immediacy of the streaming market has become the first choice for many.

Disney+, Paramount+, Hulu, and streaming alternatives by most of the television conglomerates will continue to acquire and produce content much more like television than the highly eclectic content hosted by Netflix. In part, this is because of the content ownership model of these conglomerates, which has little room for independent productions. In part, it is driven by the scale and business model of publicly traded media companies.

The difference between streaming on a premier platform like Netflix or Amazon Prime Video and self-publishing a streaming channel on YouTube or Twitch is much narrower than between producing a movie for Disney and producing an independent production. The production company must establish its approach to content distribution early, incorporate it into the business plan, and organize the marketing approach around that strategy. At a minimum, this means deciding whether the company is producing a single, feature-length project or intending to create a series of shorts or hour-long episodes. Either a feature or a series of shorts will be easier to produce than a series of hour-long episodes, and both have more market distribution alternatives.

Independent film continues to thrive, but increasingly the field is shifting to online, streamed distribution either through the large streaming services or through the self-published options provided by YouTube and similar platforms. The business plans for the filmmaker should incorporate both traditional independent distribution venues and the online options, with a realistic approach to the revenue opportunities that have shifted to streaming income.

C. Twitch, YouTube, and the Online Personal Presence

The proliferation of media platforms has opened the marketplace to the production of short-form and long-form audiovisual works as a cinematic journaling experience. YouTube channels, web series distributed through Twitch, and a multitude of other platforms and formats allow anyone with a home computer and cell phone to become a movie mogul. Add great storytelling, acting, and creativity, and the audience may come calling.

Approximately 700 feature films are released theatrically in the United States each year. Globally, YouTube shows 5 billion videos daily. The world has moved online, and the competition for the audience is in the digital space. Forbes has reported that the top YouTube earners in 2017 exceed $20 million in revenue and around the same in viewership. These filmmakers and content producers did not need to negotiate for final cut, sit through test screen audiences, or suffer the distribution strategies of commercial distributors. On the other hand, those content producers were operating large-scale business operations and marketing platforms, not merely posting content.

Video blogging, or "vlogging," daredevil stunt and extreme sports videos, and other genres of the personal online narrative often have the look and feel of cell phone productions. In practice, however, these formats can create a powerful ongoing narrative relationship between the filmmaker and the audience, much like the audience relationship created in daytime television. To the extent that these projects involve small teams of performers, the interaction and dynamic among the team members can create character relationships similar to soap operas.

Although these productions often appear rather haphazard and unedited, that may not reflect the actual production work that goes into them. As the audience for a particular title grows and the opportunities to monetize the viewership with associated advertising increases, these episodic productions will have the same issues involving locations, crew, cast, rights clearance, product endorsements, and other issues as do all short films and features.

The vlogger, however, has a very different revenue model than the feature filmmaker. Vloggers post on a regular basis, often daily or weekly. The videos do not have a market for theatrical distributors. Instead, they will be supported by advertising. Typically, the vlogger hosts these to the vlogger's own website, earning advertising revenue based on the traffic to the site. The vlogger might also earn revenue from companies that pay for commercial exposure and endorsements. The goal of these videos is to maximize the size of the audience to the vlogger's website to maximize the return on advertising and value in the commercial endorsements.

Alternatively, the vlogger may choose to distribute the videos on a channel within YouTube, Twitch, or another content aggregator. The video platforms generate much more traffic than stand-alone websites, but the competition to keep the audience attuned to the vlogger's site might be stiffer. Most vloggers tend to experiment with the mix of private sites and platforms, shifting these resources as the audience changes with new technologies and trends.

Although video blogging and distribution of video content on YouTube and similar sites is more than a decade old, the technologies and audience expectations are still in a great deal of flux. What works for maximizing audience this month may be very different from three months earlier or three months from now. Vloggers must be very active in testing and retesting their assumptions about audience preferences and move the content to follow this highly dynamic flow.

D. Planning

A filmmaker may be compared to a military general, commanding armies of cast and crew. If the plan of engagement has not been carefully developed, if contingencies have not been incorporated into the plan, the campaign will falter in the field. Once in the heat of battle, the opportunity for careful planning has been lost. Effective generals and artistic filmmakers are great at improvising because both have planned ahead and are able to incorporate any necessary changes into their overall strategy.

Well before principal photography begins, the filmmaker should have reviewed all the delivery obligations for the project to ensure that the script meets all artistic and legal needs, the right shots are taken, the correct releases are signed, the funds will be disbursed, the locations are available despite any vagaries of the weather, the materials for marketing are created, the postproduction process is ready, and the strategy to distribute or sell to a distributor is fully thought out. Even in the case of the vlogger, the arc of the storyline, the locations, and the highlights of each season should be prepared carefully in advance. For the feature filmmaker, structural planning is even more important.

1. Planning for Distribution

Good planning dictates that the filmmaker consider the challenges, demands, and expectations for exhibition and distribution of the film. At a minimum, distribution requirements dictate the running length of the film and the level of adult content. Very few theatrical distributors will accept a film that is too long or cannot receive an MPAA rating of R or lower. While runtime is not as important for online streamers, the ratings will be even more important. Countries in many regions of the world impose censorship standards on films, requiring the filmmaker to edit the film appropriately for that country. The filmmaker should plan to shoot alternate versions of potentially problematic scenes, so the story can be edited easily to address issues of alcohol, nudity, profanity, blasphemy, and other subjects likely to trigger censorial cutting.

The economics of independent film are highly volatile. Markets for feature films and documentaries change from year to year, and from subject to subject. Streaming has upended the market, creating a strong demand for content. For some filmmakers, this has led to strong sales, but these platforms often pay very poorly for many independent films. Eventually, the spending on content by these platforms will level off. Meanwhile, the streaming services have killed what was once a healthy DVD rental market, and they have nearly ended the sales of DVDs. Premium and basic cable is beginning to feel the effects of the change in consumer behavior as well.

Filmmakers should build their productions with the understanding that a feature-length, narrative film might be able to receive a theatrical distribution, but it is much more likely to go straight onto a streaming platform.

If the potential distributors believe an audience will pay for the theatrical experience, they will be much more likely to invest in the marketing for a theatrical release.

Audience engagement often begins with utilizing familiar material. There are many works quite popular that exist in the public domain, which means that the filmmaker can acquire a familiar title or story for free. Even works protected by copyright may be surprisingly low cost. Novels from 20 years ago are not in high demand by the studios, so the publishers and authors may be interested in modern updates. The name recognition from these strategies can go a long way to launch a career. It explains the long list of films about Frankenstein, Dracula, the dog from *The Call of the Wild*, Sherlock Holmes, Don Quixote, and other iconic literary characters.

Audience engagement is also helped considerably by casting recognizable stars. Realistically, most independent films do not have access to movie stars that can open a motion picture on a national platform. Nonetheless, there might be casting opportunities for performers who have built up some audience recognition, and this can often help the filmmaker. Films that tell a sufficiently important story may also gain some assistance with actors who have an affinity for the material.

The new filmmaker can also take steps to build an online presence. Based on the story, cast, locations, and genre, the independent film company should utilize social media to build awareness and gain an audience. The company might focus on background information, interviews, crowdfunding, and other content that generates interest. While social media platforms are often free, producing the content is not. Budget and staffing decisions should take these costs into account.

2. Planning for the Filmmaker's Future

Good planning requires the filmmaker to be vigilant regarding the goal of the production. For some filmmakers, the goal may be to launch a film company. For others, the goal is simply to gain experience and increase their employability in the entertainment industry. An actor-turned-filmmaker may want to prove that the performer has the artistic range to play a role, the vision to shape particular content, and the clout to have the film distributed nationally. Another filmmaker may have a passion to tell a specific story, and once that film or documentary is distributed, the filmmaker may not make another film. Some filmmakers are focused on their own artistic expressions, and they have little regard for the size of their audiences. Each of these examples reflects a very different reason to make an independent film. Each will require different choices during the process.

For the filmmaker hoping to launch a business, the development of ongoing relations with investors and vendors becomes a significant part of the planning. Such a filmmaker may wish to convince investors to prepare for investing in a few movies before making money, with protections that all investments will be repaid if the money ever does pour in. Such a filmmaker should plan a whole slate of projects and learn to always have one project in preproduction, one in production, and a third in distribution. Such a professional filmmaker will approach the business with a bit more distance than the filmmaker who has a compulsion to explore a particular story.

The actor-turned-filmmaker, in contrast, will be using the film as a calling card to reshape the performer's professional profile. Relations with the media and Hollywood will be as important as the film itself. The goal of the film is to change the nature of the scripts being offered, so the actor should be looking to accept additional film roles even before this film is theatrically distributed—protecting against career-ending unfavorable reviews.

Often the true reasons for making a movie are closely guarded personal secrets. Even if the filmmaker is not forthcoming with others, the filmmaker must be sufficiently self-aware in order to achieve the actual goals of the project. The filmmaker must acknowledge the true reasons for making the film and organize the business and filmmaking strategy to maximize this opportunity.

3. Planning Beyond the Film

Even an independent film has the potential to become a *tent pole* production, a literary phenomenon that creates multiple franchise opportunities: sequels, books, toys, television productions, video games, and other merchandise. George Lucas's *Star Wars* represents the ultimate tent pole franchise: it has generated 11 live-action movies (with many more in the works), books, streaming live and animated series, and a vast merchandizing empire. The brand's power even propelled the development of Industrial Light & Magic, Lucas's premier visual effects company. Industrial Light & Magic had been the special effects team on the original *Star Wars*, and as the franchise grew, Lucas developed the company into a separate enterprise that has gone on to set the professional standard for the industry. With the eventual sale to Disney, *Star Wars* became the backbone of the Disney+ streaming platform and expansion of the Disney theme parks.

Though filmmakers should not expect to achieve the success of *Star Wars*, they should still plan ahead to take advantage of the opportunities created by a successful film. If the film has strong graphical elements, its financial strategy should include the development of video games, graphic novels, merchandise, or other ancillary products. More than just financial opportunities, ancillary products create a relationship between the production and the audience. Independent filmmakers should seek to foster this relationship rather than allowing it to be controlled by the film's eventual distributor.

Particularly for films that might spin off video games and other graphical projects, the filmmaker must plan early to acquire the correct rights and develop the appropriate content to maximize this opportunity for the film.

E. Choosing to Make a Film or Series

While it may seem strange that a book on independent filmmaking asks whether the project should even be made into a film, this should be the threshold question for any production today. By tradition, making a motion picture—whether it's shot on film stock or captured digitally— means shooting and editing a feature-length project of 73 to 200 minutes (preferably 93 to 130 minutes) for distribution initially in movie theaters and later on the array of home viewing platforms.

Financially, this remains an extremely challenging business. Though there are notable successes in selling feature films and documentaries, the vast majority of films are never theatrically distributed—or picked up for any distribution at all. The filmmaker can place them online in the hopes that an audience will come calling, but without marketing funds, those videos uploaded for free will have little or no viewership.

In contrast, the ability to make one's content publicly available has never been easier. Anyone can shoot a one- to five-minute scene and post it on websites and social networks. In some cases, these short videos consist of scenes from the larger project, while others are original expressions of the ideas of the feature project. The popularity of these shorts can be used to build enthusiasm and financial support to launch a full-length film.

Although shorts are easy to distribute, that does not mean that high-quality shorts are easy to produce. Tight writing and powerful acting are just as important to a short as to a feature film. In fact, it can be much more difficult to communicate all one's ideas in three minutes instead of an hour and a half. Still, a good scene will communicate to investors much more effectively than a screenplay, and a popular video clip will help assure investors and distributors of audience interest in the project.

One of the best examples of an online short series was *The Guild*, created and written by Felicia Day. Over six seasons, the company produced 70 episodes that appeared on a variety of platforms, including YouTube, Microsoft Xbox Live Marketplace, MSN Video, Netflix, and Day's own YouTube channel, Geek & Sundry. It was an early winner of the YouTube Streamy Awards.

The Streamy Awards presently recognize three general categories of video: general, social good, and advertising or brand engagement. The general streams include recognition for series, performance, craft, audience choice, and other categories.

For developing filmmakers, success on these platforms may serve as an excellent introduction to the craft at a cost in time and money much more reasonable than jumping directly into a feature film. Some stories, however, need to be told via a feature film. By mixing stories and formats, the filmmaker can find the ideal mix to explore untold stories and develop the skills of cinematic storytelling.

The online media format has many more genres than traditional independent narrative and documentary filmmaking. Music, arts and crafts, how to, unboxing, video magazines, animation, videogaming, and a multitude of other content forms give performers and storytellers an unlimited range of what can be done. The ability to explore the copyrighted authorship of others through fan fiction further extends the range of what can be done online. While the technical craft necessary is described in this book for feature productions, every step can be scaled to fit the needs of online media producers and adjusted to fit the demands of shorter, and more frequent, production deadlines.

2

The Film Company

The scope of an independent film project can range dramatically from a single filmmaker walking the countryside with a digital camera to a massive business involving hundreds of employees and millions of dollars in expenses and revenue. But even the smallest film is big business. A typical low-budget feature film project must include a payroll for salaried employees, payments to independent contractors, and agreements with trade unions, property owners, lenders, suppliers, and a multitude of support services. The filmmaker may be obligated to become licensed within one or more states, pay federal and state taxes, meet employer documentation requirements and withholding obligations, execute contracts to rent property, license copyrighted works, sell securities, and obtain credit. Inevitably, the project will take on the trappings of a "real" business, so the filmmaker should organize a film company to anticipate the legal and business issues.

A. Purpose of the Corporation and LLC

1. Ownership and Control

The structure of the business will determine the relationship between the filmmaker and the investors, producer, director, cast, and crew, so thoughtful consideration of the structure should be given early in the filmmaking process. The filmmaker should select the business structure best suited to the project and the filmmaker's short-term and long-term goals. The purpose of business planning is to address four primary concerns: control, financing, liability, and tax obligations.

The first aspect of selecting a legal form is to establish legal control over the enterprise. The movie's director may have artistic control over the look of the film and the selection of shots, but only the film company can grant that authority. If the director wants to shoot a scene in Hawaii and the film company decision-maker says that a trip to Hawaii is not in the budget, the artistic control of the director will take second place to the financial control of the film company. Artistic control may even be revoked if the film company judges the director's decisions to be highly unreasonable. Therefore, for the filmmaker to retain absolute control of the film, the filmmaker must also retain control of the film company.

In a general partnership, for example, control is shared by all general partners—which can be comprised of all participants in the filmmaking process. General partnerships are very problematic for a filmmaker who wishes to maintain control of the filmmaking process. In contrast, a corporation or LLC establishes that the control vests in the senior manager of the enterprise, with some additional control vested in the corporation's board of directors. The LLC maximizes control for the filmmaker, while the laws governing corporations mean that shareholders and directors will share some aspects of control.

One of the challenges that filmmakers often face is the claims of authority by others in the filmmaking process. In the case of the copyrights involved in the screenplay, musical score, and film, copyright law's default provisions can result in claims of joint authorship brought by individuals who made only minor contributions to the project. Explicit provisions in both the organizational documents for the enterprise and in the employment or engagement agreements are essential to eliminate this concern.

Similar claims can be made by producers, directors, and various collaborators during the film project's development. The greater the number of people involved with a production, the greater the amount of structure needed to organize the production. Even if there is no money involved in the project, using a clear business model will avoid the interpersonal conflicts that often define and end film production efforts.

2. Protections from the Negligence of Employees and Vendors

Exposure to financial *liability* can be reduced through careful business planning. The film company is legally liable for the contractual obligations and any tort liability that may arise while making the film. Contractual obligations include the duty to pay bills, return rental equipment, withhold and pay taxes, and generally deliver on the promises made by the filmmaker. Tort liability generally reflects the duty to pay for any damages or cover costs associated with accidents (or intentional misconduct) that may arise during the making of the film. If a pedestrian is hit by a car while the filmmaker shoots a car chase scene, then the film company is responsible for paying the injured person to compensate for the harm. Financial exposure from tort liability can be reduced through the purchase of insurance, but the responsibility still rests with the film company.

The purpose of using a corporation or LLC is to create a legal entity that has the primary responsibility for the liabilities of the company. When a vendor signs a contract with a company, the vendor is put on notice that it is the company with which the vendor is doing business.

There are limits to the protections from liability. Some vendors will insist on personal guarantees from the filmmaker or other responsible parties so that if the company does not have sufficient funds, others are responsible to pay the bills. This is a legally enforceable promise that the individual will cover the contractual obligations in the event that the film company cannot. The effect of the personal guarantee is to render the corporate protection of only limited value. The vendor must still look to the corporation first, but if the corporation cannot pay the bill, then the guarantor will have to cover the guaranteed expenses.

Similarly, tort creditors may also be able to circumvent corporate protection. The filmmaker is often the individual conducting or supervising the activity that leads to a tort claim. For example, a filmmaker shooting the car chase would be personally responsible for the car accident if the filmmaker drove the car in an unsafe manner or took other unreasonable risks that put pedestrians in danger. If the filmmaker is found personally negligent, then the filmmaker will be personally liable for the costs to the injured party. The corporation can protect the employee through the purchase of insurance and by agreeing to pay the expenses on behalf of the employee. But if the corporation does not have any funds, then the person who acted negligently will still be responsible. No legal entity will protect a person from one's own actions.

Finally, if the corporation or LLC has no assets, then a court can choose to ignore the corporation and hold the shareholders or owners directly responsible. This is sometimes referred to as "piercing the corporate veil."

Courts will not allow the use of corporations to defraud innocent third parties, and the failure to fund the business will often lead to piercing the corporation. Courts will also be willing to pierce the corporate veil if the officers, directors, and shareholders ignored the corporation and acted as if it were merely a general partnership. As a result, while corporations and LLCs provide significant benefits, they are not magic shields. Sufficient funding and careful planning are essential to avoid liability.

3. Management of Financing, Investors, and Tax Obligations

The third area of primary importance relates to the management of the investors and the financing of the enterprise, including the revenue distributions and tax obligations resulting from the production.

Financing refers to the practical problems of funding the filmmaking process. If the filmmaker hopes to use other people's money to finance the film, then the nature of the film company must be designed to accommodate the financial participation of investors or donors. Financial participation is closely tied to the issue of control as well. Even in the arts, investors will want some say in the manner in which their money is spent and will insist on measures to protect their investments and returns.

In a general partnership, for example, each investor would automatically become a general partner, making this an inappropriate method of operating for all but the smallest of projects. A corporation, in contrast, can have any number of investors and will be the preferred model for crowd-funded projects and companies that hope to create multiple films from the same structure. There are significant differences between C corporations, S corporations, and LLCs, which focus on the types of securities the company can issue and the tax rules regarding the allocation of profits and losses, which are detailed in the sections on each type of enterprise.

Tax obligations are a specific type of liability that the film company must address. They need to be planned for separately from other financial obligations, early in the development process, because the choice of business structure will determine the amount of taxes owed and shift the tax obligations between the company and its owners—which, in turn, will affect both the cost of raising capital and the benefit of profits earned each year. The goals in tax planning are to minimize the total amount of tax due and to ensure that any tax obligations that do arise can be covered with cash payments. Since every dollar saved can be applied directly to the film and the profits will go to the film's creators and investors, thoughtful early tax planning sets the stage for good management throughout the project.

Professional tax planning is beyond the scope of this book, but it is important for the filmmaker to work with an experienced accountant or attorney. Preliminary discussions in the planning stage may save the filmmaker thousands of dollars in taxes later in the process.

The best choice of business structure will depend on the objectives of the filmmaker in balancing control, financing, liability, and tax obligations, which are often in conflict. The filmmaker must determine the nature of the project early in its existence, because the planning choices may dictate some of the subsequent choices available to the filmmaker. Still, as with everything else in filmmaking, business organizations can change as the situation evolves. If a filmmaker starts out making a small film but the project suddenly doubles in budget and scope, the filmmaker can revise the business plan to reflect the new situation.

B. Sole Proprietorship

A sole proprietor is a single person who is personally responsible for all aspects of a business. Unless the filmmaker works with a partner or adopts a more formal legal structure for the film company, a filmmaker will automatically operate as a sole proprietor. A sole proprietorship is never separate from its owner, and all control stays with the sole proprietor. All liability, including all debts, promises, and obligations, also remains the personal responsibility of the business owner.

1. Benefits of the Sole Proprietorship

The primary benefit of working as a sole proprietor is simplicity. Without any separate legal entity to manage, few if any formalities are needed to conduct the filmmaking business. A second potential benefit is that an individual has a credit history and assets that a new business entity may not have. Of the independent films financed on credit cards—like Spike Lee's *She's Gotta Have It*—most relied on the personal credit of the filmmaker (as well as the once-liberal card issuance policies of the credit card companies). If the income and expenses of the film project are relatively small, the choice to remain a sole proprietor may be a reasonable one.

The legitimate business expenses of a sole proprietorship may be tax-deductible business expenses. The filmmaker must use Schedule C on the 1040 annual tax form and report the expenses and income that are carefully itemized during the filmmaking process. Additional rules apply to ensure that the sole proprietorship is truly a business rather than a hobby. The filmmaker must show positive income in three of every five years or the IRS can treat the filmmaking costs as nondeductible hobby expenses.

2. Risks of the Sole Proprietorship

The single biggest drawback to operating as a sole proprietor is the personal liability that the filmmaker undertakes. By comparison, corporations and limited liability companies provide *limited liability*, a legal shield that protects the filmmaker from personal obligation for any contractual obligations and for any tort liabilities if the filmmaker is sued as an officer or director of the film company.

Although the legal protections of a corporation or LLC are not absolute, they are quite significant and beneficial. If a filmmaker is involved with a sizable group of cast members and crew or any significant scale of production, then a sole proprietorship would not be advisable. On the other hand, for a personal video blog or podcast or similar productions, there might not be significant benefit in a separate legal organization.

A sole proprietorship provides the filmmaker with the maximum level of control but does not accommodate equity fundraising. The filmmaker can raise money by taking out personal loans (debt financing), but the sole proprietorship is not suitable for raising capital from third parties. Since the third party cannot receive ownership in the film company and can only receive contractual rights to the film's revenue, most investors will balk at the arrangement. In addition, if an investor does contribute funds to the sole proprietor, the investment may transform the sole proprietorship into a general partnership, because the investor has joined with the filmmaker in the business enterprise. This undermines the control sought by the filmmaker and creates significant financial risk for the investor.

3. Using a DBA with a Sole Proprietorship

A sole proprietorship is not restricted to the name of the filmmaker. The filmmaker can still use a production company name by filing a Fictitious Business Name Statement—often known as a "DBA" or "doing business as" form—with the state in which the filmmaker resides. The DBA gives the filmmaker only the right to use a fictional name in a particular state. It confers no limits on liability, nor does it give the filmmaker trademark rights to the name. In the early stages of planning a film project, the filmmaker may elect to file a Fictitious Business Name Statement as the first preliminary step toward creating the film company. It may give some priority for use of the name in that state if the filmmaker later wishes to create a legal entity, and the filing gives the filmmaker the legal right to conduct business under that name.

C. General Partnerships

A general partnership is any business conducted by two or more people for profit. Like a sole proprietorship, no formalities need be followed for a general partnership to be formed. Also like the sole proprietorship, each partner is fully and completely responsible for all contractual and tort liabilities of every kind for the entire partnership. If there is a partnership of five people, for example, and the general partnership has a debt of $100,000 to a rental agency, then each of the five people could be held responsible for the entire $100,000. If all five general partners have sufficient funds to pay their share, then each will pay $20,000. But if only two of the partners have assets, then those two partners will each have to pay half of the $100,000 and make a claim against the non-paying three partners. In this way, each general partner insures the public against the other members of the partnership.

The general partnership differs from the sole proprietorship in that two or more people share control and liability. Like a sole proprietorship, there is no protection from contractual or tort debts.

1. Avoid General Partnerships

There are no valid reasons to operate a business as a general partnership (unless the partners are comprised of other corporations or legal entities). General partnerships increase the potential liability for the partners while providing no benefit to them. The law provides that all profits, like all losses, be shared equally among the partners, unless the partners have agreed otherwise. But because the legal requirement for revenue sharing often comes as a surprise to the typical members of a general partnership, even this rule of equitable distribution may sometimes cause more mischief than it provides help. Filmmakers should avoid general partnerships to the greatest extent possible.

2. Legal Presumption of Forming General Partnerships

State law creates a presumption that when two or more people come together to run a business, they have created a general partnership. Unless additional steps are taken to assign authority or limit the control of the partners, each partner shares equally in everything. This means that if any general partner agrees that the business will do something with a third party, such as a vendor or location, that contract will be binding on the partnership, even if the other partners are unaware of the contract or even if the other parties had instructed the contracting partner not to enter into the agreement. In contrast, the rule between the partners is that decision-making is conducted by majority vote. For the filmmaker, having decisions made by majority vote of the participants and investors would destroy the filmmaker's control of the project. No good management comes from a general partnership.

Filmmakers often find themselves in difficult situations in which they struggle to make last-minute decisions and are pressed to make poorly considered promises. Granting contractual power to everyone involved in the production exacerbates this problem and will undermine the management of the film company. For example, it may be that the director—in order to get one last shot at 2:00 AM—promises an actor improved billing if only the performer will do the scene one additional time. That promise will be binding on the film company only if the director has the authority to make such a bargain. If the director is the sole proprietor, then no one else is to blame if the offer was imprudent. If the director is one of three general partners— along with the producer and the screenwriter—then the other partners will be bound by a hasty bargain over which they had no say.

3. Formalizing and Structuring General Partnerships

The rules that govern a general partnership can usually be changed by agreement among the partners. The general partners can create an *Operating Agreement* to assign duties, give primary authority to one partner, and restrict the authority of each partner to particular matters.

General partnerships require tremendous trust among the parties to the partnership because each partner can legally commit the partners and partnership so easily. Because of the risks associated with tort liability resulting from harm to bystanders, proper legal advice is that a general partnership should never be used for filmmaking. Nonetheless, general partnerships are very easy to form under state law, and filmmakers often ignore legal advice out of trust for their friends and colleagues. As a result, parties often find themselves as partners without advanced planning. General partnerships may also arise in the early stages of a project's development, well before there are any contracts to sign with third parties or risks of tort liability.

If a general partnership is going to be used, the filmmaker should insist on a written Operating Agreement signed by the partners that sets out the responsibilities of each general partner. As a safety precaution, the Operating Agreement should specify that any obligation to spend more than an agreed-upon dollar amount requires the approval of all partners. Similarly, the authority to make major decisions should either be assigned to particular parties or require the approval of all parties. The written Operating Agreement will not protect the partners from contractual or tort claims brought by third parties, but the Operating Agreement is binding to control the relationships and authority among the partners as well as any employees of the general partnership.

4. Risks of General Partnerships

General partnerships are commonly used in very informal situations, so despite the advice in this book, formal partnership agreements are often never drafted or signed. In the absence of an agreement to the contrary, the partners in a general partnership all share equally in the profits and losses. They also share in the responsibility for the partnership's debts and obligations. The obligation to share in the debts does not limit the liability of any individual partner. As noted, if only one of three partners has any assets, then that partner will be responsible for all obligations of the film company. That partner can look to the other partners for repayment, but the debt owed by other partners will not reduce the obligation to creditors.

Because general partnerships are presumed under state law whenever two or more people come together to engage in a business for profit, the filmmaker and other cast and crew may find themselves forming a general partnership well before they are ready to do so. To avoid the problems created by general partnerships, the parties may consider entering a Collaboration Agreement, discussed subsequently, or creating a corporation or LLC early in their planning process to avoid the unintended consequences of the general partnership.

5. Tax Status of General Partnerships

General partnerships are not taxed. Instead, the profits and losses are allocated proportionately to the partners, who then pay personal income tax on the profits or deduct the business losses. The tax rules that allow the partnership not to be taxed are probably the best feature of the general partnership. The only difficulty is that the partners are obligated to pay their share of the taxes regardless of whether the partnership has actually distributed the proceeds. But despite the tax benefits, it should be clear that a general partnership is not a good business form for operating a film company.

D. Limited Partnerships

Limited partnerships differ dramatically from general partnerships. These are formal, documented, legal entities that protect the investors from personal liability for debts while treating the partnership's managers as general partners. A limited partnership is formed by filing the necessary papers with the state in which it will be based.

1. Participants in Limited Partnerships

Limited partnerships have two categories of participants—general partners and limited partners. *General partners* are those who actually manage the business on behalf of the partnership. A general partner may be a corporation or other business entity.

Limited partners are investors who contribute money or property as capital in exchange for ownership in the company and participation in its profits and losses. To remain limited partners, they must have very little to do with the control and operation of the business. They vote only on selected issues that affect the survival of the business or to appoint a new general partner if a current general partner has died or become unavailable or unable to act.

Limited partnerships are primarily fundraising vehicles, particularly well suited to sole proprietors who need to raise capital. Corporations can also serve as the general partner of a limited partnership, which works well to separate a production entity corporation from the investors for a particular film or project.

The limited partners participate by contributing the necessary capital for the business, but they do not interfere with its operations. As the general partner of a limited partnership, the filmmaker or the filmmaker's corporation retains most of the operational control over the film company. The filmmaker must account to the limited partners regarding how money was spent, collected, and disbursed, but such fiduciary obligations are often set at the lowest level allowed by law.

2. Risks of Limited Partnerships

The long, successful history of limited partnerships may make that structure an attractive form for the filmmaker seeking to raise funds. It combines some of the better features of the sole proprietorship and the corporation. The partnership itself has primary responsibility for all contractual and tort liability. Only if the company is unable to meet these obligations do the general partners become responsible.

The investments made by the limited partners are used to pay any liabilities of the partnership. The limited partners are not personally responsible to pay any additional money or cover debts of the partnership. In contrast, the general partners of a limited partnership are responsible for any debts that cannot be covered by the assets of the limited partnership.

One note of caution: the sale of limited partnership interests, like corporate stock, is the sale of a *security*, which is highly regulated under both state and federal law. Many filmmakers violate these laws, as well as federal Securities and Exchange Commission (SEC) regulations, by arranging for financing without consulting a qualified attorney. A filmmaker who does so may be compelled to return all the funds to the investors, incur significant fines, and even face criminal penalties. Please see chapter 10 (pp. 180–185) for an introduction to securities law and an explanation of how to safely raise funds.

3. Tax Status of Limited Partnerships

Limited partnerships may provide tax benefits as well. Like general partnerships, limited partnerships are not taxed. The profits and losses are allocated to the partners, who pay the taxes or deduct the losses on their individual returns. If the filmmaker has little income to offset the losses, the partnership agreement may make the investment more attractive to the investor by allocating a greater portion of the loss deductions to the limited partners. Unfortunately for the filmmaker, tax rules have changed over the years, so that the benefits of investing in money-losing limited partnerships have been significantly reduced, but there may still be some tax benefits for investors.

E. Corporations

Corporations are the oldest and best-established form of business entity. Each state has its own state corporate law. A corporation is created by filing the Articles of Incorporation with the state, paying any required fees, and following the other steps set out in the state law. These steps usually include:

- Adopting bylaws, which establish the governing rules of the company;
- Electing directors;
- Accepting the resignation of the incorporator, the person who filed the Articles of Incorporation; and
- Filing any state securities documents establishing the initial ownership of shares in the company.

Corporations are the legal entities that operate the largest companies in the world—and many of the smallest companies as well. They can range in size from an entity owned by millions of investors to one owned by a single person. Once formed, a corporation is managed by a board of directors, operated by its officers, and owned by its shareholders. The corporation provides the shareholders with limited liability for all acts conducted on behalf of the corporation and protects the officers, directors, and employees from many forms of personal liability. State law also recognizes closely held corporations and allows the qualifying entities to simplify the management of the enterprise by permitting the shareholders to also serve as the officers and directors.

1. Participants in Corporations

One of the key features of corporations is the separation of management from control. The shareholders—the investors who have contributed cash or property in exchange for ownership—control the corporation. The shareholders exercise their ownership authority only by electing a board of directors. The shareholders have no other authority over the management of the company and only limited rights regarding the major changes to the company, such as its merger or closure.

The board of directors, elected by the shareholders, is made up of professionals who manage the business and hire the employees of the company. The board of directors is bound by operating rules established in the corporation's bylaws. For a filmmaker, such complexity may seem extreme. This is true for many small businesses. As a result, most states allow a corporation to have a single person serve as the board of directors. Unanimous written agreements among the shareholders can bind the shareholders to elect the same person as officer and director of the corporation. Using these techniques, the same corporate form that works for General Motors can be adapted to My Film Company, Inc.

2. Risks of Operating as a Corporation

There are no significant downsides to operating as a corporation. Forming the corporation requires a certain amount of formality, but the steps are relatively simple, and thousands of books and software programs are available to guide the filmmaker through the process.

Perhaps the greatest danger of structuring the film company as a corporation is that the filmmaker will oversimplify the task. Many publishers, lawyers, and Internet resources provide standard documents for corporations, but these one-size-fits-all materials often create problems for their users. Filmmakers should avoid adopting "corporate form book" documents uncritically. Artistic and business decisions necessary to make a film are quite different from other business decisions, and as a result, the standardized corporate forms might not be the best fit for the filmmaker.

The distinction between a typical business and a film production company begins with its purpose. Most companies are intended to operate as going concerns for years or decades. Corporate law allows corporations to operate in perpetuity. But most film production companies are formed to create a single motion picture, sell it to a distributor, and dissolve. Investors in the film expect to receive returns from their investment and do not want the filmmaker to be able to retain the profits from the film for future productions, unlike shareholders of normal companies who expect the company to continue to reinvest most of its revenue in future operations.

Corporate form documents often fail to include the necessary restrictions regarding the purpose of the corporation or against holding onto the profits. This could lead to significant disputes between the filmmaker and investors, which can easily be avoided if the corporate documents are drafted to take the specifics of the film project into account.

Another risk of operating as a corporation may come from relying too heavily on the corporate form to shield the filmmaker from personal liability. As a general matter, both contractual and tort creditors must look first to the corporation for payment of any debt. But if the corporation never had sufficient assets to operate as a business, a court may disregard the corporation and compel the owners to pay the debt. In addition, the corporation would not provide immunity for a person's own negligent or criminal actions. For example, if a production assistant were to injure a pedestrian while running errands for the film company, the corporation would be responsible to pay for the accident. But if the corporation was unable to pay, then the production assistant would remain personally responsible for the accident. The corporate form minimizes financial and legal liability, but it does not eliminate it. To manage risk, the film company must still raise sufficient funds to its pay debts, and it must purchase appropriate insurance to cover the risks associated with filmmaking.

3. Tax Status of Corporations

Corporations typically fall into two separate tax categories. Most corporations are *subchapter C corporations*, which pay their own taxes on the net profits they earn. When the shareholders receive dividends or payments from the corporation, those shareholders also pay taxes on those distributions. Known as *double taxation*, this may significantly increase the amount of taxes paid each year. In addition, any corporate losses are attributed to the business rather than its shareholders, so losses do not provide investors with any potential tax benefits.

To avoid double taxation, the company can instead be organized as a *subchapter S corporation*, which is treated as a partnership for tax purposes—and therefore not taxed as a separate entity. To elect to be taxed as a partnership, the company must limit the number of shareholders to 100 and limit the securities to a single class of stock. Despite the limitation on classes of stock, the IRS permits an S corporation to issue the stock with different sets of voting rights. As long as the terms on repayment, dividends, and other attributes do not change, the control of voting rights can make an S corporation very efficient for fundraising for a film production company.

F. Nonprofit Corporations

An alternative to the for-profit corporation is the nonprofit corporation. Like for-profit corporations, nonprofits are organized under the laws of the state where the company has its primary place of business or other close ties. A nonprofit corporation is organized by volunteers for a specified public benefit, such as public educational, charitable, or literary purposes. A nonprofit corporation cannot be organized to benefit private interests or private individuals, and it does not have shareholders or owners. These limitations do not eliminate the ability of the nonprofit corporation to pay reasonable, fair-market wages to staff, including the executive director and other officers. Instead, the limitation is designed to ensure that the donations and earned income go primarily to the charitable purpose.

Although most filmmakers hope their projects create global audiences and generate wild revenues, in actuality most independent film projects lose their investments. Moreover, with the explosion of media content available for free online or as part of prepaid streaming platforms, filmmakers and other creative artists struggle to find audiences and revenue. For filmmakers who plan to make a series of projects that have a strong social agenda, a nonprofit company may be a reasonable alternative. As discussed in chapter 7 (pp. 139–142), however, even for-profit film companies can raise charitable funds for particular projects, if the project is sponsored by a charitable entity, such as a fiscal sponsor, and the project meets the sponsorship guidelines.

The nonprofit corporation works well for those seeking to establish a company to support many filmmakers or to support a number of educational, literary, and charitable purposes in furtherance of film. Charities are not well suited to be one-time, single-production entities.

1. Forming the Nonprofit Entity

To be a nonprofit corporation, the entity must be properly organized under state law and then apply to be a public charity through its federal tax filing. Some states will also require that the entity make a state tax filing for charitable status as well. The primary rules for determining charitable entity status are based on IRS regulations, and the states that have additional laws follow the IRS regulations closely.

A nonprofit corporation is created by filing the Articles of Incorporation with the state, paying any required fees, filing an application with the IRS, and following the other steps set out in state law. These steps usually include:

- Adopting bylaws, which establish the governing rules of the company;
- Electing directors;
- Accepting the resignation of the incorporator, the person who filed the Articles of Incorporation; and
- Filing the state and federal tax application to be recognized as a public charity.

Unlike the filing of the Articles of Incorporation, the filing with the IRS to become a public charity is not automatic. To be tax exempt, the IRS requires that the articles and bylaws for the organization provide the following components:

- The corporation is organized for a charitable purpose;
- No part of net earnings will be paid or distributed to anyone, though the corporation can pay reasonable salaries;
- The corporation will not be organized for lobbying or political purposes; and
- The corporation will dedicate its resources to its charitable purpose.

a. Charitable Purpose—the Organizational and Operational Test

Both the charitable purpose and the nonprofit corporation's operations must be consistent with the IRS definition of a charity. The IRS provides this definition of exempt purposes:

> The exempt purposes set forth in section 501(c)(3) [of the Internal Revenue Code] are charitable, religious, educational, scientific, literary, testing for public safety, fostering national or international amateur sports competition, and preventing cruelty to children or animals. The term **charitable** is used in its generally accepted legal sense and includes relief of the poor, the distressed, or the underprivileged; advancement of religion; advancement of education or science; erecting or maintaining public buildings, monuments, or works; lessening the burdens of government; lessening neighborhood tensions; eliminating prejudice and discrimination; defending human and civil rights secured by law; and combating community deterioration and juvenile delinquency.[1]

Film companies can fulfill the exempt purposes required by the IRS either because the companies produce literary works or because the works produced further one of the other purposes in the regulation. For example, a nonprofit documentary film company that produced documentaries on civil rights would meet the goals of the exempt purpose through its literary work, its public education, and its efforts to defend human and civil rights. The IRS often takes some convincing that an applicant is serious in its efforts to meet the exempt purpose of the regulation, so meeting the exempt purpose test in multiple ways makes for a stronger application even if it is not technically necessary.

To establish the charitable purpose, the applicant must meet the organizational and operational test. The organizational test is based on the declarations made in the Articles of Incorporation and bylaws for the organization, meaning that the documents provide that the organization operates "exclusively for charitable, religious, and educational" purposes and avoids any description of a nonexempt purpose. To meet the operational test, the charity must describe its activities that fulfill the exempt purposes of the charity.

b. Limitations on Political Activities

While the film company can fulfill its public educational role through its narrative or documentary content, the IRS prohibits the direct support for political candidates and restricts lobbying to influence specific legislation or elected officials. In the film company's application and its other materials, it must operate in a manner that follows these regulations.

For organizations that create content focused on highly political topics, the film company must take extra steps to ensure that its activities are not directed at lobbying or particular candidates. Audience members and licensees of the completed motion pictures do not have the same limitations.

c. No Private Inurement

A charitable organization must be operated for the public benefit, in contrast to the for-profit corporation, which operates to earn a return for its investors. This means that there can be no shareholders in the nonprofit corporation. It also means that there cannot be other securities that would create a private benefit to any other individual. There are, however, important limitations to this rule.

First, the rule does not prohibit a nonprofit corporation from paying reasonable salaries. Hospitals, universities, and other large nonprofits must pay the going rate for their doctors, professors, coaches, and others. The same will be true of the film company, which can certainly compensate its writers, directors, cinematographers, cast, and crew at rates appropriate for the production. The limitation is that the pay must be reasonable within the context of both the comparisons to other similar projects and to the revenue of the enterprise.

Second, the rule does not prohibit financial transactions with its volunteers. It is quite common for volunteers and donors to provide below-market cost transactions to help the charity. For example, if a member of the board of directors were to provide a lease to the charity for its office space and the cost of the lease were 50 percent of what that donor charges for-profit companies that rent space, then the lease would not trigger the private inurement rule. If instead the board member received rents above the market rates for the property, that would be prohibited by the IRS regulations.

Third, the rule does not prohibit the nonprofit corporation from hiring contractors, including attorneys, accountants, advisors, investment managers, and others, and paying professional compensation for their services. To avoid questions of private inurement, it is better that these compensated professionals do not have decision-making authority over the organization, but the transaction would still be permitted so long as the value of the economic benefit received by the charity exceeds the payments to the contractor. For example, if the contractor has an established rate for services that it receives from its general clientele, and the contractor provides those services to the charity at a clear discount, that will establish that the benefit to the charity exceeded the payment to the contractor.

Once the nonprofit corporation has established its bona fide charitable purpose and organized itself so that its operations and funding qualify as a public charity, the board of directors must authorize the filing of the tax exemption application. The tax exemption application should be filed as soon as possible after the formation of the nonprofit corporation. As IRS regulations provide, if the organization files the tax exemption application within 27 months of its initial formation, the organization's exemption will be recognized retroactively to the date it was organized. Otherwise, exemption will be recognized based on the postmark of the application to the IRS (or the date of receipt by the IRS if there is no postmark).

2. Participants in Nonprofit Corporations

A nonprofit corporation is operated by a volunteer board of directors and staff that is composed of paid employees, volunteers, or both. The board of directors must generally have three or more people. Nonprofit corporations may be organized to have a voting membership, but it is much more common for the donors to be nonvoting, even if the term *member* is used to describe their participation and role. For nonmembership nonprofits (meaning that there are no members with voting rights), the members of the board of directors are elected by the current board of directors.

Many nonprofit arts organizations operate as fiscal sponsors or central operations for smaller film production companies and other arts or educational activities. In this model, the nonprofit is run by a professional staff, including an executive director, fundraising director, and other officers. The company will provide backend support to the filmmakers and artists, raise funds for these artistic projects, provide trainings for emerging artists, and promote the artistic works.

A smaller number of nonprofit film companies will be operated directly by the filmmaker and exclusively produce the filmmaker's works. Such a company must operate carefully to ensure that the filmmaker, who likely serves as the key paid staff member, does not violate the private inurement rules. To do this, the board of directors must be independent of the filmmaker and not include any family members or employees. Provided that the board of directors remains uncompensated and independent of the filmmaker, and as long as the compensation to the filmmaker does not exceed the private inurement rules, the film company can operate successfully as a nonprofit enterprise.

3. Tax Management of a Nonprofit Corporation

Tax benefits are the primary reason for operating as a tax-exempt, charitable organization. There are three distinct tax benefits. First, the film company's net revenues are not subject to tax, provided the income is based on the charitable activities of the nonprofit. Second, the organization is eligible for grants from private foundations, which can increase the potential to raise funds for film projects. And third, contributions to the organization are eligible for a charitable deduction by the donor.

The donor deduction is the greatest benefit of the nonprofit funding model. This means that instead of seeking investors who are reminded in the securities filings of the high likelihood of financial failure, donors are guaranteed a deduction on their itemized tax returns that might amount to as much as 40 percent of the funds donated. This benefit, however, has lessened in importance since 2018, when Congress doubled the standardized deduction. Far fewer people itemize their taxes, and those that do not itemize do not get the benefit of the charitable deduction.

The charitable status also greatly reduces the difficulty, cost, and administrative burden of raising funds. In contrast to the complexity of selling securities to investors, seeking donations is much less costly and cumbersome. The film company can publicly seek donors and is not restricted by the private fundraising rules of selling investors on the project.

There are considerable obligations for reporting the nonprofit organization's annual tax returns and for the documentation for the donors' personal tax returns. The organization must file a publicly available annual tax return on Form 990. If the company has less than $50,000 in income, a simplified online Form 990-N can be used.

Tax regulations require that the charitable organization provide a written disclosure statement to donors of a "quid pro quo contribution in excess of $75." A quid pro quo contribution is defined by the IRS as "a payment made to a charity by a donor partly as a contribution and partly for goods or services provided to the donor by the charity."[2] For example, if the donor pays $100 and in return receives a DVD that retails for $40, then this is a quid pro quo donation for which the donor can only deduct the $60 not reflected in the value of the gift. Certain low-cost items are excluded from these requirements, including bookmarks, calendars, key chains, mugs, posters, tee shirts, and similar items bearing the charity's name or logo.

In the written disclosure statement provided to each donor, the nonprofit must:

- Inform the donor that the amount of the contribution deductible for federal income tax purposes is limited to the excess of any money contributed by the donor over the value of goods or services provided by the charity
- Provide the donor with a good-faith estimate of the value of the goods or services that the donor received

Since donors are required to have a written record from the charity to substantiate all gifts, the charity must provide the notice for them. This can be done at the time of each gift, or the charity can send its donors an end-of-year summary of all contributions made during the prior calendar year. Additional regulations apply to documentation for the contribution of goods, such as books, artwork, and cars.

When initially formed and throughout its operation, the nonprofit corporation will want to be recognized as a public charity to maximize the tax benefits for itself and its donors. IRS regulations presumptively categorize any tax-exempt charity as a "private foundation" and then make the applicant establish that it meets the criteria to be recharacterized as a public charity. Despite this presumption, the IRS provides that an applicant "will be classified as a publicly supported organization and not a private foundation if it can show when it applies for tax-exempt status that it reasonably can be expected to be publicly supported." To do this, the explanation of future activities and sources of income must be clear. "An organization must describe fully the activities in which it expects to engage. This includes standards, procedures, or other means adopted or planned by the organization for carrying out its activities, expected sources of funds, and the nature of its contemplated expenses."[3]

The nonprofit film corporation will need to demonstrate that it operates as a "publicly supported organization." The IRS lists examples of publicly supported organizations:

- Museums of history, art, or science
- Libraries
- Community centers to promote the arts
- Organizations providing facilities for the support of an opera, symphony orchestra, ballet, or repertory drama, or for some other direct service to the general public
- Organizations such as the American Red Cross or the United Way

A charity meets the publicly supported organization test "if it normally receives at least one-third of its total support from governmental units, from contributions made directly or indirectly by the general public, or from a combination of these sources." If a single family gives the charity more than two-thirds of its support each year, then it is a private foundation. If the charity raises at least one-third of its funds from government grants, foundations, and the general public, it is a public charity. Additional tests allow other organizations to also qualify as public charities and provide exceptions to the donor rules for extraordinary gifts.

The tax compliance is complex, and like the securities compliance discussed in chapter 10 (pp. 180–185), these efforts require good advice from lawyers and accountants who focus on these fields.

4. Risks of Operating as a Nonprofit Corporation

For an individual filmmaker, the greatest risk of operating as a nonprofit corporation is compliance with the tax regulations to maintain the tax-exempt status. The rules regarding private inurement and charitable purpose provide only a narrow window within which to operate the nonprofit film company. Failure to stay within the regulations will result in tax penalties and the end of nonprofit status. The IRS can even seek criminal prosecution if the agency considers the use of the nonprofit status to be fraudulent.

Because there are no shareholders, the filmmaker leading a nonprofit organization does not need to worry that investors in the film have a different agenda than that of the filmmaker, giving the filmmaker great latitude in completing the motion picture. That said, however, the board of directors must be legally independent of the filmmaker. Over time, the board members' interest in maintaining a healthy organization may diverge from the interest of a filmmaker with a particular vision. This has happened with dance companies, orchestras, schools, and other charities. Often, nonprofits originally founded by a single visionary have found their boards splitting with their founder. The IRS is much more likely to accept the application of an organization dedicated to film production and distribution from a wide range of filmmakers than to recognize the charitable purpose of a single filmmaker, though both are technically possible.

Another challenge for operation as a nonprofit corporation is the film company's ability to maintain its status by operating each year as a public charity. The organization needs sufficient broad-based support to be a legitimate recipient of donations and grants.

G. Limited Liability Companies

The limited liability company, or LLC, has evolved into a very popular choice for small business and likely serves as the best model for independent film companies. As defined by most state statutes, the LLC is owned by its *members* and operated through its *managers*. Like shareholders in a corporation, members have limited liability. Some states require that an LLC have two or more members, but other states do not impose this requirement, so the filmmaker should review the information on the secretary of state's website for the state where the business will be formed.

1. Forming the LLC

The required filings—the Articles of Organization—are often one-page fill-in-the-blank forms that must be submitted, along with a tax payment, to the secretary of state in the state in which the film company will be located.

While simple to fill out, the Articles of Organization provide no information about how the business should be run. To be useful to the filmmaker,
a film company LLC should have a written, signed Operating Agreement
that serves as the articles and bylaws of the organization, in addition to the
simple Articles of Organization.

The Operating Agreement establishes the rules for managing and operating the business. Many of its provisions are common to every LLC and
will be found in virtually every form book. They establish the name and
place of business of the LLC, regulate the admission and removal of participants, and provide for maintenance of capital accounts, terminations, and
transfers of interest. Nonetheless, there are a few additional issues of particular concern for the filmmaker.

In many states, the Operating Agreement may simply indicate that the
manager—the filmmaker—has sole management authority, that there will
be no meetings, and that the profits and losses will be shared in a specified
manner between the manager and the other members of the LLC. Investors
in the film company, however, may not wish to give such unbridled discretion to the filmmaker, particularly over the raising of capital or other financial decisions. One of the primary benefits of the LLC is the opportunity to
shape the business entity to reflect the nature of the investors' interests and
the filmmaker's needs. Because the filmmaker needs to encourage investment in the film—a very risky investment—the filmmaker should provide
operational protections for the investor as a way of encouraging investment
and demonstrating responsibility regarding the enterprise.

2. Risks of the LLC

The greatest drawback to the limited liability company is that the business
and investment community has had limited experience with this organizational structure. Investors may be more willing to purchase shares of a
corporation than to invest in an LLC, because they are used to financing
businesses that use the more traditional form.

A second risk flows from the need to draft an Operating Agreement for
each LLC. As with a corporation, standardized LLC Operating Agreements
found in form books may not be appropriate for independent filmmakers.
Each company will have its own investment strategies, distribution plans,
and expectations regarding sequels and other projects, and these specifics should be reflected in the Operating Agreement. Some productions, for
example, will restrict the movement of additional capital into the LLC to

protect the original investors. (More often, however, film investors are not concerned about the size of other parties' investments, as long as all the funds raised are used exclusively to make the film.)

3. Tax Status of the LLC

The LLC has become a favorite vehicle for small business planners because it gives the owners maximum flexibility regarding the structuring of control and financing while reducing not only liability but also tax obligations. The owners of the LLC have the option to be treated as a partnership for tax purposes. In 1997, the Internal Revenue Service adopted rules that allow the LLC to elect whether to be taxed as a C corporation or as a partnership. By default, LLC entities are taxed as partnerships.

3

Initiating the Film Company's Formation

The sole proprietorship, general partnerships, limited liability partnerships, LLCs, S corporations, C corporations, and nonprofit corporations provide a rather dizzying array of options for a filmmaker not familiar with business planning. Many of the choices regarding which business model best fits the needs of the film project are based on the size of the project, the amount of time the project will be ongoing, the sources of financing, and the goals of the filmmaker and others involved in the project. This chapter will explore those differences to point out the best solutions for various projects.

A. Projects for Which a Corporation or LLC May Not Be Needed

Not every film project needs to be produced using a corporate entity. The general rule is that the smaller the project, the lower the chances the corporation or LLC will be useful. Millions of people shoot home movies every day without significant legal risk. Shooting video for posting to YouTube does not change this.

There are fees, taxes, and paperwork associated with the creation of a corporation or LLC. To undertake this effort, the benefit of the legal entity must outweigh the costs of its creation and maintenance.

A person who records a video blog is not likely to get significant value out of a corporation. Any money put into the corporation would come directly from the filmmaker. The size of contracts, if any, would be quite modest. The risk of tort liability would not be reduced, because the filmmaker is the person taking all the actions. As a result, what little benefit is available with a corporation or LLC would be insufficient to outweigh the costs.

The selection of the corporate form might also be made too early in the process for some projects. In the early stages of planning a film, there are a great many different plans. The size of the project can vary considerably, the parties who hope to be involved may change, and locations, funding, and other plans will often evolve as the filmmaker's team begins to gel.

If a corporation or LLC is made too early in the process, rights may be granted to individuals who have only a limited role in the project, locking in obligations that will interfere with the production. A filmmaker should be clear with anyone who might be involved with a project that a legal entity will be formed and only when there is a legal entity and written contracts will there be binding promises. Put another way, the filmmaker must make clear that all discussions are explorations until written agreements bind the participants. Then, the filmmaker can explore relationships among those who could potentially be involved without creating any legal liability.

B. Collaboration Agreements as Alternatives to Early Corporate Formation

Effective use of contracts can go a long way to manage the relations among the participants in a film project, particularly in the stage before a legal entity is formed. This is particularly helpful to avoid the unintended formation of general partnerships and the unintended formation of joint author relationships under copyright law.

In the case of joint authorship, if two or more people come together and contribute elements of the copyrighted work with the intent to be joint authors, then the joint authorship relationship is formed. The amount contributed does not need to be equal in any way, and the nature of intent is often murky and subjective. It is quite similar to the formation of general partnerships that may not reflect the true goal of the filmmaker.

A Collaboration Agreement that specifies the nature of the relationship among the parties and clarifies the actual intent of the participants will avoid the unintended consequences in both those situations, without the need to form a legal entity. The Collaboration Agreement clarifies the relationship among the parties, creates an obligation to protect trade secrets and nonpublic information, specifies the roles and rights of each collaborator, and provides strong evidence that third parties are not additional collaborators entitled to ownership, control, and compensation.

A Collaboration Agreement does not need to be a complex contract. A sample of a simple collaboration agreement is included in appendix A. When properly drafted, the Collaboration Agreement will enable the filmmaker to work with others while retaining control until there are the resources to actually create the legal entity. It provides important benefits to the filmmaker by:

- Establishing contractual rules about additional participants;
- Stripping any individual collaborator of power to expand the group of collaborators without consultation and approval of the appropriate parties; and
- Establishing what the team requires to be a collaborator, making third party claims much harder to substantiate.

The Collaboration Agreement will explain the anticipated role for each potential participant while also including any important limitations. For example, if a project has been proposed by an actor to the filmmaker for a particular adaption of a novel, the Collaboration Agreement might include a statement that all decisions on casting will not be made until a corporation is formed and that other parties, including the owner of the underlying rights and the investors, may have the right to advise or to approve casting decisions. The actor may not like that reality, but it is preferable to the filmmaker making a promise to the actor that the owner of the underlying rights will not recognize.

If the parties already have an agreement regarding compensation or ownership, the Collaboration Agreement can specify that understanding. Again, the agreement may provide that the understanding is subject to modification when a formal corporation or LLC is formed.

The agreement should also include relevant confidentiality provisions, duties of each participant, and milestones or other measures of progress. It must include a method of modification, a specified duration, a method of resolving disputes, and a disclaimer that the parties agree they are not general partners and do not get any additional rights other than those specified in the agreement.

If one person is clearly the filmmaker at this stage, then the Collaboration Agreement should provide that the filmmaker has general authority and the role of each other collaborator is specifically to provide the services or funds listed in the agreement.

On occasion, the attempt to execute a Collaboration Agreement will result in the parties walking away from each other. This is not a bad result. The alternative is for the tensions among the parties to smolder for weeks or months and erupt in conflict when the consequences of the dispute are much greater.

C. Choosing the Best Structure

For many independent filmmakers, the LLC is the best choice for forming a film production company. It can be taxed as either a corporation or a partnership, and although its Operating Agreement is more flexible than corporate bylaws for structuring the film company's operations, it limits personal liability as effectively as a corporation does. Another advantage of the LLC and partnership forms is the ability to allocate gain, loss, deductions, and credits to participants in a way that maximizes their value to investors.

Nonetheless, a different structure may be preferred, depending on the particular makeup of filmmakers and investors. For films heavily financed by outside investors, the traditional corporate form may be best. An S corporation also combines the tax benefits of a partnership with the limited liability and structure of a corporation. Particularly because the voting rights of the S corporation can be adjusted, the S corporation provides a useful structure with many of the same attributes as an LLC. S corporations, however, are limited in size.

C corporations may serve the interests of the investors most effectively, particularly if the film company plans to use crowdfunding to create a large body of shareholders. The filmmaker can issue multiple classes of stock and draft different shareholders' agreements to achieve the same results as with an LLC's Operating Agreement. The company will lose the tax advantages of a partnership, but for some investors they will have little value, particularly if the investors are more interested in the long-term growth of their investments than in deducting short-term losses. Corporations are strongly favored for investments, such as when a technology firm has the possibility of expanding into the public markets. While going public is not a significant possibility for most film companies, the structure may further encourage investors.

Limited partnerships are well suited to individual filmmakers who need to raise capital but want to retain sole operational control over most aspects of the film company. The limited partners participate by contributing the necessary capital for the business, but they do not interfere with its operations. The filmmaker is not protected by limited liability, but since it only shields the filmmaker from liability as an officer or director of the business, and most risk of tort liability will arise from activities in which the filmmaker is personally involved, that protection would be of little value.

If an individual filmmaker is not seeking investment financing, there may not be any benefit to forming a corporation, LLC, or limited partnership. Not only is the value of limited liability negligible, but also most debt will come from personal loans or unsecured personal credit cards, and the financial risk associated with these obligations will not be changed by using a formal business structure. If the filmmaker is a guerrilla artist or shooting a short project with a small cast and crew, then remaining as a sole proprietor may be a viable option.

On the other hand, if the size of the project increases or if investors are brought in, it is very important that the filmmaker switch to a formal business entity. The worst choice is to ignore the problem and have the law treat the project as a general partnership. The decision to switch need not be made immediately. Tax laws allow the sole proprietor to exchange the business for the assets of a new entity without paying a tax penalty. But from the outset of the film project, the filmmaker should have the business management in mind and work with a lawyer and accountant as early as possible so that the necessary business entity can be created when the filmmaker is ready.

D. The Nested-LLC Model for Continuity and Protection

Many filmmakers hope to launch an ongoing film company with the creation of their first film. Yet they need to keep the investments of each film project separate to ensure that the profits from each film are distributed to the investors of the particular project. To accomplish both goals, a popular structure calls for the creation of two limited liability companies, one to serve as the ongoing film business and the other to serve as the fundraising vehicle for the particular project.

1. The Umbrella Company Organized for Multiple Projects

The umbrella company is formed as an LLC owned and operated by the production team. The team may be organized in many different ways: it may consist of a group of producers; a team of writer, director, and producer; a director and actors; or any other possible combination. This company generally has only limited financial needs, and any investors are investing in the overall success of the business, not a particular project. The structure provides for limited liability for all participants and the taxation benefits of a partnership.

The umbrella LLC then serves as the sole manager of a second LLC formed to finance, develop, and distribute a particular motion picture. The investors in the movie are members of the second LLC. This structure maximizes the control filmmakers have over the project while allowing the relationship among the filmmaking team to be carefully crafted to reflect the rights and interests of each of its members.

In the Operating Agreement of the umbrella LLC, each member of the filmmaking team will negotiate the appropriate arrangement for compensation, responsibility, and control. If the team is composed solely of producers, the arrangements may be very similar for each member of the team. If the team is organized more like a rock band, with a writer, director, actor, and producer each contributing different talents and financial resources, the Operating Agreement can be drafted to reflect those differences. In addition, these terms may be modified without having to be ratified by the film's investors, since they are members of the other LLC, not this one.

The umbrella company is only necessary when a team of people are working together to create the movie, but given the highly collaborative nature of filmmaking, these projects have a much greater chance of success than projects attempted by a single filmmaker.

2. The Subsidiary Company Organized as an Investment Vehicle for the Film

The terms of the film project LLC should establish that the company's activities are limited to the particular motion picture. The company is managed by the umbrella LLC, so the Operating Agreement should be very clear regarding the authority of the manager—the managing company must have sufficient latitude to make the movie and clear direction regarding its authority to operate, and the role of the investor-members should generally be limited. This does not mean that the filmmakers are not obliged to update investors regarding finances, production, or distribution plans.

Most film investment companies are organized to make a single motion picture. But if the filmmakers know they are making a tent pole project—involving, for instance, a film, sequels, and video game tie-ins—the Operating Agreement can indicate that the manager has authority to retain earnings to invest in these additional projects. Such authority should be very clearly specified.

It is also important that the investment LLC's Operating Agreement grant the filmmakers latitude to be involved in other projects while making the film. In the film industry, filmmakers typically work on multiple projects simultaneously, but this creates a situation in which these projects may be competing for investor dollars, time, and attention, or even film festival admission. To ensure that the investors are fully aware of the potential conflict, the Operating Agreement should specify that the services of the umbrella LLC and its members are provided on a nonexclusive basis.

Finally, the Operating Agreement should set forth all the structures for recoupment of investments and profit participation, as well as the fees paid to the umbrella LLC for the management of the film project. While the Operating Agreement does not take the place of financial disclosure documentation, the two documents will closely resemble each other in many regards. This should allow the attorney to draft the two documents together, saving time and money. And since the Operating Agreement works as a blueprint for the operations of the company, it should also make it easier for the filmmakers to meet their obligations to their investors.

Technically, the managers of the umbrella LLC have no direct relation to the investors in the film project LLC, but the parties should not rely on this legal fiction; each filmmaker should treat all duties to the investors the same as if owed to the film project LLC. The two-LLC structure is not likely to immunize the filmmakers from their ethical and fiduciary obligations and should not be used for that purpose.

Duties of the Film Company

As mentioned in chapter 2, a typical film company of even modest size quickly undertakes all the attributes of a well-established business. If at all possible, these operational duties—engaging employees, renting equipment, paying taxes, raising working capital, etc.—should be separated from the creative duties of filmmaking. Separating business obligations from artistic functions improves both professionalism and focus. While many filmmakers serve as chief cook and bottle washer, more regimented efforts tend to be more successful. That way, a filmmaker who works with an actor regarding character development does not have to discuss tax forms at the same time.

The most important business obligations the film company has are to its investors and employees. Unless the film company fulfills these obligations faithfully, the film cannot be successfully made and distributed—and the company risks violating state and federal law. The filmmaker must, therefore, pay close attention to its business operations if the filmmaker hopes to achieve any artistic goals.

A. Financial Accounting and Responsibility

The financial accounting of a motion picture is extremely detailed, complex, and vital. It is not a coincidence that Michael Eisner became the CEO of Disney by learning the business in the accounting department. Many other studio heads were lawyers earlier in their careers. A film company should assign accounting and internal auditing functions to someone early in the development of the film company. Though not a glamorous role, a good production accountant can help ensure that the film company will have the funds necessary to pay salaries, rent equipment when needed, and still edit the film after principal photography has ended.

1. Planning

Often, participants in an independent filmmaking project agree to be paid from the film's profits. For this arrangement to work, profit participants must have confidence that there will be profits to share in if the film becomes a success. This requires that the film's costs be carefully itemized and reported.

The most critical phase in filmmaking accounting is the first step: budgeting. Chapter 9 (p. 164) provides a detailed description of the budgeting process and an analysis of the items that go into a budget. The production budget provides a blueprint for the structure of the film company and the film project. It allows the filmmaker to identify the scope of the project, calculate the magnitude of the financial resources needed, schedule receipts and payments, and prepare for the long-term obligations that might arise if the film is not a financial success. For unions such as the Screen Actors Guild (SAG) and the Directors Guild of America (DGA), the film's budget also determines the film company's eligibility to utilize the unions' reduced-pay-scale contracts. The production company must submit a proposed budget to the unions. Each union will scrutinize the budgetary assumptions as a condition for allowing union members to work for the company under the terms of a low-budget contract.

Often, filmmakers will also create a business plan that anticipates each phase of the film project from financing to distribution and assesses factors such as the market conditions for the film and the likelihood of profitability. (The business plan is detailed in chapter 9.) That business plan will help map out the road ahead for the benefit of potential investors and more cautious creative participants who demand a realistic chance of success before they commit to a project. It is much more important to filmmakers who hope to develop further projects rather than those who are shooting and distributing a single film. If the filmmaker elects to create a business plan, it must be accurate and realistic. The business plan will become the framework for the Private Placement Memorandum used to raise investor funds or the marketing plan for the crowdfunding campaign, or both, so the accuracy of the business plan and the budget are essential to the production and distribution of the project.

2. Record Keeping

Keeping careful records of financial transactions is every bit as important as careful budgeting. Record keeping serves two distinct goals. First, it provides the documentary proof of the production's expenses, which is essential to calculating tax liability and compliance with contractual obligations to the unions and to determining the film company's profits. Since many participants' payments are based on the profit of the film company, failure to document expenses will lower the break-even point at which the profit participants must be paid. In addition, some financing options may require documentation to prove that the specific expenses were actually incurred.

Second, record keeping allows the filmmaker to monitor the costs of ongoing expenses. Set construction, costuming, craft services, and other costs can easily balloon if not carefully monitored. For example, if 14 days into a 21-day shoot the film company has already spent 90 percent of its set construction budget, the filmmaker will have to make some choices. Perhaps most of the money was spent on a single set that has been used throughout filming. Then the remaining 10 percent of the budget should be satisfactory. If, however, the set construction costs are generally the same for each day of filming, then the filmmaker can expect to run as much as 40 percent over budget on set construction. Knowing this, the filmmaker can choose to scale back on set construction, increase the set construction budget by reducing other costs, or plan to increase the production expense. Without the advance knowledge, the production company could be without funds and suddenly shut down in the middle of production. Careful record keeping may not improve the film, but careful accounting will improve the chances of completing the film.

3. Accountability

The budget is the road map, and the payment records are the GPS. The production accountant must serve as a vigilant navigator. When money begins to flow, the danger always exists that it may be misspent. The term *misspent funds* refers to money stolen, personal purchases improperly attributed to the production company, and expenses attributed to the wrong budget line. In the heat of principal photography, dozens of individuals may be authorized to start purchasing supplies. It is wasteful for three different production assistants to each buy bottles of glue. It is criminal for one of those production assistants to buy an extra bottle of glue for the person's own supplies and charge it to the production. The film company must be attentive and efficient so that a culture of lax accounting does not encourage the volunteers and independent contractors to take advantage of the film's limited resources.

For accounting purposes, misspent funds do not include failed creative choices, such as purchasing a wedding dress for a scene that is later rewritten to take place in a dance club. Though that may be a regrettable expenditure, the purchase of the intended costume was made, and the balance sheet reflects the value of the dress even if the finished film does not. Filmmakers must be conscientious, but accountability should be a tool in support of the artistic goal rather than an obstacle.

Whenever someone other than a sole proprietor is handling the film company's payments, a specific system of accountability must be established. The nature of the system depends on the size of the project and the number of individuals authorized to spend company money. For example, a film company can authorize its scenic designer to buy materials as necessary, as long as the expense remains within the agreed budget. Or the film company can set a limit on the authority of the scenic designer to approve a purchase, so that expenses above a certain threshold are approved directly by the filmmaker.

The key is that for each expenditure, the rules of authority are established, a receipt is obtained, and each receipt is attributed to a particular budget line. As payments are made, the receipts should be booked on a daily basis. This helps to guarantee that the designer has actually spent the money on set materials and allows the business manager to compare the expenditures to the approved budget. If a senior production team member waits two weeks before submitting receipts, the production company will not be able to manage its expenditures, and it may not have the funds to reimburse the receipts. Credit lines and company credit card expenditures must also be booked each day to ensure that there are no surprising bills at the end of the month.

The ability to maintain careful accounting becomes most difficult near the end of principal photography. As the tension mounts to finish filming on schedule, the frenetic pace often encourages frenzied choices. Late hours result in crumpled receipts piling up in ashtrays. After the frenzy, the receipts are flattened and submitted for reimbursement. The delay in submission allows the expenses to balloon, possibly eliminating the funds left for postproduction. Particularly on low-budget films, money is tight. Even a few bad choices at the end of principal photography can derail the project.

4. Reporting

The final aspect of accounting relates to the obligations to report income and pay taxes. Unless the filmmaker operates a sole proprietorship, the film company must report income or losses. That information is used to pay taxes, either directly by the corporation or indirectly by the participants in a partnership or LLC. Movies are unique assets subject to illogical and highly manipulable accounting rules. It is generally accepted that a film company will either speed up the depreciation of the film to generate business losses and reduce tax liability or slow the depreciation down by predicting long-lasting revenue from the movie, which increases the value of film as an asset on the books of the company.

Although the guerrilla filmmaker may pay little heed to the accounting possibilities, investors and financiers will. The successful film company should engage the services of a qualified accountant who can help the company establish a strategy to deal with the tax and reporting obligations for the project.

One additional note of caution: The tax reporting for a marginally successful film may continue for years, and in some cases, the tax reporting will outlast the prints of the film. When creating the film company, the filmmaker must be prepared to accept this obligation to continue to collect fees and provide tax reports.

B. Fiduciary Obligations

The record keeping and financial reporting obligations are duties owed to investors, unions, revenue participants, and the IRS. In addition, the filmmaker's role as business operator creates specific duties of care and loyalty to the investors. Because the filmmaker is also an employee of the company and a primary beneficiary of the film project, the filmmaker must take great care to respect these fiduciary obligations and to carefully disclose the various conflicts of interest to the investors before they agree to invest in the project.

1. Duty of Loyalty

Whether serving as a general partner, managing member, or corporate officer and director, the filmmaker has a primary duty to act in the best interests of the business rather than out of personal self-interest. As a general matter, this duty limits self-dealing transactions. A manager should never take a personal loan from the business, pay a bonus, divert business opportunities, or otherwise take any benefit that should go to the company. Any benefits should be documented so that investors are aware of the terms before they invest. For example, if the manager is entitled to a percentage of the film's profits, that percentage should be part of the investor's contractual agreements and not increased unilaterally by the manager.

There are many examples of self-dealing that violate the duty of loyalty. For example, if the film company owns the sequel rights to the movie, the manager should not buy those rights from the company for the purpose of reselling them at a substantially higher price. Similarly, the manager cannot agree to sell the sequel rights cheaply on behalf of the company in exchange for a highly lucrative contract to direct the sequel. Although a rights transaction might be perfectly appropriate between the manager and an unrelated party, the manager has a duty to maximize the profits from the sale for the business; the manager cannot personally take that benefit.

To honor the duty of loyalty, the filmmaker should plan ahead. First, certain situations will create clear conflicts of interest between the filmmaker and the business. As much as possible, the filmmaker should disclose the terms of any material conflicts to prospective investors. The disclosure should be in a Private Placement Memorandum or other offering document and in the language of the Operating Agreement, bylaws, or subscription agreement:

- All contracts among officers, directors, managers, and partners must be disclosed to potential investors before they agree to invest. These contracts may include the writer's agreement, director's agreement, actor's agreement, or other agreements between the filmmakers and the company.
- If the officers, directors, managers, and partners want to work on projects other than this film, they must disclose their nonexclusive status.
- If the officers, directors, managers, and partners are fundraising for multiple projects, this creates a direct conflict of interest, which must be disclosed.

- The ownership interests held by the officers, directors, managers, and partners must be clearly distinguished from the rights owned by the business. For example, if one of the managers is the original author of the screenplay who sold the business the right to film the script but retained the copyright—including rights to sequels, characters, and similar projects—then that arrangement must be made clear.

When individuals choose to invest in the business after having received full disclosure of these preexisting conflicts of interest, they cannot effectively complain that the transaction unfairly benefits the managers rather than the business. On the other hand, if the information was not made available in advance of the investment, the investors may have grounds to charge that the manager misrepresented the transaction. Once the investment is made, the filmmaker is of course restricted from making further arrangements that benefit the managers to the detriment of the business or its investors.

2. Disclosure and Approval for Conflicts of Interest

In independent filmmaking, even when a manager is scrupulous about adhering to the duty of loyalty, conflicts of interest will arise throughout the filmmaking process. To be of concern to investors, the conflict must be material. Contracts to acquire rights, to distribute the film, and to compete with the film company by working for another company are among the types of transactions that are clearly material. Eating the catering on the set is not. The manager must use common sense in determining whether a reasonable investor would consider the conflict important, erring on the side of overdisclosure.

To resolve conflicts of interest, the Operating Agreement, partnership agreement, or bylaws should provide clear provisions. For example, the bylaws might mandate that when officers, directors, managers, or partners have a conflict of interest, such a transaction can only be completed after the following steps have been taken:

1. The conflict of interest is fully disclosed.
2. A disinterested group meets for discussion and approval of the transaction without the participation of the interested person. This may mean the disinterested directors on the board of directors, disinterested managers among the managing members, or a committee formed specifically for this purpose.

3. If the conflict includes a bid to provide services, a competitive bid or comparable valuation is solicited, if possible.

4. The body approving the transaction determines that the transaction is in the best interest of the organization.

5. The decision to approve the conflict of interest is summarized in writing, to be kept in the minutes of the corporation or the records of the business.

In many situations, no disinterested board of directors or managers will be available. In such a case, the Operating Agreement or bylaws should specify that substantially similar steps are taken by the members of the LLC, partners of the partnership, or shareholders of the corporation. In that situation, the best approach is to seek unanimous written consent of all investors by providing the information in writing and seeking signatures of approval.

3. Duty of Care

The duty of care requires that the officers, directors, managers, or partners act in good faith and exercise prudent decision-making in the undertaking of the business for the benefit of the business and its investors. Whereas the duty of loyalty provides a very demanding standard, the duty of care sets a low threshold. Independent filmmaking is a highly risky enterprise, so wide latitude is given to the filmmakers to act reasonably in an uncertain business.

The duty of care essentially requires that the filmmakers avoid being grossly negligent in the operation of the business. The filmmakers must be fully informed of their obligations and make every reasonable effort to meet those obligations. The duty of care would make the filmmakers liable to the company and its shareholders for failing to keep records, failing to acquire the rights necessary to make the film, or materially violating tax or professional obligations.

Other potential breaches of the duty of care are more ambiguous. Perhaps the most interesting and difficult situation would arise if the filmmakers determined that a film project would cost $100,000 to shoot under their business plan but they chose to begin principal photography when only $50,000 was raised. Is it unreasonable and grossly negligent to hope that an angel investor will appear before the money runs out? Certainly, it would have been more prudent to adjust the shooting schedule or other expectations to make a $50,000 film or to wait until full financing was in place. It might have been more prudent to spend $10,000 to create a trailer to help raise the additional funds. Nevertheless, the filmmakers may not have been grossly negligent in going forward with the shoot, depending on how reasonable it was to expect that the additional funds would be raised. If the filmmakers' expectations were low, then such a strategy may very well have been grossly negligent, in which case the filmmakers would be personally obligated to repay their investors.

Fortunately, independent film investors know how risky the industry can be, so they are generally reluctant to seek personal reimbursement. Filmmakers can resolve this common problem by disclosure in their business plans. If a production's business plan includes the $100,000 budget and the operational plan that starts principal photography as soon as 50 percent of the budget is raised, then all the investors are aware of the plan and its attendant risks. By investing in such a plan, the investors have agreed to follow its guidelines. In contrast, if the business plan or other contracts specify that principal photography will not commence until 100 percent of the budget is raised, the change in plans will violate both the contractual agreements and the duty of care.

The duty of care should serve as a check on the risks that independent filmmakers are willing to take. If there is no reasonable likelihood of a return, then the investors' money should not be spent. If the filmmaker goes into a project knowing the risks are very high, then the high-risk strategy should be disclosed to the investors. If the filmmaker is really seeking gifts, then the financing requests should be focused on friends and family.

C. Employer Obligations

Employment and labor obligations are perhaps the most detailed and the least followed aspect of independent filmmaking. The myriad federal and state laws are poorly suited to addressing the realities of the filmmaking industry. Luckily for independent filmmakers, principal photography typically ends, and most employees are dismissed before regulators have an opportunity to object to offending business practices. In addition, the employees themselves are often focused on completing the project and indifferent to their legal rights.

Nonetheless, employer obligations can create significant headaches for the successful filmmaker. If crew members are paid only small stipends, the crew members may successfully claim that they were entitled to be protected by minimum-wage laws, including overtime pay for working in excess of a 40-hour week—or even an eight-hour day under the law of some states. Filmmakers are not permitted to characterize every employee as an independent contractor if the individuals are working under the direction and control of the film company for an extended period. Employers must pay particular attention not only to wage and hour laws but also to hiring practices and antidiscrimination policies when managing the significant labor force involved with even the most modest of film projects.

1. Hiring

For a motion picture, hiring includes both very subjective choices regarding casting and much more routine decisions regarding support staff and technical personnel. Although casting is a form of hiring, the subjective nature of casting gives employers more discretion to be arbitrary in their hiring choices than employment laws might otherwise allow.

To fill the remaining positions, the filmmaker must adhere to a broad range of legal rules and limitations designed to ensure that job applicants are treated fairly. Recent changes in the attitudes throughout Hollywood have made pay equity and inclusion a high priority, and these priorities should be reflected by independent producers and directors.

An employer may not discriminate on the basis of categories such as race, national origin, gender, sexual orientation, age, or disability. In particular, the Americans with Disabilities Act requires that the employer make reasonable accommodations for an employee's disability unless that disability affects an essential job function. So, for example, the filmmaker would not have to consider a deaf candidate for the job of sound engineer, because hearing and judging sound quality is an essential function of the position, but that same candidate, if otherwise qualified, should be considered for the job of stunt person.

To deny a job on the basis of a disability, that disability must affect an essential job requirement. A deaf stunt person could not properly be passed over for a less-qualified applicant who is not hearing impaired merely because the person might be given a few lines of dialogue later in the production process. Similarly, an employer must make reasonable accommodations for an employee's disability, so the film company would be required to find a method to provide visual rather than auditory cues to begin and end action during filming.

Because discrimination is illegal, the company must avoid asking interview questions that could give rise to discriminatory practices. According to the Equal Employment Opportunity Commission, on both written questionnaires and in oral interviews, the interviewer should focus on issues related to the applicant's experience and skills, availability, and ability to fulfill the job requirements and avoid questions unrelated to those issues. Often interviewers make small talk to break the ice during an interview, but questions regarding marital status, religion, or other personal issues that might be used to discriminate are inappropriate and impermissible. The rules apply whether the person being hired is the film's director or the assistant script supervisor.

The hiring process also involves a significant amount of salesmanship by the film company. Often with independent film production, the company must convince the applicant to work for a deferred salary or minimum wage in exchange for a chance to participate in the potential windfall if the movie hits it big. While such optimistic projections are part of the vision of the independent filmmaker, the company must take care not to misrepresent the financial status of the project or the professional expertise of the participants. Filmmakers commonly lie about such matters, but doing so constitutes unfair trade practices under state and federal law, and it may be grounds for lawsuits if the project fails to meet employees' expectations.

Once the applicant has been hired, the film company must also verify the person's eligibility to work in the United States by following the instructions on Form I-9 from US Citizenship and Immigration Services. Employees must complete this form within three days of beginning work and provide documentation within three weeks. The I-9 form is not submitted to any government agency but must be retained by the company and presented in case of government inspection. The company must retain the I-9 for one year following the termination of the employee or three years from the date of hire, whichever is later. In addition, all employment applications and resumes must be retained for one year, even if the person was not hired.

2. Employment Status: Independent Contractors and Employees

One of the common techniques to avoid dealing with employment laws in the independent film community is to treat everyone as an independent contractor instead of an employee. This approach is only occasionally appropriate, and the overuse of the independent contractor designation can lead to significant tax and insurance liability for the film company.

An independent contractor is a self-employed person who provides service to the hiring party by taking it on as a client. For example, the catering company would typically be an independent contractor, providing craft services for a number of clients, including the film company. In recent years, the IRS and state regulators have made it a priority to protect workers who have been unfairly classified as independent contractors and denied their employment rights.

Although there are no precise standards, the IRS and the courts first look to the company's ability to control the activities of the worker. If the hiring party dictates the hours, the manner of the work, and the location where the work will be done, that level of control will generally indicate that the worker is an employee. If the person controls those factors, it suggests that the person is an independent contractor. Another significant characteristic of independent contractors is the ability to provide services for multiple clients. Similarly, ownership of one's own tools and equipment suggests status as an independent contractor.

Under these general parameters, most participants on a film project are not independent contractors. The cast, director, and designers work under the direction of the film company using equipment rented by the film company. They should be considered employees. On the other hand, caterers, costumers, sound engineers, and special effects teams tend to be on a shoot part-time, to bring their own tools, and to service multiple clients when the work is available. For these individuals, independent contractor status may be more appropriate.

The difference between the two categories is significant. The employer must pay Social Security taxes and withhold employment taxes on behalf of the employees. Independent contractors have no deductions taken from their paychecks and retain responsibility for all taxes. However, if the IRS or a state's labor department discovers that an employer has improperly treated an employee as an independent contractor, the company will face significant consequences, including not only the payment of back taxes but also interest and penalties.

In many states, employers have another reason not to overuse the independent contractor designation: it lessens the protection of workers' compensation insurance. An employee is covered by workers' compensation insurance in the event of a work-related injury, and in exchange the injured employee may not sue the employer for negligence. An independent contractor does not have the benefit of this insurance and has no restrictions on suing the film company in the event of a personal injury on the set of a production.

Workers' compensation may also be an issue for a third class of worker common on film projects—unpaid assistants. Depending on state laws, these assistants may or may not be covered by workers' compensation insurance. Unfortunately, due to long hours, dangerous equipment, and crew inexperience, independent film productions have a high risk of accidents. A company may find it is cheaper to pay volunteers a minimum wage, qualifying them for employee status and thus workers' compensation, rather than to purchase separate liability insurance to cover their risk of injury on the set.

3. Employment Status: Exempt or Salaried Employees

Like the difference between independent contractors and employees, the distinction between exempt and salaried employees affects the employer's obligations toward workers. Minimum-wage laws protect salaried employees, providing overtime pay for work in excess of 40 hours per week, or even eight hours per day in some states. Exempt employees, on the other hand, are not bound by wage and hour laws and are instead paid for the scope of the project rather than the hours worked.

To qualify as exempt, employees must earn at least $684 per week and fall into one of the following categories: executives, administrators, professionals, and salespeople. The creative professional exemption must meet the salary requirement, and "the employee's primary duty must be the performance of work requiring invention, imagination, originality or talent in a recognized field of artistic or creative endeavor."[1] Actors, musicians, writers, and similar categories of work qualify. These regulations have been changing more frequently in recent years, so the production company must pay attention to the regulations enforced at the time of production.

Executives include employees who supervise at least two other individuals, have management duties, and play a significant role in the decisions about hiring and staffing their departments. Historically, anyone with supervisory duties on a film will be working in an executive or professional capacity. Changes by the Department of Labor have tightened the rules, however, reducing the availability of the exemption. *Administrators* must exercise independent judgment in their administrative duties. This category may sound unnecessarily vague since, one hopes, every employee exercises independent judgment throughout the day. Maybe this is less true outside of the film industry.

Although stretching the definition of exempt employee does not carry the same magnitude of risk as misapplying independent contractor status, a film company should make every effort to comply with the law wherever possible.

4. Tax and Withholding Status

The film company has a number of specific obligations regarding employee tax payments. Immediately upon being hired, the employee should complete IRS Form W-4 to determine the amount of money to be withheld from the payroll to pay federal, state, and local income taxes. The employer must deduct the appropriate amount of money from each employee paycheck and deposit this money in a separate account. Severe fines and even potential criminal liability can be incurred for withholding an employee's tax payments and failing to submit those payments to the government. The W-4 must be kept for four years following the termination of the employee.

The company must withhold not only income taxes but also Social Security and Medicare taxes. For 2020, the Social Security tax is withheld at a rate of 6.2 percent for the first $137,700 earned per year. Medicare taxes are withheld at a rate of 1.45 percent on the entire amount earned each year. The company must also pay the employer's portion of Social Security and Medicare taxes, which is equal to the amount withheld from the employee. For Medicare, employers are responsible for withholding an additional 0.9 percent for an employee's wages paid in excess of $200,000 in a calendar year.

Following the end of each calendar year, the film company must submit a statement to the IRS reflecting the annual payment and taxes for each employee. The employee must receive Form W-2 by the first of February each year, and the IRS must receive Form W-3 by the first of March. Failure to file these forms can result in fines. More important, the former cast and crew need these forms to complete their own taxes, and the film company has an obligation to provide them with this information. The company should do whatever it can to maintain goodwill with former employees so that frustrations do not arise, and the former employees do not provoke investigations into the myriad employment and labor violations that regularly occur in independent film companies.

At some point the independent filmmaker may be required to take legal risks to continue the production. If no money is left in the production account and 12 pages of script are left to shoot, then the film may be completed by volunteer labor—since everyone was technically laid off when the funds gave out. The bottom line is that the filmmaker must make well-informed, pragmatic choices based on the associated risks. For example, a filmmaker should never fail to submit payroll taxes, even if the only way to afford it is to treat three salaried employees as exempt. Most accountants and attorneys would further recommend that a filmmaker forgo a scene involving an expensive wind machine before ever considering failing to pay withholding taxes or mischaracterizing the employment status of the cast and crew—which reflects why accountants and attorneys rarely become guerrilla filmmakers.

5. Loan-Out Employment Services

For independent filmmakers who want to sidestep many of these concerns, the best solution may be to handle employer obligations through a loan-out employment service. Such a company becomes the employer of record for the employees. The employment service collects and distributes the withholding taxes, and it collects and pays the obligations to the unions, guilds, and talent agencies. For some production companies, the cost of such services may be prohibitive, but for a production of even modest budget, a loan-out employment service may be a very sound investment in the stability of the film project and the longevity of the film company.

A less costly alternative is a payroll service, which handles the administration of employee payments but does not actually serve as the employer of record. It is useful for handling the details of bimonthly employee payments, but it does not relieve the film company of its primary duties as an employer, nor does it solve the longer-term issues of record keeping.

Increasingly, small production companies can obtain the same basic payroll services equally well using commercial software, for a fraction of the cost. A payroll program requires that someone remember to operate it and make the payments, but it offers sufficient information and support for a small filmmaker armed with a checklist of the proper forms to submit and a schedule of submission.

6. Profit Participants

For guerrilla filmmakers, the notion that minimum wage will be paid—or even that basic employment records will be filed—stands as little more than wishful thinking. While these fundamental duties should be fulfilled, practical guidance is the art of the possible. For those companies that would not otherwise attempt to meet their hiring obligations, another approach is to include all the participants in the risks and rewards of the film.

Unlike employees, the owners of an enterprise are not generally covered by hour and wage laws, nor are they included in workers' compensation insurance. The owners—general partners, managers, officers, or corporate directors—assume the risk and participate actively in the enterprise, so these legal protections are less necessary. If the film company truly consists of the cast, the director, and the producer, it may be appropriate to organize it as an LLC, with an Operating Agreement that treats all the participants as managing members. Thus, the filmmaker avoids many of the state and federal employment obligations while allowing everyone to share in the risks (minimized to the extent possible using the LLC) and rewards of the project. The portions need not be equal; the filmmaker can retain a larger share, reflecting the filmmaker's primary role in the production.

This technique should not be abused. As the scope and budget of a project increases, the reasonability of this approach diminishes. Nonetheless, for guerrilla filmmaking, this structure may at least serve as practical justification for looser employment practices.

D. Decision-Making

For the sake of both employees and investors, the film company has a responsibility to practice good decision-making by communicating effectively and creating clear lines of responsibility. If the filmmaker, business manager, and other senior staff all work closely to explore the impact of significant decisions, they have a common basis for decision-making. If their respective responsibilities are clearly delineated, they will be more capable of sharing the load.

The decision-making model provides the structure for planning all aspects of the film production, from making artistic choices about locations, cast, and story to navigating business decisions regarding equipment rentals, film permits, and service agreements. Except in the case of a sole proprietorship or general partnership, it is very important that the film company and not the filmmaker be the entity responsible for every contract and negotiation. Planning becomes the purview of the film company as a whole, and the decision-making process must allow for some delegation of authority.

As the production grows, responsibility for more decisions is delegated, so it becomes even more critical that information is shared among the affected parties. If possible, production meetings of the senior management should be held regularly. A delay in notifying the costume designer of a casting change may result in wasted effort and money. Location changes may cascade through the production, impacting every other art department. Conversely, if everyone knows of a cash shortage, then every department can look to find the least harmful ways to cut expenses and defer payments. Together, communication and delegation allow the production company to improve the chances of successfully completing the film and free the filmmaker to focus on the important artistic issues.

Good decision-making is fostered by having a clear business plan, realistic contingency planning, and ongoing communications among all key personnel.

E. Business Continuity

The film company provides the continuity for the film as it moves through the completion phase, the markets and festivals, and the various distribution windows. A successful film might continue to offer licensing opportunities, earn revenue, and demand the fulfillment of legal and contractual obligations for decades. The film company must be organized to anticipate this long-term commitment. To this end, the company maintains consistency regarding employment and tax record keeping, the regular distribution of revenues, the distribution of payments for unions and gross income participants, and the legal ownership of the film. Again, delegation may become critical.

A successful film often propels many of the production team into increasingly larger projects. This may make it difficult for them to manage the often more modest revenue from their early independent films. Delegation to a professional involved with the project, such as the accountant or attorney, may allow the film company to continue to meet its obligations while allowing the filmmakers to grow their careers.

5

The Property of the Film Company: The Film Concept

Once the film company is formed and its business obligations prepared for, the production company can finally turn its attention to the true purpose of any filmmaking project: telling a compelling story. As an artist, the filmmaker is concerned with discovering an engaging story concept and transforming it into a visual and auditory experience. As a business, the film company must be concerned with acquiring the legal rights to that story and respecting the legal interests of its owners or those depicted in it. By carefully crafting agreements with the rights holders, the company can maximize the filmmaker's artistic flexibility while minimizing risks of future legal problems.

A. Sources

Comic books, plays, newspapers, novels, and the filmmaker's imagination are among the many sources that serve as the basis for new film concepts. From a classic short story to a taxicab conversation, no bad source exists. The source material should not limit the creative choices of the filmmaker. From a business and legal perspective, however, each of these sources has certain limitations and certain advantages.

1. Original Ideas

From a legal perspective, original ideas are the easiest source material to develop, since there are no preexisting legal rights to consider. As long as the idea is truly conceived by the filmmaker, then the resulting story, which uses only the filmmaker's fictional characters and plot points, can be developed without limitation.

Borrowing general ideas from other sources does not violate copyright laws, but such use may run afoul of the filmmaker's preexisting duties under agreements not to use ideas that have been developed by other people. Detailed plots are more than mere ideas, and those are protected by copyright.

The business disadvantage of basing a film on an original idea is that the film lacks a "hook," or preexisting awareness of the story, making it more difficult to market. This may increase the difficulty not only in developing the film's marketing campaign but also in raising capital for the production of the film. Despite the ultimate success of the movies, filmmakers and distributors had less difficulty promoting the film *Ali* than earlier boxing films *Rocky* or *On the Waterfront*.

2. True Events

True events are tremendous sources of material. True stories cannot be "owned" by anyone. The First Amendment grants the filmmaker the right to retell a true story using original expression. Whether presented in documentary form or dramatized into a narrative film, true stories have a natural resonance for audiences, which in turn provide excellent marketing opportunities. And many true stories need to be told to promote ideas and impact society. Movies such as *12 Years a Slave*, *Schindler's List*, *Milk*, and *Boys Don't Cry* are award-winning for the truth they reveal.

Nonetheless, adapting true stories presents important legal complications. Unless the people portrayed in the movie have given their permission, or the accuracy of their portrayal can otherwise be established, the filmmaker risks being sued for libel. *Charlie Wilson's War* provides a fascinating glimpse into American politics and also serves as a stark reminder of the governmental policies that led to the rise of the Taliban. In that film, Mike Nichols and Aaron Sorkin had former congressman Wilson's blessings to tell his story and to show him drinking constantly, admitting to drug use, and fornicating with a married woman. Most filmmakers are not so fortunate. Without such permission, the risks for the filmmaker are much higher.

Despite the care taken by filmmakers, *When They See Us*, *The Laundromat*, *The Wolf of Wall Street*, *Boys Don't Cry*, *The Perfect Storm*, and *The Insider* are just a few of the many films that resulted in lawsuits or threats of legal actions over unflattering portrayals.

While it is often not possible to gain permission from all the participants in a true story, particularly if the adaptation paints them in an unflattering manner, the filmmaker can limit risk. Careful choices made throughout the writing and filming process, as well as contractual agreements with some participants, will allow the filmmaker to reduce exposure to crippling lawsuits or liability that could scare away distributors from otherwise brilliant films.

3. Comic Books

Comic books have become one of the most important sources of tent pole or blockbuster films, including the Marvel Cinematic Universe (MCU), which began with *Iron Man*; DC Comics' Superman and Batman franchises; the *X-Men* films; and Dark Horse Comics adaptations such as *Hellboy*, *The Mask*, and Frank Miller's *Sin City*. As an intensively visual medium with strong characters, the comic book naturally translates well into motion picture storyboards and scripts with little alteration. As with other previously published sources, comic books have a powerful relationship with a pre-existing audience; comic book fans are especially passionate about their favorite characters and stories. However, this does put pressure on the film producer to respect the audience's expectations.

The replacement of celluloid film with digital filmmaking and the ubiquitous use of computer-generated imagery (CGI) has eliminated the limitations of physical laws onscreen. Big budget studio films rely very heavily on CGI, but tools are available for special effects and digital effects to fit any budget.

What was once a small genre for science fiction and fantasy aficionados has grown into the largest market segment of motion pictures. Many of the top earning films and streaming episodic series developed from the MCU or from titles first developed by DC, Dark Horse, Image Comics, IDW Publishing, or other comic book publishers. Marvel is a division of Disney, and DC is a division of WarnerMedia (which is itself owned by AT&T). Dark Horse is independently owned but has entered into production arrangements with various film studios during its highly successful career. For the independent comic book companies, the audiovisual rights are usually negotiated at the time a comic book title is first acquired.

4. Novels and Short Stories

Novels, novellas, and short stories are a staple of feature filmmaking. Of the various forms of written literature, the short story is the best dramatic form to transfer to film, since time constraints and other limitations on motion pictures tend to oversimplify novels. Still, filmmakers often purchase the rights to both books and short stories to serve as the basis for their films. The business advantage of doing so is that a known story may help to attract financing and talent. The literary work can also serve as a starting point for the film's marketing campaign.

The filmmaker will need to purchase the film rights to any book or short story protected by copyright. The author of the story or the author's estate generally holds these rights. The filmmaker may choose to purchase all rights in the story by acquiring the author's copyright ownership, or instead purchase a limited license granting permission to make and distribute a single film production. If the book or short story is based on true events, then the filmmaker must acquire both the rights to the story and any additional rights necessary to fictionalize a true story.

5. Song Titles and Music

Song titles and musical lyrics can also serve as the creative element at the heart of a film. Using a recognized song in the film's title can lead to increased recognition for the movie; if the song is famous, then the movie appears famous as well. Songs may be less expensive than other source materials as a method of purchasing instant recognition, particularly if the song has not been heavily licensed for use in commercials or other film productions. Neither film titles nor song titles are protected by copyright, but oftentimes they are protected as trademarks, so permission is still required.

In addition, to include the song in the soundtrack, copyright permission must be obtained from the songwriter or the songwriter's publisher. If any popular recording of the song is to be used in the film, then the permission of the record producer or record distributor, often called the *label*, is also required. Permission is generally given in exchange for a licensing fee. Separate permission is required if the filmmaker plans to release a soundtrack album.

6. Stage Plays

Plays are another popular source of film ideas. Legally, plays are treated just like novels and short stories. And as with literary sources, audience familiarity can serve as a hook. Plays are also like film remakes in the sense that the story has already been told in a dramatic medium. But because plays tend to generate drama using stylized language rather than arresting visuals, translating them to film may be much more difficult than one would expect. Some play-to-film adaptations, such as the Oscar-winning *Driving Miss Daisy*, transfer successfully, but many are financial or artistic disappointments. For motion picture adaptations of musicals, the track record is even spottier. *Dreamgirls*, *Chicago*, and *West Side Story* have been financial and artistic successes, but many are not. The long-awaited adaptation of *Cats* became a financial disaster and one of the most reviled big budget films ever released.

In the world of independent filmmaking, plays are a mixed blessing. The stage history can help to raise funds and draw media attention for marketing purposes, but films based on plays are often treated differently from other films, which may limit some of the financial potential and turn off distributors. Nevertheless, making films and videos of classic plays in the public domain can provide a production company great experience at a very low cost.

7. Movies

Increasingly, filmmakers turn to studio vaults for interesting stories to retell. Remakes have instant recognition for investors and audiences. Once, such projects were generally limited to color updates of black-and-white films, but today remakes of all kinds are extremely common. *The Incredible Hulk* (2008) essentially remade *Hulk* (2003), which may set a record for the shortest time between versions. The Batman franchise retells the same group of stories on a regular basis. Occasionally a remake may be created as a shot-by-shot reproduction, as when Gus Van Sant remade the Alfred Hitchcock classic *Psycho*. More typically, however, a remake takes substantial liberties, updating the story and characters.

Remakes may be the most difficult projects to structure legally. Since the film that is the subject of the remake may itself have been based on another work under copyright, a series of permissions may have to be obtained. Further, since film companies often change hands or sell their libraries, researching the chain of title for a film may prove difficult.

The legal issues are especially tricky for films from the 1930s through the 1960s. Before the advent of television, film companies were not as aggressive about retaining every possible legal interest in a film. For example, the owners of a 1940s film might have sold the right to distribute the original film on television to another company, and that sale might have included the television rights to any remakes and sequels as well. A filmmaker who wanted to pursue a remake would have to acquire those television rights separately. Since the rise of television, and especially since the dawn of the Internet, film rights have become much less diffuse. Often, it is easier to acquire all necessary rights to a newer film than an older one.

8. Video Games, Websites, and Podcasts

The newest additions to the entertainment media are also the latest sources of motion picture content: video games, websites, and podcasts. Angry Birds was a breakout hit as a phone app and, to a lesser extent, as a movie franchise. Simple websites, like published literary diaries or blogs, may be treated like short stories or other literary works. In contrast, obtaining the rights to adapt a complex interactive website, phone app, or video game is like negotiating to remake a black-and-white movie. These projects' creators may have overlooked the potential of motion picture adaptation and failed to acquire the rights, so securing them requires careful analysis and contracting. Separate owners may control the rights to the story of the game, the artwork, and potentially the game play; each element to be incorporated into the motion picture must be identified and acquired separately. Similarly, if actors contributed their likenesses to the game, their permission may also have to be obtained, depending on the needs of the filmmaker and the actors' contracts.

The order of development might also be reversed, with websites, apps, and other interactive digital media often developing as supporting content for motion pictures. Because of these reciprocal relationships, the production company should be sure to acquire the necessary downstream rights to allow these ancillary products to be developed.

9. Industrials, Fan Fiction, and Everything Else

There was never a production category for television's *America Funniest Home Videos*, and yet the show has been in production since 1989, collecting pratfalls, pranks, animals, and baby videos. The cat videos that were the dominant theme of the Internet for a decade have given way to unboxing videos, fashion and makeup tutorials, how-to instructions for every conceivable project, fan fiction, video games, and product marketing. These activities are very different than their predecessors, but the film, television, and theatrical industry have been doing this since their inception.

Much of theater developed through the Passion Play and other staged performances dedicated to religious education, just as much of Greek theater had begun as celebrations of the Greek deities. Fiction has always been used to educate, indoctrinate, and train. In the golden age of theater, the industrials were large musical productions that were presented at conferences and trade shows. The industrials provided training and entertainment to large corporations' workforces and kept the Broadway talent working throughout the offseason. Hollywood also had its filmed industrials, with A-list talent working along with many others to create shorts and training videos for corporate clients.

The online media marketplace has reinvented all of these genres. Online production companies create corporate training content and self-help, promotion, and tutorial videos on all popular subjects, such as health, fitness, hygiene, language, literature, and pop culture.

In addition to these, the growth of fan fiction[1] and the acquiescence by the copyright holder to non-feature-length "nonprofessional productions" has led to an increase in productions by filmmakers exploring areas and themes not previously explored in traditional film.

B. Copyright Limitations on Source Material

In a number of ways, laws affecting copyright, trademarks, privacy, libel, and contract rights determine the availability of source material, limiting the options of the filmmaker. The most important of these factors is copyright. For independent filmmakers, copyright is both a blessing and a curse. It protects the filmmaker's ownership of the work being developed, but it also creates barriers to the source material that may be used to create that work. Filmmakers find themselves on both sides of copyright transactions: they need to acquire source material and to license their finished products.

1. Exclusive Rights Under Copyright

Copyright provides an author the rights of ownership for an original work. The author has the exclusive right to reproduce the work, publicly display the work, distribute copies of the work, publicly perform the work, and prepare *derivative works*.[2]

A "derivative work" is a work based upon one or more preexisting works, such as a translation, musical arrangement, dramatization, fictionalization, motion picture version, sound recording, art reproduction, abridgment, condensation, or any other form in which a work may be recast, transformed, or adapted. A work consisting of editorial revisions, annotations, elaborations, or other modifications, which, as a whole, represent an original work of authorship, is a "derivative work."[3]

A film based on a preexisting copyrighted work—a novel, play, earlier film, etc.—is considered a derivative work. For example, the Hitchcock thriller *Rear Window* is a derivative work based on the short story "It Had to Be Murder" by Cornell Woolrich.[4] The filmed version of *My Fair Lady* is an adaptation of the Broadway musical of the same name by Lerner and Loewe, which was itself based on the George Bernard Shaw play *Pygmalion*.[5]

The various exclusive rights of the copyright holder may be licensed separately to others. For example, the author of the short story "The Paleontologist" licensed the first publication of the story to a science fiction magazine but retained all other rights, including the rights to any filmed version of the story, audiobook, or other adaptation. The author could then choose to sell the movie rights to a filmmaker at a later date. The scope of the license depends on the language used in the contract. These contracts vary considerably, though generally literary authors are able to retain their motion picture and television rights to their work, even when signing with major publishers.

A license may be given free of charge, but more typically the copyright holder will require a fee in the form of an immediate payment, the right to receive some percentage of the proceeds from the film, or some combination of both. An author could sell the movie rights to a short story for a fee such as $5,000 and 1 percent of the gross profits of the film. If the filmmaker agrees to these terms, the short story author will sign a license agreement that transfers the film rights in exchange for the agreed-upon payment.

If the author is granting exclusive rights to use the copyrighted work, the assignment must be in writing, dated, and signed.[6] By law, nonexclusive permission may be granted either orally or in writing, but the filmmaker will find that exhibitors and distributors will insist on written documentation for each copyright assignment, license, or release. Every written license should include a signature and date.

As copyright holder on the film, the production company will possess the exclusive rights in the film. This gives the production company control over the shooting of the film, editing, distribution, and exhibition. The production company will typically sell the distribution rights to a distributor, which will then license the rights to theatrical exhibitors, television networks, and streaming services.

The copyright interests may be limited by any factors chosen by the copyright holder, including geography, time, language, and medium. The short story author, for example, might assign the exclusive publication rights in the English-language version of the story to one publisher for North American distribution, the exclusive publication rights in Spanish to a second publisher, and the rights for English-language publication of the same story in Europe to a third publisher. Since none of these publishers acquired the film rights, a filmmaker can still acquire worldwide rights to the motion picture.

For United State filmmaking, the production company should always acquire the worldwide rights to all audiovisual uses of the underlying material, in all languages. Given the global reach of the United States film industry, any limitations will undermine the ability of the independent film company to sell the project. In fact, the contractual rights should provide for "anywhere in the universe," because the long length of copyright will likely mean that there will be exploitation of films beyond the earth before the copyright of a new work will expire.

Copyright protects the author of the motion picture, which is typically the production company, and the law protects the copyright owner for every copyrighted image or piece of music utilized in the production. The need to acquire permission for the use of source materials goes well beyond simply licensing the short story or comic book on which the film is based. Every piece of set decoration that includes copyrighted material should be used only if the filmmaker has acquired a written release. Works of art from posters and on T-shirts are protected by copyright, and the rights to those items must be licensed, unless the use is a *fair use*, as described in chapter 14 (pp. 271–272).

The written agreement provides documentation that the production company has the right to use the copyrighted material in the film. The distributors and exhibitors will require this documentation for all copyrighted material incorporated into the film and for all performances used in the film.

As discussed in chapter 15 (pp. 290–294), documentaries and news gathering projects can use fair use to give them some flexibility. When documentary filmmakers, journalists, or web producers record actual events that are not staged or recreated by the filmmaker, fair use offers them more latitude in filming the copyrighted background images on T-shirts, posters, and billboards. The creators of fictional works do not have this flexibility.

2. The Term of United States Copyright and the Public Domain

Copyright provides lengthy, but limited, rights to published works. For works created beginning January 1, 1978, the term of copyright is the life of the author plus 70 years. In the case of a work-for-hire, the term is 95 years from publication or 120 years from the date of creation, whichever is earlier. Corporations use the 95 years from publication rule, since there is no "life" from which to measure the life plus 70 years. For any work created before that date, the time period varies depending on the date the work was first published and the laws applicable. For example, all published works more than 95 years old have fallen into the *public domain*, the term used for anything that has had its copyright expire or was never copyrighted. Anything less than 95 years old must be carefully screened before it is assumed to be in the public domain.[7]

Congress has often extended the length of copyright. The last extension, known as the Sonny Bono Copyright Term Extension Act, added 20 years to the length of copyrights for works that had not already fallen into the public domain. Before this act, the length of copyrights for works created before 1978 had been extended to 75 years. After 1998, the term became 95 years. This means that works published prior to 1923 (75 years old in 1998) are in the public domain—all works published in or before 1923 are free for use in the United States without copyright protection.

In addition, any work published in the United States more than 95 years old is in the public domain. There generally should not be any works protected for a longer period elsewhere in the world, but countries sometimes amended the general rules to grant term extensions (for example, during World War II), which may make the time for some works slightly longer. Before substantial investment is made in a work, the history of the copyright should be analyzed to determine whether it is in the public domain or it remains under copyright.

While famous works such as published novels by Charles Dickens or Cervantes are clearly in the public domain and free for all filmmakers to adapt, most works published in the 20th century and unpublished materials potentially hundreds of years older may remain protected by copyright in the United States or abroad. Works by Arthur Conan Doyle are now largely in the public domain, while most of the works published by Agatha Christie remain protected by copyright.

Plays by Shakespeare are in the public domain because they were written before copyright existed. Similarly, a play such as George Bernard Shaw's *Pygmalion* (made into a number of films and adapted for the musical *My Fair Lady*) is now in the public domain because the play's copyright expired in 1988 in both the United States and Great Britain.[8] Once a copyright has expired in the United States and abroad, the filmmaker is free to utilize that material as the source or basis for any work.

3. Copyright as a Barrier to the Film

While copyright is the primary source of protection for filmmakers, it is also a curse. For the independent filmmaker, the ability to use public domain material has tremendous advantages. The material is free. There is no need to ask permission to use the material. There are no delays waiting for a response to the request. The material can be altered without the need for any additional consent.

For some materials—particularly unpublished works or those written by foreign authors—the reliance on the public domain will always include a significant amount of risk. For example, a novel may have fallen into the public domain in the United States but may still be protected by copyright in another country, such as Canada or France. Unfortunately, there are no central registries of copyrights, so the status of a novel published in Canada, Europe, or elsewhere in the world must be researched in each country.

In Europe, the situation is particularly complex, because the European Union member countries are required to extend the greatest protection to any European citizen that any other member country provides. As a result, copyrights that might otherwise have fallen into the public domain in those countries with shorter copyright terms are now automatically extended to the longer German copyright period of life of the author plus 70 years. As a general rule, therefore, a European work cannot be assumed to be in the public domain unless it has been more than 70 years since the death of the author. For any other work, expensive and time-consuming research must be conducted to determine the status of the copyright. To limit this expense somewhat, the filmmaker may wish to limit the research to the most important major foreign film markets, such as Canada, England, France, Spain, Italy, Japan, and Mexico.

Despite their limitations, public domain plays in particular serve as a valuable source for independent filmmaking because the story, dramatic structure, characters, and many other literary elements are provided for the filmmaker. Translating public domain plays into film may serve as an excellent method of learning filmmaking, creating a solid self-education program for the filmmaking student.

4. Subject Matter of Copyright

Copyright ownership covers, with limited exceptions, "original works of authorship fixed in any tangible medium of expression."[9]

Fixation is merely the requirement that the expression be recorded in some manner. It can be written, recorded, videotaped, filmed, digitized, or fixed in an entirely new way. Screenplays, novels, and all writings are fixed as soon as the words are typed into a computer's memory or written on paper. A stand-up comedian's act is not protected by copyright unless the comedian writes it out or records a performance. (A written notation, however, can be in shorthand, such as is used for choreography.) An improvisational rehearsal process is not protected unless the stage manager's notes carefully record the session or the session is videotaped. Sheet music is sufficient to protect a new musical score, and a detailed choreographer's notation will be enough to protect a new dance. There is no requirement that the copyrighted work display a copyright symbol (©) or other notice of copyright, though there are certain benefits of using the copyright notice and registration with the US Copyright Office within three months of publication.[10]

5. Ideas

Copyright does not protect the underlying idea or concept, however, only the expression of such an idea.[11] In practice, this means that basic plots, themes, and general subjects are not protected by copyright. No one can own "boy meets girl," since the idea is the basis for thousands of plots. But the written or filmed story of one such boy and girl, including the description of scenes, the dialogue, and the narration, is protected by copyright once it has been fixed on paper or in digital memory.

The line between the idea and the expression of an idea is often a difficult one to conceptualize. Dialogue, unless it comes from trial transcripts or other public domain sources, is invariably copyrightable expression, but copyright covers more than just a film's dialogue. Stopping a runaway bus is an idea. Add well-developed characters, a number of plot twists, and interesting locations, and it becomes the specific expression behind the movie *Speed*. A man-made monster run amok is an idea. Add a struggling scientist, a love interest, and unsolved local murders, and it remains an idea; *Frankenstein*, *Dr. Jekyll and Mr. Hyde*, *Hulk*, and many others fit the bill. Specific characters and plot twists unique to the story and its characters help transform the idea into protected expression.

6. Other Matters Not Protected by Copyright

In addition to ideas, copyright does not cover facts, historical information, titles, the typeface that may appear in the film's credits, or short phrases such as "I'll be back," "I've got a bad feeling about this," or "*Hasta la vista, baby.*" Any filmmaker is free to use them without fear of copyright violations. The Robert Wise movie *The Hindenburg*, based on the destruction of the famous German zeppelin, violated no copyright, even though the historical information it dramatized was first published as a rather speculative conspiracy theory instead of an official statement of fact. The same is true of factually based movies about the sinking of the *Titanic*, the assassinations of President Kennedy and Malcolm X, and the many other historical dramas.

C. Other Legal Limitations on Source Material

In addition to the laws of copyright, a number of other legal concepts limit the free use of source material. Most of these limitations can be overcome if permission is granted from the rights holder. Whether substantial payment is necessary for the permission will depend on the nature of the rights sought, the size of the film being made, and the relationship between the rights holder and the filmmaker.

1. Trademarks

Trademarks are words, symbols, or other indicators that identify a particular source for the goods or services of a business in commerce. They range from simple product names such as Diet Coke®, to identifying marks such as the roar of the MGM lion or the pink color of Owens Corning roof insulation. Trademarked products are often licensed for use in films, providing the filmmaker free access to the product along with permission to film it.

Increasingly, many product manufacturers will pay for the opportunity to have their products featured.

Trademark law does not generally give the trademark holder rights to control the depictions of the trademarked item in film or television. No one asks permission of clothing manufacturers to clear everyday shirts and pants when used on a set. Despite this general rule, there are a few areas where the filmmaker must be cautious in using trademarked items without permission.

The first such area is in the advertising and marketing materials of the project. If the effect of the trademark use in the advertising is to suggest an endorsement from the trademark owner, that use might trigger a claim for trademark infringement. Such an analysis will depend on how the trademark is portrayed and featured in the advertisement, but highlighting trademarks in the ads for a film without permission should generally be avoided.

The second concern regards the *disparagement* of the trademark, meaning the use of the trademark in a way which brings embarrassment or criticism to the product. Like the use in advertising, this is very fact-specific, and the trademark laws protecting trademarks from disparagement are limited by the First Amendment interests of the filmmaker. Nonetheless, disparaging uses are likely to invite litigation from the trademark holder, and the factual nature of the cases make these very expensive to defend against.

A concern related to disparagement is misuse of the product that suggests a harmful or unintended use. For example, if a scene depicts a character sniffing glue to get high, the filmmaker is better served by not showing a particular brand of glue. The potential for the trademark holder to bring an action will be even higher if the filmmaker chose a brand of glue formulated to remove the chemicals that could make a person high, since the example would then have the potential to mislead the public regarding the nature of the trademark owner's product.

Chapter 14 (pp. 269–275) provides a more detailed explanation of how to obtain the necessary rights to use trademarked products or to reduce the potential for legal disputes. In addition, many trademarks utilize copyrighted artwork, allowing the trademark owners both a trademark and copyright claim. As a result, if an unauthorized trademark is to be featured in an independent film, it must be used carefully, in consultation with the filmmaker's attorneys.

2. Misappropriation and Ideas

Legal protection for ideas remains a controversial topic in intellectual property law. Fueled by high-technology fields and issues of trade secrecy, the legal limits on when someone is liable for the use of another's idea have never been well defined.

Filmmakers are pitched ideas from friends, family members, and restaurant staff on a constant basis. The law provides that an idea is not protected by copyright, and unless it is the subject of an enforceable contract between the parties, a person has no obligation to pay for an idea. On the other hand, if the filmmaker made statements or took actions to suggest that "if I use your idea, I'll pay you for it," then the later use of that idea might be subject to a legitimate contractual claim.

The safest way to hear new ideas is to be sure a release is signed, clearly stating that while the filmmaker will not violate any copyright in the submission, many similar ideas are often presented, and the filmmaker cannot provide compensation for any ideas. For the writer, the safest suggestion is to refrain from sharing ideas until they have been developed sufficiently to enjoy copyright protection.

3. Defamation

Defamation is a false statement of fact that injures a person's reputation in the manner defined by statute or case law. A statement is defamatory if "it tends so to harm the reputation of another as to lower him in the estimation of the community or to deter third persons from associating or dealing with him."[12] At common law, a statement was defamatory if it held one out for hatred, ridicule, or contempt. Only a living person may be defamed; once the person has died, the heirs may not pursue the claim. A related doctrine known as *trade libel* applies to businesses.

To be defamatory in the United States, the person alleging the defamation must prove that the statement is both false and harmful, that it pertains to the person suing, and that it has been made available to someone other than the person claiming to be defamed. Defamation requires only that the defamatory statement was shared with at least one person, so it can be done orally or through publication in a script, on a website, through a letter or email, or via some other recorded form. Republishing a defamatory statement will give rise to a new claim for defamation. As a result, a filmmaker is responsible for any defamatory material depicted in the motion picture. A filmmaker cannot rely on source material to assume that the content is not defamatory.

Filmmakers face different legal challenges depending on the nature of the party who objects to the characterization. Public officials, such as the president or state officeholders, and public figures, such as O. J. Simpson or Ralph Nader, can only win a defamation lawsuit if the filmmaker is found to have published defamatory material intentionally—with knowledge it was false—or recklessly—with reckless disregard toward the truth or falsity of the statements.[13]

A person is considered a *public official* only if the official holds a significant public office. Merely being a public employee is not sufficient. The person must have some position of influence or importance or be subject to ongoing public scrutiny—for instance, most elected officials and others who are in the position to direct public policy. Although the United States Supreme Court itself has been somewhat vague as to the standard, other courts have developed a series of tests. In California, for example, a four-part test has been used:

A "public official" is someone in the government's employ who:
1. has, or appears to the public to have, substantial responsibility for or control over the conduct of governmental affairs;
2. usually enjoys significantly greater access to the mass media and therefore a more realistic opportunity to contradict false statements than the private individual;
3. holds a position in government which has such apparent importance that the public has an independent interest in the person's qualifications and performance beyond the general public interest in the qualifications and performance of all government employees; and
4. holds a position which invites public scrutiny and discussion of the person holding it entirely apart from the scrutiny and discussion occasioned by the particular controversy.[14]

The purpose of this test is to distinguish the rank-and-file employees from those government officials who are in the public eye.

The same standards have been extended to famous individuals and those who actively engage in public discourse on controversial matters. They have made themselves *public figures*, subject to the same legal standards for defamation as public officials. As one court explained, "public figures are those who command sufficient continuing public interest by their position or their purposeful activity amounting to a thrusting of their personality into the 'vortex' of an important public policy and have a realistic opportunity to counteract false statements."[15]

Many interesting films based on true events are not about public officials or public figures, however. Instead, they deal with "little people" who change the system or serve as whistleblowers. Many of the characters in films like *Norma Rae*, *Schindler's List*, and *Erin Brockovich* are *private figures* whose stories deeply impact us all. If the film is about a private individual involved in some matter of public interest, then the filmmaker can be liable for being merely negligent in failing to ascertain the truth[16] or in the manner in which the truth was altered to fit the dramatic needs of the film.[17]

Finally, the person suing the filmmaker for defamation must prove that the statements or depictions are untrue, and that the statements or depiction are harmful to the person's reputation. If the jury believes the film is accurate, the filmmaker will not lose the lawsuit. If the film is inaccurate and harmful and the person suing is a private figure, the filmmaker will be held accountable for the damages if the research or depiction was made without reasonable care regarding the facts. If the person suing is an official or public figure, the research or depiction must be the result of intentional lies or reckless disregard for the truth. A filmmaker should not be held liable for honest mistakes involving public officials or public figures.

One particularly insidious form of libel is to falsely attribute quotes to a person. The Supreme Court has held that otherwise unobjectionable statements can be deemed libelous when they are transformed into quotes.[18] When a film character is based on a living person, the dialogue sometimes includes statements that were originally made by critics of that person but are now portrayed as self-deprecating comments made by the character. This practice can increase the amount of material in the film to which objections may be made.

Fictionalization may also result in the creation of *composite characters*—fictional characters that embody attributes of a number of live individuals. Because of the requirement that the statement be of or concerning the person claiming defamation, a common practice is to create fictional characters to stand in for unsavory conduct that may have been undertaken by real people. If the fictional character or composite character is identifiable as a real person involved in the situation, then the fictionalization only adds to the potential for liability.[19] Litigation over this practice seems to occur most frequently when the character's name bears some resemblance to the living person's name or if the role played by the person is closely identified by a person involved in the underlying incident.

Fortunately for filmmakers, United States courts disfavor defamation awards. This may be a result of their strong respect for the First Amendment, but it may also reflect their respect for the detailed investigative process that major motion picture studios and television networks follow for their docudramas and other fact-based works. Needless to say, the latter will not extend to guerrilla and other independent filmmakers shooting on-the-fly films on shoestring budgets. For this reason, it is vital that when producing a fact-based motion picture, the filmmaker documents every step taken to verify the truth of the story before creating the script and shooting the film. As discussed subsequently, if the people involved in true stories sign agreements with the filmmaker, they are less likely to sue for defamation, but unless every person depicted in a fact-based story has signed a release, the risk of a defamation claim remains.

Filmmakers should be mindful that the United States is much more protective of the rights of free expression than other countries. The standards for defamation and libel are very different in Europe and Asia, so a project that is not libelous in the United States may still draw defamation claims abroad. Even if the filmmaker intentionally avoids distribution in libel-friendly countries, the sale of copies or international streaming may provide a sufficient basis for a lawsuit in a foreign jurisdiction—particularly if it is the home country of the person offended.

4. False Light Privacy Invasion

The common law doctrine of false light creates liability for invasion of privacy if a published work provides a person with "unreasonable and highly objectionable publicity that attributes to him characteristics, conduct, or beliefs that are false," and thereby causes that person to be "placed before the public in a false position."[20] The depiction may be laudatory, but if it is highly objectionable and false, it may be actionable. False light provides a second basis for objecting to false and harmful content, even if the statements would not appear to hold a person up to ridicule or contempt. A good example would be a story that incorrectly attributed a heroic self-defense shooting to a particular police officer. Since shooting in self-defense is not illegal or immoral, the claim would not be defamatory, but it may still be deemed highly offensive to the officer and a reasonable person, depending on the situation. A docudrama that falsely connected a New Jersey firefighter to the World Trade Center rescue effort could result in injury to the person's career because it made it difficult to live up to the false impression caused by the suggestion. If the firefighter suffered financial or other damage as a result, the film company may be liable for those damages. Unlike alleged libelous statements made against private persons, false light claims require intent or reckless disregard of the truth rather than mere negligence.[21]

5. Invasions of Privacy

Not all statements have to be false to be actionable. The right of privacy goes further than defamation or false light to protect a private individual from having unfavorable information published or presented to the public, even if the information is true. The right to privacy is limited in scope. It will not protect either a public figure or a private individual if the information is newsworthy, but the law does offer limited protection "to keep a man's business his own."[22]

Under common law, an individual may be entitled to damages if unauthorized, highly offensive details of that person's private life are widely disseminated.[23] A filmmaker can be held liable for broadly publishing information about a subject's physical or mental health issues, identifying the individual involved—or even for creating a well-meaning public service notice, intended to promote social responsibility, that identifies a family in dire financial need.

Generally, if a person is out in public, the person cannot claim to have any protections for intrusion into seclusion. But this may overstate the situation, and filmmakers should be respectful of "private" public areas, such as locker rooms or bathrooms, and be wary of using cameras to zoom in on uncurtained windows. In such cases, the defense that the filmmakers themselves were in public may not withstand the growing protections of personal privacy.

Privacy law has grown extensively in the United States as an expansion of laws and regulations at both the state and federal level. In certain industries, such as finance and health care, information provided to service providers is protected as private information. If a documentary or narrative filmmaker were to collaborate with one of those providers, the film company could face potential claims for common law invasion of privacy or violations of state and federal privacy laws if the filmmaker used the collaboration to publish protected information. Filmmakers would not be obligated to protect the private information if it had been disclosed publicly by someone other than the filmmaker prior to the production.

Privacy laws are very specific and will only impact those productions dealing with information that is confidential or protected by privacy. Nonetheless, if a film crew tried to intrude into a medical examination, for example, the patient's right to medical privacy would generally trump any claims by the film crew of its First Amendment rights to broadcast the story. The use of a telephoto lens to shoot the medical records of a star athlete for purposes of a newscast or documentary would still run afoul of the patient's right to medical privacy, and the efforts by the filmmakers could also trigger common law claims for intrusion into seclusion.

6. Publicity Rights

The right of publicity is the right to control the commercial exploitation of a person's identity, name, or likeness.[24] This right has also been extended to protect a person's performance. Publicity differs from privacy because it recognizes that individuals have the right to make money from their good name. New York, California, and many other states protect publicity rights very broadly. The California statute is representative:

> Any person who knowingly uses another's name, voice, signature, photograph, or likeness, in any manner, on or in products, merchandise, or goods, or for purposes of advertising or selling, or soliciting purchases of, products, merchandise, goods, or services, without such person's prior consent . . . shall be liable for any damages sustained by the person or persons injured as a result thereof.[25]

The law generally limits publicity rights to the selling or advertising of goods or services. Publicity rights protections do not extend to the editorial content of newspapers, magazines, literature, film, television, radio, or DVDs, all of which is protected by the First Amendment. A newspaper could run an article about Beyoncé and illustrate it with a photo of her eating a famous brand of popcorn without obtaining her permission. On the other hand, the popcorn manufacturer could not purchase the rights to publish the photo and use it to sell the popcorn without also acquiring the rights from Beyoncé to use her image for the sale of the product.

Further, most states do not just afford publicity protection to famous people.[26] For instance, if a photograph shows recognizable individuals from corporate events or panels, it creates the impression of association with a company's products or services. When that photograph is used to advertise or otherwise commercially benefit the product or service, permission must be obtained from each person who is identifiable in the photograph.

Publicity rights should not interfere with a filmmaker's interest in making a biography or even of introducing real persons into fictional drama. The 101-year-old Dame Olivia de Havilland brought an action for both invasion of her right of publicity and for defamation regarding the docudrama entitled *Feud: Bette and Joan*, about her part in the rivalry between Bette Davis and Joan Crawford. Her claims were summarily dismissed.

Unfortunately, publicity rights law varies greatly from state to state, so there is some ambiguity as to the potential risks. Therefore, insurance companies and distributors are sometimes quite conservative about these potential risks and demand that anyone who is identifiable provide a written release. As a result, filmmakers must anticipate not only the legal limitation placed on their expression but also the additional reservations that may come from distributors or insurance carriers.

D. Literary Tools: Treatments, Storyboards, and Screenplays

Movies have been sold to distributors based solely on the posters shown at film markets, but more commonly, films are developed using treatments, storyboards, and screenplays. These are tools for the filmmaker to capture the story before it is shot on film; to communicate with the investors, buyers, cast, and crew; and to keep all parties wedded to a common vision for the project. Ultimately, however, no matter how much time and effort are placed in their development, they are merely tools, scaffolding to allow the movie to be made.

These tools may be created in any order, depending on the filmmaker's needs and the audience for whom a tool is intended. For example, investors often find a full screenplay to be difficult to read and understand; they may respond better to a short synopsis rather than a lengthy treatment. For a highly visual story, the storyboards may communicate more than any other tool.

1. Treatments and Synopses

The essence of the motion picture is usually described in a *synopsis* of 3 to 10 pages. This document simply introduces the movie's plot, characters, and theme. In contrast, a proper *treatment* of a script is typically an extensive scene-by-scene narrative summary that often runs one-third the length of the finished screenplay. Investors and others often use the term *treatment* to describe both this detailed summary and the briefer synopsis.

The synopsis is a teaser, drafted to pique the curiosity of the reader and create a hunger for the screenplay. It will be used to introduce the film to prospective investors, production companies, performers, and crew. Because the synopsis is the document most heavily relied upon by investors, it has more impact on the project than anything other than the completed film.

The treatment, on the other hand, serves more practical purposes. Writers will consult it while revising the screenplay, and it can help producers and department heads to visualize the budgetary implications of the project. A good exercise is to continue to update the treatment to match the screenplay as the development progresses.

Tremendous care must be taken not to distribute a synopsis or treatment too freely or hastily. Filmmakers seldom have a chance to present a film project twice. If an early synopsis or treatment is drafted in a rush, or if it is written by a producer or other participant who does not possess the ability to capture the essence of the script, it may end the interest of a potential investor, cast member, or other principal.

2. Storyboards

Storyboards provide a scene-by-scene visual outline of the motion picture, almost like a comic book. Because of their visual impact and the increasing ease with which they can be produced via computer-based imaging, storyboards have become more and more common as a tool to communicate with both investors and the creative team being assembled for the film. Well-crafted storyboards, however, are still time-consuming and expensive to create. They are most critical for science fiction, horror, and other genre films in which the imagery is exotic or expressionistic. For films that are more realistic in style—for instance, a movie set in a New York apartment— storyboards may be less valuable to communicate the action.

3. Screenplays

The screenplay remains the most important tool for making the film, serving as road map, guide, and final authority. The screenplay includes everything needed to complete the film, including all the dialogue, action, sets, scenery, and characters. A typical screenplay runs between 90 and 120 pages in length.

Screenplays follow a very stylized and specific format, to which even the independent filmmaker should adhere. Innovation should be seen on the screen, not in the page layout. Many guides have been written about screenplay formatting. In addition, computer programs such as Final Draft and Movie Magic provide helpful tools to write in the correct style—but once a writer learns the basics of the screenplay format, any word processor can generate a properly formatted script.

A screenplay must serve many roles, depending on the reader:

a. Literature

First and foremost, a great screenplay will work as a piece of writing. Like a short story, it must capture the atmosphere of each scene with only a few words. The merits of the story, the characters, and the structure must be strong, powerful, and believable. This is true of even the silliest of parody films. If the script does not make for a compelling story, the film is unlikely to succeed.

b. Character Guide

The screenplay must include sufficient information about each of the characters so that casting decisions and costume choices can be made. The script should also tell the actors about the characters they are portraying and provide them information and tools to develop those characters.

c. Visual Guide

Since film is a visual medium, the screenplay should create snapshots of each scene that a graphic artist could translate directly into storyboards. (For a film that actually utilizes storyboards, the artist will draw them based on the screenplay.) The screenplay creates the visual style that controls all the other visual elements of the project.

d. Screen Stopwatch

The screenplay is often used as a guide to timing the film. As a rule of thumb, one page in the script equals one minute on the screen. While this may not work page for page, a 120-page script translates fairly consistently into a two-hour film. This is not an absolute rule, but the principle is sufficiently common that writers generally use it when structuring screenplays.

e. Production Clock

Another rule of thumb for the timing of traditional feature film scripts is that one page of script equals half a day's filming. Television scripts shoot five pages a day. Although digital filmmaking does not yet have any established guides, once a pace is established, it is often followed closely. The writer can improve the accuracy of time estimates by using more text to describe longer, more difficult shots and briefer language to describe shorter, simpler setups.

f. Calling Card

Finally, every actor, investor, production company, or other person who considers becoming involved with the film will use the script to evaluate the project. The script becomes the point of introduction for many key participants. It becomes part of the contractual relationship, binding the filmmaker to deliver a movie that is substantially similar to the script.

Because the screenplay takes on so many different parts in the filmmaking process, before any other work is done, the screenplay must be substantially completed. Even though stories abound of movie projects in which the script is hastily rewritten on the set, this practice wastes time and increases editing costs. The independent filmmaker does not have this luxury.

This should not suggest that the finished screenplay will exactly match what appears on the screen. A host of changes, compromises, and new ideas will force the movie to evolve from the original script, but it remains critical that the script be as strong as possible before shooting begins. Even if the choice is made to improvise the story, a script remains important for establishing the dramatic structure, locations, emphasis, and relative timing of scenes. The only obvious exception would be a documentary, but even many documentaries are well structured and partially scripted before shooting begins.

E. Protecting the Filmmaker's Property

As the concept of the film is developed into a screenplay and eventually into the film, the filmmaker must protect the material from theft. For screenplays and treatments, protection will come from federal copyright law as well as from well-drafted contracts. The Writers Guild of America also provides an evidentiary service.

1. Copyright Protection for the Unpublished Screenplay

Because federal copyright law protects a script or film as soon as it is written down or otherwise recorded, as an unpublished work, a screenplay does not have to be registered with the United States Copyright Office. A lawsuit for copyright infringement may not be filed until the copyright registration is issued, however, so the screenplay should be filed as soon as there is a hint of difficulty with anyone involved with the project. The money spent on the copyright filing buys a strong negotiating chip.

Generally speaking, it is also a good idea to put a copyright notice on the work. The notice is only necessary for a published work to be registered, but it may serve as a good reminder to discourage theft even when used on an unpublished work. A proper notice includes the copyright symbol © and/or the word *copyright*, the year of the copyright, and the name of the copyright holder. For example, the notice on this book reads "Copyright © 2021 by Jon M. Garon."

Proper registration creates a presumption of a valid copyright. For most purposes, copyright registration can now be completed online at http://www.copyright.gov. The US Copyright Office provides very helpful guidance, and most filers should not require an attorney or other assistance.

2. Writers Guild Registration

The Writers Guild of America (Writers Guild, or WGA) has a system by which a treatment or screenplay can be placed in deposit, to serve as evidence if there is a dispute over its authorship. Any treatment, television script, or screenplay may be registered. The Writers Guild will also accept stage plays and other written ideas prepared for audiovisual works. Registration lasts for five years and may be renewed.

The Writers Guild registration does not replace copyright, but it does create evidentiary proof of the existence of the work as of the date of registration. When the submission is received by the Writers Guild, it is sealed in an envelope, and the date and time are recorded. The Writers Guild then returns a numbered receipt to the author that serves as the official documentation of registration. The work remains in a sealed envelope that the WGA can forward to a court, unopened, as evidence. The Writers Guild also accepts electronic deposits, providing a similar process for digital submissions by authors.

Many independent film companies that accept unsolicited submissions insist that the Writers Guild registration number be marked on the script, so that there is documentary proof of the material submitted.

3. Film Titles

Although neither copyright law nor the Writers Guild protects titles, the Motion Picture Association of America (MPAA) provides a title registry for its members and contracting film companies. Film distributors must avoid duplicating the names already taken on the MPAA registry. To consult the registry, the filmmaker must sign the Non-Member Title Registration Agreement. The proposed titles are distributed to all members, and members may file objections to the use of titles. Since titles are often changed by distributors, the filmmaker may not need to check with the MPAA prior to production, but if a title is derived from a memorable piece of dialogue or significant action in the movie, then it may be wise to know of any potential conflicts before it is filmed.

Availability in the MPAA system should not be the only review. Motion picture titles are really trademarks and may compete with similar trademarks in other literary works, including novels, songs, albums, and video or computer games. As the marketing and merchandising campaign for the film is being first developed, the filmmaker or the distributor should enlist the service of an attorney or otherwise conduct a trademark search. One useful source for such a search is CompuMark. The company will provide a comprehensive trademark search, including use in film titles and in other media.

6

Contracts

Throughout the filmmaking process, the filmmaker will negotiate and enter into a wide range of contracts, starting the process with an agreement to purchase the literary rights or other underlying rights upon which the screenplay and film will be based. The terms of that agreement will set the stage for the financing, employment, and many other agreements that follow.

Although each agreement has its own particular terms, the purchase agreement can serve as a model for negotiating and structuring the other contracts. The parties to any of the film company's agreements are likely to be engaged with each other throughout the life of the film production, and possibly for decades following the initial release, as the film continues to be shown. The negotiating strategy should take into account the long-term nature of the parties' relationships.

The goal of the agreement should be to provide what each party needs to be successful. All information should be as accurate as the filmmaker can provide. The film company should build professional and economic incentives for the other parties into each contract to encourage the success of the film. This does not mean that the film company should be unduly "soft" or overly generous, but rather the parties should understand that there are many reasons people support independent films and incorporate those motivations into the contracts. Payments, residuals, credits, thank-yous, copies, screening invitations, and other incentives should all be utilized by the filmmaker to help make the movie possible. When approached from this perspective, negotiating contracts becomes much simpler, and success is much easier to achieve.

A. Purchasing a Literary Property

To obtain the right to make a movie out of an existing short story, novel, comic book, or play, the filmmaker must license the movie rights from the author or copyright owner. Once the proper copyright owner has been identified, a license must be negotiated that awards the filmmaker the right to produce and distribute the motion picture. The nature of the license may vary significantly depending on the type of source material, its commercial value, and its age.

1. Identification of the Copyright Owner—Ownership and Work-for-Hire

The first step is one of the most important: confirming who actually owns the interests needed by the filmmaker. Copyright generally vests initially in the author of the work. The author can then sell or license the copyright. If the author sells the copyright, then the new owner of the copyright has all the exclusive rights to the copyright other than certain termination rights that are not transferable. If the author licenses the copyright, then any party that acquires the exclusive rights to the copyright has the authority to further license those rights unless the contract between the author and the licensee restricts additional licensing. The author of a novel, for example, is the copyright holder. If the author sells the novel's copyright to a publisher, then the publisher may own the film adaptation rights. If, instead, the author licensed the publication rights to the publisher, then the author will have retained the film adaptation rights. For the filmmaker, it is important to review the filings in the copyright office and the contracts between the author and publisher.

A second category of ownership rules exists for works made for hire. The term refers to works that are made under an employment relationship. The law provides for two very different methods of establishing copyright ownership as a work made for hire (or work-for-hire). The first is when the work is authored by an employee as part of the employee's regular duties. To be a work-for-hire under this first test, the author must be an employee of the company for which the work was made, and the person must be creating the work as part of the person's regular employment. For example, all the artwork created by salaried employees at motion picture studios falls within this work-for-hire rule.

The second type of work-for-hire involves non-employees. An author can enter into a work-for-hire agreement with another party, provided that the agreement is in writing and signed by both parties and the work falls into a specific list of nine types of works listed in the Copyright Act. Works made "as a part of a motion picture or other audiovisual work" are listed among these nine types, along with contributions to collective works, supplementary works, translations, compilations, and other categories.[1]

When a copyright is created as a work-for-hire, the copyright owner is the employer. The employee has no rights to the copyright.

Determining the ownership of an underlying work starts with learning whether the author of the work was the initial copyright owner or whether the author created the work as a work-for-hire. Based on the law and industry custom, plays, novels, and musical works are almost never works made for hire. In contrast, screenplays, comic books, films, and television are typically authored under work-for-hire agreements.

As a result, the apparent rights holder may not be the person with authority to grant the necessary license. Although it is standard practice for the license to include warranties from the seller of the literary work that the seller is the owner of the work and has full authority to sell the rights, the filmmaker should take steps in advance to avoid any problems.

For example, if a short story author transferred the film rights to the publisher of the book collection in which it was included, then an agreement between that short story author and the filmmaker will fail to grant the filmmaker the rights needed for the film. The filmmaker may have a valid legal claim against the short story author, but that will be little solace when the film project grinds to a halt and litigation begins.

If the work is based on literary characters that appear in more than one work, the filmmaker should research the origin of those characters and be sure either that the characters are in the public domain or that the seller of the works is the owner of those characters and has not sold those rights to other parties. This may be particularly important for a comic book, since characters may have moved from one work to another. If the comic book publisher failed to properly purchase the characters, then it may not be the sole copyright holder of the literary property in question.

Licensing a film based on a Broadway musical will also raise complex ownership issues. The musical may have three authors: the "book" writer who created the story and dialogue, the composer who wrote the songs, and the lyricist who wrote the lyrics for those songs. Depending on the agreement between the book writer, composer, and lyricist, the group may operate by majority vote or may require unanimous consent to transfer the film rights. In addition, the producer of the musical will have acquired some interest in the motion picture production.

The filmmaker must identify everyone with a stake in the project to ensure that the license covers all possible claimants in order to guarantee there will be no surprise obligations. Though it may be preferable to have an attorney experienced in copyright searches research the rights holders, some self-help is available. The Copyright Office provides guidance and information on copyright searches in Circular 22.[2]

The filmmaker should first find out as much information as possible from the work itself. For example, if the work is a novel, the filmmaker should look up the name of the author, publisher, location of the first publication, and first publication date. Novels provide this information in the introductory pages. For a short story, this may be more difficult, since publishers commonly place a copyright notice for the entire work rather than separate notices for each short story. Nonetheless, the more information the filmmaker can obtain from the source, the more efficient the subsequent searches will be.

Google Books, IMDb, Wikipedia, and other online resources provide a wealth of additional information about titles and authors. In addition, since card catalogs have been replaced with digital directories, library searches will often provide a wealth of information on the provenance of titles.

The US Copyright Office's Catalog of Copyright Entries is also available online through numerous libraries. An excellent source is the Online Books Page hosted by the University of Pennsylvania at https://onlinebooks. library.upenn.edu/cce/. The catalog will reflect all the information that was given when a work was registered for copyright; unfortunately, it will not provide much detail beyond that. It does not include information on assignments and transfers, and because film rights are transferred by assignment, the most critical information will not appear. But the information available will speed up the subsequent searches.

Publishers may also be excellent sources of information. Because publishers of books and music collect their authors' royalties, they often have an ongoing relationship with the copyright holders. In addition, the Ransom Center at the University of Texas at Austin has created the WATCH File

(Writers, Artists, and Their Copyright Holders), an online database containing contact information for American and English authors at https://norman.hrc.utexas.edu/watch/. This ongoing project should prove to be a very useful resource for independent filmmakers.

The last step in the copyright investigation is to have a professional search conducted. The US Copyright Office can do the cheapest search itself. The office charges an hourly fee, so the more information the filmmaker can provide, the cheaper and quicker the search. To improve the search, the Copyright Office suggests the following information be provided:

- the title of the work, with any possible variants
- the names of the authors, including possible pseudonyms
- the name of the probable copyright owner, which may be the publisher or producer
- the approximate year the work was published or registered
- the type of work involved (book, play, musical composition, sound recording, photograph, etc.)
- for a work originally published as a part of a periodical or collection, the title of that publication and any other information, such as the volume or issue number, to help identify it
- the registration number or any other copyright data

Motion pictures are often based on other works such as books or serialized contributions to periodicals or other composite works. *If you desire a search for an underlying work or for music from a motion picture, you must specifically request such a search. You must also identify the underlying works and music and furnish the specific titles, authors, and approximate dates of these works.*[3]

If the search shows no assignments, it is time to contact the copyright holder. On the other hand, if the search shows that there has been a transfer, then a lawyer may be necessary to determine whether the rights might still be available.

2. Negotiations for the Motion Picture Rights

Once the filmmaker identifies the owner of the film rights, the next step is to enter into negotiations to acquire those rights. If possible, the filmmaker should approach the author directly instead of communicating through an agent. An author will often be more flexible on pricing and other terms. The film company needs to explore if the movie rights are legally available and what the author wants for them.

This begins the process of negotiating the *literary property agreement.* At the time the literary property is purchased, the film company can choose to purchase the rights or to option the rights for a future purchase. Option agreements are very helpful because it allows the filmmaker to spend a small percentage of the total amount negotiated for the cost of the underlying rights while obtaining exclusive control of the rights for a specified period of time.

Properly drafted, an option agreement should specify all the terms and conditions for acquiring the rights to the property along with additional provisions that create a payment for the exclusive rights to exercise the rights in the contract for a specific period of time, often one to three years. Some production companies choose to use very simple options that do not specify the rest of the terms of the agreement, but such agreements to agree often fall apart, leaving the filmmaker with nothing but wasted time and money.

The consequences of not reaching an agreement go up dramatically once the filmmaker is financially committed to the project and has begun filming. The filmmaker should not put off negotiations until a time when the film company is at a strategic disadvantage. Instead, all relevant terms of the acquisition agreement should be included from the outset.

The negotiations generally focus on the following terms:

- The scope of rights—including length, geographic scope, language, and other attributes
- The extent to which the literary property rights holder will participate
- The discretion of the filmmaker to alter the facts and dramatize the story
- The amount of money being paid for the rights
- The risk of noncompletion of the filmmaker's project

These negotiations will proceed differently for an independent filmmaker than for a studio production company. Typically, the studio would demand all rights of every kind from the literary property rights holder and absolute discretion over how those rights are exploited. In exchange, the cost of those rights can be expected to be much higher for a studio than for an independent filmmaker. In the latter case, the negotiations can better reflect the filmmaker's ability to make the film and the rights holder's interest in protecting the work.

a. The Scope of Rights

At a bare minimum, the filmmaker must acquire the right to use the literary property to make the current production. Such an agreement, however, would limit the use of the literary property to the single production currently being planned by the filmmaker. Instead, it is better for the filmmaker to acquire rights that are more broadly defined.

First, many independent films are produced with very low budgets and many challenges to production quality. If the story is compelling, the filmmaker may have the opportunity in the future to remake the film on a grander scale. The right to make a film does not include the remake rights unless the contract includes that right.

Second, the studio film industry is financed by the success of sequels, prequels, and narrative universes. Television and series production are fueled by spin-offs. Like the potential for remakes, the ability to expand the story by making prequels and sequels will increase the opportunities to sell the completed film. Investors and distributors want to know they have the potential to mine the material if the project turns from sleeper to blockbuster.

Third, the medium in which the movie is made may not be film. Since independent "films" are often photographed digitally, any confusion over terminology should be removed early on. The audiovisual work might be a single, narrative story, or it might be told in a miniseries or longer series. At the time the filmmaker is acquiring the rights, these are unknown choices that will be driven by financing and distribution as much as by artistic storytelling.

The best scope-of-rights clause states that "the filmmaker hereby acquires the exclusive right to exploit the [literary property] in any media now known or hereafter developed, including without limitation the right to make motion or audiovisual pictures, sequels, prequels, remakes, live, interactive, or episodic versions." In a separate sentence, the contract should also provide that "the filmmaker may produce and distribute the work using any media now known or hereafter developed." The first sentence says that the story can be captured using any technology or media. The second sentence provides that the film, TV show, or Internet broadcast can be sold, broadcast, or packaged in any fashion.

"Literary property" should be broadly defined so that it includes any copyrighted work, characters, story, plot, theme, or action embodied in that property. In this way, the filmmaker exclusively owns the rights even to elements of the story that are not copyrightable. While this might not stop a third party from creating a similar plot, it will stop the author of the plot from recycling it into a competing project.

With an independent film project, it is possible to negotiate these terms to provide more limited rights for the filmmaker. The seller of the literary property may require it if the work is already being used in other media. The broader the scope of rights, however, the better for the filmmaker, because it reduces the chances of two or more similar projects competing in the market at the same time and gives the filmmaker a bigger bundle to sell to the distributor.

b. Participation of the Literary Property Rights Holder

The authors of literary works often want to remain involved in the development of their work. Similarly, if the work is really the life story of an individual, the subject of the story may demand certain approval rights. In the studio setting, these considerations are rarely entertained. Like an uninvited extra cook, the seller of the literary property and the subject of a true story are often considered threats to the project and are given very little chance to participate. For the independent filmmaker, however, these participants may be a resource rather than a burden, especially if the film is based on true events. The participation of the rights holder may also provide some marketing and press opportunities. The cost for such access is greater interaction between the filmmaker and the person whose story is being adapted.

The willingness to work with the underlying rights holders and the subjects of true stories can often provide independent filmmakers leverage to acquire stories that a studio is unable to purchase. The intimacy and collaboration of independent projects are quite valuable for some story owners.

c. The Discretion of the Filmmaker

The biggest advantage an independent filmmaker has over the studios is the ability to earn the trust of the literary rights holder. While the filmmaker generally wants unbridled discretion in telling the story, some rights holders will only make their material available to a sympathetic filmmaker, particularly if the material is based on true events. The filmmaker must negotiate before the work has begun to determine the limits regarding the subject's control and discretion in the project by allowing the rights holder to observe, participate, or veto decisions of the filmmaker.

At the same time, the involvement with rights holders creates significant limits and constraints on the filmmaker. The legal power to observe, participate, or veto should be given away very sparingly. The filmmaker can provide the opportunity for the rights holder to observe and participate without contractually promising access, but if the contract provides for such access, the decision cannot be undone.

The filmmaker can grant other parties the right to review choices at any of various stages in the development of the film. The participation can occur in the approval of casting, script, filming, or finished film. The right of approval is a valuable commodity, which filmmakers should generally not give up. However, the offer of approval rights may allow the filmmaker to acquire rights to a story which would otherwise be too expensive or too difficult to acquire. More frequently, the rights granted are those of consultation, while the contracts specify that the filmmaker retains final say on all decisions. In most cases, consultative rights are sufficient, since they are still far more generous than the rights available from studio productions.

d. The Amount of Money Being Paid for the Rights

The payment provisions are often the point of greatest interest to the parties. Negotiators do well to consider payments based on the amount of money being provided, the timing of the payments, and the contingencies that trigger payments. By utilizing all three factors involved in a payment, there is room to add flexibility in the negotiation process. Typical financial arrangements include the following:

- Outright cash payment at time of purchase
- Partial cash payments at each stage of financing, production, and distribution
- Deferred payment of a fixed amount, paid out of financing
- Deferred payment of a fixed amount, paid out of distribution income
- Deferred payment of a percentage of adjusted gross distribution income received by the production company
- Deferred payment of a percentage of net distribution income received by the production company

These different payment schemes may be used singly or in combination. For example, the filmmaker may offer the rights holder a payment of $100 for the literary property, with an additional payment of $4,900 if the production company secures a specified amount of financing, as well as 1 percent of the adjusted gross income from all distribution income of the film. A token up-front payment often helps to inspire trust between the filmmaker and the rights holder, while deferred compensation allows the filmmaker to reduce the cost of making the film.

If the literary property is the screenplay itself, this technique is particularly attractive. It ties the screenwriter's financial interest to the completed film, since that is when the primary payments will occur, which may create an additional incentive for the writer's participation in revisions even if the money has run low.

e. The Risk of Noncompletion of the Filmmaker's Project

Very few of the stories acquired by filmmakers are actually made into feature films. This is true in both the independent and the studio film industry. But rights holders are even more concerned about selling their rights to an independent filmmaker than to an established film company, since the rights holders generally receive less compensation for their rights from independent filmmakers, and independent films tend to receive less promotion. To overcome these limitations, the independent filmmaker should include specific provisions in the contract to address this risk.

First, the contract must be clear that the filmmaker is under no obligation to exercise any option or to complete the finished project. The contract should recite that both parties understand the difficulty of completing and distributing a finished film so that the film company is responsible only for the payments owed under the contract and for nothing else.

Second, in fairness to the seller of the underlying rights, the contract may include provisions that allow the rights holder to reclaim the rights in the event the film is not made. This right—often referred to as the right of *reversion*—allows the rights holder to either reclaim all literary rights sold to the filmmaker or transfer those rights to a new studio.

Under the typical studio conditions regarding reversion, the rights holder must return the money the filmmaker paid to secure the rights, and the new film production company must reimburse the filmmaker for the costs incurred in preparing the abortive film. The right of reversion often does not begin for five years following the sale of the literary rights to the studio. The studio approach may meet with a good deal of opposition and may not set the proper tone for the relationship the filmmaker is trying to develop.

For that reason, the independent filmmaker may elect to vary these terms in a number of ways. The rights can be returned to the rights holder without charge, or a reimbursement payment can be tied to the completion of the film adaptation by another company. This allows the rights holder to give the independent filmmaker a chance without making a decision that becomes financially impractical to fix.

The length of the reversion term can also be varied, but as long as some progress is being made, the term should continue to run. Independent film projects often start and stop for years, so the filmmaker should not promise that the movie will be completed in six months or the project is finished. Instead, the rights holder may give the filmmaker the rights to the material for one year, but if an agreed-upon amount of money is not raised, then the rights revert. If the money is raised, then the filmmaker has three years to begin principal photography. Once principal photography has begun, the rights are generally irrevocable.

The timing of any reversion should be based on the date when the rights are actually purchased by the filmmaker; it should not count the option period. For example, the deal could specify that the filmmaker pays an option amount of $1,000 per year for a maximum of two years. When the option is exercised, the filmmaker pays a purchase amount—say, $5,000—to complete the acquisition. At this point, the filmmaker is the owner of all film and media rights in the work. Additional payments are due at various stages of production—e.g., the start of principal photography and distribution. If principal photography does not commence within a particular time period (e.g., three more years), then a reversion provision would give the author the right to return the $5,000 and reclaim the rights to the work.

Typically, the option payments are not required to be returned, but the filmmaker and rights holder can make any arrangement that meets their needs. This is just one example of a structure that balances the interests of the filmmaker and the rights holder.

Reversion provisions put pressure on the filmmaker while providing the rights holder some protection. Rights holders may be more willing to enter into a transaction or accept a lower price if they know the opportunity is less likely to be squandered on a languishing project. As such, reversion provisions reflect a compromise approach to the bargain that may benefit both parties.

3. Provisions of the Purchase Agreement

The purchase agreement gives the filmmaker the right to use or exploit the literary material for any of the stated purposes, including making a film, television show, streaming service, downloads, videotape, or anything the contract writer can think to include. For the filmmaker, the most important provisions for the literary purchase agreement are the following:

- The grant of rights for the broadest form of license to make movies and related types of shows using any technology
- The *representations and warranties*, or contractually binding promises that the author owns the material being licensed, that no one else has any right to the material, and that no other party has any interest in the transaction
- The purchase price for the literary rights
- Any royalty or percentage of net profits or gross revenues
- Screen credit

If the seller of the rights is an author, that person may want to add terms such as:

- The right to write the first (or more) drafts of the screenplay
- The right or option to write any sequels, prequels, or television versions
- Terms reserving the rights to live stage versions, novelizations, and other writings

4. Option Agreement Provisions

The option agreement gives the filmmaker the power to buy the film rights to a movie in the future and stops the rights holder from selling the rights to anyone else during the option period. To be enforceable and useable, it must be more than an agreement to agree. All of the material terms and conditions of the literary purchase agreement must be included. Option agreements can range in length from 2 to 17 pages.

The option agreement is essentially a literary purchase agreement with a few additional provisions:

- The length and starting date of the option period
- The amount to be paid if the option is exercised and the literary property is purchased
- The price of renewing the option, the length of the renewal, and the number of times the option can be renewed

In addition, the agreement should include a recital by the author that all the rights are available and have not previously been transferred. This recital will be of some help if the filmmaker cannot afford the copyright search immediately.

In the simplest case, for example, an author has a written a short story entitled "Rosebud, the Sled of Youth." The author ("Author") published the short story once in a small magazine, retaining all other rights in the work. The contract would state that the filmmaker ("Producer") is acquiring an exclusive option to all rights in the short story entitled "Rosebud, the Sled of Youth" (the "Work").

A different section of the agreement would provide that the Author retains the literary publishing rights to the Work. The option agreement would include a payment of $500 for the exclusive right to develop the Work as a film (and in all other media now known or hereafter created) for the next year and may be renewed for up to an additional three years by additional annual payments of $500. The Author would represent and warrant that the author has all the rights to the Work and can sell the rights to the Producer.

This option agreement would also include the final sale price and the payment schedule for the film. There should be no clause that says that payments or other key terms will be mutually agreed upon; all obligations must be decided in the option agreement. Otherwise, the filmmaker may find there is no final agreement with the literary rights holder when the time comes to exercise the option.

While option agreements are generally preferred over literary purchase agreements because less money must be spent initially, a tremendous amount of money may be saved by purchasing the rights in full up front. Many rights holders will accept $5,000 in hand rather than the promise of $50,000 if the movie is made. Buying rights with cash remains a potent strategic choice for any filmmaker with the money to implement the strategy.

5. "Based Upon" Provisions for Synopsis and Treatment Submissions

Well before the script is finished, a screenwriter will often develop the story for a film project in a brief synopsis of 3 to 10 pages or detailed 30- to 50-page treatment of the screenplay. Filmmakers often prefer to purchase the literary work at this stage, because it allows the filmmaker to have control over the development of the work. Filmmakers typically acquire treatments through the same option agreement structure used for other literary works. The filmmaker pays a modest advance and agrees to pay the writer a specified amount or percentage of income if the finished film was "based upon" the treatment.

This type of arrangement was made famous when writer Art Buchwald sued Paramount Pictures over the Eddie Murphy film *Coming to America*. Paramount had entered into an agreement with Buchwald, paying him for a movie treatment and providing him with profit participation if it was used as the basis for a film. Paramount and the project's producer, John Landis, used Buchwald's work as part of the development of *Coming to America*, but the screenplay was ultimately written by Eddie Murphy, who testified that he had not read the treatment nor used it to write his script. The film was unquestionably different from Buchwald's original concept. Nonetheless, the lawsuit was decided in Buchwald's favor; he was entitled to payment.

This was the proper result of the lawsuit. The treatment had been used by Paramount and Landis to keep the production going, and it had served as a reference for the producers as Murphy developed his independent screenplay. Similarly, any contract that provides for payment if a film is "based upon" a treatment should be interpreted to mean that the treatment author will be paid unless the treatment is wholly unrelated to the subject matter of the finished film.

A film may be based upon a preexisting treatment or other work because of the production history and contractual relationships. This is very different than claiming the finished film was a "copy" of the work for copyright purposes, meaning that the finished film was substantially similar to the original work. Buchwald's treatment had little in common with Murphy's screenplay. There was no copyright infringement. But Paramount did use Buchwald and his writing to help secure financing and keep the momentum of the production going. "Based upon" is not a copyright standard; it is only based on the contractual relationship.

Because of the vague nature of "based upon," a producer should try to avoid using the term in contracts. Instead, the producer can offer a percentage basis to the author of the treatment if the final film is *substantially similar* to that treatment as provided under copyright law. Since "substantial similarity" is the copyright test for infringement, this contract essentially provides that if the final shooting script or the finished film uses the copyrighted work, then the writer receives the agreed-upon payment. For a simple arrangement, this provides the easiest contractual framework.

Nonetheless, there are working relationships for which the "based upon" approach is the understanding between the parties and appropriate to use. If the filmmaker chooses to use the "based upon" terminology, the production company should expect to be obligated to pay the treatment writer even if only the most general ideas in the two works are similar.

B. Submission Agreements

The basic purpose of a submission agreement is to allow a production company to review treatments and screenplays written by writers who are not employees of the production company. Often, these are *spec scripts*—scripts written as pet projects by writers hoping to break into the motion picture industry or to move up in its ranks. Spec scripts are particularly prevalent immediately after a prolonged strike.

Submission agreements are designed to protect the production company from claims by submitting writers that the company has stolen their ideas or copyrighted materials. Since themes, ideas, and characters are often based on cultural influences, and many authors may independently be developing stories along similar lines, it is important to have a contract that sets out the expectations of the submitting writer and the film company before the company receives a screenplay or treatment.

1. Significant Terms of a Submission Agreement

A submission agreement limits the contractual claims of the submitting author. The production company should insist that no script be accepted unless the submitting writer first signs one. Typically, submission agreement contracts do not limit a writer's copyright claims but focus on claims to ideas, characters, themes, and other materials that do not rise to the level of copyrightable expression. The primary provision of the agreement states that there is no contract or promise to compensate the submitting writer for use of ideas, regardless of the similarity with any ideas that may eventually be exploited.

Although ideas are not protected by copyright, those same ideas and plots may be protected by contract. Producers must be careful to avoid making promises or otherwise creating any form of contract on which a writer providing a submission could rely. Oral contracts and public statements could give the wrong impression. Instead, before accepting any submission, a producer should require an agreement specifying that in exchange for accepting a submission, the writer agrees the producer is not obligated to pay for submitted ideas, plots, or characters. Instead, the producer will only pay to acquire the rights necessary to secure copyright in the author's submission, should the producer agree to produce the work.

a. This contract represents the only understanding between the parties regarding the submission of any treatment, story, idea, screenplay, or other work (collectively "Work"). This contract supersedes any oral agreement, and it may only be modified in writing when signed by both parties.

b. The production company will accept submission of writer's Work only in exchange for entering into this agreement.

c. Because many writers submit materials, and often similar ideas are submitted or otherwise available in the public domain, the production company does not pay writers for Work submitted, except to the extent copyrighted content will be used for productions.

d. The production company is under no obligation to pay the writer for the Work submitted. The production company is free to use all material not protected by the laws of copyright. The production company is not obligated to keep the materials submitted.

While it is important to protect the production company from untold claims by writers who may have hit upon similar ideas, a production company should comply with copyright law. A general submission agreement should not be used to force a writer to transfer copyright ownership from the writer to the production company or to give the production company the right to make a screenplay or film from the submission. The submission agreement can explain this, in part, as a means to soften the otherwise harsh tone of the agreement.

e. In the event that the writer submits a Work protected by copyright, the writer grants permission to review the Work and make copies of the Work for its evaluation. The writer shall retain all copyright in Work unless such rights are transferred to the production company as part of a written agreement.

The submission agreement should also explain that it is the general practice to review all submissions within approximately six months, or such time as is realistic for the producer, but that because of the number of submissions, the production company will contact only those writers with whom it is interested in developing a working relationship. While it is certainly more professional to thank every author, and even to respond with comments if possible, the production company is better off simply doing so than promising to do so in a contract.

> f. The production company is not obligated to return the materials. The writer will at all times retain an original copy of the materials submitted and hereby releases the production company from any claims that may arise as a result of the production company holding the Work.

The contract might also note that materials will only be returned if the submitting author includes a self-addressed stamped envelope. Given the low price of copying and the increasing cost of postage, many authors may forgo the return of their materials.

These suggested provisions are similar to the language that a larger production company would use. They help courts dismiss frivolous lawsuits—before trial preparation becomes very expensive—from authors who send unsolicited materials.

2. Solicited Ideas and the Nondisclosure Agreement

General submission provisions must be modified to fit the particular situation. If the production company wishes to solicit a plot or an idea from a particular author, then it must be prepared to protect that author's ideas through the form of a nondisclosure agreement. Nondisclosure agreements are frequently used in business—they have become ubiquitous in the software and other intellectual property industries—and they essentially require that both parties agree to share information in exchange for the promise that neither party will use or disclose the other party's confidential information without permission. Indeed, if the previous sentence were written on a napkin and signed by both parties, it would probably be sufficient.

In the context of solicited ideas, the nondisclosure agreement is slightly different than in the traditional business context. The essential component of the agreement is that the idea, story, plot, characters, or other elements are treated as confidential unless they were already known by the party who receives the material, or they become known in a manner that does not breach the film company's duty of confidentiality. The following contract clauses illustrate the core of the agreement.

a. Confidentiality. Producer shall not directly or indirectly disclose, disseminate, publish, or use for its business advantage or for any other purpose, at any time during or after the term of this Agreement for a period of seven (7) years, any information received from Writer deemed confidential by the other party ("Confidential Information").

(1.) Definitions. For purposes of this Agreement, Confidential Information shall be defined as any information not generally known in the industry about Writer's story, characters, ideas, themes, plots, writings or expressions, products, trade secrets, services, or any combination thereof, whether or not such information would be recognized as proprietary absent this Agreement.

(2.) Limitations. Notwithstanding any other provision of this Agreement, Producer shall not be liable for disclosing, disseminating, publishing, or using information which (i) was already known prior to the receipt of the Confidential Information; (ii) is information similar to the Confidential Information of Writer so as to make such Confidential Information no longer unique to Writer; (iii) is now or becomes public information through no wrongful act of the Producer; (iv) is independently developed or acquired by Producer without any use of the Confidential Information in such development; or (v) is required to be disclosed by law. Producer shall, within 30 days of receipt of Confidential Information, inform Writer of that material Producer deems not confidential pursuant to this paragraph.

b. Documents and Materials. The documents and materials of Writer (including but not limited to all data, screenplays, treatments, records, notes, lists, specifications, and designs) are furnished in accordance with the terms of this Agreement and shall remain the sole property of Writer. This information (collectively known as "Evaluation Material") shall, upon the termination of this Agreement, be promptly returned to Writer, including all copies thereof, which are in the possession or control of Producer, its agents, and its representatives.

c. Term and Renewal. The term of this Agreement shall be one (1) year commencing as of the date hereof; provided however, that Paragraph (a) of this Agreement shall survive termination of this Agreement and shall remain in full force and effect for a period of seven (7) years.

Using these terms, the producer provides significant protection to the writer for any ideas and other materials that are not protected by copyright while still retaining the ability to avoid paying for material that has become public or that is already owned.

3. Submissions by Joint Authors

Many of the fiercest fights break out between two people who had been jointly developing a work. A simple contract that explains the duties of each party helps to eliminate these problems. The contract should have a sentence requiring that all ideas developed during the partnership may only be used by mutual consent. If the filmmaker hires someone to develop an idea, the contract should require that all ideas become the property of the filmmaker.

C. Contracting and the Authority of the Filmmaker

Studio films are created and financed by producers, who seek the maximum flexibility to hire and fire the artistic talent involved with a film. Similar interests are held by *producing distributors*, those companies that invest in a film so that they can acquire it for distribution. They seek to maximize their ability to change the film to suit their distribution needs. If they substantially disagree with the choices being made by the director, they may want replace the director with another choice.

More often than not, the filmmaker on an independent project is the director. The independent filmmaker will want to structure all agreements to provide much less authority for the producer to replace the director. Fortunately, when an independent filmmaker raises private funds to make a movie that does not yet have distribution, the filmmaker remains in charge. The investors are not as well positioned as studio producers or producing distributors and generally are not as interested in asserting authority over the project. The relationship between the filmmaker and the investors is very different than the president of the company and its shareholders. As a result, many of the standard forms available for running a business give far too much authority to the shareholders and too little protection for the filmmaker. Only film-specific contracts should be used.

1. Identifying the Authority in the Project

For an investor-financed independent film, all parties must agree on which of them is the filmmaker, the person with final authority on the project. Without this agreement, conflicts can never be properly resolved, and the filmmaking process is likely to end with significant frustration. This is not an issue in studio-financed filmmaking. When studios or established production companies finance a film, the studio acquires final approval over every decision in the project, including the employment of writers, director, cast, editor, and crew.

If the filmmaker is a team of writer and director, then the issues that arise must be resolved through the mutual agreement of those two parties. If, instead, the director has the ability to replace the writer, then the writer is not truly a partner of the director on the filmmaking team. Similarly, if an actor serves as final authority for a project, then that actor will retain the authority to hire the other participants. If an actor invests fame, time, and energy to launch an independent film but the contracts vest authority in the producer because the lawyers did not understand the project, the actor could be betrayed, and the project will likely languish.

The contracts employing the participants, structuring the film company, and acquiring the rights must all reflect a common perspective on authority. Any party can be the filmmaker with final authority, but all the contracts and agreements must be drafted in concert to ensure that the same party plays that role. This is done most efficiently in the organizing documents of the production company. The production company Operating Agreement or bylaws vest maximum authority in the filmmaker, and all other agreements are drafted between the production company and the various cast, crew, and vendors.

2. The Limits of Form Agreements

With the explosion of information available on the Internet, filmmakers increasingly search for sample agreements online to provide low-cost alternatives to hiring lawyers and revising agreements. Others rely on the sample contracts in books such as this. Standard or form agreements are an extremely helpful tool for verifying that the important topics of each contract are addressed. However, form agreements necessarily lack the point of view of the particular filmmaker.

In some cases, the agreements between the parties are closely managed by unions through collective bargaining agreements, and the standard wording will apply without adjustment. In other situations, however, the sample language was drafted with specific other parties in mind, and agreements may not provide the filmmaker with the right balance of interests. As a result, sample contracts should be used as checklists and points of comparison but not adopted as the operating language without careful legal review.

Form agreements are particularly unsuited to an independent project's needs regarding the authority of the filmmaker. Most forms will assume a studio-based model of producer control, which is the least common approach to independent and guerrilla films. Filmmakers who seek to save a few dollars by using form agreements may find themselves giving away their movie as a result.

3. What Can Be Standard in an Agreement?

Once the source of authority in the film project has been identified, it is very helpful to standardize the key agreements. First, all key agreements should use a common language and approach so that the defined terms of each agreement are the same. Second, each *category* of agreement should be standardized. For example, all the actors' agreements should have identical language, except where unique needs arise. Similarly, all the crew agreements should use the same language and, whenever possible, the same language as the cast contracts.

Also, as described subsequently in section D, many provisions are standard in every agreement. Though labeled *boilerplate*, these provisions have important legal effects.

4. Assigning the Filmmaker's Story Rights

In the studio setting, writers are required to create any script as a *work-for-hire* so that the film studio becomes the author of the screenplay. Studios also demand that they be assigned all the rights to make the film, as well as the rights to create an unlimited number of additional works, known as *sequel rights*. These sequel rights include sequels, prequels, adaptations, spin-offs involving one or more characters or settings, television versions for both episodic (weekly) television and television specials, streaming, downloading, and every other entertainment imaginable that could be based upon the film.

For the filmmaker who has created an original story, the studio approach may not be the most advantageous. If an independent film company is organized for a single production, the company may not be in a position to exploit sequel rights, and the filmmaker's desire to write sequels may be stymied. Retaining these rights gives the filmmaker a measure of leverage to control future opportunities. However, such reservation of rights must be clearly spelled out so that investors are not misled about the potential for their investment. And if the film acquires studio financing, the studio will automatically insist that these rights be transferred to it.

One possible compromise is for the filmmaker to give the film company an option to exploit sequel rights but limit the option to a particular time span. If the rights are exploited within the first three to five years, then the film company should be in a position to participate in sequels. (The filmmaker should also receive some compensation as the author, even in this case.) If the rights have not been exploited in that time, then the film company has little direct financial interest, so the rights can reasonably return to the filmmaker. This compromise allows the filmmaker to return to the material without having to clear the rights with a long-defunct production company. In the event the film rights are sold to a studio or major producing distributor, however, such arrangements are likely to be renegotiated to meet the purchaser's demands for subsidiary rights.

D. Boilerplate: Understanding the Rest of the Contract

In almost every contract, the significant terms are followed by a series of provisions that control most of the rules for enforcing and operating under the contract. Regardless of the key negotiated terms of the agreement, these provisions—often referred to as *boilerplate*—are quite similar in every contract, from manufacturing cars to selling cable service, and they apply to the thousands of different agreements into which the filmmaker will enter during the production. The following subsections provide examples of boilerplate terms and their meaning.

Although these terms are repeated over and over, they have important legal significance. Parties to contracts are bound by these provisions, and they can have significant impact on the meaning of agreements.

1. Term and Renewal

The term governs the length of the contract. Unless another provision allows the contract to continue after the termination date, the contract itself ends, and the future relationships are governed by a new agreement, whether in writing or by oral understanding.

> The term of this Agreement shall commence as of the date hereof and continue for a period of one (1) year; and provided neither party shall not be then in breach of or in default under any term or provision hereof, this Agreement shall automatically renew for additional one (1) year periods thereafter, unless either party gives written notice of its election to terminate this Agreement not less than sixty (60) days prior to the expiration of the term or any renewal thereof.

This provision provides that the contract starts beginning with the date on the top of the page, which is preferable to relying on two possibly conflicting dates accompanying the signature lines of the parties. The contract has a one-year term, but that term automatically extends each year unless either party decides to terminate the contract. This automatic renewal is quite typical for ongoing relationships. For project work, an event should be specified. For example, the contract may terminate upon the completion of principal photography.

Termination provisions can also allow that some provisions of the contracts survive termination. For example, if an agreement provides for financing the film, the contract may automatically terminate if insufficient funds are pledged by a specified date; nevertheless, the contract may provide that the provisions relating to nondisclosure of the film idea will survive for an additional period of years.

2. Representations and Warranties of the Parties

The representations and warranties are the basic promises that serve as the basis for the agreement. They generally go to the ability of the parties to enter into the agreement, but may become very specific depending on the nature of the agreement.

Each party to this Agreement hereby represents and warrants that it has the right and authority to enter into this Agreement and that it is not subject to any contract, agreement, judgment, statute, regulation, or disability which might interfere with its full performance of all of the covenants and conditions hereunder.

It is common that the representations and warranties for the two parties to the agreement be somewhat different from each other. For instance, the representations and warranties of the author of a story will include the following additional issues:

The Seller [of the novel, screenplay, play, or other literary work] hereby represents and warrants as follows:

The Property has been written solely by and is original with Seller; neither the Property nor any element thereof infringes upon the copyright, publicity rights, trademarks, story rights, or other interests of any other literary property.

The Property is wholly fictional, no portion of the Property has been taken from any other source (other than the public domain), and the Property does not constitute defamation against any person or violate any rights in any person, including without limitation, rights of privacy, publicity, copyright (whether common law or statutory, throughout the universe), trademark, publication, or performance rights, or rights in any other property, and any rights of consultation regarding the Property or any element thereof.

The Property has not previously been exploited in any medium except the following [identify what rights have been used], and no rights have been granted to any third party to do so.

In addition, for some projects it is important that nothing interfere with the ability to market the personality involved in the project.

Neither party has committed, and throughout the term of this Agreement neither party shall commit, any act or omission which constitutes a felony or could be deemed an act of moral turpitude. Any breach of this paragraph shall be deemed a material breach.

In such a situation, the representations and warranties need to include a *morality clause*, guaranteeing good, honorable behavior both before and throughout the term of the contract. The most important aspect of this provision is that it allows the buyer to revoke the contract if the misconduct of the seller makes that choice appropriate.

3. Indemnification

Indemnification is the legal obligation to pay compensation to the other party to the agreement for damage, loss, or injury suffered as a result of a breach of the contract or any duties that arise under it. For example, a screenwriter will be required to indemnify the film producer for any material copied from other sources in violation of copyright law and of the representations made by the screenwriter under the contract.

It is not sufficient that each party promises to abide by the obligations laid out in the contract. Each one runs the risk that third parties may make claims against that party as a result of what it has done. For example, the filmmaker wants to be protected from anyone claiming the screenwriter improperly copied that person's story. To provide such protection, the screenwriter must agree to defend the filmmaker, meaning the writer must provide a legal defense for the benefit of the filmmaker. The screenwriter must also indemnify the production company, meaning the writer must agree to pay any damages if the script is found to have violated some other person's or company's rights.

> Screenwriter hereby indemnifies and holds harmless [Film Company] and its employees, independent contractors, agents, and assigns against any loss or damage (including reasonable attorneys' fees) incurred by reason of any claim based upon any breach of the representations and warranties of Seller contained in this Agreement and any documents contemplated hereby.

In contrast, the filmmaker is generally in the better position to defend the screenwriter for any lawsuits that might arise as a result of the making of the film. Therefore, the filmmaker has a similar obligation to protect the screenwriter from liability.

> [Film Company] hereby indemnifies Screenwriter against any loss or damage (including reasonable attorneys' fees) incurred by reason of any claim based upon its exploitation of the Property which does not involve the acts or omissions of the Screenwriter.

Finally, a very simple but effective provision is a general statement that each party will protect the other for any actions that it caused.

Each party agrees to indemnify the other and to hold the other harmless from and against any and all claims, action, cause of action, liabilities, damages, judgments, decrees, losses, costs, and expenses, including reasonable attorneys' fees, arising out of any breach or alleged breach of any representations, warranties, or agreements made by it hereunder.

These sample clauses do not include the requirement that the party defend the lawsuit. Defense language is common and can readily be added to these paragraphs merely by inserting the term "and defend" after the word "indemnify" wherever applicable.

The difficult issue—which of the two actually created the situation that allowed a third party to be able to bring a lawsuit—is often highly contentious, with the result that the two parties to the contract often end up suing each other to determine which has the obligation to pay for the litigation and any damages caused by the lawsuit.

4. Resolution of Disputes

Because of the costs and delays involved in litigation, many people prefer to use some alternative, including arbitration or mediation. *Mediation* involves a person who tries to help the parties to the dispute work out the issues among themselves. *Arbitration* involves an independent person who acts much like a judge, who will listen to both sides in the dispute and make a determination. Although arbitrators in some jurisdictions may not have quite the discretion of the courts to award injunctions or punitive damages, they have substantial power to craft final remedies. In addition, if the arbitration is *binding*, then the decision of the arbitrator is as enforceable as that of a judge.

The choice to forgo the right to go to court should be considered carefully. Many protections are given up by waiving the right to use the traditional legal system. On the other hand, the independent filmmaker probably does not have a great deal of money or time to fight a legal dispute through trial and appeal. Also, the ability to choose the arbitrator allows the parties to use the services of a decision-maker familiar with the film industry and the issues involved. As a result, arbitration may be a useful alternative for filmmakers. In fact, it is required in most agreements with union personnel (directors, actors, writers, etc.). Each union will have specific language that it requires be used.

Dispute resolution provisions vary greatly, but the following is an example:

Any and all disputes hereunder shall be resolved by arbitration in accordance with the American Arbitration Association ("AAA") under the rules then obtaining. Any party hereto electing to commence an action shall give written notice to the other party hereto of such election. The location for such arbitration shall be Los Angeles, California, subject to the convenience of the parties, and any and all rights of discovery available pursuant to such arbitration shall be limited by the applicable arbitration provisions of the California Code of Civil Procedure. The award of such arbitrator may be confirmed or enforced in any court of competent jurisdiction. The costs and expenses of the arbitrator, including the attorneys' fees and costs of each of the parties, may be apportioned between the parties by such arbitrator.

5. Assignment

Most business contracts are freely assignable, or transferable. In contrast, most contracts calling for a person's individual services are not assignable. In the filmmaking scenario, both issues are occurring at once. The duties of most of the participants are personal in nature, but the filmmaker may create a film company or sell the existing company as part of the financing process. As long as the filmmaker remains involved in the project, none of these activities should trigger the assignment clause.

The services and obligations under this Agreement are personal in nature and cannot be assigned or delegated. The services of [Film Company] may be assigned upon consent, which consent shall not be unreasonably withheld. Notwithstanding the foregoing, the transfer of this Agreement to a company owned in whole or part by [Filmmaker], a related company, or to another entity with substantially the same executive and principals of [Film Company], or to a company that employs [Filmmaker] as [producer/director], shall not be deemed an assignment requiring approval under this paragraph.

The limitation on assignment of the various personnel do not limit the ability of those employees to assign their right to receive income. If a party had to assign income to another party or entity for tax purposes, marital obligations, or other reasons, the clause preventing assignment of the work would not interfere with the separate assignment of the right to receive revenue.

6. Amendments

Things change. Actors may get sick, locations become unavailable, funding increases and decreases. Nonetheless, when the filmmaker goes to the trouble of creating a written agreement, it is important that any changes be put into writing, so that quick, last-minute promises do not undermine the thoughtful management of the production. As a result, every contract should include a statement that written amendments are required. The requirement is simple.

> This Agreement may be modified or amended only in a writing signed by both parties.

Even with this language, some jurisdictions will allow for oral modification of the agreement. Further, courts will often find that a party has waived its rights to require a written document as a result of statements made about or conduct relating to the transaction. Despite this risk, the provision should be included in the agreement and adhered to by the parties throughout the course of their relationship.

7. Severability

In some situations, a portion of the contract cannot be enforced. The court (or arbitrator) must then decide whether to throw out the entire contract or just that provision. That choice can be provided for directly in the contract. In most situations, half a contract is better than none, as the severability provision reflects.

> If any provision of this Agreement shall be held to be invalid or unenforceable for any reason, the remaining provisions shall continue to be valid and enforceable. If a court finds that any provision of this Agreement is invalid or unenforceable, but that by limiting such provision it would become valid and enforceable, then such provision shall be deemed to be written, construed, and enforced as so limited.

8. Entire Agreement

To control the issues that may be swirling around the filmmaker, everything should be in writing. A provision that specifies that all the issues have been incorporated into the written agreement may help to overcome claims that side agreements and other promises were made. Even the most well-meaning people hear what they want to hear, so the more exact and structured the contract, the fewer the misunderstandings.

> This Agreement contains the full and complete understanding between the parties hereto with reference to the within subject matter, supersedes all prior agreements and understandings, whether written or oral, pertaining thereto, and cannot be modified except by a written instrument signed by both of the parties hereto. Each of the parties acknowledges that no representation or promise not expressly contained in this Agreement has been made by the other or its agents or representatives.

9. No Obligation

Unfortunately, many films do not get made, and opportunities are often lost. All employment contracts and contracts for purchasing literary properties and other services should be sure to protect the filmmaker from claims that the production company is responsible for the losses incurred because the project was not successful.

> Notwithstanding the rights granted herein, [Film Company] is under no obligation to utilize [services/property] in any manner whatsoever, and failure to exercise any rights contained herein shall not constitute a breach of any covenant, express or implied.

This provision will not determine what payments or other obligations the filmmaker must make; the payment terms will specify under what conditions the payments are due. If the payments are due for entering the contract, then the payments are owed, even if the film is not made. However, most payment obligations are based on using the services, in which case failure to start the film results in no financial obligation.

10. No Partnership or Joint Venture

The financial and business relationship should also be specified. Courts may ignore these self-serving declarations, but at least they remind the parties how they are supposed to relate to each other, and they may have some effect on the courts if any problems do arise.

> [Screenwriter] is an independent contractor with respect to [Film Company] and not an employee. [Film Company] will not provide fringe benefits and [Screenwriter] shall be responsible for all income tax and withhold-

ing required which due by [Screenwriter] as a result of this Agreement. Nothing in this Agreement shall be construed as creating a partnership, joint venture, or employment relationship between the parties hereto, and each party is solely and exclusively responsible for that party's own debts and obligations.

11. Further Documents

Throughout the course of the filmmaking process, a wide variety of financiers, distributors, government agencies, unions, exhibitors, and others are going to request legal documentation regarding the film. Some of those documents will have been created during the production process, but others will not have been necessary or will not be in the form needed. The filmmaker must be able to compel the other participants to continue to sign documents necessary for the production and distribution of the film and the exploitation of related rights. This provision makes the willingness to sign additional papers an affirmative promise of each party.

> Each of the parties agrees to execute, acknowledge, and deliver any and all further documents which may be required to carry into effect this Agreement and its respective obligations hereunder, all of which further documents shall be in accordance with and consistent with the terms of this Agreement.

12. Notices

The contract should specify the form of delivery allowed for subsequent correspondence. Email is typically not included in these provisions, but increasingly it is a useful tool. If it is used, then the sender should confirm that the email has been received. Many notice clauses include the address to which all notices should be sent and often include the attorney or agent as a second address, entitled to a copy of the correspondence. Often these are left blank, however, so this paragraph provides more flexibility in selecting the applicable address.

> All notices, statements, or other documents which either party shall desire to give to the other hereunder shall be in writing and shall be deemed given as when delivered personally or by email (with confirmed receipt), telecopier (with confirmed receipt), or 48 hours after deposit in the U.S. mail, postage prepaid, and addressed to the recipient party at the

address set forth in the opening paragraph of this Agreement, or at such address as either party hereto may designate from time to time in accordance with this Paragraph.

13. Governing Law

The parties can choose which state's laws govern the contract, as long as that state is related to the agreement. If one of the parties to the contract is from a particular state, or if most of the work will occur in that state, then the selection will usually be respected by the court or arbitrator.

> This Agreement shall be governed by and construed in accordance with the laws of the State of California applicable to agreements entered into and wholly performed therein.

The choice of a particular state may depend on the laws of that state—for instance, a state may have particularly favorable laws regarding the contract in question. The choice varies dramatically depending on the states under consideration and the issues involved, so it should be based on the advice of a lawyer familiar with the issues.

14. Signature Line

The signature line should indicate who is signing the agreement and in what capacity. For example, if the filmmaker has formed a film company, then the filmmaker should sign only in the capacity as president of the company, manager of the LLC, etc. The contract should also identify that the film company is the party to the agreement rather than the filmmaker in a personal capacity. This will limit the personal liability that would otherwise attach to the filmmaker if the filmmaker signed in a personal capacity. Without properly drafting and properly signing the contract, the value of creating the film company will be lost.

7

Financing the Film Project

Film financing is often the most difficult aspect of independent filmmaking—both raising the funds and complying with the applicable state and federal laws. When raising capital, even small mistakes can result in the end of the production, fines, and criminal liability, and as the amount of money raised increases, so does the importance of working with an experienced attorney. The process requires extreme care and attention to detail.

For all but the smallest projects, funds are going to be required to make the motion picture. Expenses may range from a few dollars for out-of-pocket expenses to hundreds of millions of dollars for top-name stars, on-set special effects, and postproduction effects and editing. The more typical amount for independent filmmaking ranges from a few thousand dollars for digital cameras, computers, software, food, costumes, makeup, and set decorations to a few million dollars for a union-cast project.

A. Survey of Financing Tools

Three main categories of financing are available: debt, equity, and advance sales. With *debt financing*, the filmmaker takes out loans to make cash available for the production. With *equity investment*, outsiders fund the film company in exchange for financial participation in the particular film. In the third category, *advance sales financing*, the filmmaker raises production funds by selling, prior to the film's creation, the right to distribute and exhibit the film.

In a debt financing arrangement, a lender such as a bank gives the borrower money in exchange for a promise to repay that loan on time. The bank makes profit by charging interest on the loan. Debt financing places the risk of failure on the borrower, because the lender expects to be repaid whether the film is successful or not. (And the filmmaker is generally going to be responsible for the repayments if the film's income is insufficient to cover them.) On the other hand, although the borrower must pay back the principal and interest regardless of the outcome of the film, the lender receives only a fixed rate of return and is not entitled to any additional profits. As a result, the borrower stands to make significantly more profit if a successful film is debt financed rather than equity financed.

Equity financing distributes the risk of the project, because the investor only receives money back if the film shows a return. If a filmmaker sells 50 percent of the film's interest to an investor, for example, then the investor will lose the entire investment if the film is a complete failure. If the film is a tremendous success, the investor will receive 50 percent of every dollar of profit—far more than a lender would have received.

Assume that a particular digital film can be successfully shot and completed for $100,000 before the interest payments, if any. The table on the next page shows the profit and loss associated with equity financing and debt financing, with different revenue results. In the examples in the left column, the filmmaker sells 50 percent of the LLC created to produce the film to an equity purchaser for $50,000 and retains 50 percent of the ownership. In the examples in the right column, the filmmaker takes out a loan repayable in one year at 10 percent interest, for a $5,000 expense.

The investor shares the risk and reward in proportion to the filmmaker. In contrast, the lender must be repaid in full, plus interest. Equity financing softens the losses of the film project but also reduces the profits. Debt financing maximizes the profits but places the entire cost of loss on the filmmaker—and adds the cost of interest to boot.

The filmmaker will do substantially better if the investors provide 100 percent of the funds in exchange for the investors' 50 percent of the profits. This is also quite common, since the filmmakers are providing the skills and effort to produce the film. In that case, in the first scenario the revenues would be the same for the filmmaker as for the investors, but any losses

Scenario 1 $400,000 Revenue	50% Filmmaker	50% Investor	Cash Flow	100% Filmmaker	Lender	Cash Flow
Contribution	$50,000	$50,000		$50,000	$50,000	
Gross Revenue			$400,000			$400,000
Production Costs			($100,000)			($100,000)
Loan/Interest						($55,000)
Net Income to Production Company			$300,000			$245,000
Final Gain/Loss	$150,000	$150,000		$245,000	$5,000	

Scenario 2 No Sale	50% Filmmaker	50% Investor	Cash Flow	100% Filmmaker	Lender	Cash Flow
Contribution	$50,000	$50,000		$50,000	$50,000	
Gross Revenue			$0			$0
Production Costs			($100,000)			($100,000)
Loan/Interest						($55,000)
Net Income to Production Company			($100,000)			($155,000)
Final Gain/Loss	($50,000)	($50,000)		($105,000)	$5,000	

Scenario 3 $50,000 Revenue	50% Filmmaker	50% Investor	Cash Flow	100% Filmmaker	Lender	Cash Flow
Contribution	$50,000	$50,000		$50,000	$50,000	
Gross Revenue			$50,000			$50,000
Production Costs			($100,000)			($100,000)
Loan/Interest						($55,000)
Net Income to Production Company			($50,000)			($105,000)
Final Gain/Loss	($25,000)	($25,000)		($55,000)	$5,000	

would all be absorbed by the investors. This is the best result for the filmmakers, who can avoid financial risk and complete their projects.

Nonetheless, many independent filmmakers, including successful directors such as Spike Lee and Francis Ford Coppola, have used their personal funds to finance all or part of their films. There are no legal limits or restrictions on this practice. Despite the adage that a filmmaker should only spend other people's money, personal funds are invariably part of the film financing mix.

In addition, it is common for productions to mix these approaches, using a combination of both equity and debt. If the lenders are friends and family rather than banks, the film company may also offer some revenue participation to encourage the lender to make the loan. For the filmmaker, the combination of a loan with a revenue participation may prove to be a very good arrangement if the lender would agree to make the loan "non-recourse," meaning that the loan would be made only to the film company without any right to seek a guarantee from the filmmaker or otherwise claim payment from any party other than the production company.

B. Financing Based on Distribution Deals and Presale Arrangements

Unlike other industries, the motion picture business presents a second type of financing sale in addition to the typical model of equity financing. It involves selling the film's distribution rights. In this form of financing, the company sells its assets in exchange for a present or guaranteed payment. For example, if the film company sells its rights to European distribution in exchange for $50,000, then its future revenue will exclude any monies made in the countries identified as European, whether those markets generate $5,000, $50,000, or $500,000. This arrangement reduces the potential for future income, but also reduces the risk of loss. Potential distribution formats can also be sold in advance, such as streaming rights.

From the filmmaker's standpoint, cash for the production is the most critical requirement of any financing structure; no number of future promises will cover rental fees or payroll. Unfortunately, the business realities for presale agreements often require that the completed film be delivered prior to any payment. To actually produce the film, the filmmaker must borrow from a lender, using the presale agreement as collateral. Under this structure, the interest costs are not avoided, and the filmmaker may still shoulder the residual risk that presale fees will not materialize. Nonetheless, since a presale agreement allows the filmmaker to finance a project without risking personal funds, it remains a very attractive option.

Presale and distribution deals may vary significantly. Some of the more common structures are briefly described as follows.

1. Advertising Revenues

For the online media company, revenue can be generated by participating in various platforms such as YouTube to accept advertising. Uploading content does not automatically generate any revenue on YouTube or on any of the other platforms. For example, filmmakers (or content producers) on Twitch who become members of the Twitch Partner Program can allow ads in their streams. The filmmakers share in the revenue based on the viewership of the advertising. YouTube producers initially earn revenue by enabling the monetization settings in their accounts. The benefit of the advertising dollars is that the funds are revenue, meaning that no ownership interests are granted in exchange for the income. The difficulty is that the revenue is generated in response to large audiences watching what generally needs to be a significant amount of content. A production company may choose to "follow the money," and start with low-cost video that drives viewership online to build the cash reserves and the audience to leverage more ambitious productions later in the company's production cycle.

2. Cash Deals

Only in the rarest of situations or with the lowest of budgets will a filmmaker be able to fund the production with a cash advance on a guaranteed distribution. There was a time when companies such as Cannon Films would create *one-sheets* (theatrical advertising posters) to exhibit at the international film markets. If it was successful selling enough territories based on the poster, Cannon would contact the talent named in the posters and begin the process of producing the film. If a film didn't attract enough interest, the remaining posters would be discarded and those projects never started. Today, modest cash advances may sometimes be available, but this is the exception to the rule. The growth of online streaming services has created a demand for content that has resulted in cash deals, but these are generally reserved to well-established producers with attractive track records or libraries for the streamers.

3. Negative Pick-Up

Although the details can vary greatly, *negative pick-up* means that a film studio or distributor pays for the cost of the film to be finished to the point that a completed negative or digital files are ready to use. Generally, the filmmaker sells the film to a studio in exchange for reimbursement of production expenses and some form of profit sharing from the eventual proceeds of the film. For example, if a filmmaker had a budget of $1 million for a film project, the film company would "sell" the film by promising to deliver a completed motion picture substantially the same as that described in the screenplay in exchange for a payment of $1 million. Once the film was delivered, the film studio would then have the obligation to finish the prints for the film, pay for its marketing and distribution, and split profits, if any, with the filmmaker on the agreed-upon percentage basis.

The negative pick-up arrangement often operates very similarly to studio financing. Each major decision may be subject to review by the distributor. The distributor will require that the script be followed, the agreed-upon casting not be changed, the length of the film be acceptable, and the film be eligible for a particular MPAA rating, typically a PG-13 or R. Any major deviations must be approved by the purchaser or the filmmaker risks the company stopping payments or claiming the production company is in breach of the agreement.

The amount paid for a negative pick-up need not be the same as the production cost of the film, although the distributor will often seek to cap the payment at this amount. If so, the filmmaker must be sure to include budget items for all the participants who have invested sweat equity in the project. In other words, the filmmaker, along with all key personnel, should be included in the budget used to negotiate with the studio or financier in a negative pick-up arrangement. Once the price has been agreed upon, further compensation will be very difficult to add.

The actual payment structure can vary from arrangement to arrangement. In most cases, the purchasing studio will provide funds on a weekly basis as necessary for the production company to meets its regular obligations. Each payment will be conditioned on the filmmaker demonstrating that the project remains on budget and on schedule. In other cases, the funds will be paid on delivery of the final product, so the filmmaker must use the negative pick-up agreement to obtain commercial loans to cover production expenses.

4. Distribution Guarantee

Closely related to the negative pick-up arrangement is the *distribution guarantee agreement*. In this case, the distributor agrees to purchase the completed film's full distribution rights in exchange for a fee and an agreed-upon royalty or gross participation amount. A distribution guarantee does not eliminate the risks to the filmmaker, because the funds are generally not made available until the filmmaker has completed the film.

Since the sale of distribution rights does not immediately result in cash to the filmmaker, the film company must use the sales agreement as a form of collateral against which it can borrow money from a bank or other lender. Under the distribution guarantee agreement, the film's distributor serves as guarantor of the loan. Since the lender is entitled to repayment regardless of the film's revenue, the distributor's guarantee may put the lender in a position of much greater security than if the filmmaker is solely responsible for the loan. If the distributor is a stable, well-established company, lenders are generally willing to finance this type of arrangement.

Invariably, the lender will require that the film company furnish a *completion bond*, which insures against the film not being completed as required by the purchasing distributor. Together, the loan interest and the premium cost of the completion bond could add 20 percent to the cost of completing the film. Short-term financing may further increase this cost substantially.

5. Foreign Distributors, Markets, and Territories

Foreign distribution has grown to become the single largest category of theatrical film distribution income, exceeding both domestic theatrical exhibition and broadcast rights for revenue. Despite its importance, however, foreign distribution is risky territory for independent films, because the language, currency, and legal enforcement barriers often make it difficult to collect royalties or enforce contract rights. If a production company seeks an advance and a royalty payment in exchange for foreign distribution rights, currency exchange rates and the difficulties of collection may still result in the production company receiving far less than it was promised.

Even if royalty payments are forthcoming, the difficulties of auditing foreign receipts and dealing with clever accounting practices make foreign income highly volatile for independent filmmakers. Without the leverage of an ongoing business relationship, the cost of collecting small royalties from foreign distributors in small territories can exceed the payments due. Where possible, the filmmaker is best served by selling the rights to a foreign territory outright. More modest prepayments will result in greater cash in hand for the filmmaker and should be the preferred strategy with all but the most reputable distributors.

Nonetheless, independent filmmakers have been increasingly successful in selling the rights to foreign territories in exchange for advance payments and using these payments to finance all or most of the film's budget. These transactions can be conducted through direct cash payments or through letters of credit that are deemed sufficiently sound by US lenders.

Often the strategy in these sales follows that of Cannon Films: filmmakers invest early in the poster art so that the purchaser knows what it is marketing. Few people have the skill necessary to read a screenplay (or even view a rough cut) and successfully visualize a final film. On the other hand, most people have attended films solely on the basis of the poster. Perhaps this form of financing seems artistically impure, but commercial success for a film requires commercial techniques.

During the independent film boom of the 1980s, the combination of new marketing opportunities and supportive tax regulations led to an infusion of foreign capital. This financial resource disappeared as a result of changing economic conditions and substantially more restrictive tax regulations.

Since foreign markets make up such a large component of film distribution, many opportunities remain to collaborate or coproduce with production companies outside of the United States. Occasionally these coproduction arrangements will provide financing to the US company, but more often the foreign company enjoys subsidies for its local production and will provide services in exchange for the co-ownership of the project. Although such an arrangement entails a number of unique risks, it may also afford the independent filmmaker some attractive side benefits: opportunities to travel and to benefit from the coproducers' expertise.

6. Studios

Traditional Hollywood studios manufactured motion pictures as product. They purchased the raw materials—stories and talent—and produced finished films that they exhibited in the theaters they owned throughout the world. Over time, antitrust laws required that production activities be separated from the exhibition of films. The movie palaces became independent companies and exhibition chains. The studios reduced their reliance on their back lots and increasingly served as financing companies for a schedule of films produced by other companies.

Today, with the exception of Disney, the major motion picture studios are primarily distributors rather than film production companies. Instead of directly purchasing stories or scripts, the studios work through existing relationships with established production companies. These production companies package the script, develop the budget, and manage the production. The budget will include a negotiated fee for the producer's own expenses and income. The agreement between the producer and studio will also determine the producer's participation in the film's revenue. The studio will finance the project on an incremental basis, providing the necessary funding for each step of the process. In exchange, the studio has primary control over the project and the ability to terminate it at any point in its development.

This incremental approach, known as a *production and distribution deal*, allows the studio to maximize its control while minimizing its risk. The producer will typically receive a fee for early preproduction activities. Although the costs of script and budget preparation often exceed this payment, the producer rather than the studio covers this risk. If the studio is interested in developing the project further, it will release funds to the producer to pay for selected key aspects of preproduction. Locations will be scouted, the script rewritten or polished, and key personnel identified. Throughout this process, the producer will receive little or no additional pay.

Eventually, however, the studio may commit to the project. It "green-lights" the film and commits to principal actors, a director, and designers. (For some directors and actors, the studio will be obligated to pay them whether or not the production is ever filmed—the "pay-or-play" obligation to compensate the person for the right to rely on the person's participation.) During this phase of preproduction, the studio will typically distribute a small portion of the producer's fee. The bulk of the producer's fee will be paid during principal photography, with small payments withheld until the delivery of the first rough cut of the picture and the delivery of the final picture.[1]

For the independent filmmaker, making a film under a studio-financed production deal is both a blessing and a curse. A well-made studio film has the potential to greatly exceed the success of any independent film. The studios' marketing budgets and promotional savvy can make a household name out of anyone, opening the door for tremendous professional control on subsequent projects.

The curse is that the independent filmmaker gives up control immediately. Rarely do studio screenplays resemble the writer's first drafts, and novice directors will be second-guessed at every turn—if the filmmaker is allowed to remain attached to the picture at all. Still, that is where the money is. For most artists it is commercial success that buys them the luxury of later artistic control.

C. Crowdfunding, Crowdsourcing, and Crowd Financing

In recent years, a new form of independent financing known as crowdfunding has become available. Crowdfunding combines the best aspects of social media with the power to create engagement opportunities for the filmmakers' audiences well before the final feature is complete. Kickstarter, one of the leading crowdfunding platforms, claims it has helped more than 100 successful independent films. StudioBinder has identified 15 Kickstarter films that have been nominated for an academy award, including the 2019 Best Documentary Short Film, *Period. End of Sentence*. These numbers highlight that crowdfunding is an important strategy for independent film.

At the same time, crowdfunding is not a magic wand that will make money appear from the sky. Well-designed crowdfunding campaigns require a great deal of time, effort, and engagement. In many ways, the crowdfunding exercise will require as much effort as the motion picture itself.

There are many different approaches to crowdfunding, although most popular press discussions of crowdfunding do not distinguish between the various types. Crowdfunding allows members of the public to learn about interesting and worthwhile products, services, artistic endeavors, and causes and then provide money through a third-party platform such as Kickstarter or Indiegogo. The platforms help market and promote the various projects being funded on their sites, and they take a small percentage of the revenue earned by the project in exchange for hosting the activities.

There are both nonprofit and for-profit crowdfunding platforms. The nonprofit platforms raise money for charitable causes, with both the platform and the recipients meeting the tax exempt charitable status standards. The majority of crowdfunding activity, however, is in the for-profit sector.

Crowdfunding is particularly useful as part of an online media company's outreach strategy. Some video hosting platforms also provide *tipping services* so that viewers can make small donations to promote the efforts of the filmmaker. The ability to accept small amounts of money, either as thanks or in exchange for small rewards, and to connect regularly with an online, engaged audience, creates a very positive feedback loop that encourages stronger support from the audience.

1. Crowdfunding

In a typical crowdfunding campaign, a film company would set a target amount it wishes to raise to complete the film project or a particular component of the film project, such as finishing funds or editing. The film company would market the project on the platform website in addition to its own media outreach. The campaign would use production stills, interviews with cast and crew, story logs, artwork, and other creative elements of the project to invite the public to become interested in the film.

In exchange for giving the production company funds, the people paying to help the film project might receive a thank-you recognition in the end credits or a DVD or digital download of the film, to be delivered when production is completed. For more generous participants, the film company might give tickets to a showing of the film at a film festival or other public premiere. Other production companies have even included invitations to the wrap party for the production or walk-on parts as rewards for high-level purchases.

The money paid by the public in these crowdfunding examples are either gifts or purchases, depending on whether the member of the public paying the film company is receiving a tangible value in exchange. The copy of the completed film and the tickets to a showing of the film at a public event both have a tangible value. The film company has therefore sold goods and earned taxable income. In contrast, the thank-you recognition in the credits has no tangible value, and the money exchanged is merely a gift.

As of 2020, gifts received through crowdfunding by small businesses do not get reported to the IRS until they exceed the threshold of 200 transactions or $20,000. Even then, there is no taxable income unless the funds were paid in exchange for some benefit or exchange. Single donors who gift more than $15,000 may be subject to the gift tax, suggesting high-level gifts might be better arranged outside the crowdfunding platform where additional tax planning can reduce or eliminate any liability.

For the recipient film company, the tax characterization will depend on whether the funds are true gifts or are more like payments. Corporations do not generally receive gifts, and most crowdfunding campaigns include some form of thank-you or value back to the donor. In such cases, the gift will likely be treated as income by the IRS. In contrast, if a family member uses the platform to make a personal gift, the familial relationship will make the transaction fall outside of corporate income and be treated more like a gift. Any revenue earned will then be offset by the operating expenses of the film company, so in most campaigns there is still no tax obligation.

2. Crowdsourcing

Crowdsourcing is very similar to crowdfunding. It takes advantage of social media platforms to arrange for goods or services to be used in a project. The members of the public generally offer their time and effort rather than funds. For example, if an independent film needs a crowd scene, it can use Meetup or another social media platform to bring the needed volunteers. By putting together a campaign similar to a crowdfunding one, the film company can promote the event that needs to be filmed and arrange for a large group of people to appear for the shoot.

Crowdsourcing might also enable a production to acquire expensive or hard-to-rent sets and props. The production company may need to reach out for antique cars and their drivers, Civil War reenactors, or a wide selection of jugglers and mimes. Whatever the filmmakers can imagine, the use of crowdsourcing may overcome the challenges of finding the resource.

Like with donors, however, merely having a platform may not be enough to get people to actually volunteer. The crowdsourcing campaign must be compelling to get members of the public to spend their time and effort to participate.

3. Crowd Financing

Crowd financing is quite different from crowdfunding and crowdsourcing. Instead of offering copies of the film to the people who support the campaign, the film company sells offerings with debt, equity, or other securities instruments in exchange for payment. That is, the film company uses the services of an online platform to sell investments in the production company to the public rather than raising investor money through private transactions.

For some productions, this opportunity provides a great resource to raise capital. For others, it can lead to confusion, the distraction of managing shareholder relations for a large group of unsophisticated investors, and liability for violation of poorly understood securities laws.

Crowd financing was authorized by the 2012 JOBS Act and the Securities and Exchange Commission Regulation Crowdfunding rules that enabled the selling of federal securities using the JOBS Act exemptions to federal securities registration. A film company issuing securities using crowd financing is permitted to raise a maximum aggregate amount of $1,070,000 in a 12-month period. The amount eligible will continue to be adjusted for inflation. The amounts raised outside of Regulation Crowdfunding are not counted against this amount.

For individuals who have an annual income and net worth of more than $107,000 (adjusted for inflation), the individual can invest up to 10 percent of the person's income or net worth, whichever is less, but cannot exceed an investment of $107,000. For individuals with either an income or net worth less than $107,000 (again, adjusted annually), the person can invest up to either $2,200 or 5 percent of the lower of the person's net worth or annual income. The investment caps are for a 12-month period. The typical investor in a crowd financing investment will likely be purchasing far less than the maximum amount.

There are a number of additional regulations regarding the disclosures that must be followed by the film company issuing the securities, including a requirement to use audited financial disclosures. Most important, while Regulation Crowdfunding allows the film company to issue shares to large numbers of people without registering the securities, the film company and its management remains responsible under Rule 10b-5 of the Securities and Exchange Act of 1934.

Crowd financing has heavy overhead. A 2019 report by the SEC found significant costs associated with the efforts. The SEC survey reported that "the average issuer employed three people who collectively spent 241 hours to launch a crowdfunding campaign. Based on the survey estimates, the total cost of creating a campaign page, issuer disclosures, film, and video, and hiring a marketing firm, a lawyer, and an accountant amounts to approximately 5.3% of the amount raised."[2] The median amount earned by the crowd financing issuers was $25,000, well below the maximum amount sought in most of these offerings.

Rule 10b-5 makes it illegal for any person to defraud, make false statements, omit material information, or otherwise conduct business in a manner that would deceive another person regarding the purchase and sale of securities. This rule requires that everything said about the film project and the securities offering is true and complete. While this has always been true for statements made to investors, the fundraising under Regulation Crowdfunding has the potential to increase the number of investors significantly and to offer the film company's securities to individuals who are much less sophisticated—and therefore much more easily defrauded—than the sophisticated and accredited investors who have traditionally funded independent film. As a consequence, crowd financing is a tool for only the most sophisticated producers, those that have the resources to mount a credible crowd financing campaign and have the ability to manage the investor relations for the remainder of the life of the production company. For most filmmakers, those resources can be put to better use elsewhere.

4. Incorporating Crowdfunding in the Business Plan

While crowd financing is a challenging and difficult strategy rarely worth the costs and effort involved, crowdfunding and crowdsourcing provide excellent vehicles to promote the film and build an audience. The successful crowdfunding strategy should use the crowdfunding approach as a feature of the broader social media and commercial marketing strategy for the project. The crowdfunding platform should be an extension of the websites, social media tools, and other communications platforms used by the filmmaker to tell the story about the making of the film and to tease the audience with the story in the film.

The degree of script confidentiality will vary considerably. Filmmakers involved with *Star Wars* and the Marvel MCU have become obsessed with confidentiality, as online blogging has turned spoilers into daily fare on many sites. On the other hand, there are many films based on literary works or cinematic remakes where the story is widely known. The joy in those projects is to see how the well-known content is scripted, shot, and performed rather than to worry about minor plot twists. The willingness to share content will inform the filmmaker how much of the story to reveal in the crowdfunding campaign as well as in the trailers and other marketing materials.

More than the story told by the film, the crowdfunding campaign also tells the story about the filmmaker's journey to make the film. Potential supporters will come from those directly and closely involved in the project. The most successful crowdfunded projects have devoted fan bases for the underlying content, the director, or cast members. Other successful projects may be based on support from the locale in which the project is shooting or from a particular community whose interests the work highlights. For example, narrative and documentary films dealing with difficult medical issues or social justice concerns, such as wrongful convictions, climate change, or animal rights, all tend to have potential for an audience willing to donate to have a story brought to the screen.

The production company should establish its strategy for engaging with the audience early in the process and create the materials needed to tell a compelling story throughout the process. For films needing hundreds of thousands of dollars, production companies may do well to seek campaigns for specific, incremental steps in the film process rather than making an ask for the entire budget. A target of $5,000 to storyboard a script is likely to be reachable. The production company can provide the donors a digital copy of the storyboards (after the release date of the film, if confidentiality is an issue) in exchange for payments above a certain level. T-shirts and hats are also good thank-you gifts.

With the completed storyboards and script, along with a business plan and 100 or more crowdfunding supporters, the filmmaker can raise some funds outside the crowdfunding campaign. If additional funds are needed to travel to a location, add special effects, or acquire music, the production company can run a new campaign for that step. Hopefully, each step engages more participants and grows the interest.

Another very common strategy is to use the initial crowdfunding campaign to make a short film, which provides the filmmaker with the best possible tool to convince potential investors about the project. Much more than a script or storyboard, a compelling short tells the viewer that the cast and crew have come together and are able to make a worthwhile story. At the same time, this strategy highlights that the use of crowdfunding can often double the amount of work needed. The crowdfunding campaign and the short project may together require as much time and effort as the proposed independent film.

Since a $50 donation is a fairly typical amount for a gift, the filmmaker must have a very large and dedicated following to raise sufficient funds to make most projects. One rule of thumb is that a campaign must know it has at least 100 supporters before a film company should risk launching a crowdfunding campaign. In part, this is because a failed online campaign might dampen a potential distributor's interest in the project. After all, if the film could not gain attention in its crowdfunding campaign, why should it attract attention for a theatrical launch? Crowdfunding, though helpful, should be used strategically and thoughtfully.

D. Cash Management of Sales Financing

In most funding scenarios, the film producer must bear the burden of both controlling the costs and paying the bills as they accrue.

Although the filmmaker may have sold the right to distribute the film (or assigned the copyright in the completed film), these future transactions do not translate into production funds. Instead, the filmmaker must apply to a lender to provide the cash to make the movie.

1. Film Lenders

A few commercial banks regularly provide this form of independent film lending. The experience and knowledge of these banks allow them to assess the credit risk of an independent production. The film company must present credible evidence that it will be able to repay the loan and that it has sufficient collateral to cover the principal amount borrowed. Just as a home purchaser must show the intended property is worth at least as much as the loan, the filmmaker must demonstrate that the value of the financed project exceeds the loan requested.

To demonstrate the value of the project to the lender, the film company must present a film package that lays out its existing collateral. Since filming has not yet begun, that will include the screenplay and story rights; legally binding commitments by the key personnel to participate in the film; the production budget, including a draw-down schedule for the use of the proceeds as they are paid to the filmmaker throughout production; and any binding agreements regarding the sale or distribution of the film.

Of these assurances, the most important are the legally binding guarantees for the territory sales, negative pick-up, or other financing arrangements. To be effective, these contracts must specify the guaranteed minimum the filmmaker will be paid, which is the amount that can be used as collateral to be pledged against the value of the loan. If the film's distribution agreements, negative pick-up contracts, or presales involve non-US territories, the financing becomes a bit more complex. (Issues involving fluctuating exchange rates, governmental stability, and creditworthiness can frustrate the lending process.)

To get the collateral ready for the bank, there may be significant expenses, particularly with regard to key personnel—cast and crew who require an advance payment to legally bind themselves to the project. The bank will also require a security agreement that puts a lien against the developed (and the exposed) film stock and the copyright in the film, so that the lender can foreclose on the assets in the case of nonpayment.

Film lenders typically make their payments weekly, upon proof of satisfactory progress during the prior week's shooting. This short-term bridge financing may be substantially more expensive than other financing sources, and the cost of the interest payments must be included in the budget for the project.

2. General Commercial Loans

All commercial banks provide other forms of commercial loans, including unsecured loans. Even though these lenders may lack a sophisticated team experienced in entertainment or media-secured financing, they may be of assistance to an independent filmmaker seeking modest additional funds. Unless the transaction is for an unsecured loan based on the filmmaker's personal creditworthiness, the lender will require the following elements to be in place before it will agree to finance the film:

- A reputable distributor that has entered into an agreement to distribute the finished film

- A completion bond company's guarantee that the film will be completed for the agreed-upon budget
- A budget that accurately reflects the anticipated costs of the film's production
- Sufficient general liability and other insurance
- Adequate security agreements between the lender and the production company so that the lender holds a perfected security interest in both the physical and intangible property of the production company
- Written, enforceable contracts committing the principal cast members to appear in the production

When the filmmaker can package these elements, some lenders may be willing to provide credit to the film company.

For a company that has received significant cash investments, lenders will be willing to provide small lines of credit. In these cases, the lender may reduce the demands for documentation, completion bonds, or other requirements because the risk to the bank is minimized by the investor's participation. The company's assets, including the copyright to the film and its cash reserves, provide sufficient security for the lender to accept the risk of providing the modest loan. The creditor will have priority for repayment over the investors, so in the event of default, the bank will be repaid in full before the investors receive any of their funds.

E. Nonprofit Financing for the Filmmaker

For guerrilla and digital filmmakers, nonprofit grants often go unnoticed. Many nonprofit organizations are willing to participate in independent film projects. Some invest in film as an art form regardless of content, while others support particular projects because they want to promote the message of the filmmaker—this is particularly true for documentary film.

Raising funds for a nonprofit film from charitable donors may be much easier than raising investment funds from investors. Investors understand that most independent films are high-risk investments with little chance of financial success. The worthiness of the project is secondary to the financial considerations. When asked for a charitable donation, in contrast, the same individual will focus on the merit of the project and the people involved without any expectation of return other than the guaranteed tax deduction. Moreover, the tax deduction occurs at the time of the donation, so the return is immediate and without risk. For first-time filmmakers, particularly documentary filmmakers, charitable support is a very legitimate way to enter the business.

For the filmmaker, a further benefit is the level of appreciation afforded by the sponsors. Nonprofits often recognize that most of the work done on an independent film is essentially volunteer time, donated to complete a worthwhile project. As a result, they may offer the filmmaker wide latitude and a great deal of respect.

A limitation on nonprofit fundraising is that the money is often quite modest. The donors may also lack any sophistication regarding the project, unlike sources connected with the film industry. When funds become available from industry sources, they may often lead to other opportunities to promote the film or to valuable connections essential to the casting or production of the project.

1. Sources for Nonprofit Financing

Organizations that provide resources to filmmakers include the Sundance Institute Documentary Fund, assisting the development of documentaries on social issues; the Fund for Jewish Documentary Filmmaking, focusing on Jewish history and culture; the Black Public Media (formerly known as the National Black Programming Consortium), focusing on films emanating from the African diaspora; the Astraea Lesbian Foundation for Justice (formerly known as the Astraea National Lesbian Action Foundation), addressing issues in the communities on the margins of society; and many geographic programs, dedicated to local arts, including documentaries and narrative filmmaking.

In many other cases, a nonprofit organization may not specifically look to finance a film project but rather to provide funds for community outreach, training, or other goals. If the film being developed promotes those goals, the film project may become a valuable investment for the organization.

2. Fiscal Sponsorships

Nonprofit organizations may raise money from private donors or from grant organizations to fund those who support their exempt charitable purpose. As charitable organizations, they do not pay federal income tax, and they allow their donors to receive a charitable deduction against personal tax obligations. These charities are often referred to by their IRS tax designation, *501(c)(3) organizations.*

 A few 501(c)(3) organizations have the development of noncommercial film and video as their charitable purpose. Organizations such as the Independent Filmmaker Project (IFP), The Film Collective, and others accept donor funds to promote film projects. Under the typical fiscal agency relationship, a filmmaker applies for fiscal sponsorship by providing information on the film project, the filmmakers, the budget, and the distribution strategy. If approved by the fiscal agent, that charity receives the donations. The charity then provides the donated fees to the filmmaker. The fiscal agent typically charges a 5 to 10 percent fee for its services.

 The filmmaker is responsible for careful financial accounting and for compliance with all applicable tax laws. For example, the donor cannot be given any financial interest in the film, because this would transform the charitable gift into a for-profit investment. Donors can be given tokens of appreciation, but if these gifts have any significant monetary value, then the donor must be informed of the value of the gift and deduct that from the value of the donation listed on all tax returns.

 Some of these charitable endeavors have been operating for decades, but others may stay in business for only a few years. Filmmakers should be sure to check the history of the particular charity, particularly if the filmmaker is also encouraging that donors contribute to the charity as part of the charity's commitment to the filmmaker's project.

 For projects that have a strong social justice or charitable agenda, the use of charitable dollars as the funding vehicle makes very good sense. It allows the filmmaker to complete the film and achieve the goals of the project while avoiding the challenges of fundraising from accredited investors or crowd financing.

3. Partnership Projects and Agenda-Based Films

Fiscal sponsorships are not limited to arts organizations. Any 501(c)(3) organization may elect to serve as a film's fiscal agent, provided the film meets its charitable purpose. For example, a charity dedicated to promoting the elimination of a particular rare disease may find that a documentary highlighting the devastating consequences of the disease would help promote awareness and encourage pharmaceutical research to find a cure. A filmmaker hoping to make such a documentary could enter into a relationship with that charity by which it served as the project's fiscal agent.

The filmmaker would be responsible for attracting new donations to the charity earmarked for the documentary, and the charity would be responsible for assuring that the tax and reporting obligations are fully met. The agreement should provide for the filmmaker's salary, whether paid up front or deferred, and also stipulate that any donations in excess of the production and distribution costs be retained by the charity. The charity may charge a small fee to cover the expenses it incurs. The filmmaker retains the ownership of the film and its copyright, and all revenue from the film.

Even without becoming a fiscal agent, a nonprofit may serve as a conduit for additional funds donated by supporters of the film project. For example, if a church were willing to sponsor a production based on the life of one of its former pastors, the church would probably provide a modest grant toward the production costs (and perhaps provide the use of the church without charge as a shooting location). In addition, the church could collect funds for the film project from other donors. So long as the payments were consistent with the charitable purpose of the organization, a nonprofit could choose to use its resources to underwrite the film project.

4. Accounting and Accountability

If the fiscal agent, which is responsible for ensuring the film project's fundraising meets its tax obligations, is a film-arts charity, it will likely have little or no control over the content of the film. (Non-arts charities are likely to participate as fiscal agents only in those situations where the charity and filmmaker have agreed in general terms about the content of the project.) To meet IRS regulations, however, the fiscal agent must have a legal right to control the use of funds related to the project in order to ensure that the funds are used in a manner consistent with the agreed-upon budget and that financial record keeping and reporting occurs properly. Charities with ongoing fiscal agency programs will have operational guidelines that the filmmaker must agree to follow. The filmmaker remains responsible for any liabilities of the production.

The film company does not itself become a 501(c)(3) charity. Instead, it should receive an annual tax form from the fiscal agent identifying the funds donated to it. Since the amount should be offset by the costs of production, there should be no taxes owed on these payments. If the film company is a sole proprietorship, however, and the budget includes the filmmaker's salary, then this will constitute personal income to the filmmaker.

F. Nonprofit Financing for the Nonprofit Organization

Film companies often consider undertaking the obligation to become a nonprofit, charitable organization in order to produce multiple projects. As described in chapter 2 (pp. 31–32), the formation of a charitable entity to produce the films should only be selected if the filmmaker intends to get donor support for activities that meet the charitable rules of IRS and if the nonprofit will operate for many years in promotion of many artistic works and other charitable purposes.

1. Creating a Public Charity to Fund the Film Project

As explained in chapter 2, the new company must meet the organizational and operational test to be a charity. This requires that the purpose fall into one of these categories: "charitable, religious, educational, scientific, literary, testing for public safety, fostering national or international amateur sports competition, and preventing cruelty to children or animals." *Charitable* has its own meaning. It includes relief for the poor or underprivileged, addressing discrimination, promoting human and civil rights, and similar activities. It is not enough that the earning be spent to the exempt purpose. The income must be earned in a manner that is itself a charitable purpose.

For a filmmaker considering the formation of a public charity to support production work, there are two primary reasons that the formation of a new charity is preferable to working with a fiscal sponsor or preexisting charity: sustainability and control. The choice to operate as a new charity is primarily undertaken because the projects will continue for a long period of time, rather than for a single motion picture production. A great example of a charitable production company is the Children's Television Workshop, which produced *Sesame Street* and other children's educational television, primarily for low-income families. (Children's Television Workshop was renamed Sesame Workshop in 2000.)

The charitable model enables the production company to seek federal grant money and foundation support for its projects. Sesame Workshop, for example, was a recipient of sponsorships from the Corporation for Public Broadcasting, US Department of Education, MacArthur Foundation, LEGO Foundation, and many others to expand *Sesame Street* globally and to develop other educational resources for children's education, including those in refugee camps.

The second reason to adopt the charitable approach is to ensure independence from any fiscal sponsor regarding the mission and focus of the content being developed. Most fiscal sponsors use a very light touch in the relationship they have with their funded projects, acting much more as a resource than a reviewer. Nonetheless, if the people involved in making the fund are hoping to expand into other charitable activities beyond the project, then the limited expansion afforded by the fiscal sponsor may be too limiting. For example, if the filmmakers hope to expand from a single production to a series and then to live workshops and in-school programs or live, charitable fundraisers, then the additional steps might not fit within the fiscal sponsorship relationship.

A production company with the need for long-term sustainability and organizational control might be one dedicated to addressing a charitable need or social issue that uses films and audiovisual series as one among many charitable outreach efforts. Such an organization would bring together both a charitable and an artistic purpose. Some production companies, for example, are dedicated to Christian missionary work. Other production companies might be focused on efforts to promote educational resources. Such companies are primarily focused on the underlying goal of the organization but use short films, documentaries, and audiovisual works as a method of promoting the message of the charity.

In the UK, for example, the Charity Film Awards recognizes the best short films and full-length films produced by charities. In 2019, the competition received over 300 entries. In addition, as Charity Film Awards noted, there were "over a $\frac{1}{4}$ million extra views of the videos that entered, dozens of press stories and in excess of 2 million page impressions related to the awards on the internet."[3] The use of audiovisual storytelling to promote the charitable purpose of the organization can have a far-reaching impact.

2. Differences Between For-Profit and Nonprofit Film Companies

A nonprofit film production company will operate very differently than its for-profit cousin. Because of the private inurement rules described in chapter 2, the individuals who operate the production company do not own the company. There are no shareholders or members with any ownership interest. All net profits of the production company are kept by the nonprofit.

To stay compliant with the private inurement rules, the nonprofit production company should treat any contractual relations with insiders very differently from those contractual relationships with outsiders. For IRS purposes, the insiders described here are the company's officers, directors, major donors, and their immediate family. Those insiders who are employees of the company can receive a reasonable salary for their work. A reasonable salary should be measured against industry norms and the company's resources. A person does not have to take a vow of poverty to work at a nonprofit organization, but generally the wages are lower than in the for-profit sector for similar work. Directors are generally uncompensated.

Any financial contracts with the insiders should be for the benefit of the charity and cannot provide inappropriate financial benefit to the insider. For example, it is common for major donors to also provide the occasional loan to the charities they support. These loans must be at or below standard market rates. Payment of rates above market would result in a private inurement to the donor. The same holds true with any property rental agreement. A board member might offer low-cost space to a charity to assist it in its growth. But the board member cannot charge above-market rates for the space.

Because of the private inurement rules, insiders should generally not be profit participants involved in the projects. First, profit participation is very similar to corporate dividends in structure, and the IRS might disallow the payments. Second, it is very difficult to establish reasonable market rates for profit participation, making any amount presumptively unreasonable.

But there may be some limited exceptions, particularly if production resulted in a small actual payment. For example, if the daughter of a nonprofit director were cast in one of the films, thereby receiving the same small profit participation percentage as all other cast members, then although she would be considered an insider (or *disqualified person* under IRS regulations), the amount paid would be based on the external measure for all participants providing identical work and considered minor in relation to the effort provided. So the payment would be reasonable and would not be disqualified. For most companies, however, the time and effort to defend such payments would not be worth the challenge. The production company would still be better off disqualifying insiders from most payment.

For productions that do not rely on volunteers, there is an exception. The state and federal wage rules continue to apply. The same child of a board member would be entitled to receive at least minimum wage for hours worked on a film if the charity was not relying on a volunteer cast. These payments would be reasonable because they represent the least the company could pay any employee for the services actually rendered.

3. Paying Reasonable Fees for Production Services

In contrast to contractual relationships with insiders, the nonprofit production company is free to engage in business with outsiders and other corporate vendors (not controlled by insiders) as it would with any arm's-length agreement. Nonprofit organizations such as the American Public Media Group, Corporation for Public Broadcasting, National Public Radio, and other large nonprofit distributors of film, radio, and television content pay market rates to their filmmakers and production personnel.

In the theatre world, for example, there are thousands of nonprofit professional and community theatre companies. All of them pay the rights holders for the stage plays to produce the works. Most pay their directors and production personnel. Among them, the professional companies pay the actors while the community theatres rely on volunteer actors and crew members.

If the new production company has a salaried executive director and a voluntary board of directors, then the non-insider directors, cinematographers, producers, designers, cast, and crew can be paid through both salary and profit participation for the specific projects on which they worked. Jim Henson, for example, developed certain characters for *Sesame Street* and retained the trademark rights and other rights in some of the other characters. Henson's company and Children's Television Workshop collaborated on licensing arrangements to promote both companies. The need for Children's Television Workshop to jointly license with Henson did not interfere with the nonprofit status of Children's Television Workshop.

Nonprofit production companies should develop clear internal procedures to separate those participants governed by insider rules from those with whom the organization has the ability to contract more freely. In addition, all activities must benefit the charitable purpose, so the decision-making structure of the nonprofit should have sufficient safeguards to ensure that each of its undertakings remain consistent with its mission and charitable purpose. By following these guidelines, the nonprofit production company can serve as a very valuable alternative to for-profit filmmaking.

As technology has increased the access to audiovisual content production, it is reasonable to expect a shift toward nonprofit productions in much the same way that professional Broadway theatre is complemented by professional and amateur theatre production companies. Local playhouses could partner with audiovisual production companies to bring a new generation of volunteers onto the stage to produce community film and television in addition to live theatre and music.

4. Serving as a Fiscal Sponsor

A nonprofit production company can choose to produce its own artistic content, or it could choose to work with filmmakers in the community by serving as the fiscal sponsor for other productions. As noted previously, many arts-related fiscal sponsors are also focused on promoting equality and addressing discrimination by providing opportunities for women and filmmakers of color. Others are focused on a religious mission or on addressing a particular social need.

To transition into the role of being a fiscal sponsor, the nonprofit company should develop clear guidelines for working with potentially sponsored productions. The National Network of Fiscal Sponsors provides an excellent set of guidelines available to its members and the public. In the guidelines, the organization notes that although "many nonprofits engage in fiscal sponsorship activity on an occasional basis," it warns that the "practice carries certain inherent risks."[4]

The sponsored organization is primarily responsible for carrying out the project in the manner promised to the fiscal sponsor and the donors. At the same time, the fiscal sponsor is the charitable, tax-exempt entity responsible for reporting the donations to the IRS and assuring that the expenditure of its funds has been used in a manner consistent with the charitable purpose. If a filmmaker were to seek funds to make a film dedicated to childhood education but then produced an R-rated zombie movie, the filmmaker would have breached the commitment to the donors and the fiscal sponsor.

This creates tension between the freedom generally provided by the fiscal sponsor to let the filmmaker control all artistic and production-related decisions, and the fiscal sponsor's responsibility regarding financial accountability and tax reporting. The plots of *The Music Man* and *The Producers* exemplify flimflam fundraising, though neither is in the nonprofit setting.

To keep flimflam fundraising from occurring, most fiscal sponsors look at the nature of the leadership behind the proposal, the commitment to mission demonstrated in the package presented to the fiscal sponsor, and the communications with the donors. Typically, it is the leadership supporting the project that engages in public solicitation for donations. The success or failure of the sponsored project will depend on the integrity of the film-makers and their ability to convince donors of their ability to achieve their mission. But the fiscal sponsor will still be required to address any misallo-cation or other misuse of funds. Through explicit contractual relationships between the fiscal sponsor and the sponsored program and ongoing moni-toring of the project's progress, these risks can be mitigated. Nonetheless, as the National Network of Fiscal Sponsors admonishes, "nonprofits should engage in fiscal sponsorship only if their executive leadership and boards of directors are fully aware of the obligations and liabilities they legally assume as fiscal sponsors."[5] This is good advice both for existing charities and for those seeking to launch new fiscal sponsors.

G. Other Opportunities for Financing and Cost Management

1. Product Placements

A very popular revenue source for independent filmmaking is financing opportunities generated by placing products strategically in the motion picture. Even though product placement opportunities have always been a part of film and television financing, changes in audience viewership of commercials has led advertisers to seek product placement opportunities with greatly increased frequency. The potential is even greater for series productions, since the arrangements can take the size of the audience and the distribution platform into account.

Perhaps the most famous product placement story is the decision of candy manufacturer Mars not to work with Steven Spielberg to feature M&M's in his movie *E.T. the Extra-Terrestrial*. After being turned down by Mars, the director contracted with Hershey to use Reese's Pieces, and E.T. later starred in some Hershey advertising. Today, automobile companies, including Audi and BMW, have invested heavily in films featuring their vehicles. In addition to cross-licensing film content for Audi advertising and paying for product placement, Audi invested heavily in developing a concept car featured in the film *I, Robot*.

Independent productions are unlikely to receive this same level of sup-port, but advertisers are increasingly interested in product placement in independent films and even YouTube videos. The advertiser may pay a fee for having a product in a shot. Filmmakers can negotiate a larger fee if the product plays a featured role in the story. Generally, any such arrangement requires that the product be shown in a positive light. Advertisers will rarely pay to have their products disparaged.

For on-location productions that feature their locale, the neighborhood shops may be the easiest to approach and the most willing to participate. Featuring a local coffeehouse or store as a location adds verisimilitude to the production and creates a potential windfall for the advertiser if the film is successful. Movie locations generate significant tourism, so featuring the actual name and location of a retailer can inspire a boom.

Moreover, if the film can generate a following on YouTube or other popular social networking websites, the opportunity may appeal to companies interested in viral advertising. The product placement agreement can include provisions that earn the filmmaker additional payments from the advertiser if video clips hit specified thresholds.

If the filmmaker hopes not just to receive payments for product placement but also to license the film content for standalone advertisements for the product in question, then the production company must obtain the right to do so in its agreements with cast members. These agreements generally give each cast member the right to opt out of a particular ad appearance. Cosponsored advertisements could lead to additional revenue for the performers, so most actors will choose not to opt out if the ads are done appropriately.

A somewhat different scenario may occur in postproduction, if the opportunity arises to use clips from the film in commercials unrelated to product placement or cosponsorship deals. For those, the production company should make clear that both the production company and each cast member depicted have the right to approve or disapprove the use and that the cast members are entitled to payment for their depiction in the ads.

2. Sale of Incentive Tax Credits

As states and foreign jurisdictions compete to lure film companies into their locations to promote their territories, add employment opportunities, and increase tourism, production companies are provided with an additional financing tool. Some states and foreign governments provide incentive tax credits.

A tax credit allows the holder of the credit to deduct that amount from the taxes owed. This is much more valuable than a deduction or exemption, which serve to reduce the amount of taxes owed. In some jurisdictions, these credits can be sold to other companies in the state.

An incentive film tax credit typically allows the company to receive a portion of its budget back from the state as a credit. Credits are typically applied against taxes due, providing a significant tax benefit. For example, the Ohio credit allows eligible productions to "receive 30 percent on production cast and crew wages, as well as other eligible in-state spending."[6] Since the value of the credit is based on the employment practices and payment activities of the film, the value of the tax credit will be established by the end of principal photography and should be able to be projected with a fair degree of accuracy.

Each jurisdiction has its own set of regulations that require the production to be based, in whole or in part, in that jurisdiction; that identify which expenses will qualify for the tax credits; and that provide other payment structures. The rules are complex, but the incentives can greatly reduce the cost of shooting in certain locations.

With sophisticated accounting and legal assistance, the tax credit may be able to be sold in exchange for funding that can be used to produce the film. Such sales can only occur in those jurisdictions that permit the transfer of the tax credits, so advance planning and close cooperation with the state film office are required. In jurisdictions that allow for the sale of tax credits and provide high incentives, this may be a significant financial resource.

3. Noncash Contributions

Often, the film company receives not only cash contributions of investors but other forms of contributions as well: professional services, equipment, cast participation, locations, and many other attributes of the filming. They can help alleviate the filmmaker's financial burden—but they may also have unintended tax effects.

The general rule of the IRS is that bartering goods and services is the same as conducting transactions. The IRS uses the example of "a plumber exchanging plumbing services for the dental services of a dentist."[7] A filmmaker could certainly barter the making of a commercial for a local business in exchange for that business providing the film company with necessary equipment or services. Some companies use a barter exchange to swap goods and services while others engage directly in transactions. These are taxable exchanges, as if each party received income equal in value to the goods or services received.

A production company may offer profit participation for the exchange.

Generally, a share of the film's future profits or revenue should not be taxed until the revenue is actually earned. The significant risk that no actual profits will be earned should be taken into account in valuing the transaction.[8] Instead, if the production company provides stock, partnership, or LLC interest, then the payment is likely to be presently taxable.[9]

H. Self-Financing the Production

The simplest form of self-financing is for the filmmaker to take cash from a savings account and transfer it to a business account. While this certainly works, few filmmakers have sufficient savings to use this system. In addition to personal cash, filmmakers can seek nonprofit grants, personal loans, and other avenues to help complete their film projects.

1. Guerrilla Financing: Discretionary Money and Gifts

For a true guerrilla film, presale arrangements and studio financing—with its attendant studio control—simply will not work. A guerrilla film is not fully realized until finished. The guerrilla artist thrives on the energy generated from the chaos that a lack of funding can foster, even if this environment takes its toll on everyone else.

A guerrilla filmmaker's primary source of personal financing will be *discretionary income*—savings that will not be missed—and loans. A guerrilla filmmaker who can finance a film exclusively from discretionary income needs little financial advice. Tell the story, make the movie, and suck as much of the marrow from the production's bones as possible.

Most guerrilla filmmakers, however, do not have the luxury of sufficient discretionary income. To raise additional funds, the best approach is to rely on small gifts. These need not be tax-deductible gifts to a nonprofit fiscal agent, but simply small checks from friends, family, and supporters of the filmmaker's work. For example, the guerrilla filmmaker can arrange a party at a local bar and invite everyone the filmmaker knows. Each guest pays a cover charge that provides at least a $20-per-person profit to the filmmaker. In addition, the filmmaker asks for gifts of $50 to $250, offering a thank-you credit and premiere tickets or a copy of the finished project. Even better, the filmmaker can ask a local band to play at the event and donate a copy of its latest album to the film's larger contributors.

While offering to sell interests in the film is a clear violation of securities laws, requesting gifts or selling advance copies of the project is not.

These same steps can be done on a crowdfunding platform, but that takes additional time, effort, and production value. If, instead, the cast and crew just announce the date of the production kick-off party on all their other social media platforms with a series of short posts, the filming can follow.

2. Personal Debt: Credit Cards and Home Loans

When self-financing without cash in hand, the filmmaker often turns to available sources of debt financing. Personal credit cards and personal collateral often provide emergency money for filmmakers. These sources are generally expensive because of their high interest rates. They are also highly risky: the debt comes due whether or not the film is completed.

A common use of personal collateral is to obtain a *home equity line of credit*. In home equity lending, the filmmaker borrows money from the bank by securing a primary residence as collateral. Historically, a bank would only lend to someone who maintained at least 20 percent equity in the property. Although banks had substantially relaxed these rules, the mortgage crisis of 2008 compelled lenders to tighten all lending rules.

If the filmmaker is married, the spouse will typically be a co-owner of the property. The bank will require that all parties who own the property sign the loans, which makes both the filmmaker and the non-filmmaking spouse personally responsible for the loan. The danger of borrowing against one's primary residence is that if the film does not sell, the filmmaker's home would be in jeopardy. This is a significant burden for the filmmaker to impose on the non-filmmaking spouse, particularly when added to the time commitment and personal sacrifice that the guerrilla filmmaker's work extracts from family commitments.

The filmmaker should carefully consider the expenses required, both the interest and the principal payments. If the only way the filmmaker can cover the payments from the loan is to successfully sell the film, then the filmmaker should restructure the budget or take other steps to avoid this risk.

I have never given different advice to any student or client, nor have I ever heard of anyone who has gambled a house on a film and won. Change the budget, change the project, or find another way to tell the story. If, on the other hand, the filmmaker can cover the interest and principal payments, then using a home as collateral is merely an unwise, highly risky choice that should be avoided if possible.

The other personal source of funds for financing the film is *revolving credit*—credit card debt. Because of questionable lending practices, a moderately successful individual with a reasonable amount of personal debt could be offered up to hundreds of thousands of dollars' worth of credit cards. The bank regulations enacted in response to the 2008 economic crisis had slowed this practice, but the banks are starting to offer loose credit once again, making this expensive and risky alternative available for unwise guerilla filmmakers.

Credit cards are unsecured and generally offered for personal rather than commercial use; the cards are usually in the filmmaker's name rather than in the name of the film company. The filmmaker should carefully consider the consequences before committing personal assets by financing the film through short-term, high-interest credit card loans. The attraction is obvious, and filmmaker Spike Lee built his early success on credit cards, but the downside can be financial ruin.

If used at all, credit cards should be a method of last resort. The filmmaker may decide to keep a credit card available as a rainy-day fund, to cover the final costs of editing when the investments and production expenses go slightly over budget. They should also be paid off first to avoid the high costs of the loans.

Finally, some guerrilla filmmakers convince the cast and crew to "lend" the production their credit cards. This practice is unethical and should be avoided, no matter how tempting the idea. The party named on the card is the person responsible for the debt, and even a promise or written agreement by the filmmaker to cover the costs on the card cannot change that fact in the eyes of the bank issuing the card. Since a crew member's credit card would not be used unless the production itself had no assets, the effect is to make the other participants in the film financially obligated for the debts of the project.

If members of the cast or crew have the financial ability to become investors, then they should be properly informed and rewarded as such. The so-called borrowing of their credit cards offers them no protection while exposing them to significant financial risk. If the filmmaker makes empty promises about quick repayment when trying to borrow credit cards, then the filmmaker could be committing criminal fraud that could result in prison. Borrowing of credit cards from cast and crew should never be done. Any authorized expenses paid for by cast and crew members should be promptly reimbursed. No one should be encouraged to make purchases for the production if the expenses may not be reimbursed.

8

Operating the Film Company

The basic structure of the film business entity must provide the core ownership and management for the filmmaker with limited protections for the investor. Depending on the form of the business (see chapter 2, p. 18), organizational papers may have to be filed and submitted to the secretary of state along with a tax payment. Additionally, a film company must have written and signed articles and bylaws or an Operating Agreement that sets out the rules for operations, governance, and payments.

A. Planning with the Future in Mind

1. Short-Term and Long-Term Project Planning

With the rapid changes to media distribution and distribution models for film, television, streaming, and downloading, the role of the producer is more important than ever before. Today, the producer for an independent project has the opportunity to create multiple revenue streams but will face challenges because the traditional distribution windows and markets are undergoing such significant and unanticipated changes.

The most successful production companies emphasize the importance of the business practices of the project as much as the artistic aspects of their productions. These companies work to keep cast and crew together for multiple projects, and some will incorporate projects of different scale in order to manage workflow and ensure ongoing opportunities for everyone involved in the project.

The organizational approach will be very different for those companies focused on creating a single work from those designed to remain in business for an indefinite period. One of the benefits of the myriad new distribution platforms is that it opens up an ability for production companies to remain in business, creating long-form features and short-form videos and series productions. The decision to create an ongoing production company should shape the contractual agreements between the production company and its employees. While the company will likely not bring on cast members or crew members unless there is sufficient paying work to hire them on a regular basis, it can structure employment agreements to provide for a system of payments when cast members and crew are needed. In this way the contracts do not need to be executed each time new work is available. Instead, the agreements would provide that the work will be based on need and the payments established on an hourly, daily, weekly, or per-project basis.

2. Finance and Business Leadership

In the typical independent film company, the filmmaker makes most decisions, and all business choices are pursued in furtherance of the primary film production. In contrast, in the studio setting, the publicly traded company is primarily focused on earnings, making most of its business choices based on cash flow and revenue rather than artistic merit. An independent production company that seeks to operate as an ongoing business must balance these two extremes. The company must fulfill its artistic and storytelling goals while also assuring sufficient cash flow and operational needs to keep the concern going.

To run a company with this longer-term goal as its focus, there needs to be a shift in importance for the financial and business leadership of the organization. The filmmaker may be considered the leader of the key project for the production company, but decision-making for other aspects of the operation is under the management and supervision of the business leadership. Such a structure will necessarily add tensions and conflicts within the organization as scarce resources are divvied up among the competing concerns, and the shift in staff from one project to another will sometimes put the promised delivery at stake. Nonetheless, with clear advance planning and a commitment to a stable operation, such a business approach can be accomplished.

3. Decision-Making

For a film company dedicated to making a single motion picture or series, the decisions of the filmmaker should take precedence, provided there are sufficient funds to meet the needs of the production. When the funding is short, as is often the case, the filmmaker must be able to balance the artistic and operational choices to implement any compromises. The filmmaker must remain responsible to the overall production and its investors and employees, of course. Spending everything in the hope that money will be found is generally not the artistically responsible choice any more than it is the responsible business choice. The filmmaker cannot ignore the bills coming due and spend the cash on hand, since that will bankrupt the production and result in the failure of the film.

For a production company dedicated to creating an ongoing working operation for its feature film and its other media projects, the compromises are much more complex. Telling the filmmaker that funds are unavailable because staff is being hired for an unrelated project can cause frustration. Competing demands among multiple projects often lead to conflict among the team members and competition for organizational leadership.

There are a few solutions to mitigate the conflict. The first step is to make clear where the authority rests for financial and operational decisions. This may no longer be the filmmaker, and that must be agreed upon from the outset. With authority established, the senior leadership should meet regularly in briefing sessions so that the status of each project is clear and the priorities are highlighted. The potential for conflicts over time and resources should be discussed early and regularly so that no member of key leadership is surprised by the challenges. Budgets and business plans should be in writing for each project and agreed upon within the senior leadership. The successful company should also have some long-term reward strategies available to keep everyone aligned with the goals of the company. For example, this might include modest resources for the filmmaker for the preproduction efforts of the next film. Knowing the production company is committed to helping with films number two and three will encourage the filmmaker to accept some of the compromises needed to complete film number one while allowing the production company to also keep on schedule with its weekly series productions.

B. Organizing the Operating Agreement

1. Business of the Company

The business documentation should match the goals of the production team. The first question to answer is whether the film company is being created for the purposes of one particular film project or whether it may be used for multiple projects—sequels, unrelated films, or other projects entirely. Today, a typical corporation's bylaws state that it can conduct "any lawful business," meaning any business that exists. For Disney, that makes sense. To protect small investors, however, the better choice is to limit the investment to a single film project, unless the commitment from the outset was to build a company dedicated to multiple platforms and content. The filmmaker can always try to amend this decision later—but, of course, the investors will then have a voice and a vote in such a modification.

An open-ended business purpose poses a risk for the investors. If the purpose of the company is not limited, the filmmaker can continue making movies until the money runs out; even if the first film returns a nice profit, the income is retained for future films. In such a case, the investors may still receive nothing. Given the risks involved in motion picture investing, the more equitable approach may be to limit the investment to the production or productions agreed upon at the time of investment.

2. Control

As described in previous chapters, the filmmaker's authority must be carefully and expressly delineated, and the documents organizing the business must reflect that. For the single project film, the filmmaker must retain management control, at least throughout the initial production and distribution of the project. The Operating Agreement of the film company should be drafted to guarantee that the filmmaker retains control of the film company's management to the greatest extent permitted by law. Even so, this authority cannot be absolute. The filmmaker will eventually die or become unwilling or unable to manage the company's operations.

3. Personal Obligation of the Filmmaker

By its nature, an independent film is a highly personal undertaking. The Operating Agreement should thus reflect the importance of the filmmaker's role and include specific provisions in the event the filmmaker becomes disassociated from the project. For example, the death or incapacity of the filmmaker may terminate the project. Similarly, if the filmmaker becomes professionally unavailable—whether because the filmmaker has become too famous or too frustrated is irrelevant—the project should end in most cases. In many ways this also is a form of protection for the investors. Survival of the project after the death or withdrawal of the filmmaker should require the consent of each investor.

4. Project Milestones

It is not uncommon for independent films to languish for years while money is found to complete them. The Operating Agreement must be very clear regarding the rules about the availability of the investors' money. The investors should be obligated to pay immediately and should receive no interest in the company until that payment is received. If the budget sets the minimum amount of cash available at $150,000, either the investors must agree that the funds can be spent prior to the company raising the entire $150,000 or the investors' purchase payment should be put in escrow until the film company has raised a specified amount.

Most typically, the terms of the Operating Agreement stipulate that the investors' funds will be released when enough is raised to make meaningful progress. For example, if the film can be made for $150,000, then the agreement may provide that the funds will be released when $100,000 is received, because that is enough to get through preproduction and principal photography.

5. Management Fees

The filmmaker, as manager of the film company, may choose to receive some portion of the revenue as payment for services provided. The choice to pay oneself is neither a good nor a bad choice. So long as the payment structure is fully disclosed, rather than hidden in fine print or unstated, the investors can have no legitimate complaints. Such payments are akin to the producer's fees charged to a studio. However, if all participants in the project worked without pay and the investors assumed a very high risk, then it may be appropriate to forgo any producer's payment. Both approaches have been used. The key is for the Operating Agreement to explain specifically the basis for the investors' return on capital and participation in net revenue.

6. Wrap-Up of Ownership

The Operating Agreement should also provide for a mandatory repurchase of the investors' interests at some point in the future. For example, this may be triggered by a lack of production company revenues for a three-year period. Such a clause would provide that if the production company has not made more than a minor amount of income (say, $5,000), then the company can repurchase the interests of the investors by paying a preset fee, or by providing for mandatory arbitration if the parties cannot voluntarily agree on a price.

7. Limitations on the Managers

As the person in charge of a legally recognized business, the filmmaker undertakes business and professional obligations toward the investors as well as the employees and other participants of the project. And if the film-maker enlists other individuals to serve as managers of the LLC or directors of the corporation, those individuals have a similar duty to act in the best interests of the business.

Further, the law does not like to vest unbridled discretion in a single businessperson's hands. State laws will protect the investors in some situations, requiring that the filmmaker provide the investors with information and an opportunity to vote on suggested changes. For example, if the company has insufficient funds to start its movie and another film company has insufficient funds to complete an unrelated picture, the filmmaker might wish to merge the two companies in order to receive producer credit and associate director credit on the second picture. Nonetheless, the merger can take place only if the shareholders or members of the LLC agree. Similarly, the filmmaker could not take the money invested in the first film and put it into the second film, because that would breach the duty of good faith to the investors and the film company.

In the same vein, the Operating Agreement will generally limit the amount of debt the company can acquire without member approval, set the minimum and maximum amount of equity that the film company can raise, and prevent the sale of the company's assets other than through agreements to distribute the motion picture. In this way, the interests of the investors are protected from excesses of the manager or director.

8. Deferred Compensation for Some Participants

Most independent film companies are unable to pay all their expenses. Instead, they rely on locations, cast, crew, and service providers to work on deferred compensation. In exchange, to balance the risk of nonpayment, filmmakers often promise revenue or profit participation to those parties as well. The company must plan carefully regarding deferred payment obligations. They must be incorporated into the budgeting process and clearly identified when defining the revenue returns to which the investors are entitled.

For example, it is common to grant the investors a return of capital before the producer takes any portion of gross revenues. Often, investors are entitled to as much as 125 percent of their initial investment before the producer receives payment. The Operating Agreement must specify whether the cast, crew, and other service providers are entitled to deferred compensation payments prior to the investors' payment. If the motion picture has a total cost of $150,000, an investor may think the film has a reasonable chance to return the majority of the investment and the potential to return far more. If, instead, the picture has a "cost" of $150,000 because those are the expenses that could not be deferred, but an additional $250,000 in deferred compensation, then the investor may not receive the first dollar until after $400,000 in revenue has been earned.

Deferred compensation dramatically changes the risk of an investment and is therefore highly material to the structure. The Operating Agreement should specify whether the deferred compensation is paid first, the investors are paid first, or both are paid proportionately at the same time. In this example, if the deferred compensation was paid on a pro rata basis with the investors, each dollar earned would be shared equally among each person or group in proportion to the amount that each party is entitled to receive.

C. Returns and Distributions

For the investors and the participants who have an interest in the revenues in the project, the returns and distributions play a key part in the business structure. The amount due to each revenue participant will be deducted from the operating income of the company. Any funds left over become potential dividends that can be paid to the investors.

Most financing agreements prioritize the position of the investors considerably. The agreements do this by providing that revenue from the income earned on the project is repaid to the investors to reduce the amount of the investment. In some cases, the investment is recouped at an amount exceeding 100 percent of the funds invested, moving part of the profit ahead of other obligations owed by the production company.

For cast and crew, the deferred compensation and revenue participation are also based on the schedule of distributions. In studio contracts, these definitions can be ten or more pages in length. In a very simplified model, the revenue participation can be based on gross income, net profits, or adjusted gross income—which is something in between gross and net. If the contingent fees are based on *gross income*, then the payments are due before money is paid to investors or other parties. If they are based on *net profits*, then the fees are paid only after all other expenses are paid.

Even gross income may not be every dollar owed to the film company. The distributors and exhibitors will take their share of the revenue before providing the funds to the film company, and there may be charges for credit cards, taxes, and other fees that reduce the amount it would otherwise receive from its distributors. A film company should never contract to pay a percentage based on an amount greater than the production company actually receives.

In addition, there is no standard definition of the relevant terms on which to rely. Instead, the definition of *income*, *expenses*, and *net profits* adopted by the film company will establish whether payments to the investors are expenses to be deducted before the film has earned net profits. The film company should adopt a single standard for these terms that is used in every disclosure document and agreement that covers how profits are distributed. The production company can negotiate for the number of points each participant gets, but it should avoid using different definitions for different parties. The production company is also best off avoiding the terms *gross* and *net* entirely, since they may evoke meanings not intended by the parties. Using terms such as *adjusted gross* or *defined profits* more clearly indicates that the order of payments will be derived from the project's agreements rather than from theoretical accounting procedures.

The order of payments will vary depending on the nature of the project and the needs of the parties; the following provides a general guide. The flow of the revenue is sometimes described as the waterfall of funds that flow from the film exhibitors down to the profit participants and shareholders.

Before any funds are paid to the production company, the *distributor* will collect the revenue owed for exhibition and sale from various markets.

The distributor collects the funds earned from theatrical distribution and other pay windows, including video-on-demand, home video, streaming, downloading, pay television, cable television, and airlines, as well as ancillary income through music and merchandise. This is typically 40 to 60 percent of the box office income for the production.

The distributor's fee will range from 15 to 30 percent of the income, and the distributor's expenses will then be deducted from the revenue owed to the production company. The production company will generally use a sales agent to find and negotiate with the distributor and may also use a producer's representative. The sales agent will also take 15 to 30 percent of the income, and the producer's representative will be a more modest 5 to 15 percent.

So far, the distribution on $200 in box office receipts will look like this:

- Exhibitor $100
- Distributor fees $30 (30%)
- Distributor Expenses $5
- Sales Agent $13 (20% of $65)
- Producer's Rep. $2.6 (5% of $52)

The production company is receiving roughly one quarter of the box office receipts for the project. In this example, the production company earned just under $50 on the $200 taken in at the box office. These numbers will vary, but the percentage generally holds true from project to project.

Next comes the distribution of the funds that have come into the production company's coffers. The payments must be made. The vendors who are owed payments, the debt service on the production loans, and the ongoing salaries for employees must be paid on time. Ideally, those costs were fully covered by the funds raised from the investors, but if that is not the case, then the advances and revenues will go first to cover these expenses rather than to repay investors or cover other deferred salaries.

Thereafter, the payments will likely be made in this order:

1. Debt repayment
2. Investors until recoupment, or as much as 125 percent of recoupment
3. Cast and crew deferred salaries
4. Producer's and filmmaker's deferred participation
5. Profit participants—shared among investors, producer, and key personnel

Depending on the willingness of the cast and crew to drop to the bottom of the waterfall and the difficulty of raising investor funds, the order of repayments among investors, cast, and crew can be adjusted. In addition, the filmmaker and key personnel might need living expenses. In that situation, the filmmaker can be offered a *minimum guarantee*—a small percentage, such as a 10 percent producer's fee, that is paid before the investors but after the debt repayment. Similarly, if the production relies on A-list talent, the producers may have conceded that the star is guaranteed payment based on the distributor's gross payments, pushing the star well above the rest of the waterfall.

The payment profile will look very different if all of the budget was covered by the investment funds raised. In that case, the guaranteed minimum payments from various markets will begin to cover recoupment and deferred salaries. If the recoupment and deferrals will not be covered until revenue in excess of the minimum guarantees is earned, then the likelihood of profitability becomes much smaller.

9

Budgeting and Business Planning

The need for a business plan is much greater today than it had been in earlier eras of independent filmmaking. In the past, almost every independent film followed the same strategy of raising capital from investors, seeking presales of foreign markets, using the film markets and film festivals to sign a sales agent, having the sales agent find a theatrical distributor, and moving from theatrical (if the project was very fortunate) into home video, video-on-demand, pay television, broadcast television, and cable television. A few projects also had music and merchandise as ancillary revenue.

With the advent of streaming and downloading, the shift to global day-and-date releases, the erosion of distribution windows (exacerbated by the coronavirus pandemic of 2020), the weakening of television, and the importance of mobile connections, every audiovisual project has the potential to be produced and distributed in its own, unique manner. As a result, having a business plan establishes the map the production company will follow. It will likely become part of the offering documents to investors, and although it will not create contractual promises, major divergences from the business plan will have to be supported by significant changes in circumstances or approved by investors.

A. Business Planning

A useful business plan provides a blueprint for the operations, direction, and growth of a business. It explains the needs for funding, anticipates the cash flow operations of the business, highlights strategic partnerships, and serves as a proof-of-concept for key stakeholders. The credibility of the business plan will help investors, cast, crew, and vendors assess the thoughtfulness and planfulness that has gone into the production.

The business plan is not a disclosure document. The business plan does not have sufficient information to counsel a potential investor regarding the many risks associated with the investment or offering. That task is left to financing documents. In modern business transactions, however, all the information provided by the business owner must be accurate and truthful.

1. Role for a Business Plan

Perhaps the most valuable aspect of the business planning process is the actual planning and exploration of building the business. Many software products are now available to assist filmmakers in the creation of business plans.

Although it is not a disclosure document, neither should the plan be an investor's sales pitch. It should be accurate and reasonably objective. Any material mistakes in the facts must be corrected, including statements that might have been true at the plan's drafting stage but are no longer true because circumstances have changed. One common mistake in business plans is to highlight the success of one or two similar projects without acknowledging the risks associated in the field as a whole. Most independent films do not recoup their investments. A realistic business plan should not highlight only the few that became blockbusters because that does not provide an accurate picture of the financial risks involved for investors. The company is better not making comparisons than making them in a misleading manner.

The drafting of the business plan will help the production company make decisions about the relationship of the financing goals to the distribution channels and purpose of the project. When done well, the business plan will also help convince investors that the filmmaker and the production company are thoughtful in undertaking what is known to be a very speculative enterprise.

2. Elements of a Business Plan

Business plans for film companies are much simpler than for many other industries. The business plan must explain whether the production company seeks to produce a single film, multiple films, a series, or some mix of different audiovisual works. For most film companies, the key behind the business plan of a single-title business is the compelling nature of the story and the film it will support. For the business plan of a multiple-title business, the key feature will be the leadership of the company and the importance of supporting the filmmaker involved with the company.

The elements of the business plan will likely follow the same basic sections as are typical of most business plans. But the focus on the stories being told and the filmmaker's vision must remain front and center of each section. Here is a list of the typical sections of a business plan, with some small adjustments for the typical film production company:

1. *Executive Summary*—1.1. Objectives; 1.2. Mission; 1.3. Keys to Success
2. *Business Activities*—2.1. Primary Productions in Development; 2.2. Additional Products and Ancillary Activities
3. *Production Strategy & Implementation*—3.1. Cast, Writer, Director and Key Artistic Personnel; 3.2. Locations; 3.3. Other Production Elements
4. *Marketing and Distribution Strategy*—4.1. Target Audience; 4.2. Distribution Channels; 4.3. Distribution Support; 4.4 Ancillary Opportunities
5. *Company Summary*—5.1. Company Ownership; 5.2. Financing Structure
6. *Management*—6.1. Organizational Structure; 6.2 Management Team; 6.3 Key Agreements; 6.4 Personnel Plan; 6.5 Decision-Making Process of Management
7. *Key Risks and Risk Mitigation Strategy*—7.1 Key Risks; 7.2 Strategies to Control Risks Associated with Locations, Cast, and Key Employees; 7.3 Strategies to Control Risks Associated with Financing; 7.4 Additional Risk Management Strategies
8. *Financial Plan*—8.1 Balance Sheet; 8.2 Equity Stakes; 8.3 Projected Income & Expense Report—Cash Flow and Profit and Loss.

Unless the most important questions are answered on the first page of the business plan, few readers will turn to page two. Like good journalistic writing, the business plan cannot bury the lead—it must establish the strength of the business in its introductory section. The executive summary must make the case that the film under production must be made by this team as soon as possible. All of the remaining sections of the business plan need to support that compelling statement.

3. Integration with the Private Placement Memorandum and Crowd Financing Campaign

The business plan for a film production company can be a short document ranging from three to ten pages. For investors it can be provided as part of a larger package that includes the Private Placement Memorandum, described in chapter 10 (pp. 186–187), which includes all the key disclosures about the securities offering and details the investment repayment structure. For public investors, the business plan can be used as part of a crowd financing strategy to help the public investor understand what the production company is, what it is making, and why the project should be funded.

The business plan is not a stand-alone document. It should not be provided to a potential investor separately from the entire Private Placement Memorandum or other offering document. For key personnel, however, it provides a blueprint for the vision and structure of the business. Along with the budget, the business plan should enable the both the artistic and business teams involved in the project to start with a common vision and objectives.

B. Introduction to Budgeting

Though sometimes it is the most creative part of a film, a carefully crafted budget provides the pivotal road map for the entire film project. It is the most carefully read component of the production company's business plan. Whether the film is expected to cost $2,000 or $200 million, its budget must account for every dollar to be expended on the production. In addition, the budget is a comparative tool, assuring that all pieces of the film are proportionate or at least carefully planned. If each cast member receives tens of millions of dollars, then the film should not have homemade special effects.

The budget will be shaped by the filmmaker's specific choices: locations, size, and prominence of cast, stunts, and the effects needed both during and after principal photography. For independent and guerrilla filmmakers, the key is to identify the cornerstone elements of the film and build the budget around those items. If a particular location must be used to tell the story, a particular cast member becomes essential to the financing, or a certain special effect defines the film, then that element should be identified early and its costs determined. Thereafter, the remainder of the budget can be structured to keep the production in harmony with that item.

The budgeting process continues from the inception of the project through the completion of the finished negative. Neither the cost of prints used to show the film theatrically nor the advertising and promotional budget are included in the budget numbers used for production. For studio films, print and advertising costs often equal the production costs, and for an inexpensive film, they may greatly exceed those costs.

There are excellent software programs to assist filmmakers with the detailed budgeting and accounting process, including Entertainment Partners' Movie Magic Budgeting and Jungle Software's Gorilla Budgeting. These programs can handle a great deal of detail and generate extremely helpful reports. The approach to the budget, however, must come from the filmmaker rather than the software.

C. Purpose of the Budget

The budgeting process is important for a number of reasons, both internal and external. The screenplay may be the most important filmmaking tool, but only the budget can set the financial framework for all the decisions regarding the film. It provides a material foundation on which every party involved in the project relies.

An accurate and complete budget must be provided to the investors, lenders, completion bond company, and unions. Once the filmmaker obtains a commitment, few significant alterations can be made without their approval. A filmmaker may not unilaterally decide to film for an extra two weeks to capture the light, no matter how artistically compelling it may be. Nor can the filmmaker drop a name star to pay for those two weeks, unless permission is granted by the lender and the completion bond company. Even investors might get upset by such changes, so the documents must be very explicit regarding which budget decisions are subject to change and which are not.

1. Independent Review of the Budget

Many of the recipients of the budget will undertake an independent review of its assumptions. For instance, if a low-budget production seeks to use

WGA or SAG-AFTRA reduced-scale agreements (see section E.3, p. 174), the proposed budget is part of the document package provided to the unions. They assess the anticipated cost of equipment, locations, cast size, and number of days and may reject the budget if they do not believe it accurately reflects the cost of the shoot. In addition, the unions will require the actual expenses to be submitted at the end of principal photography to ensure that the filmmaker has stayed within the financial limits of the low-budget agreements.

The completion bond company will also review the budget carefully, in combination with the script, to determine the feasibility of delivering the film within the projected budget. The company will only be willing to provide a completion bond if it believes the budget is reasonably conservative in its estimates of cost and schedule. Since the completion bond is a requirement for many entertainment lenders, this budget review can make or break a production.

2. The Budget as the First Disclosure Document

As will be discussed more fully in chapter 10 (p. 179), the film company is required to provide the investors with a series of disclosure documents that are accurate, complete, and sufficient to give the investor a full understanding of the risks involved in the production. No document is more important for this purpose than the budget. It details the costs to complete the film and acquire a distributor. If the film company seeks to raise substantially more money than this, the additional money raised will likely go into the pockets of the filmmakers. If the film company does not raise enough money to meet the budget, then the filmmakers must explain what combination of loans and personal funds they are committing to the film. Otherwise, the project is doomed from the start.

Investors have no information other than the budget to understand the relationship between their potential investment and the costs of producing the proposed film. Despite the ease with which the filmmaker can adjust the presumptive costs in the budget software, the filmmaker must understand that the budget represents a commitment to those parties who have relied upon the document.

3. Working and Reworking the Budget

Because a budget is an important source of information for investors, the time to adjust and experiment with the budget is before they have committed to the film. Until the budget has been presented to investors, lenders, or the completion bond company, it represents nothing more than numbers on a page.

Budgets often are changed during the planning stages of the project. For an independent filmmaker, there may be a variety of budget scenarios based on best-case financing and worst-case financing. Certain scenes may be noted for possible revision based on the financial outcome. Like a modern theatrical writer, the filmmaker writing a low-budget film must treat the financial limitations as a structural framework around which the story is crafted. If no flashback to the Eiffel Tower is possible, a close-up of a toy replica in a store window might do the trick.

If an independent film will be made on a minimal budget, then certain expenses must be eliminated. Because the budget cannot accommodate travel expenses or other costs, the movie may be filmed locally or in areas that can easily double for other locations so that multiple scenes can be shot without moving. A high-speed car chase may need to be revised to take place on foot or on bicycles. The science fiction genre has become so effects laden that low-budget science fiction films have nearly disappeared.

4. Budget Coverage

When studios or production companies review scripts for possible purchase, the script is put through a *coverage review*. The result is a two-to-five-page report in which the potential purchaser quickly summarizes the project; assesses the strengths and weaknesses of the concept, story, and writing; and provides an estimated cost of production.

The estimate reflects what this particular production company believes it should spend to bring this script to the screen. Embedded in this analysis are the production company's choices regarding the quality and budget for lead cast members, scale of special effects and visual effects, and approach to international locations. A studio or major production company with a roster of A-list talent and films will incorporate those types of costs into the analysis and coverage. A small art house will assume a different pool of actors from which to choose and different strategies for managing costs. Each will provide budget coverage for the script that is accurate for that company's production, but that coverage will not necessarily be relevant to any other producer.

The majority of the coverage process is focused on the script rather than the budget. The coverage report will separately rate the script and the writer, along with the key elements of the content: concept, plot, story structure, characters, dialogue, and visual impact. This grading, along with the company's own synopsis, will become the document used to assess the film.

D. When Not to Disclose the Budget

Although many parties to the film financing will rely on the budget, the filmmaker may not find it helpful to disclose budget figures when selling the distribution rights in a film market or film festival setting. The film company is seeking the largest possible advance for the rights to the film, because a large advance provides cash to the film company and motivates the distributor to work diligently to recoup its investment in the film. The distributor, in contrast, rarely wants to provide an advance greater than the budget of the film. Since the filmmaker would violate the duty to negotiate in good faith if the budget were to be misrepresented, the best strategy is to keep information regarding the budget secret and refuse to respond to inquiries regarding the budget during the negotiation process.

Nonetheless, unfinanced films, such as Kevin Smith's *Clerks* or Robert Rodriguez's *El Mariachi*, do create a certain rough ambience about them. Modest success can often result in large-percentage returns, which bolster the credibility and bankability of the filmmakers. In contrast, high-budget films must be blockbusters to justify the expense, resulting in ever more lavish productions and increasing expectations. As a result, although independent filmmakers often want to create the impression that their film cost more than it did when selling it, they frequently *understate* the cost once the film is being exhibited, to suggest that they are more creative and resourceful than the actual budget would suggest. For example, it was rumored that even though the reported budget of *The Blair Witch Project* was only $30,000, Artisan Entertainment spent close to $1 million to finish the film.

E. Anatomy of a Budget

A budget consists of the summary page, known as the *top sheet*, and a series of department-by-department itemizations for that budget. Even if a film's expenses top $200 million, every roll of tape must be budgeted, receipted, and credited to its particular account. The numbers may get large, but the need for attention to detail never diminishes. Each day throughout the course of the production, the actual expenses are reconciled with the budget to calculate the production's accuracy in planning and to make the necessary adjustments to keep the project on time and on budget.

Every budget contains several different types of expenses. *Above-the-line expenses* are the major costs that set the scale of the production; they include the salaries of the director and leading cast members, the cost of the script, and the producer's fee. In the studio world, they are often negotiated in coordination, so that A-list talent salaries are proportionate, and the director has a deal somewhat similar to those of the other above-the-line participants. *Below-the-line expenses* are typically the production expenses, which include the remaining cast, locations, sets, costumes, permits, and equipment rentals. These costs tend to vary less than above-the-line expenses; the cost of a location permit, for example, does not change based on the fame of the cast. The budget must also reflect postproduction expenses, including the editing, sound, addition of special effects, and titles.

In addition to the production and postproduction expenses, other significant budget items include the various forms of insurance, legal fees, accounting expenses, and a small budget for capturing film and video content to be used in the publicity of the film and as extras on the DVD or website.

Traditionally, the scale of a film was set by above-the-line costs, which represented the most significant portion of the budget. In today's moviemaking environment, however, this may not be the case. The visual effects added in postproduction can equal or exceed the cost of production and may represent expenses as great as the salaries of top-name A-list talent.

1. Deferred Compensation

Deferred compensation represents income earned but not paid to cast, crew, or other parties. In reality, deferred compensation represents a form of an unsecured loan made to the film company by its employees. If the film company does not obtain sufficient funding or earn sufficient income, then the employee will forgo this portion of any income.

Deferred compensation is an expense, and like all expenses it should be included in the budget, itemized in the appropriate category. If a film has cash needs of $200,000 and deferred compensation of $300,000, any contracts or other provisions reflecting return to investors would be based on a $500,000 budget amount rather than the $200,000 cash needs, so the budget should make this clear.

However, the budget should also identify deferred compensation as such. The average investor will be much more likely to respect additional royalties paid to the deferred income participants if the investor can see that it reflects the risk that they will not receive their $300,000 in earned income.

2. Special Considerations: Music

Music has always been an important part of filmmaking. The film score can influence the emotional impact of a scene, shaping audience reactions at a subconscious level. Featured songs can carry the audience's emotional associations with those songs into the film's world of suspended disbelief. For instance, when *WALL·E* incorporated a video clip from *Hello, Dolly!*, it helped bridge the audience age gap and was instant shorthand for the values learned by the main character, a self-aware robot, during its 700 years of isolation.

The details of music licensing for the film score, featured songs performed for the movie, and *needle drops*—prerecorded songs played during the film—are described in chapter 16. But with regard to the budgeting, because music has become not only a vital aspect of independent filmmaking but also an expensive one, the filmmaker should pay particular attention to its role. The budget should separate out the payments to the composer of the film score from the budget for featured songs and needle drops.

Budgeting for needle drops requires the filmmaker to identify the rights holder, which is typically the record label. The record label will want information on the planned use of the recording: "opening credits," "end credits," "background," or "featured in the scene." The label will also want to know the budget for the film and the planned distribution.

The record companies understand that motion picture promotion can lead to great sales for songs and records. But their goal is to maximize revenue, so songs that are already more popular among filmmakers demand a high premium. In addition, it costs money for the companies to review the music license rights for each song, so they tend not to be particularly helpful unless the filmmaker already has a distribution agreement in place.

For filmmakers who do not have distribution agreements, the record companies' compromise is to offer a *festival license*. For a modest fee, the record company gives the film company permission to use its song in one or more film festivals. This gives the film company the authorization it needs to proceed, implying permission to copy the song onto the audio tracks of the film, edit the song to the appropriate length, and otherwise exploit the song enough to prepare the film for its festival release and screen a rough cut to potential distributors.

The significant downside to the festival license is that it does not state the cost the filmmaker will have to pay to use the song in theatrical distribution or in any of the other media for which a license will ultimately be needed. The festival license leaves the filmmaker at the mercy of the record label, perhaps even creating a risk that the film rights will be sold for a price below the cost of the music rights. Unfortunately, few record labels are motivated to provide complete fee schedules to low-budget filmmakers.

Filmmakers must anticipate the financial challenges of music acquisition. If they hope to use popular recorded music, they must set aside a budget for this purpose. Wherever possible, they should avoid relying on popular recorded music unless they can establish the price for the music's use. If the music is featured in a scene, then the film is put at great financial risk unless the filmmaker can rely on a fixed price to acquire the music. Filmmakers should use other music sources to the greatest extent possible to avoid the licensing trap created by the festival license.

3. Special Considerations: Low-Budget Union Agreements

To encourage low-budget filmmaking and promote the employment of union members, the various industry trade unions have authorized a series of low-budget agreements to reduce costs for production. A number of low-budget agreements exist for various trade unions, including SAG, WGA, and IATSE (International Alliance of Theatrical Stage Employees). These rates increase periodically, so the information included here provides only a general guide. The production company will need to contact the union to determine eligibility and the appropriate contracts. The production payroll company Topsheet provides an excellent set of resources to help clarify the myriad different hiring categories.

The rates are determined based on the budget of the project, the length of the project, and the nature of the production. Under the SAG-AFTRA agreements, for example, all the work must be completed in the United States, and various budget caps set the eligibility to participate:

Short Film Agreement (40 minutes or less)—Total budget of less than $50,000
- Salaries are negotiable and can be deferred
- No consecutive employment required (except on overnight location)

- Allows the use of both professional and non-professional performers
- Background performers not covered

Ultra–Low Budget Agreement—Total budget of less than $250,000 (Including deferrals under $500K)
- Day rate of $125
- No step-up fees
- No consecutive employment required (except on overnight location)
- Allows the use of both professional and non-professional performers
- Background performers not covered

Modified Low Budget Agreement—Total budget between $250k and $700k
- Day rate of $335
- Weekly rate of $1166
- No consecutive employment required (except on overnight location)
- Reduced overtime rate

Low Budget Agreement—Total budget of less than $2,500,000
- Day rate of $630
- Weekly rate of $2,190
- No consecutive employment required (except on overnight location)
- Reduced overtime rate
- Reduced number of Background Performers covered

The WGA low-budget provisions are similar, reducing the minimum payments and allowing for some deferred compensation. The WGA agreements tend to be renegotiated on a three-year cycle with the current schedule from 2017. That contract has expired, but the parties are continuing to use it until a new agreement is reached. Under the 2017 agreements, the production company must still provide payment to the writers for residuals and contribute to the union's health, welfare, and pension funds.

The basic agreement provides that low-budget films, those below $5 million, have a minimum for 2019–20 at $76,341 and films above the $5 million have script fees starting at $143,319.

Low-budget minimums for films budgeted between $500,000 and $1,200,000 are $51,290 for original screenplays and $41,740 for nonoriginal screenplays. An additional $5,000 script publication fee is payable to the writer who receives credit on the film, after writing credit is determined under the WGA rules.

For lower-budgeted productions, the minimums are calculated as a percentage of the low-budget amount due, for work-for-hire agreements that include the first and second draft of the screenplay, as follows:

- *Below $200,000*: $12,823 (25 percent of minimum) and no $5,000 script publication fee—or $51,290 and $5,000 script publication fee, but all fees may be deferred
- *Between $200,000 and $500,000*: $25,645 (50 percent of minimum) and no $5,000 script publication fee—or $51,290 and $5,000 script publication fee, but all fees may be deferred

The low-budget agreements, which provide considerable budget relief for low-budget producers, increase the need for accuracy in the budgeting process. Moreover, because the actual production expenses must be reported to the unions, the agreements put additional pressure on the filmmakers to stay under the budget caps set out in the various union agreements. Often, the low-budget agreements provide guidelines (and in reality ceilings) for the negotiations between low-budget productions and screenwriters who typically are not members of the union.

F. Managing Risk: Contingency, Insurance, and Completion Bond Requirements

In addition to the costs associated with the mechanical processes of filmmaking, the budget must account for other expenses that are part of the risk management of the production. In the budget, the filmmaker should set aside an amount of money, typically 10 percent of the total budget, to cover whatever contingencies may arise, and should allot additional funds to insurance coverage and often a completion bond.

1. Insurance Coverage

Except for the tiniest productions, each film company must carry a variety of insurance, including workers' compensation insurance; cast insurance; liability insurance on the negative and videotape, sets, equipment, and property; and errors and omissions insurance to cover problems with the script such as defamation or copyright infringement.

Liability insurance can cover many aspects of the production. The insurance is typically *short-term*, as the coverage is only necessary during principal photography. These policies may include:

- General liability
- Rented equipment
- Props, sets, and wardrobe
- Negative and faulty stock
- Third-party property damage
- Extra expense
- Automobile liability and physical damage
- Umbrella
- Certificates of insurance (including special certificates)

A film company may need only some of these policies. Every project should have general liability insurance, automobile liability insurance, and workers' compensation coverage. Other policies will depend on the nature of the shoot and the risks the film company is willing to undertake. Any specialty items, such as boats, planes, and antiques, require separate coverage.

2. Completion Bond

Many film projects must be protected with a completion bond, by which the bond company agrees to pay unforeseen costs in excess of the project's 10 percent contingency. This insurance is expensive in both financial and practical terms. The completion bond company retains veto control over cast and crew and can take over the production if either the shoot begins to fall behind schedule or reshoots are necessary. Its concern is focused on the budget, so an aesthetically bad but efficient production has little to worry about.

To obtain a completion bond, the production company must have full financing; complete, unambiguous ownership of the story and script rights; full insurance coverage for the production; agreements for use of the primary locations; and a feasibility study or coverage report showing that the script and budget balance. The steps necessary to obtain a completion bond make it significantly less likely that it will be needed, so for many filmmakers the process simply serves as an exercise in good planning. A completion bond is essential, however, if the film company requires a loan for cash flow based upon a distribution agreement.

G. Contingent Fees

Royalties, residuals, and profits are not considered deferred expenses of the production; instead, they come out of the income earned by the film. *Royalties* refer to the ongoing payments for the use of the copyrighted film script or other intellectual property rights. *Residuals* are percentage payments provided in exchange for services, and can be earned by anyone in the production, depending on the contractual arrangements. *Profits* refer to the earnings of the company after its expenses are paid, which may be distributed under employment contracts like residuals or as dividends to the investors and company owners. Contingent fees do not need to be incorporated into the production budget. They effectively reduce the cost of completing the picture, but they must be spent carefully and wisely.

The order in which the various contingent payments are made to the parties must be clearly established in the employment contracts and disclosed to the investors. Absent an agreement to the contrary, royalties and residuals are operating expenses that would be paid before profits are distributed. This means that as owners of the film company, investors are generally the last parties to receive a share of income. To protect investors, it is not uncommon to treat the return of the investment as a separate category of obligation and to reimburse some or all of the production investment at the same time other contingent obligations are paid.

10

The Investors' Package

Film investors purchase an ownership interest in the film company. Whether the interest is sold as shares of company stock or limited liability company membership interests, the transaction involves the sale of securities. This stands in stark contrast to selling (or preselling) the distribution rights in the movie. When the film company sells the distribution rights, it is selling the product the company makes, and the purchaser does not acquire any interest in the company.

If the filmmaker is going to finance a project independently by receiving investments from relatives and qualified individuals, the filmmaker has to determine what *must* be disclosed and what *should* be shared with the potential investors. The hardest decision is how to convey the story. Few professionals, and even fewer nonprofessionals, can read a treatment or screenplay and interpret what it will look like as a completed motion picture. As with the sale of distribution rights, the filmmaker may often elicit a greater visceral reaction by creating small poster mock-ups, or one-sheets, than by sharing the written treatment or completed script.

Regardless of how the story will be sold to the investors, there remains a great deal of information the investors should know.

A. Prerequisites to Soliciting Investments

Because investors acquire rights in the company in which they invest, the transaction is a complicated, sophisticated business arrangement involving securities laws, federal disclosure requirements, and complex tax and reporting obligations. The various documents provide information to the investors regarding the transaction and set out the terms of their ownership. Although quite common, selling interests in a film company requires careful planning, diligent execution, and ongoing maintenance. The basic rules discussed subsequently apply to all formal business structures: corporations, limited partnerships, and limited liability companies.

1. Basic Requirements and the Meaning of "Disclosure": Making a Federal Case Out of Film Financing

Under both state and federal law, a business seeking to raise capital has as its first obligation a duty to provide full disclosure. In other words, the filmmaker must reveal all the material facts regarding the investment and its risks. This simple rule is often overlooked at the filmmaker's peril. Failure to fully disclose all material terms can result in the investor being entitled to a complete return of the investment directly from either the film company or the filmmaker, depending on which of the parties has assets. The filmmaker may also be held criminally liable for knowingly misrepresenting the risks involved in the investment. All other planning done by the accountants and lawyers will be worth nothing if the filmmaker hides information or misrepresents the facts regarding the production.

Not only must all information provided to investors be accurate when made, but it must be updated as well. Therefore, investors need to be kept informed throughout the life of the project.

One challenge for properly meeting disclosure requirements is identifying what facts and issues are material. At its heart, *material* means information that is important to the investor, information a reasonable person would consider important in deciding whether to invest.[1] Put another way, information is material if there is a substantial likelihood that it would be considered to have significantly altered the "total mix" of information available to the potential investor. Thus, material issues include not only all terms of any investment deal but also information regarding the film, the production, the competition, and anything else the filmmaker thought was important to say when promoting the project to the investor. Furthermore, the filmmaker must avoid puffing in the resume, overstating the potential chances of profitability, or otherwise painting an unrealistic picture.

2. Overview of Federal Securities Restrictions

Because the sale of interest in the film company is governed by state and federal securities law, there are a number of important limitations on the way a filmmaker can raise investment funds. These limitations do not typically apply to presale arrangements and other distribution-based financing—which is yet another reason such financing is preferable to soliciting investor funds. Still, if Aunt Betty's investment is the only way the film can get made, this section will identify when it is fair to ask Aunt Betty for funds and when it violates the law even to ask.

Offers to sell and sales of securities are governed by the Securities Act of 1933 and the Securities and Exchange Act of 1934. Unless exempt from the federal rules (see subsection 3), an offer to sell securities must be accompanied by a detailed disclosure document called a *prospectus*. In addition, every state but Nevada has its own laws governing securities offerings and sales, generally known as *blue sky laws*. The state laws set forth specific rules for the offers to sell securities and often allow the state to judge the fairness of the offering to residents of the state. Again, certain offers may be exempt from these rules (see subsection 4).

Because of the costs and difficulties involved with preparing these offering documents, virtually all film financing projects are structured to fall within one of the exemptions to the federal and state laws. Even if they are exempt from the documentation requirements, however, state and federal laws still protect the investor from fraudulent statements or failures to disclose material information.

Since the laws cover the *offers to sell* as well as the sales themselves, the filmmaker must be careful to avoid casual conversations about the availability of interests in the film. In other words, posting on social media, sending emails, creating websites, or taking similar other steps to publicly offer to sell interests in the film company should never be part of the film financing strategy.

3. Exemptions for Certain Types of Securities Transactions

Although federal law covers all securities, it categorically exempts a variety of transactions from documentation registration. If the offering falls into one of the exemptions, the documentation does not need to be reviewed by the SEC prior to the sale of the security. This does *not* mean that the film company should not provide documentation regarding the sale of the shares, membership interests, or limited partnership interests; it merely means that the form and content of the documents will not be specified by federal regulations.

Under federal law, the company does not need to register securities if they are offered by the company in a transaction not involving any public offering.[2] At a minimum, nonpublic transactions are those conducted directly by the issuer (the company) without any finder's fees or other fees paid for identifying investors and without any public advertising, broadly defined. Although this definition appears to cover a wide range of offerings, the interpretation of various state and federal securities laws and regulations limit it significantly.

Nonpublic offering exemptions often apply to securities sold to the company's senior officers, directors, or managers—individuals in a position to have sufficient knowledge of the company's situation because of their professional association. Similarly, the exemption may be available to close family members. A sale to Aunt Betty would most likely not be governed by the federal securities registration requirements if she were truly a blood relative. If, instead, she was a family friend called "aunt" out of respect, however, the answer under the securities laws would change. The nonpublic exception is rather narrow and difficult to rely on.

In addition to nonpublic offerings, the federal laws generally do not govern transactions that occur completely within one state.[3] To meet this test, the business entity must be formed in the selected state, every offer and sale must occur exclusively in that same state, a significant portion of the business activity must occur in that state, and the interest must come to rest in that state. For example, if all offers to finance the film took place in California, the sales were in California to residents of California who did not move during the next nine months, the film company was formed in California, and much of the production occurred in California, then only California law would apply regarding the sale of securities and no federal registration would be required. Federal antifraud provisions, however, would continue to apply even for an entirely intrastate exemption as long as an instrument of interstate commerce was used—such as telephone, email, or US postal communications involving the offer or sale of the securities.

In addition, and perhaps most significant, federal law exempts from documentation and registration the transactions limited to *accredited investors*, those with the financial resources and personal savvy to take care of themselves under Regulation D (or Reg D). Accredited investors include the following:

- Individuals with income of at least $200,000 annually in each of the two most recent years, or joint income with a spouse exceeding $300,000 for those years, and a reasonable expectation of the same income level in the current year
- An individual who has individual net worth, or joint net worth with a spouse, that exceeds $1 million at the time of the purchase
- A director, executive officer, or general partner of the company selling the securities
- A charitable organization, corporation, or partnership with assets exceeding $5 million[4]

This is not a complete list. Some banks, specialized nonprofit organizations, and other entities are also accredited investors. Federal law presumes that these people and organizations are sufficiently sophisticated, that they will ask the right questions and protect themselves from poorly understood business transactions. The law also assumes that only those with substantial income can afford to take the significant risk involved with these types of small offerings. If someone falls within this category, federal law does not require that the information regarding the financing be in any particular form, as long as the information is fully disclosed to the investors' satisfaction.

In addition to these examples, the SEC has promulgated rules for a variety of transactions involving nonpublic offerings and sales of securities. Each rule has its own disclosure requirements regarding the amount of information the issuer must provide to the purchasers, which vary depending on the size of the offering and the description of the individuals receiving the offers. Companies selling securities have substantially less risk of violating the law if they follow these SEC rules than if they rely on the general exemption for nonpublic offerings.

For example, the federal exemption known as Rule 506(b) provides a series of clear guidelines regarding persons to whom private interests can be sold without having to register with the SEC and without any limitations on the dollar amounts raised. Rule 506(b) allows for an unlimited number of accredited investors and up to 35 *sophisticated investors*. It has the further benefit of preempting most state blue sky laws, although certain state filings are still required for those states in which the securities are sold.

A sophisticated investor is a nonaccredited investor who is nonetheless considered capable of evaluating the risks and merits of the investment under the SEC rules. As Rule 506 puts it, "each purchaser who is not an accredited investor either alone or with the purchaser representative(s) has such knowledge and experience in financial and business matters that he is capable of evaluating the merits and risks of the prospective investment, or the issuer reasonably believes immediately prior to making any sale that such purchaser comes within this description."[5] (The purchaser's representative must be a sophisticated investor capable of evaluating the risks and merits of the investment.)

For these sophisticated investors, however, the SEC rule requires that the film company make a more detailed disclosure of information, making the inclusion of one or two sophisticated investors potentially more difficult than their investment is worth. Given the high-risk nature of film investment, private solicitations are better left with those in the accredited investor category, to the extent the filmmaker has that choice. Rule 506(c) reinforces this distinction and permits general solicitation, provided the company restricts offerings to accredited investors and takes reasonable steps to verify the accredited investor status of those being offered the securities.

Revisions under the JOBS Act have also increased the potential to invest funds. Rule 504 now permits issuers to raise the value of securities sold to $5 million in any 12-month period. Rule 504 requires compliance with the state blue sky laws.

As an alternative, although generally a dangerous choice because of the lack of any limits on liability, general partnerships have one primary benefit. Because of their access to information and control of the organization, all general partners are usually treated as exempt for purposes of mandatory disclosure documents.

4. Additional Filing Required Under State Securities Law

The rules governing securities sales grow even more complex when dealing with state laws. For offerings not involving publicly traded companies, state law often plays the more important role in governing the nature of the transaction. Because state laws vary so greatly, there are few generally applicable rules.

The first step is to consult a qualified securities attorney in the state where the offering will take place. Generally, if the offering is nonpublic, with no advertising and no commissions or finder's fees paid, then the sale to sophisticated investors will require a minimum amount of mandatory documentation under state law. Similarly, if the interests are provided only to those people who have a direct working relationship with the project, there may be few mandatory requirements for documentation. As discussed subsequently, however, the company always has the obligation to provide the investors with all material information. Many of the states' laws simply assist the filmmaker in meeting this obligation and should serve as a guide rather than a burden.

B. Requirements for Creating Nonpublic Offerings

The key to properly structuring disclosure documentation is that all the information must be accurate, complete, and sufficient to give the investor a full understanding of the risks involved in the production. For the sake of both the investors and the filmmaker, the money should only come from people who can afford to invest the funds. The documents should properly alert potential investors to the significant risk involved with independent film financing.

The form and substance of the investment documents will depend on the legal structure of the film company, amount of money sought, state laws, and federal exemptions used to reduce or eliminate federal registration of the securities. As a result, no single document can be used for all film financing transactions.

1. LLC or Financing Agreement

For motion picture financing, the LLC is an excellent vehicle, because the Operating Agreement, which dictates the rights and interests of the managers of the company, can also serve as the disclosure document in many transactions. In corporations, a disclosure document known as a *subscription agreement* or *financing agreement* must provide the same detail. Whatever the form, the guiding principle of the process is the need to provide full disclosure of all the material facts regarding the project.

Among the material details, the agreement must state the total amount of money to be raised and the ownership interest in the film company received in exchange for each payment. It must also state the ownership interest retained by the filmmaker and what was given in exchange for that interest (services, the screenplay, etc.). It must clearly state how these numbers can be modified by the film company if necessary.

The agreement will also provide information on the transferability of the interests, the payments to the managers (typically the filmmaker), the other income or deferred compensation paid to the managers and to other participants, and any other financial arrangements already made. If any pre-sale arrangements have been entered into, any loans have been obtained (even through credit cards), or any other material contracts have been signed, they should also be disclosed.

2. Private Placement Memoranda

Depending on the amount of money involved and the nature of the participants, the filmmaker may elect to use a Private Placement Memorandum to describe the investment opportunity. This memo should be used exclusively for sophisticated or accredited investors who have the financial resources to risk a total loss of their investment in the film.

The Private Placement Memorandum should include information regarding the business entity, the risks involved in the production, the film, the filmmaker, the production team, and the offering—including the financial opportunity and structure, the use of the investment proceeds, the allocations and distribution of revenue, and fees and expenses. It should also provide information regarding the independent film market in general and those films most comparable to the filmmaker's particular project. Finally, the document should outline tax issues, procedures for the termination or dissolution of the company, conflicts of interest for the filmmakers or other principals, and the effect of taking on additional financing. Such a document is quite detailed and must be completed by an experienced attorney with the help of the filmmaker.

The Private Placement Memorandum contains only disclosure information; the investor receiving it has no obligation to invest. Instead, in a traditional corporate stock transaction, the actual sales document is typically a subscription agreement, which provides contractual language for the obligations described in the Private Placement Memorandum similar in detail to that of an Operating Agreement. Such terms may include limitations on the transferability of the stock, identification of the obligations of the investors, the rights and returns expected, and any other contractual protections offered by the film company or waived by the investors.

Private Placement Memoranda and subscription agreements provide much greater detail regarding the business and the transaction than may be necessary for a small-budget independent film. Ultimately, the form of disclosure will depend on the amount of information necessary to explain the transaction adequately, the expectations of the investors, and the sophistication with which the investors spend their money.

The disclosure documents are *anti-sales* documents. By outlining all the details and highlighting all the risks, these documents should discourage investment unless the person investing has the financial ability to take a complete financial loss on the project and yet is still willing to back the film. The investors' motivation must come not from the potential financial return—which is extremely speculative—but from the commitment to telling the filmmaker's story or otherwise support the filmmaker's career.

3. Contingent Planning

Disclosures must be accurate, complete, and sufficient, but they need not be unduly limiting. If the film company has developed contingency plans, then it should explain them in the Private Placement Memorandum or other disclosure documents. For example, all commitments by cast members are subject to the possibility that the cast member will become unavailable for health reasons or take higher-paying work. Union actors cannot be bound to perform without being paid, and filmmakers cannot pay the actors until the funds have been raised, so the actors' commitment is always subject to change.

Other contingencies may involve the budget and the ability to raise funds. These may include issues involving the casting, locations, special effects costs, equipment selected (particularly if additional funds are being allocated to shoot on 35mm stock rather than using digital equipment), and other material expenses. The filmmaker can share that certain funding levels will allow the production to add beneficial, but not essential, costs. By disclosing these options, the filmmakers can seek funds for the $2.25 million project but elect to go forward with as little as $1.5 million. This may be preferable to amending the offering documents and asking each investor to sign an amended agreement when the decision to change course occurs.

4. Other Documents

The investors' package must also include a finalized budget that accurately reflects the anticipated production expenses. A statement should be included to indicate that the budget reflects the good-faith plans of the filmmaker but that it is subject to change throughout the project.

Similarly, a production schedule should be provided to give the investors an idea of the time involved in preproduction, principal photography, and postproduction. The planned distribution strategy should also be out-lined. Again, these documents must clearly explain that they are good-faith planning devices, and that the filmmaker expects them to change as circum-stances dictate.

C. Optional Information

In addition to the foregoing requirements, the film package can be aug-mented with information generally designed to encourage the investors. There is no standard or set package. If a movie is to be based on a play, then reviews of the play might be helpful. If the movie will be a documen-tary, then newspaper stories about the topic might provide the potential investors with insight into the project. The more the package is creatively tailored to the filmmaker's vision, the more likely it will elicit positive responses.

The information must meet the same test as the disclosure and contrac-tual information: all information must be accurate, complete, and sufficient to give the investor a full understanding of the risks involved in the pro-duction. A document cannot describe the play on which the film will be based as "stunning" when taken out of context from a quote that found the play to be "a stunning example of what is killing Broadway." While the statement is accurate, it is not complete, and it materially misrepresents the true statements in the review. When added to the investor package, this puffery may invalidate the entire offering.

1. Director and Cast Information

Cast information and photographs are often a movie's strongest selling point, and investors react to them like any other audience. Even if the cast is relatively unknown, strong backgrounds may instill confidence. The same holds true for the director and other key production personnel; if a per-son has professional expertise that enhances the film, then that information should be included in the package. Nonetheless, remind the cast and crew that embellishing their resumes can be costly and that all information they provide must be accurate. In addition, casting often evolves, so the disclo-sures must provide details that the final casting choices will be subject to change. The filmmaker should keep the investors informed of these changes on a regular basis as well.

2. Distribution Information

Any distribution guarantees must be disclosed, particularly if they affect the possible returns the film company will see. If no distribution agreements are in place, then the film company may be wise simply to explain that it will seek distribution of the finished film in all media. Describing the best-case scenario would be misleading, and describing the range of possibilities would ultimately prove fruitless and depressing. Assuming that the risk has already been explained elsewhere, there should not be any need to identify the particular odds of selling the film or receiving an award from a film festival.

3. Comparisons with Other Films

Like the discussion of distribution possibilities, the comparison with other films is a dangerous addition to the investors' package. Offering documents that list the top five independent films and their return on investment is wholly inadequate unless the documents also provide information such as the average return or the number of films that do not receive any paid distribution at all (a number that has reached into the thousands annually). Like describing a lottery jackpot without disclosing the odds of winning, comparing the current project to the most successful independent films is misleading at best. For any sophisticated investor, it demonstrates a lack of professionalism on the part of the film company.

In contrast, comparisons with other films for the purpose of communicating the story, the genre, or the visual style have far fewer drawbacks. Describing a spoof comedy as "in the tradition of *Airplane!* and *Scary Movie*" does not suggest that it will have the same box office success, but it does convey the nature of the content well.

Independent filmmaking is an incredibly high-risk financial proposition. The information to investors should stress the passion and commitment rather than trying to sell the wild but quite rare successes. The investors should never be led to believe that the occasional blockbuster is typical of independent filmmaking.

D. Getting Hold of the Money

Whatever financing structure and disclosure strategy is selected, most of the money will not be used until principal photography commences. Only a modest portion of the financing should be allocated to the early prepro-duction process. The film company will thus have time to continue raising funds while engaged in preproduction.

1. Escrow Accounts

The greatest risk for any investor is providing seed capital for a business that fails to get started. In that situation, the investor has no collateral to provide a return. Most investors, therefore, are less willing to provide funds to the production company unless they know that the other money sought will also be collected and the project can at least attempt to meet the spec-ified targets.

Although promises are nice, nothing is as secure as cash in the bank. A subscription agreement often provides that each investor's participation is due when the minimum investment amount has been sold. When that mile-stone is reached, the company notifies all the investors, and they send in their payments. This strategy may work well in a large commercial setting, but for most small ventures, the risk is simply too great that an investor will renege, whether for personal or for financial reasons, resulting in the film-maker's failure to secure the minimum amount of capital.

An *escrow agreement* provides an excellent alternative. It stipulates that the funds raised from the investors will be deposited and held in a segregated account (or with a separate escrow company, if necessary) and that the funds can only be released for use once the milestones are met. The most typical milestone would be that the minimum capital investment has been raised. Milestones may also relate to casting or other key elements of the film.

The agreement need not require that every penny be raised before the funds are released. Instead, it may provide that if, for example, the capital sought was $1 million, reflecting the amount necessary to complete the film, then the escrow funds could be released at $800,000 raised, the amount sufficient to complete principal photography. Presumably, a filmmaker will have an easier time raising editing money if a high-quality shoot has already produced sufficient footage to create a good movie, and investors may feel sufficiently comfortable to agree to escrow provisions with such a clause.

Alternately, the reduction in budget may mean the elimination of cer-tain scenes. The documents can give the filmmaker discretion to begin with a budget of a lesser amount or wait for the larger amount, as long as the investors can understand the choices involved.

The escrow agreement should be tied directly to the contingencies disclosed in the offering documents. If the filmmaker reserved the option to shoot using less expensive equipment or to otherwise save funds, then the escrow provisions should be drafted to allow the company to make that election and to release the funds.

2. Waivers

While some investors may require the protection of the escrow accounts, others may be more generous. If investors support the film project as their primary purpose and view any return on investment as secondary, investors may be willing to release their investment even prior to the funding of the entire minimum capital amount. The filmmaker may request that such an investor waive the protections provided by the escrow accounts. The investor should sign a waiver of any rights for the monies to be held in escrow and explicitly grant the film company permission to use the funds for the purposes of raising capital and conducting necessary preproduction activities. The filmmaker may consider structuring the offering so such investors receive a premium for their additional risk (such as their interest being sold at a 10 percent discount from the price of the other investors).

The access to funds and the ability to gather enough capital to begin the project should be the final business issue in the making of the movie. With full disclosure, complete financing, presales, and loan agreements in place and the investment money released from escrow because the target amount has been raised or waivers have been signed, the filmmaker is finally ready to merge the creative process with the business process. The filmmaker is one step closer to making the movie.

E. Soliciting Investments and Sales in Crowd Financing

The solicitation and sale of securities for a crowd financing campaign must be conducted on a portal registered with the SEC and a member of the Financial Industry Regulatory Authority (FINRA) or a registered broker-dealer. There are dozens of authorized portals, though an increasing number are starting to become inactive as the shine has started to come off of crowd financing.

1. Marketing and Crowd Financing

Under the SEC Regulation Crowdfunding (a.k.a. Regulation CF or Reg CF), an issuer is severely limited in what it can advertise publicly about its crowd financing offer. It can only publish a notice that directs potential investors to the registered portal. The notice can have only three components:

- A statement that the issuer is conducting a Reg CF offering
- The terms of the offering, which are defined as the amount, nature, and price of the securities offered and the closing date
- Factual business information about the issuer, which is limited to the name, address, phone number, and website of the issuer; an email address of a representative of the issuer; and a brief description of the business

The restrictions are stringent and need to be respected. Most important, the film company must avoid any statements regarding predictions, projections, forecasts or opinions with respect to valuation of a security, or information about past financial performance of any kind. These types of promotional statements have been identified as violating exemption disclosure requirements by the SEC and will likely trigger a violation of Regulation Crowdfunding.

The filmmaker must walk a fine line when promoting the project and the offerings. That is, the filmmaker must continually promote the development of the film and create a buzz regarding its production and release while not allowing this excitement to bleed into the investment opportunity in the production. So long as this distinction is vigorously followed, the marketing will pose no difficulties. On the other hand, if the filmmaker or others promoting the film on the production company's behalf suggest that investors can get in on the ground floor for investment or ownership of the project, then that statement will violate the Regulation Crowdfunding limitations.

2. Types of Offerings

Although the film company generally sells either equity investments or debt securities in the form of loans, many ways to create security interests have some combination of both debt and equity. Also, some investment offerings have the characteristics of profit participation rather than ownership in the underlying company. In most financing for independent film, the acumen of the accredited investors and the relatively small number of potential investors allows the issuers to negotiate directly for the terms of the offering with the key investors. In a crowd financing transaction, in contrast, all the terms are published prior to the creation of the offering.

An emerging security is the Simple Agreement for Future Equity (SAFE). A SAFE security is an option to purchase equity only if a triggering event occurs, which gives even more control to the company and puts investors at a very high risk of total investment loss. Given the high risk of failure from independent film, the issuer will be challenged to disclose both the risks of the offering and the additional risks that the triggering event does not occur. As such, attempts to use SAFE securities for independent film productions will invariably end in failed financing campaigns or high risk of later litigation. These offerings should probably be avoided.

To manage the size of the shareholder pools, the issuers will sometimes offer the securities without voting rights to avoid needing to hold large shareholders' meetings and invest the time and effort in shareholder relations.

3. Application of the Financing Agreement

The SEC requires the issuer to provide information very similar to that suggested for the business plan in chapter 9 (pp. 166–167). The disclosure requires information about the company, officers and directors; a business description; an explanation of how the money will be spent; and information about the offering itself, including the minimum and maximum amount the offering will accept, deadlines, risks specific to the film production, and general financial information about the company if it has any history. The information is also quite similar to that required in any Private Placement Memorandum. The detail might not be as specific for the Regulation Crowdfunding as for a Rule 506 filing, but in all cases the information must be accurate and sufficiently complete that no material information is omitted.

The risk factors to be described by the issuer include "the material factors that make an investment in the issuer speculative or risky."[6] This language was adopted directly from the SEC Forms S-1 and 10-K used for publicly traded companies. For large publicly traded companies, the risk factors are highly structured and formulaic. For independent films, the language can be somewhat simpler if the issuer acknowledges that every aspect of production, distribution, and exhibition involves significant risks of noncompletion, nonpayment, and the loss of all investments. The actual language will take more words, but the issuer essentially explains to investors that they should plan on losing all their money, since that is what happens for most independent film productions. (See chapter 7, pp. 140–141, on fundraising by using fiscal sponsors.)

4. Application of Other Securities Laws to Crowd Financing

The SEC regulations allow issues of securities to use the various exemptions from registration as discrete selling opportunities. So the film company can generally use the Reg D funding for its accredited investors and another exemption, such as Regulation Crowdfunding, for its nonaccredited investors. By stacking the investment vehicles, the production company can maximize its fundraising reach and minimize its documentation requirements and liability exposure. This might work particularly well if the crowd financing is used to secure debt rather than equity. The issuance of nonrecourse debt securities has far fewer investor management challenges and could complement the financing from accredited investors.

As stressed throughout the financing sections of this book, all information must be complete and material. Any information made publicly available or provided through private methods must be accurate and up to date. Private information cannot be available to public investors, but the private investors also have access to all the public information. As a consequence, the accredited investors who may have received a Private Placement Memorandum or other offering documents will also have access to all the information on the crowdfunding platform. Those investors can rely on both sets of disclosure documents regarding the statements made by the issuer of the securities.

Filming the Movie:
Preproduction and Production

(11)

Assembling the Production Team

With the business structure in place, the rights secured to the story, and the money raised, the next step in the filmmaking process is the lengthy but critical process of preproduction. An axiom of good filmmaking is that 90 percent of the work is good casting. This is true for the people both in front of and behind the camera.

The production team will be defined by the budgetary and creative choices the filmmaker makes for the film. For example, if the production employs only union cast and crew, the salary expenses for the film will rise, but the film company also will be able to hire employees with greater experience. Low-budget and guerrilla filmmakers may not be able to afford union personnel, and many independent films elect to work with some unions but not others.

In structuring agreements with members of the production, there are only three significant points of negotiation: credit, compensation, and control. In the independent film world, the amount of compensation is necessarily modest. As a result, both credit and control become more important in the negotiation process for landing cast and crew. Fortunately, neither credit nor control has a direct effect on the cash available to complete the movie, so thoughtful choices by the filmmaker can still provide positive incentives for all the film participants.

A. Diversity, Inclusion, and Cultural Appropriateness

The opportunity to make movies in new and different ways should be exploited whenever possible. In the independent filmmaking arena, filmmakers simply do not have the luxury of indulging in counterproductive, inappropriate discrimination on the basis of sex, race, or other insidious stereotypes. Therefore, independent films may provide the most important vehicle for professionals looking to expand their skills into new areas, and for women and minority filmmakers seeking the opportunity to prove themselves.

The odds for success in Hollywood continue to be painfully low for all participants, perhaps especially for women. There are role models, however, in every aspect of the industry. Sherry Lansing, Jennifer Lee, Lili Zanuck, and Kathleen Kennedy, among many others, exemplify quality producers. Many other women have moved from actor or writer to producer or director or both. Again, strong examples abound: Liv Ullmann (*Faithless, Private Confessions*), Nora Ephron (*You've Got Mail, Sleepless in Seattle*), Diablo Cody (*Juno*), Sofia Coppola (*Lost in Translation*), Kimberly Peirce (*Boys Don't Cry*), Ava DuVernay (*A Wrinkle in Time*), Jodie Foster (*Money Monster, Home for the Holidays*), and Kathryn Bigelow (*The Hurt Locker*). They are just a few of the many productive women who have leveraged independent productions to redefine their career paths and overcome the additional hurdles faced in Hollywood because of gender stereotypes and residual discrimination.

Independent films have served the same role in helping filmmakers surmount racial barriers. Filmmakers such as Spike Lee (*Do the Right Thing, BlacKKKlansman, Da 5 Bloods*), Steve McQueen (*12 Years a Slave*), John Singleton (*Boyz n the Hood*), Amma Asante (*Belle*), Robert Townsend (*Hollywood Shuffle*), Forest Whitaker (*Waiting to Exhale*), Ava DuVernay (*Selma*), Mario Van Peebles (*New Jack City*), Ryan Coogler (*Creed*), Haile Gerima (*Sankofa*), and many more have staked their claim by creating strong identities in themselves and their work through independent film.

Documentary filmmaking in particular has felt the increasing influence of strong female and minority teams. And as the documentary genre itself expands, this helps develop talent and opportunity for feature films. Independent film projects in general are well suited to fostering the professional growth of individuals struggling against barriers to their development. These projects create opportunities to tell stories that would struggle to receive approvals and backing through a corporate Hollywood system, affording the filmmakers the independence essential to be authentic in their narrative.

1. Changes to the Status Quo

Although there have been efforts to promote diversity in film for decades, concerns over diversity, inclusion, and cultural appropriateness moved to the forefront of the motion picture industry beginning in 2018. The combined studio success of Jordan Peele's *Get Out*, Ryan Coogler's *Black Panther*, and Jon Chu's *Crazy Rich Asians* awakened the marketing and budget departments to the economic potential of works highlighting stories from outside of the Upper West Side or Middle America.

The box office support for diversity and inclusion is matched by rigorous academic research. For example, Professor Stacy L. Smith at the Annenberg Inclusion Initiative in the USC Annenberg School for Communication and Journalism has documented the modest steps being taken in Hollywood. The research has shown that the percentage of women taking significant roles in film has remained low and unchanged for decades.

More generally, the percentage of women on screen in film has not increased in decades. It's time to change these statistics. The *inclusion rider* was created to do just that. The inclusion rider is an addendum committing the production company to equitable hiring practices of both cast and crew. The goal of the inclusion rider is to promote productions that look like the world we actually live in—not a small fraction of the talent pool. It does this while also protecting story sovereignty.

2. Race and Gender Diversity Goals in Hiring

The Annenberg Inclusion Initiative, for example, has noted that "across the 100 top-grossing films of 2016, 47 did not feature a single Black woman or girl speaking on screen, 66 movies were devoid of Asian female characters, and a full 72 films erased Latinas. Very few females from the LGBT community, native and indigenous females, Middle Eastern females, or female characters with disabilities are seen in our cinematic stories."[1]

To progress toward the goal of systemic equity in the entertainment workforce, the Annenberg Inclusion Initiative collaborated with Kalpana Kotagal at the law firm of Cohen Milstein Sellers & Toll to create the contractual inclusion rider. By demanding its incorporation into their contracts, top talent can promote the hiring of underrepresented groups in Hollywood, which the rider defines as "people who identify themselves as females, people of color, disabled, Lesbian Gay Bisexual Transgender or Queer, or having a combination of these attributes."[2] By footnote, the rider suggests that the definition is flexible and can include other attributes of nonrepresentation, such as age.

The rider commits the project to auditioning underrepresented people for lead and supporting roles as well as to interviewing them for key leadership positions throughout the production process, including:

- Development and production: director of photography/ cinematographer, production designer, sound, first assistant director, second assistant director, costume designer, and line producers
- Postproduction: editor, visual effects, composer

The inclusion rider could be transformative because of its potential to expand the pipeline of underrepresented talent and crew who will gain experience and move up the ranks throughout the industry. In other respects, however, it is a relatively timid step that calls merely for interviews and auditions rather than more explicit demands on diversification of the production.

Diversity riders are likely to have the most impact within the studio system, where A-list talent has great leverage. For an independent production, diversity riders may not be the right tool for increasing diversity. Instead, these commitments can be incorporated directly into the business plan and operating documents of the production company. It will be far more impactful for the inclusion commitment to be part of the Private Placement Memorandum or crowdfunding statements. In independent filmmaking, it is the filmmaker's own commitment that will drive change, and documenting that commitment in the offering documents will help keep the filmmaker focused on it throughout the entirety of production and postproduction.

3. Compensation Equity and Workplace Culture in Front of and Behind the Camera

The opportunity to hire must also be matched by true equity in the valuation of compensation, credit, and control afforded to members of the cast and crew. While there are certain realities about what A-list talent can demand to open a picture, those considerations are rarely relevant to budgets for independent and guerilla films. Nonetheless, there is a systemic gender pay gap. Female leads who carry films are often paid significantly less than men with the same reputation and following.

SAG-AFTRA, for example, has created additional incentives in its Moderate Low Budget Project Agreement, allowing producers to use the rates of the moderate low-budget contracts for projects with slightly higher budgets if the casting includes underrepresented people:

i) Diversity in Casting Incentive . . .

  (a) A minimum of 50% of the total speaking roles and 50% of the total days of employment are cast with Performers who are members of the following four (4) protected groups:

  (1) Women;

  (2) Senior Performers (sixty (60) years or older);

  (3) Performers with Disabilities;

  (4) People of Color (Black/African American, Asian/ Pacific Islander and South Asian, Latino/Hispanic, Arab/Middle Eastern and Native American Indian) and;

  (b) A minimum of 20% of the total days of employment is cast with performers who are People of Color.

To clarify: A Project with a cast of ten (10) speaking roles, each of whom work one (1) day, should have at least five (5) Performers from any or all of the protected groups and two (2) of whom must be People of Color. Under no circumstances should an individual be counted in more than one category.[3]

If these casting minimums are met, the production cost maximum can be increased from $700,000 to $950,000.

Many independent films already provide all cast members the same economic package, and this practice should be lauded and expanded. Particularly if the film has an ensemble cast or if the leads are already taking a significant pay cut from what they would make in a non-low-budget project, the filmmaker and producer should be very mindful to ensure that the pay scales are equitable for the work being provided rather than based on any historical discrepancies that devalue underrepresented talent and staff.

4. Cultural Appropriateness of Casting and Content

Independent films empower storytellers to explore their own stories and engage with material that the filmmaker finds compelling. Telling a compelling story is vital, but there are other important considerations. For documentary filmmakers in particular, there is also an obligation to be truthful and accurate. In both narrative and documentary filmmaking, the public increasingly expects the filmmaker to reflect the realities of diversity.

Diversity in the creative arts is addressed in two very different ways. In theater, and increasingly in television and film, storytellers intentionally ignore or manipulate historical racism by employing multiracial casting. This is sometimes done to expand access to roles for minorities, but in other projects, the multiracial casting adds a layer of cultural critique and insight to the production. The result has been an explosion of multiracial casting that has reimagined history. Lin-Manuel Miranda's Broadway musical *Hamilton* has shattered box office records and reconceptualized multiethnic projects. Shonda Rhimes's Netflix series *Bridgerton* has reinvigorated the costume drama.

At the same time, audiences are increasingly critical of casting choices that ignore race, gender, or ethnicity of significant roles. In particular, efforts to whitewash characters and content is viewed with increasing disfavor. Although Laurence Olivier's *Othello* was a highly praised production in its day, the notion of performing the role in blackface today is anathema. The Chinese detective Charlie Chan was played often by Warner Oland, but the role also went to Manuel Arbó, Sidney Toler, Roland Winters, Ross Martin and Peter Ustinov. None of these men was Chinese. Similar controversies have erupted over Jonathan Pryce's role in *Miss Saigon*, Johnny Depp's role in *The Lone Ranger*, and of Scarlett Johansson's acceptance of a role as a transgender man in *Rub & Tug* and playing a Japanese woman in *Ghost in the Shell*.

The lessons from *Hamilton* and *The Lone Ranger* suggest that decisions to cast against type or culture must be made as artistic choices designed to further the storytelling, and generally are best received when they are imbued with efforts to expand inclusion. Comic books, in particular, have a long history of revising character history, gender, race, and ethnicity. This theme was explored quite effectively in the animated film *Spider-Man: Into the Spider-Verse*, which portrayed different worlds as having the character with many different backgrounds.

As with casting choices, the decision to tell stories that are embedded in particular cultures is sometimes received quite poorly if the public feels the filmmakers have exploited that story and appropriated it from another culture. Many action thrillers have used generic desert sets, Arab and Muslim garb, and minarets to shade their stories of heroes thwarting terrorism.

Most of these are very disrespectful of Arab and Muslim cultures and traditions. Other projects use Latino gang members or Hasidic diamond merchants to replace sound storytelling with racist tropes. Animation has its own issues, including criticism of DreamWorks Animation's *Kung Fu Panda* series and Wes Anderson's *Isle of Dogs*, which was criticized for its treatment of the Japanese humans in the film.

Films that celebrate and recognize challenging boundaries will generally fare better than those that make the storytelling and casting choices with a deaf ear and blind eye. For the independent filmmaker, the opportunity exists to bring stories to the public that make a positive impact and balance these concerns thoughtfully.

B. Who, What, and When to Hire

Perhaps the single greatest flaw in American filmmaking is the overwhelming number of people involved in the production process. Independent filmmakers do not have this luxury, and, as a result, they can avoid some of the pitfalls of overblown productions.

The preproduction team creating the film should evolve as the project nears principal photography. Qualified individuals should be identified early and kept up to date on the preproduction process, but they should not begin employment on the film until their particular services become essential. This both reduces costs and streamlines the information flow of the project. Since most film shoots operate in barely contained chaos, the better the information flow, the less time is wasted on distractions or costly mistakes.

The initial team is typically made up of the producer, director, and screenwriter. On an independent film, these may all be one person, but to move forward on the project, even the solo filmmaker needs someone with whom to collaborate. The process is far too lonely not to share the tensions and triumphs with someone. Filmmaking teams such as Joel and Ethan Coen and James Ivory and Ismail Merchant have had longstanding success in part due to their healthy collaboration. On the other hand, many tasks identified for preproduction can be carried out by one or two people, if they have the skills to accomplish the task (or if the filmmaker cannot afford to hire anyone else to help).

The team should be expanded as the necessary preproduction tasks exceed the abilities of the personnel already in place. For example, if the producer cannot provide the skills necessary to estimate the scope and costs of the production, then the first critical hire on the project is someone to create the budget. After all, as described earlier, the accuracy and completeness of the budget is crucial to the film's operations. Similarly, since casting is often a long process, the person in charge of casting must be identified, and if it is neither the director nor the producer, then a casting director must be brought on board early in preproduction as well.

The next round of hires often involves locations for the filming. The settings are often integral to both the story being told and the costs of telling that story. A location manager and location scouts must be assigned the task of finding interior and exterior locations where the film may be shot, identifying the proper parties for arranging permission to shoot at those locations and creating a feasible production schedule. On smaller films, the director typically serves as location manager, enlisting volunteer location scouts to help with the early legwork.

Next, the directors of the creative elements must be identified and incorporated into the process. If there is to be a director of photography separate from the director, the director of photography's early input into the locations, lighting, and visual style of the film becomes crucial. Similarly, if costumes, sets, props, lighting, special effects, or stunts play heavily in the film, then the person in charge of each creative area should become a central figure in the preproduction planning. For low-budget projects, however, these departments are often luxuries. Actors wear street clothes, apply their own makeup, and manage their own action. There is no need to add directors and designers when the scope of the project does not call for their services.

C. Introduction to the Key Unions

Whether because of the prevalence of people trying to break into show business or despite it, Hollywood remains one of the more heavily unionized industries. Nonetheless, production companies are not required to become signatories to union agreements, and the decision to become a signatory to one union agreement does not require a company to become a signatory to agreements with other unions.

The decision to work with union or nonunion labor will depend on the quality of the talent pool available, the costs to the production, and the benefits of working with an experienced workforce. Use of unions generally increases as the budget increases, since the complexity and visibility of higher-budget shoots tends to increase the need for experienced union members.

1. Unions' Benefits for Hollywood

Through collective bargaining agreements with the signatory production companies, the key Hollywood trade unions provide their members with guaranteed minimum payments for various jobs; contributions by employers to health, welfare, and pension funds; minimum health and safety procedures; and grievance procedures to simplify any disputes between a member and the production company that employs him. The unions provide important benefits to their members and to the professional quality of the entertainment industry.

2. Union Representation and Eligibility

Individual union members are free to negotiate deals with production companies that are more generous than the terms of the minimum agreements. The collective bargaining agreement merely establishes a floor for such contracts. In other areas, however, the unions exact more control. As described in section D (pp. 208–209), the unions exert a good deal of authority over the form of screen credits, even in situations in which all the parties would prefer a result other than that dictated by union rules.

Many of the industry unions maintain very high membership standards. At the same time, under the Taft-Hartley provisions of the union collective bargaining agreements, if a person becomes a "principal performer" by performing dialogue in a film shoot governed by SAG-AFTRA or otherwise becomes employed by a production company in a position subject to a collective bargaining agreement, that person becomes eligible to join the union for 30 days. The production company cannot employ the person beyond 30 days unless that person joins the union, so the eligibility must be used or the person terminated. The production company may also face union sanctions for hiring a person who is not a member of the union, unless specified conditions are met.

3. Union Members Prohibited from Nonunion Work

A member of a union is barred by union rules from working on a nonunion production. If a union member works on a nonunion shoot, the union may later issue a permanent ban on that person's future union employment.

Usually, the union will give the member violating this rule the opportunity to convince the nonunion company to become a signatory company, curing the problem created by the member.

If this situation arises during production, the union member is likely to pressure the film company, arguing that the production company must sign the union agreement or lose the services of the union member. Particularly when the member is an actor, the costs associated with having to reshoot previously completed footage may put tremendous pressure on the production company to sign a collective bargaining agreement that would likely affect the employment and union status of the entire cast.

4. Listing of Key Unions

The following are brief introductions to each of the significant trade unions for the motion picture industry:

Screen Actors Guild–American Federation of Television and Radio Artists (SAG-AFTRA) https://www.sagaftra.org/
- SAG-AFTRA represents the professional actors in film, television, industrials, commercials, video games, music videos, and other new media.
- SAG is the primary talent union for the film industry.
- AFTRA represents performers in broadcast, public and cable television; radio (news, commercials, hosted programs); sound recordings (CDs, singles, Broadway cast albums, audio books); nonbroadcast and industrial material; and Internet and digital programming.

Directors Guild of America (DGA) http://www.dga.org
- DGA represents directors, associate directors, and stage managers in motion pictures and in broadcast, public, and cable television.
- DGA guarantees the right of a film director to provide the first cut of a motion picture.

Writers Guild of America East and West (WGA) https://www.wgaeast .org and http://www.wga.org
- WGAE and WGAW represent writers in negotiations with producers to ensure their rights in screen, television, and new media.

International Alliance of Theatrical Stage Employees, Moving Picture Technicians, Artists and Allied Crafts (IATSE) http://www.iatse-intl.org

- IATSE represents below-the-line film craft professionals such as camerapersons, lighting crews, sound technicians, editors, live-action storyboard artists, set designers, art directors, and scenic artists.

American Federation of Musicians (AFM) http://www.afm.org

- AFM represents musicians working in recording; broadcast, public, and cable television; music videos; commercials; films; video games; and traveling theatrical productions.

Actors' Equity Association (AEA or Equity) http://www.actorsequity.org

- Equity represents actors and stage managers performing in live theater: Broadway, touring companies, professional theaters throughout the United States, and Walt Disney World.
- Equity does not have jurisdiction over film productions, but its collective bargaining agreements may impose limitations on the ability to film works produced for the stage, as in a "Live on Broadway" movie.

The Animation Guild and Affiliated Optical Electronic and Graphic Arts, Local 839 IATSE (TAG) http://www.animationguild.org

- TAG represents cartoonists, animators, and animation writers.

International Brotherhood of Electrical Workers (IBEW) http://www.ibew.org

- The IBEW represents electrical workers in telecommunications and broadcasting as well as in construction, utilities, manufacturing, railroads, and government.

Motion Picture and Theatrical Trade Teamsters (Hollywood Teamsters Local 399) https://www.ht399.org

- Hollywood Teamsters Local 399 represents workers in motion pictures; broadcast, public, and cable television; commercials; and live theatrical productions. Members include animal trainers, auto service personnel, casting directors, chefs, couriers, dispatchers, drivers, location managers, mechanics, warehousemen, and wranglers.

Alliance of Motion Picture and Television Producers (AMPTP)
http://www.amptp.org
- The AMPTP represents motion picture and television producers.
  Member companies include independent producers and the
  production entities of the studios, broadcast networks, and certain
  cable networks.

Producers Guild of America (PGA) http://www.producersguild.org
- Although once a union, the PGA is now a trade association for
  producers of film, television, and new media, including producers,
  associate producers, line producers, coproducers, segment
  producers, and production managers.
- Since it is not a trade union, it is not involved in any collective
  bargaining agreements, but it may still provide a useful resource for
  independent filmmakers involved with contractual and labor issues.

D. Screen Credit

Providing an onscreen credit in a motion picture acknowledges the fundamental need for personal recognition. It serves as a thank-you, and it permanently recognizes the work done by the person named. For professionals
in the film industry, the size and placement of the credit on their most
recent project plays a significant role in helping set their fee and credits in
their next role. More generally, a screen credit promotes the individual or
company named, conveying the status of the entity to future employers and
peers. It is a valuable commodity that should not be squandered.

Screen credits fall into two basic categories: those on "card" at the
beginning of the film and those in the scrolling credits at the end of the film.
End credits are usually provided in a single typeface, moving relatively
quickly across the screen; as a result, few serious negotiations are over the
format of the end credits. In addition, many of the end-credit obligations
are dictated by union agreements.

The opening credits are much more contentious. Accepted industry
standards attach importance to the placement of individual names within
the credit sequence. The first name shown is considered the "star" of a
film—certainly the actor with the most clout regarding the production. If
two names appear at once, the upper left is considered to be in first position. And names that appear before the film's title carry significantly more

weight than those that follow the title. Because these are industry standards, cast members, other professionals, and even audience members interpret the credits in this way, even if the filmmaker would like to ignore the implications.

In addition to rules regarding placement, the size of the typeface can also suggest importance. If the cast credits listed after the film title are in smaller type than that of the stars who precede it, the filmmaker is further highlighting the importance of the stars over the remainder of the cast.

Cast members are not the only parties who seek to have their names in the opening credits. Film producers (perhaps including individual investors), writers, and the director are all typically credited. Rarely do these names go before the stars or the title, but all placement is subject to negotiation.

1. Union Requirements

Credits are one of the most important keys to continued employment in the entertainment industry. For a writer, director, or actor, the receipt of a credit helps establish a benchmark for future employment negotiations. As a result, trade unions such as WGA, DGA, and SAG-AFTRA all set policies that require that their members receive minimum credit and, in the case of DGA and WGA, govern who can receive credit at all.

Under DGA and WGA rules, any dispute over directing or writing credits must be resolved by an arbitration process run by the applicable union. For WGA members, the writers must all agree to the proposed tentative writing credits or protest the tentative writing credits and seek a credit arbitration. The finished film and all the written submissions made by each of the authors are submitted to the arbitrator, who makes a determination regarding the contribution of each individual. For most writing credits, no more than two writers can be credited. DGA uses a similar process for disputes among directors, but it is used much less frequently.

2. Optional Suggestions

For film companies that are signatories to union contracts, these rules must be followed. The good news is that the union arbitrator, rather than the filmmaker, must decide which writer or director deserves the name recognition for the work. For nonunion films, the union processes can serve as a guide, but making highly contentious credit decisions is likely to create trouble. Contrary to union policy, there is no reason for a nonunion film not to offer everyone who legitimately worked on the film some credit or recognition. If the movie was inspired by a person who did not otherwise participate in the film's production, the filmmaker should feel free to give the "inspired by" credit, regardless of whether the WGA would approve.

The employment contract should, therefore, guarantee that the person's name will appear in the end credits of the film as long as that person was not in breach of the contract. The contract can also provide that the individual will receive sole credit for the task, such as a writer, if that person was the only one to provide the service, and that credit will be shared if others provided a similar service. The contract should also provide that the determination of the credits is solely at the discretion of the film company and not subject to appeal or arbitration. Taken together, a generous approach and clear contract provisions should limit the problems over credits for most independent film companies.

3. Credits as a Marketable Commodity

Credits can be valuable to a host of other participants in the filmmaking process besides the cast and crew. New York City, for example, requires that films using the valuable and free services of the New York City Film Office give the office an end credit. Independent films often offer a "special thanks" credit to the individuals and companies that provided service, but this undervalues their assistance and blunts the recognition provided. Being able to tell a lawyer, accountant, or restaurateur that the person will be given a substantive credit in the film may have more than passing value. The promise of a screen credit for "legal services provided," combined with a promise of at least deferred compensation, is enough to convince some attorneys to assist independent filmmakers.

Again, a nonunion project need not be bound by rigid union credit rules, so if the film is based on a stage play, then prominent screen credit may be the way to induce the playwright to risk allowing an independent production company to have the film rights. The key is to recognize the high value and low cost that credits provide for the filmmaker. This is one of the few advantages nonunion movies have over union productions, and the filmmaker should use it.

E. Compensation Packages: Making the Deals

To many participants, an independent film project is a professional stepping-stone that provides concrete evidence of their professional skills and serves

as their first paid work experience. Therefore, offering even modest payments can be the key to securing many individuals' participation. Nonetheless, as mentioned in chapter 4 (pp. 57–64), truly modest compensation raises
legal concerns, because of minimum-wage laws and other employment obligations. For many participants, however, these legal concerns take second
place to the psychological and professional importance of working rather
than volunteering on the film project. This need should be respected.

1. Salaries and Per Diems

The basic payment system for most films is a flat fee. The cast members and
crew members involved in the entire production are guaranteed a certain
amount of money for their work. Payments of the fee are typically apportioned based on the planned number of weeks for the production. Except
for those production members actively involved in preproduction, payments generally do not begin until principal photography has commenced.

The norms for payments conform to the traditional structure for most
filmmaking, which assumes little rehearsal time and tightly scheduled
shoots. For independent filmmakers, these conventions may not reflect the
production's actual schedule. To the extent the production differs from the
norm, the payment systems should be adjusted to fit the actual employment experience. For example, if the filmmaker adopts a theater model for
preproduction, extensive rehearsals of the entire script may be done over a
period of four to six weeks. The filming can then take place over a period
of a few days rather than weeks. This model works best in a film that uses
few sets and camera setups. If the director plans a shoot using handheld
cameras, walking with the cast through the sets as the scenes unfold, the
filming process will need to be well choreographed, but once it is staged,
the natural flow of the action will seem organic to the film. For such a shoot,
the rehearsals become integral to the production process while the length
of principal photography is substantially reduced. The timing of payments
must be varied to reflect these choices.

In addition to salaries, the cast members and crew members may be paid
per diems, or modest payments based on the number of days worked. With
the possible exception of the above-the-line participants, the per diems are
the same amount for everyone on the film. The amount is intended to cover
food, gas, and lodging (if the shoot is away from the production center). For
nonunion productions, per diems are not required, but they often supplement craft services (food service on the set) or assist with significant travel

to the shooting location. Even if salaries themselves are entirely deferred, per diems often help ensure that the cast and crew can afford the gas to get to the set.

2. Deferrals

One very effective way of extending the amount of money on hand to complete principal photography is to defer payroll expenses. Theoretically, if all the costs were deferred, then the film could be produced for no money, and all budget expenses would be paid from the film's future revenues. Though this is not typically possible for third-party vendors, participants in the film project are often willing to defer all or part of their salaries. A true deferral simply puts the payments off until the film begins to receive revenues. Since the deferred salaries are budgeted costs, they must be paid before any capital is returned to the investors or profits are paid to any parties.

A common source of confusion is the order of deferral payments. If the film is sold for an amount greater than the total of deferred expenses outstanding, then everything is paid simultaneously. If, however, money trickles in, then it is important that the priority of payments be clearly spelled out in the employment contracts or in other agreements incorporated into the employment agreements by reference.

First, each class of deferment should be treated *pro rata*, or in proportion. That is, all salary deferrals for all participants are pooled together. If the film company receives $5,000 to be applied to the salaries, then the $5,000 would be distributed to all the participants on a percentage basis. If the total pool was $50,000 in deferrals split in various salaries for 20 people, then each participant would receive a payment of 10 percent of the amount owed to that person.

The filmmaker could instead choose to divide the deferrals evenly among all participants on a *per capita* basis, with the understanding that some participants would be paid in full before others. In this example, let's say the 20 people who have deferred their salaries will make from $1,000 to $10,000. The $5,000 earned under this scenario would be split into 1/20ths, with each individual receiving $250. The person who was entitled to a $1,000 salary would receive 25 percent of what was owed, while the person with a $10,000 salary would receive only 2.5 percent of the salary. The benefit of this approach is that those who typically earn much less in annual salary will be likely to receive their salary sooner. A sum of $250 is much more important to the livelihood of someone making $50,000 than someone making $500,000, so this might be the more equitable approach. Both the pro rata approach and the per capita approach work, as long as the system is applied consistently and agreed upon in advance.

Second, any other classes of payments should also be spelled out. For example, it may be that all expenses, including equipment leases, credit card expenditures, invoices, etc., must be paid in full before any of the deferrals are paid. If this includes ongoing expenses such as office rent, then that must also be specified. Theoretically, all costs other than the deferrals should have been covered by the capital investment, but in case (as frequently occurs) there are budget overruns or not enough capital, the agreement should state whether the credit cards are paid before or after the deferrals. In addition, the producer's fee may be treated as a separate payment, to be made either before or after the other deferrals, depending on the needs of the producer.

Finally, the filmmaker may be receiving payment for many different aspects of the project. To the extent the filmmaker is wearing different hats (director, actor, screenwriter, editor, producer, etc.), the tasks that entitle the filmmaker to additional compensation should also be clearly identified in advance. The filmmaker may specify that the producer's fee is deferred until after all the other deferrals are paid in full, but payments due as a cast member and as screenwriter will be treated the same as those due to the other cast members. To avoid bad feelings and legal problems, such a structure must be quite explicit in both the budget and the contracts. As long as the system selected is clear, fewer problems will arise later.

3. Profit Participation

The other source of payment to the film participants flows from profit participation in the film. Studio films are notorious for definitions of profit participation 20 or more pages in length that make it almost unheard-of for even the greatest blockbuster to actually turn a profit as defined by the convoluted agreement. For independent films, however, the successful project will return a profit that is not hidden in the studio overhead or other charges to the film.

Profit must still be defined. As suggested in chapter 8 (pp. 160–161), it may be preferable to use the term *adjusted gross* or *defined profit* rather than *net* or *gross profit* to avoid unintended meanings of those terms. Defined profit is distributed after the expenses are paid in full, the entire investment is returned to the investors (often at 110 to 125 percent of the amount invested), and a reserve fund is made for ongoing operations of the film company. The remaining earned income should be profit. Except as provided in the profit participation agreements, all profits belong to the film company and, in turn, to the shareholders or members of the company. As a result, profit participation arrangements must be carefully specified in the offering documents for the film company.

Filmmakers may find it helpful to create a profit participation pool of some percentage of the profits, anywhere from 10 to 25 percent. In this way, the investors can be told that, say, 10 percent of all profits are apportioned among the members of the cast and crew. That number will not change even though the exact participation within the pool may continue to fluctuate as shares are assigned to particular individuals during negotiations. The filmmaker designates that the pool has a certain number of points— say, 100 or 1,000—which are then allocated to cast and crew in the employment agreements. The points not allocated can be returned to the investors, retained by the filmmaker, or paid pro rata to the pool. Any of these options work, as long as the choice is made in writing as part of the initial employment contracts.

Although even more contingent on the film's financial success than deferred salaries, profit participation has the potential to be the most valuable aspect of the compensation package. For those rare blockbuster films, the profit participation points can amount to exceptional income. The contract, therefore, should also be very clear about when the right to profit participation vests—upon successful completion of the employment duties rather than upon signing the employment contract. If an actor leaves the film because a paying job is suddenly available, that actor should not remain a profit participant. Instead, if the director can negotiate to shoot sufficient coverage to work around the actor in exchange for keeping some of the deferrals and profit participation, the contract provides the filmmaker with negotiating leverage.

4. Union-Defined Minimums

For union productions, each union requires that a guaranteed minimum amount be paid as compensation, consisting of salaries and per diems. The collective bargaining agreements allow union members to negotiate higher pay and profit or revenue participation above those minimums. Under their low-budget agreements (see chapter 9, pp. 174–176), the unions now allow for limited deferrals.

Despite the flexibility afforded by the low-budget agreements, some independent film companies still find they are unable to meet payroll and complete principal photography. To fulfill both their obligations to the union and the need to fund the film, union members may choose to invest their entire net salary in the film. This should not be a condition of employment, but the film company can provide generous deferrals and contingent payments for those union members who elect to invest in the production in this fashion. Such an arrangement must be established early in the negotiations, and the union participants should receive both generous profit participation in their compensation package and the same return as other cash investors.

Given that many actors working on low-budget films are more concerned with remaining eligible for union health benefits, financial concessions that protect those minimums are treated favorably. By reinvesting the actors' net income, all union financial obligations are met, the cast members do not risk jeopardizing their union status by working on a nonunion shoot, the professional quality of the production is generally improved, and the resources needed to make the film are not substantially reduced. Finally, as members of the production company, the participants should be sufficiently involved in the production to avoid most restrictions on the sale of securities.

5. Morality Clauses and Postcompletion Liability

The social media age and the concerns about a person's misconduct on and off the set has redefined many social norms in Hollywood. Bill Cosby and Harvey Weinstein are in prison, but many more individuals have not been held legally accountable for their conduct. The "casting couch" was once the source of movie humor but has since been recognized for the sexual abuse it represented.

Production companies are taking allegations of sexual misconduct and other forms of inappropriate behavior very seriously. Independent producers have the same obligations to provide a safe and harassment-free workplace for all employees, contractors, and volunteers. The low-budget and often informal nature of independent production companies should not be an excuse or an opportunity to permit predatory conduct or inappropriate behavior.

The independent film company must therefore have a code of behavior applicable to all employees, contractors, and volunteers who work on the project. SAG-AFTRA has produced its own code that can serve as a model for the independent production company.[4] The definitions of *sexual harassment* are helpful for the production company:

1.1 **Quid Pro Quo Sexual Harassment**

Quid pro quo sexual harassment occurs when your job or work assignments depend on your submission to sexual or romantic requests from a superior, or you are denied work or given less favorable work assignments because of your unwillingness to engage in sexual or romantic behavior

1.2 **Hostile Work Environment Sexual Harassment**

A hostile work environment is characterized by unwelcome verbal, visual, or physical conduct of a sexual nature that is severe or pervasive and which creates a hostile, offensive or intimidating work environment. Conduct directed at others can nevertheless generate a hostile work environment.

1.3 **Retaliation**

Retaliation in any form is also unlawful. Retaliation occurs when an employer takes an employment action against someone who makes a complaint of sexual harassment. Retaliation against someone who assists another in making a complaint or who participates in an investigation into inappropriate behavior is also unlawful. Retaliation can take many forms, including firing, denial of work assignments, loss of extra hours, offering less favorable work opportunities or exclusion. Report retaliatory behavior in the same manner you would harassment.

SAG-AFTRA notes that children involved in productions are particularly vulnerable to misconduct, and efforts to protect the environment for children are the obligation of the production company.

Sexual harassment is not the only misconduct that should be identified in the code of conduct. The production company should also be aware of claims involving racial or gender discrimination, as well as any other actions that are harmful to other persons and could result in either liability or disrepute to the film and the production company.

Misconduct can hurt the production company's ability to complete its independent film whether it happens on set or after hours. Although the production company has more direct responsibility to ensure a safe workplace, the backlash to a cast members' sexual or racial misconduct is not limited to the employer's legal role. The production company may have direct liability for misconduct by one of its employees directed at another employee at work. But even if the production company has no direct liability, the bad press and interference with the work product could be significant.

Production companies must take steps to vet the potential employees prior to engaging them. While respecting the privacy of individuals, the company must do its due diligence for publicly available information regarding the criminal backgrounds and published material put forth by each person taking a leadership role in the cast and production team.

In addition, the engagement agreements should contain a provision obligating the person to adhere to the conduct code and to represent and warrant that the individual has not taken actions that would have violated terms of the production company's conduct code had it been in effect. The provision must also include that any misconduct that occurs while engaged with the production company or that comes to light during the terms of the engagement constitutes grounds for terminating the relationship with cause.

The provision should make clear that the engagement is for the purpose of completing the film, and if the production company determines that the allegations have the potential to harm the business of the production company, it can terminate the relationship rather than having an obligation to determine the merits of the claim. In other words, the morals clause will give the production company the ability to part ways with a senior member of the production or a cast member in the event that allegations surface that the person had engaged in inappropriate conduct. Given their fragile economic status, most independent film companies do not have the resources to be forced to retain a cast member or director accused of misconduct in a manner that may be impractical to investigate, particularly if the decision to retain the person on set would result in other cast members quitting or triggering a controversy that will make the finished film unsalable. A morals clause gives the production much more discretion to let cast and crew members go than would have been typical in earlier eras, but the changes in expectations in Hollywood and the heightened sensitivity to these issues make it necessary.

F. Control During Production

The third primary negotiation point for most major hiring decisions concerns the allocation of control over the film project and how the balance of control may change throughout the production process. Perhaps one of the most famous of film legends is that Sylvester Stallone received offers from producers interested in his screenplay for *Rocky* that he turned down because the offers did not include a guarantee that he would play the title role. The studio offered him substantially more money to sell the script without that guarantee. His perseverance reflected his understanding that the role was far more important to his career than the credit and money he would undoubtedly have earned for the screenplay.

For the filmmaker, control should be a primary concern. In decisions involving the business structure, hiring of the management team, financing, and distribution, the filmmaker should be sure to insist on control to the greatest extent possible. Control over the film should be the touchstone for all decisions unless the money or other rewards become so great that the filmmaker is prepared to take them and run.

If the filmmaker assumes ultimate control, then the other participants in the filmmaking process necessarily will not have it. Nonetheless, the other professionals will have many of the same concerns that the filmmaker does, and as a result, reasonable authority and responsibility must be delegated by the filmmaker to these professionals as well. Further, to be successful, the filmmaker must assemble a competent, professional team. Professionalism includes respect for others and requires that the filmmaker trust the assembled professionals to make competent decisions.

1. Artistic Control

The filmmaker, often the director, must establish the mood and tone of the film. As the filmmaker shares this vision with others—the cinematographer, the location manager, the designers of sets, costumes, props, lighting, sound, and music—the filmmaker should allow those individuals to suggest ways of achieving the film's goals. Even the writing must be shaped carefully to fit within the desired tone and mood. Casting choices are based on the decisions that shape or reshape the script and will inform every choice in direction and editing.

If the filmmaker is not the director, then the collaboration must be even more closely structured. Directors are often hired to fulfill the vision of the producer or story writer, but this relationship can easily turn into conflict if the two visionaries do not have the same goals. Schedules for collaboration must be agreed upon in advance. If the director proves unwilling to accept the intrusion of the filmmaker, then the filmmaker should select another director early in the project, before such a choice dramatically affects the budget or morale of the film.

Artistic control should not be left to unspoken assumptions. In the larger-budget union films, rules of control have evolved over decades into complex provisions in the collective bargaining agreements that balance the interests of the writers, directors, crafts, and talent against the interests of the producer and financial backers. These models may not be relevant for independent films and are particularly unrepresentative when the filmmaker plays more than one of these roles. Nor are these norms laws. They simply will not govern the film company's employment relationship if the film company is not a signatory to the collective bargaining agreement in question.

The film company should instead adopt explicit job descriptions for the key participants, clearly explaining to whom each employee reports. The contracts should specify that the employment is "at will." Although the compensation is most likely based on a fixed amount, the contract should provide that if the employee is terminated prior to completion of the project, then only the portion of the fixed amount that has accrued to the date of termination is paid. This is true for both paid salary and deferred salary.

The filmmaker should also specify whether or not the proportionate amount of any revenue or profit participation accrues.

Once the filmmaker and the film company have adopted a structure, the organization should empower the leadership and work in a hierarchal manner to ensure that each department head has the support of the filmmaker and the respect of the workers in that department. The director should work closely with the cast, directors, and designers. The directors and designers, in turn, should be responsible for and have full authority over the workers within their areas. For example, if the job descriptions place costumers under the supervision of the costume designer, then the director should work through the costume designer rather than giving inconsistent orders directly to one of the costumers. The information flow is thus maximized, confusion is minimized, and the designers are given the courtesy and professional respect they deserve, while the director retains ultimate control and the ability to terminate employment, if necessary.

2. Management Control

Like artistic control, management control requires a strong command system. In a very short period of time, a company that did not previously exist will suddenly employ dozens (or hundreds) of people and spend thousands or even millions of dollars, only to once again collapse down to a few people with little or no activity following the end of principal photography. The most popular person in the company becomes the person with the checkbook. The most important person becomes the *comptroller*, the person supervising the accounting and financial reporting for the film company.

Professional titles should be matched to business duties, since legal obligations attach to titles such as "president of the corporation" or "managing member of the LLC." Such positions should be reserved for the people who have the authority to carry out their obligations on the project; they should not be used as credits with which to bargain or reward. To clarify the ultimate management and control of the production, the filmmaker should hold a key management position in addition to an artistic title, putting all other employees within the filmmaker's professional jurisdiction.

The producer has the business responsibility for managing the organization. If the filmmaker is the director of the film and holds the position of president of the film company, then the producer may be a vice president. When the filmmaker is not the producer, the company's Operating Agreement must be explicit that the filmmaker still has primary authority, with the producer deriving all authority from the filmmaker.

As a practical matter, however, the director will be busy enough making the movie and should welcome assistance managing the operations. The producer must manage the business decisions. This may include coordinating with the line producer, location manager, and others to ensure that schedules continue to function, that each expenditure is within the budget and fully authorized for payment, and that all laws, regulations, and agreements are signed and followed.

Occasionally, decisions will meld the art and commerce of filmmaking. Weather can wreak havoc on film schedules, and decisions to postpone, relocate, or eliminate scenes are necessarily a compromise between business and artistic interests. Most decisions, however, tend to be either artistic choices (e.g., the color palette for a set) or management ones (e.g., the budget to build a set). The producer and director must both know when they must consult each other. They should meet regularly to keep each other apprised of the ongoing progress. Separately, each manages a team of people and a multitude of decisions. Adopting a collaborative structure encourages the most efficient and least contentious planning process possible. This is not to suggest there will not be problems, merely that the problems will not be caused by simple confusion and misunderstanding.

3. Audience Control

In keeping with the ongoing engagement needed to maintain an online media company or to position an independent film for successful festivals, screenings, and sales, it is critical that the production company has an online presence from the beginning of its existence. That means having a website; a channel on YouTube, Twitch, and additional media platforms; and an engagement strategy to share with the growing audience for the content and to empower the audience to share and reshare the content coming from the production company. All of this must be accomplished while the production company stays on the task of creating its original content.

To manage the social media and audiovisual presence for the production or series, the company should engage in this third vector of control and management from the beginning of operations. Much like the filmmaker and the producer, the media and community engagement director plays a critical role in the planning and organizing the production. If the production company relies on advertising revenue to support or supplement its budget or if a crowdfunding or crowd financing campaign will require substantial marketing, the failure to have a dedicated senior leadership position focused on these goals will strangle the film company and make it much more difficult to succeed.

These essential steps to market and monetize the project will often be treated as distractions by both the filmmaker and the producer. The consequences of ignoring the social media opportunities and media platform needs will become much more apparent only when the completed project is languishing without public interest. Even for the most traditional of narrative feature projects, attention to these elements will increase the likelihood of landing a sales agent and distributor. For projects that are predominantly or entirely designed for digital distribution, these elements are essential building blocks for its later monetization.

4. Resources to Outsource

Some of the more important but mundane tasks of the film can be readily outsourced for arguably less money and certainly greater efficiency. The management of the film company remains responsible for these outside providers, but their services make the process more professional and better structured.

The most important area to outsource is the payroll function. As mentioned in chapter 4 (pp. 57–64), payroll has a host of legal obligations regarding taxes, insurance, withholding, and reporting requirements. All of these obligations can be transferred to a payroll house rather than being handled internally. Many firms handle basic payroll, including a number that specialize in the motion picture or entertainment industry. Their services should be able to accommodate any union obligations the film company has undertaken, and some will be able to continue to provide residual payments due as income flows from nontheatrical media.

Either as part of the bundled payroll service or separately, employment taxes should be outsourced as well. This increases the chance that proper tax filings will be made not only in the first year of the film production but also in years to come, when fewer people remain professionally associated with the project. Similarly, legal and accounting services are typically outsourced.

To the extent that a professional with experience in the industry can provide any management function for a price comparable to that of internal personnel, the filmmaker should consider outsourcing the task. If the failure to perform the task will result in legal liability or risk of injury, then outsourcing becomes the better choice.

G. Insurance

In addition to the completion bond (see chapter 9, pp. 176–178), a number of other types of insurance should be considered by every film company. Ultimately, the amount of insurance purchased depends not only on the budget but also on the level of protection the participants in the film deserve. Insurance is a fundamental obligation of the production company. All but the smallest of projects need insurance to protect the employees and volunteers from accidents that can occur while making the film.

1. Workers' Compensation

Required in many states, workers' compensation insurance provides automatic medical insurance for work-related injuries. In some jurisdictions, this coverage is mandated by law and must be included in the production budget. Even where voluntary, participation in a state workers' compensation system provides an essential protection for the cast and crew at a cost much lower than that of most private insurance systems. In some states, workers' compensation insurance will extend to volunteer crew members. In others, supplemental coverage can be purchased to ensure that the unpaid members of the company are provided this minimal level of protection. Workers' compensation also protects the employer from lawsuits resulting from personal injury. It is an extremely inexpensive and valuable form of insurance that should be purchased to extend to all participants on the set.

2. Property Damage Liability Insurance and Auto Insurance

For any production shooting on location, property damage liability insurance must be purchased to protect the film company and the locations on which the company operates. For each private location, the property owner will be added to the policy as an additional insured. Most municipalities will also require this protection for the use of public areas. Similarly, for production vehicles used both on and off camera during filming, comprehensive general liability and auto liability insurance remain a necessary part of doing business.

3. Equipment Insurance

The rental cost of film and lighting equipment represents only a tiny portion of the total value of the equipment. As a result, the rental fees may include equipment insurance. If not, the equipment owner will invariably require that the film company purchase its own insurance to protect these assets. Given the number of things that can go wrong, this is certainly valuable coverage for most productions.

4. Errors and Omissions Insurance

Errors and omissions insurance protects the distributor (and potentially the exhibitors) from liability based on the content of the film. The insurance company defends lawsuits and indemnifies or pays for the cost of any losses that arise from defamation, invasion of privacy, or copyright liability claims, along with other claims based on titles, piracy, plagiarism, or theft of ideas. Particularly given the more controversial nature of many independent films, the purchase of errors and omissions insurance is critical.

Often, purchase of errors and omissions insurance may be left to the distributor or at least until the time of distribution. The danger with deferring the purchase is that any content changes required by the insurance company may cause minor inconveniences during principal photography but will become much costlier and more difficult to make after the cast has dispersed and the sets are no longer available.

5. Other Coverage

In addition to the four categories of insurance listed, a number of other policies may be necessary depending on the shoot and the budget, including specific insurance policies for aircraft, watercraft, animals, and flights. These additional protections may be useful—and occasionally even required—but only in select situations.

The elements of the production may also be insured, including the props, sets and wardrobe; the cast; the film negative; and other media. Finally, insurance may even be available against the weather. Given the size of the investment, the filmmaker can select the degree of risk and the benefits of insuring against likely risks. Considering the other uses of funds in an independent film production, however, most insurance policies are not particularly popular with independent filmmakers.

12

The Key Members of the Independent Film Company

Although many jobs that must be filled have already been introduced in the context of financing and planning the production, brief job descriptions may be helpful to understand the broader role each plays in the filmmaking process.

The variety of jobs does not necessarily require the same variety of personnel. A truly guerrilla documentary can be created by a single person. Nonetheless, that filmmaker still fills each role, alternately serving as producer, director, writer, and editor. The cast, sets, costumes, and other elements are taken as they are found, but decisions regarding their inclusion are continuously being made by the director. As a result, the filmmaker takes up many of these tasks as well.

Every production will mix and match the personnel hired and the roles that must be filled, depending on the skills of each individual and the depth of the budget. Regardless of who performs each activity, most of the activities themselves are essential to the successful completion of the picture.

A. The Producer

1. Job of the Producer

The *producer* provides the key leadership, management, and supervision for the entire film project. This includes the "creative, financial, technological and administrative [process] . . . throughout all phases of production from inception to completion, including coordination, supervision and control of all other talents and crafts, subject to the provisions of their collective bargaining agreements and personal service contracts."[1] Like the CEO or president of a corporation, the producer is responsible for all final executive decisions and personally participates in many choices made in every aspect of the project.

A good producer must have a solid grasp of the financial, artistic, and technical aspects of filmmaking. Often the task requires that the producer bring strong-willed professionals together to make hard decisions that balance the filmmaker's vision against the financial resources and technical limitations of the project. Experience, problem-solving skills, and strong management techniques are the essential qualities of a good producer.

Executive producers, on the other hand, are generally involved in the project only indirectly, helping raise funds or coordinating multiple films at the conceptual level. Few independent films have executive producers, except as a way of securing additional capital by providing the credit to inactive but essential financial participants. Occasionally, executive producer credit is provided to important cast members who use their influence to sign the remaining members of the cast and crew. By taking an extra hand in the production, these actors empower the film to go forward.

The *associate producer* title is often liberally distributed to production participants who undertake many of the producer's duties, whether in coordination with the producer or by their own initiative. Although this credit is sometimes used in bargaining, independent filmmakers may wish to grant associate producer status to the individual who stands out throughout the production process, the unsung hero who went well beyond the job description or who paid to ensure that the project was completed.

2. If the Producer Is Not the Filmmaker

The Producers Guild of America distinguishes between entrepreneurial producers and employee producers. In the independent filmmaking context, the *entrepreneurial producer* is the filmmaker—the person who initiated the project. An *employee producer* is a person hired by the financier of the project to manage the film's production.

If the filmmaker is not an entrepreneurial producer, then an employee producer must be hired. The employee producer must have clear direction to follow the leadership of the filmmaker, reinforced through the hierarchy of the business and the employment contracts. The producer's control of the budget gives the producer significant authority over the film, so the filmmaker can retain control only to the extent that the producer answers directly and exclusively to the filmmaker.

This is not to suggest that the filmmaker should avoid hiring a producer. Most artists lack the experience, problem-solving skills, or management expertise to serve as producer. A professional producer will add perspective to the project, enabling the filmmaker to make prudent, responsible choices. Provided the producer can be overruled by the filmmaker in appropriate situations, the advice and alternative viewpoints will prove invaluable.

3. How to Select

Unlike some other independent film roles, an employee producer is only worthwhile if truly qualified. On-the-job training can occur, but an experienced producer adds incalculable value to the production company. If no such individual is willing to work within the production budget, it is better to forgo the employee producer and spend whatever money is available (whether in salary, deferrals, or revenue participation) on an experienced consultant who can provide some regular guidance throughout the film project.

If no experienced producer is available, the job will fall to the filmmaker. There is nothing inappropriate in the filmmaker retaining the credit as sole producer—or credit as coproducer if that is the reality of the production—as long as the sole producer credit has not been granted as part of anyone else's employment agreement.

When choosing to hire a producer, the filmmaker should do more than review the candidate's prior credits. A producer's level of participation can vary dramatically from one project to another, so have extensive conversations with the producer's former directors and other colleagues. These conversations should help the filmmaker better evaluate whether the producer is qualified and whether the style and approach to filmmaking is compatible with the filmmaker's goals and expectations. More than any other relationship on the film, the compatibility between producer and director is critical; it will set the tone for the rest of the production. The filmmaker may find it helpful to meet with the prospective producer on a few occasions, discussing the project and soliciting advice.

A prospective producer should be willing to invest a little time up front as a way of doing due diligence on the film. (Remember, the producer also has to decide whether this film is a good fit based on the potential producer's interests and career choices.) This trial period provides a good opportunity to test the strengths and styles of both the producer and the filmmaker, so that each can assess whether the combination will be successful. The most successful producer/director relationships can last decades, enhancing the careers of both participants.

4. Deals for the Producer

The entrepreneurial producer is invariably among the most highly compensated participants in the film project. Often the producer's salary is relatively modest, but the producer will seek a significant percentage of the revenues. A filmmaker who can serve as producer should expect to see a much larger return than one who works with an employee producer.

Producers are committed to the project for the long haul. They should agree to be available for all of preproduction, principal photography, and postproduction and, as reasonably necessary, to oversee all the marketing and distribution issues thereafter, including the supervision of the foreign language versions, dubbed editions, special edits, and other longer-term projects.

A producer may be interested in a long-term relationship as well, including a right of first refusal on the director's next project or at least on any sequel or prequel undertaken during the three years following the initial theatrical release of the film. The compensation package may even extend to a small portion of any sequel and prequel rights or rights exploited in other media, such as television or live theater.

B. The Writer

1. Job of the Writer

The motion picture screenwriter may be the loneliest person in Hollywood. Although the job may include the development of the story, the preparation of the treatment, or the writing of the shooting script, each of these tasks is done in relative isolation. To protect its members from loss of credit and status, the Writers Guild insists that the writer's work be highly restricted and noncollaborative. While this does not stop collaboration from occurring, it does illustrate the solitary nature of the writer's role in the process. The job for the writer will depend significantly on the relationship of the story to the screenplay. The writer of an original screenplay will typically play a much more central role than a person adapting a novel or dramatizing a true story.

a. Spec Script

The screenwriter's *spec script* is a work created on speculation. The author completes a screenplay without any prior agreement from the owner of the story, which the author then offers to producers, directors, and companies to produce. A spec script may be based on a story idea original to the writer or an existing story in the public domain. Occasionally, the spec writer will actually purchase the literary rights to a copyrighted source work—but given the low chances the project will be produced, the costs associated with purchasing the underlying literary rights make this approach infrequent and rarely successful.

Many independent projects use another form of spec script. In this case, the filmmaker approaches a writer with an opportunity to pen a script for the project. Any payments for the script are dependent on whether the filmmaker likes the submission. This form of writing on spec is prohibited for members of the Writers Guild, since the screenwriter assumes all the risk of the script not being accepted, and, if the finished script is rejected, the writer cannot take it to a different producer because it is based on the story provided (hopefully, in writing) by the filmmaker.

b. Original Screenplay

For the majority of film projects, a screenwriter is hired to write an original screenplay based on an idea the filmmaker or production company provides. The screenwriter works as an employee of the film company. In this process the writer usually submits a first draft, meets with the producer and possibly the director to review their thoughts on the script, and, based on their notes and the subsequent discussion, revises the script into a final draft. There may be multiple interim versions before the screenwriter considers the work the final draft, although multiple submissions are not contemplated under the Writers Guild minimum structure.

In this scenario, the production company is the copyright holder of the script, and the writer is paid for the submissions pursuant to the agreed-upon payment schedule, whether or not the film is eventually shot or distributed.

c. Nonoriginal Screenplay

A nonoriginal screenplay differs from an original screenplay in that the story idea or source material already exists. If the film will be based on an existing stage play, for instance, then much of the story and dramatic structure will already be in place. Even some of the dialogue may be taken from the play. The film adaptation may be significantly different from the stage version, or it may change only the physical attributes of opening the scenes up from the confinement of the stage.

To develop a nonoriginal screenplay, the production company must own the rights to the source material or at least have nonexclusive permission to use it. The company may have purchased the film rights from the playwright or novelist or be using true life stories compiled from newspaper accounts. In any case, the screenwriter bases the work on the materials and rights acquired by the production company.

d. Rewrites and Polishes

The writing process seems never to end. Final scripts are often revised on a daily basis for a variety of reasons. Casting and location choices each dictate certain script changes to better reflect the people and places that will actually appear in the film. Cast members frequently offer suggestions to reshape and grow their characters. Humor that works in print sometimes fails to translate to the screen. Personnel changes among the producers, directors, designers, and cast can alter expectations. Finally, some people always tinker, not knowing when to leave well enough alone.

A film polish should be focused on details: refining particular lines of dialogue or punching up the script with some added humor. The polish should not be a comprehensive rewrite of the film, but there is no specific dividing line. Both rewrites and polishes are often provided by additional screenwriters who revise the earlier writer's final draft of the script. The process can continue indefinitely.

Invariably, even filmmakers who do not serve as their own screenwriters become involved in script revisions, at least to some extent. For union productions, advance notice and other guidelines exist to protect union writers from losing screen credit to this tinkering, but true collaboration or rewriting by the filmmaker can meet union muster, if done properly.

2. Protecting the Filmmaker as Story Writer

Often, the filmmaker will write the initial treatment for the project well before engaging a screenwriter. The filmmaker must be cautious, however, to protect against losing any advantage in the creation of the work. Stories abound in which similar projects by different production companies race through production to be first to market. This can happen because public domain literature has become popular on stage and in print, because historical stories gain modern relevance, or just by random chance.

If a filmmaker were to meet with a writer and suggest a story for the writer to create as a spec script, there is no legal limitation on the writer regarding the script eventually created. Instead, the filmmaker must take concrete steps to protect the project. First, the more concrete the story provided by the filmmaker, the more likely the story will be entitled to copyright protection. As explained in chapter 5 (pp. 77–78), copyright law does not extend to ideas, merely their expression. The law will protect a detailed plot or treatment but not a mere story or idea. In addition, copyright will protect the filmmaker to the extent that the treatment is written down in a tangible form. So an oral pitch will not be entitled to copyright protection, but the written treatment will. The filmmaker may wish to register the treatment with the Writers Guild (see chapter 5, pp. 90–91), because it provides dated evidence of the treatment's content. Writers Guild registration does not provide any additional legal protection.

In meetings with prospective screenwriters, the filmmaker should also make it clear that the filmmaker is retaining "story by" credit. The filmmaker should be willing to share that credit if the story is significantly enhanced or altered by the screenwriter, and should explain this to the prospective writers as well. A written invitation to the meeting—even in the form of an email—should be enough to document this position. The email or other written note explaining the "story by" credit will help clarify the agreement between the film company and the writer when a contract is ultimately drafted.

Finally, in rare cases the filmmaker may wish to require that the writer (as well as producers and others) sign a nondisclosure agreement (see chapter 6, pp. 108–110). The nondisclosure agreement merely provides that the information disclosed will not be used except for the filmmaker's benefit, unless the information becomes generally available to the public through no fault of the recipient of the disclosure.

Nondisclosure agreements are not common in Hollywood, but they have become ubiquitous in the software industry and other fields devoted to intellectual property. Realistically, few producers, distributors, or financiers will be willing to sign a nondisclosure agreement, but the spec writer should be willing. For the filmmaker, it provides protection for the idea behind the film in addition to the copyright protection that extends only to the expression.

3. How to Select

The selection process for the writer or writers depends on where in the production cycle the film presently stands. The best way to know whether to buy a script is to read it—to commission a spec script and hire the writer only if it meets the production's needs. Despite the position of the Writers Guild, many writers are willing to write scripts on spec, even for a production company that owns the underlying story idea and rights. In fact, the writer's speculative risk is not significantly different from the risk taken by the filmmaker who will sell the finished film through a film festival only if the audience receives it warmly. However, the filmmaker should not commission a spec script from more than one writer at a time. To do so shows a lack of respect, if not bad faith, on the part of the filmmaker. The writers should not be bidding or competing against each other.

The primary alternative to commissioning spec scripts requires that the filmmaker evaluate prospective writers on the basis of previous screenplays and credits received. When applicable, the filmmaker should compare the writer's script to the finished film to better gauge the work actually contributed by that screenwriter. Since screenplays are rewritten constantly, judging a screenwriter by the filmed work may not show the true picture. Many new writers, however, are not likely to have produced many films with credits. By reviewing their own spec scripts (as opposed to a newly commissioned spec script), the filmmaker can assess their writing styles and skills.

To help evaluate the body of work submitted by the screenwriter, the filmmaker may request sample pages for the current project rather than a full script. In this way, the writer can demonstrate writing skills and the approach to the project but not be forced into the labor-intensive process of creating an entire screenplay. The filmmaker can assess the writer's timeliness of delivery, style of writing, ability to listen to suggestions, and artistic sense for the filmmaker's material. Otherwise brilliant writers may fail on any given project if they do not have the right eye for the imagery, ear for the dialogue, or taste for the story. The request to review sample pages works particularly well with an up-and-coming screenwriter who has only a modest body of previous work. In contrast, for a seasoned veteran writer, such a request may not be appropriate.

4. The Role of the Union

If a writer is a member of the Writers Guild, then union rules prohibit the union member from working with a nonunion company. Whether the individual writer chooses to follow this rule, however, is the writer's choice more than the concern of the production company. The only danger in working with a union writer on a nonunion production is that union member could later refuse to deliver a script unless the film company signs the WGA Theatrical and Television Basic Agreement (commonly called the Writers Guild Minimum Basic Agreement, or WGA-MBA). On the other hand, the filmmaker could easily walk away, so the risk of a writer repudiating the agreement is small.

A film company may become a signatory to the WGA-MBA simply by contacting the Writers Guild. The WGA-MBA provides an excellent structure for negotiations whether or not the writer is actually a member of the union.

5. Deals for the Writer

The minimum writer's fees outlined in the WGA-MBA can help the film company determine appropriate compensation. Fees are linked to the type of writing requested, with the writer earning a greater amount of money for writing both the treatment and the screenplay than for writing the screenplay alone. Similarly, writing an original screenplay is worth more than writing a screenplay based on literary rights owned by the production company.

The payment should be based on delivery of both a first and a final draft. The number of iterations between them should be specified in the contract, such as a *first draft*, *intermediary draft*, and *final draft*. If the production has cash available, then the writer should be paid a portion of the total amount at the delivery of each installment. A schedule should be used that offers incentives for early delivery and stipulates the right of the production company to reduce payments for late delivery or to terminate the agreement.

Even if the majority of the screenwriter's salary will be deferred, the production company should provide some cash payment at each delivery point, unless all other salaries are also deferred. The screenwriter should not be singled out for complete deferment. When all or most of the writer's fees are deferred, depending on the size of the budget, it may be appropriate to provide some percentage above WGA-MGA minimum. In this way, the writer may earn, say, 150 percent of minimum in the event the film fully covers its deferred costs.

Under the WGA-MBA, the screenwriter's minimums are automatically increased if the production budget exceeds the low-budget minimum. Even with a nonunion writer, tying the deferred salary to the production budget (with both a floor and ceiling) allows the screenwriter to benefit proportionately from any significant increase in the project's scale. Though highly imprecise, paying the screenwriter a minimum of 1 percent of the film's total production budget may reasonably approximate the negotiated fees for films in the low-budget and blockbuster range alike.

As mentioned in chapter 11 (p. 209), another important provision of the WGA-MBA provides a means for establishing writing credit in the event of a controversy over which writers contributed to the finished film. The WGA-MBA includes mandatory arbitration provisions, but even without a union writer, the filmmaker should retain the right to award credit based on each writer's contribution, limit the number of parties entitled to screen credit (perhaps subject to the producer's discretion), and incorporate an arbitration clause, so that the determination can be made without resorting to a court proceeding in the event of a dispute. Additional interests, such as profit or revenue participation, should be available only for the credited screenwriters. The total participation may be divided among the credited writers or earned by a single writer if that writer receives sole writing credit.

In addition to salary minimums and credit guidelines, the WGA-MBA also provides that the screenwriter should have some access to the shooting set. A nonunion contract should retain this provision as a professional courtesy to those writers who receive writing credit. Similarly, the writers receiving credit should be afforded the opportunity to screen the movie at a time when any feedback may still be valuable to the filmmaker and the editors. The writers should also be included in the promotion of the film;

they should be mentioned in all written materials and potentially included in junkets and film festival appearances as well.

Despite some competition between writers and directors over the paternity of a project, the writer is often a highly dedicated part of the creative team who provides a great deal of additional, uncompensated assistance to help get the project completed and distributed. Industry custom provides much helpful guidance to filmmakers, but participants and resources should not be lightly dismissed simply because of those customs.

C. The Director

1. Job of the Director

According to the Directors Guild of America, the job of the *director* is "to contribute to all of the creative elements of a film and to participate in molding and integrating them into one cohesive dramatic and aesthetic whole."[2] This somewhat vague description nonetheless captures the essence of the director's role. The director (typically the filmmaker but not always, as described previously) supervises all the creative elements of the production, imprinting a particular vision of the story, sound, design, and essence of the film onto the project. Technically, the director need only be responsible for the actions of the cast and the camera; in reality, the director remains integral to the entire production.

Though many projects rely on multiple screenwriters, few employ more than one director. In those unfortunate situations in which it is required, it results in significant confusion. The director is usually attached to the project early and thereafter participates in all the other employment arrangements for the production. The director should know about, or help decide, virtually all issues involved with the production, including the casting, employment of other creative personnel, and creative decisions involving the script, locations, set design, scheduling, and postproduction editing. The producer generally has authority over the director, but throughout most of preproduction and principal photography, the director has practical control over much of the project.

If the director joins the production after a final screenplay has been delivered, there is a strong chance that the director will request additional script revisions. The director will work with the producer and location manager on locations, revising the budget to accommodate the choices made. The director should also participate closely in the casting decisions. During principal photography, the director will coordinate the creative elements of the film, directing the action and filming each day and typically reviewing the rushes of the day's shooting each night.

When the filming is completed, the director will assemble the cut of the film. If the director is someone other than the filmmaker, the director may not have the right to determine the final cut of the film, but the director should be given the opportunity to create an initial version. The producer or filmmaker should provide comments to the director, who may wish to act on those comments to revise the edit of the finished film. If not, the director will have completed the work, leaving final tweaking (or more significant editing if the parties do not agree on the film) to the filmmaker. The director will also participate in the promotion of the film in all venues.

2. How to Select

If the filmmaker is not the director, then the selection of the director is a critical step in the production process. The wrong choice can cripple or kill the project. Because of the practical difficulty in terminating a director, the filmmaker must work closely with the candidate to determine whether their visions are compatible.

There is no meaningful way to conduct a tryout for the filmmaker's particular project. Filming is dependent on too many choices, and early work may not be indicative of later decision-making. Instead, the filmmaker should review the previous projects helmed by the potential director and speak directly with those projects' producers, along with cast members, production crew, and others.

Thorough due diligence is a must. The filmmaker should pay particular attention to the comments of former cast members who have worked with the director; they may be in the best position to gauge overall effectiveness and temperament. If former cast members are reluctant to work with the director again or have significant doubts about the director's abilities, the filmmaker should be very attuned to these concerns in determining whether there is a pattern of troubling behavior.

3. The Role of the Union

Since its inception in 1939, the role of the Directors Guild has traditionally been to provide representation on issues of credit, control, and finances. The DGA represents directors, assistant directors, and unit production managers. Because the motion picture has evolved into a director's medium more than the medium of any other artist, the union focuses primarily on its relationship with the studios. Within the independent filmmaking arena, the filmmakers are typically the directors, so the union has little to do in that respect. Nonetheless, the DGA Basic Agreement (DGA-BA) can be a useful guide even in the context of low-budget nonunion filmmaking and is mandatory for any union production. The DGA-BA provides for compensation minimums, mandatory credit, and rules on the relationship between the director and the production company.

The DGA also offers the DGA Low Budget Agreements with schedules ranging from under $500,000 to under $11 million. The DGA has significantly improved its flexibility, allowing for directors to negotiate without union minimums for projects below $2,600,000, including the initial compensation, daily rate, and preparation time. This improves the opportunities for union directors and for independent filmmakers to work with more experienced directors.

4. Deals for the Director

Whether or not the production is governed by the DGA-BA, the agreement provides useful guidance on the proper relationship between the director and the filmmaker. To the extent that a nondirector filmmaker wishes to retain control of a nonunion project, certain protections may be modified, but most of the director's creative rights are essential to a quality production and should be honored.

Before hiring the director, the filmmaker and the candidate should go over the key issues of the production. Unless the director comes into the project knowing these issues, the relationship may get off to a rocky start. The DGA-BA provides excellent guidance on the important discussion points:

- Budget for the film, or at least its top sheet (see chapter 9, p. 171)
- Proposed shooting schedule
- Names of creative personnel already employed
- Shooting methodology
- Any rights of script approval or cast approval contractually reserved to any person other than the filmmaker and producer
- Story and scripts presently available
- Any other artistic and creative commitments

These points really detail the significant issues that the director and the film-maker must agree upon when structuring the film project. The scheduling, budget, and creative decisions will dictate as much about the film as any choices made during the filming process. A director who does not participate in these decisions is at a severe disadvantage, one that might not be overcome.

In addition to forging a common understanding, the filmmaker must also address the director's concerns regarding compensation, credit, and control. The director's compensation package will most likely include some combination of salary (paid and deferred) and either profit participation or revenue participation. Unlike producers, directors only occasionally participate in revenues rather than profits. If the filmmaker is attempting to lure a well-respected professional director to work on a low-budget independent film, revenue participation can make up for substantially lower budgets and resources than the director earned on higher-budget projects. On the other hand, the filmmaker can offer very modest compensation to a relatively inexperienced director, who will likely jump at the opportunity to direct a feature film.

Director credit has not historically proven controversial. If a director must be replaced partway through production, a choice must be made as to who is awarded the credit. The general assumption is that the second director is the person with the greater influence on the final look of the film and has the better relationship with the production company. A subsequent director who shoots as little as 25 percent of the footage may still dramatically reshape the project and therefore be awarded shared or even sole directorial credit. The DGA-BA requires that the initial director receive credit if that individual had completed at least 90 percent of the film, though a choice can be made to award credit to both. Similarly, a nonunion contract should provide that the first director will be guaranteed director credit only if 90 percent of principal photography is completed prior to the end of employment and only if there has not been a material breach of the director's contractual obligations. Otherwise, the filmmaker should retain discretion on how to award the credit.

Unlike a straightforward director's credit, the "a film by" credit has proven to be more controversial. When first conceived, this credit was reserved for filmmakers who both wrote the screenplay (or at least the story) and directed the film. A trend has emerged to grant this additional credit to directors even if they were not writers on the project, but there is no obligation to do so, and giving the film by credit to a person who was not the filmmaker would be inconsistent with the role of the filmmaker in an independent production. In the independent filmmaking world, "a film by" should be the credit of the filmmaker, if anyone.

The most controversy involving directors' contracts stems from issues of control. The producer controls the budget and authorizes expenditures, while the director is responsible for determining the *need* for all expenditures. The same division of authority applies to hiring, selecting locations, and many of the production decisions. As a general matter, the contract may simply provide for consultation by the director with the producer on these issues, but that contract will be highly unsatisfactory if relied upon. For salary expenses, the DGA-BA identifies which support staff can be selected by the producer (such as the unit production manager) and which by the director (the first assistant director). To be effective, the producer must provide more than cursory consultation with the director and instead collaborate closely so there is a common understanding of the film's budget as it is used to shoot the film. Consultation rights also extend beyond the budget. For example, significant changes to stunt work require advance notice to the director, who may object to the change based on any legitimate concern. Perhaps more important than the right to consult on significant changes is the right to be notified in advance of any producer-ordered changes.

Finally, under the DGA-BA, the director must have some assurance regarding participation in the postproduction process. The union agreement requires that the director be allowed to assemble a *first cut* of the film, without interference from producers. Once this initial edit is done, the director might have *final cut* authority over the film; if not, the producers may step in and reedit the film. Final cut is a contractual right not protected by union agreement. Regardless of the director's final cut authority or the union status of the film, the director must be allowed to create the first cut and should be invited to participate in the rest of the postproduction process. Since the final look of the film is so essential to a director's future, offering anything less than reasonable consultation seems highly inappropriate. Unless the director has been terminated for cause or has become an obstruction in the editing process, the director should at least serve as an advisor to the producer or filmmaker throughout postproduction, including the final cut.

D. The Media and Community Engagement Director

As described in chapter 11 (p. 221), the media and community engagement director has evolved into a leadership position that sits outside of both the production's artistic process and the production's operations. It is the third leg of the overall production stool, responsible for audience engagement and creation of the collateral written, print, and audiovisual content needed to support online media demands. The title for such a position varies significantly for the position in different business sectors, and there is no real consistency yet in the entertainment industry. This book uses *media and community engagement director* because the traditional duties include overseeing the production of collateral material used by sales agents and distributors to market the film to the exhibitors.

Another possible title is *manager of direct response giving*, which describes a crowdfunding, fundraising, or development officer. Other titles include *brand specialist, business development representative, marketing director, communications director*, and *outreach and engagement director*.

1. Job of the Media and Community Engagement Director

The media and community engagement director is responsible for furthering the vision of the filmmaker through the production of collateral material to be used throughout the preproduction, principal photography, postproduction, and distribution phases of the company's operations in order to build and engage an audience for the film or series; to coordinate all aspects of any crowdfunding activities and engage the public in the campaign to support the project financially; to monetize the production company's online presence through advertising revenue, donations, and product sales; and to build an audience base of passionate friends and followers that will demonstrate the importance of the film or series to distribution partners.

The media and community engagement director should operate like other creative department heads on the project, overseeing a staff that includes a still photographer and videographer who are dedicated to the marketing effort rather than being primarily involved in the actual show production. If the scale of the project is not sufficient to have a staff, then the media and community engagement director may also serve as photographer or videographer. In other situations, the production videographer may have specific duties assigned by the film director to support the media and community engagement director, but this requires good coordination and communications. Also, like other creative departments, there should be a Media and Community Engagement department with an established budget to enable the media and community engagement director to be successful.

The media and community engagement director may consult with the director and producer regarding content for trailers, use of production elements, and other film or series content. The goal, however, is to build resources that complement the film and do not cannibalize the production or harm its eventual distribution.

For production companies that choose to self-distribute the film, the media and community engagement director can become the point person at this stage in the company's production cycle. That authority will empower the media and community engagement director and likely free the film-maker from duties that the filmmaker would prefer not to undertake.

2. How to Select

The duties of the media and community engagement director are quite varied, and the emphasis will vary significantly depending on the online media strategy selected for the production company as well as the role of any crowdfunding activities. For example, if the production hopes to use crowdfunding as a significant part of its financial strategy, then hiring a person with significant crowdfunding experience is a great benefit. Similarly, if the company is looking to build an online community and maximize its advertising revenue, then it should be looking for individuals who have extensive backgrounds with these revenue streams. Regardless of the strategy, the individual should have had some experience running social media campaigns for other organizations.

The position has subsumed the traditional work of creating production collateral in support of the distribution efforts, but this position is not primarily a content position. The role of engagement is the most critical function for the position.

In addition to having the technical skills for the social media, web revenue, and crowdfunding outreach, the person filling this role must understand that the work is at once essential to the success of the project and secondary to the creative work of the filmmaker. There have certainly been the occasional "making of" shorts that were better films than the features they were intended to market, but the goal is to support the creative vision of the filmmaker rather than to compete with the filmmaker or the film. This requires a person who is adept at managing from below and collaborating with a team while also being able to work without much direction from either the producer or the director. In short, the ideal person has strong interdependent leadership skills that enable the person to be wholly independent one moment and a staff officer the next.

3. Deals for the Media and Community Engagement Director

Positions related to the media and community engagement director are loosely organized and generally outside any of the unions. Promax is a membership organization that caters to this segment of the entertainment industry, but it has only a general connection to the role.

The production company should value the position as senior leadership, with the level of seniority tied to the emphasis on either the crowdfunding campaign or the advertising and online media presence. If either of these was intended to be 100 percent of the production financing, then the media and communications engagement director would likely be compensated with a package substantially similar to that of the producer. If these represented less than half the revenue or if the production was not using streaming except as a fallback if theatrical distribution failed, then the position would likely be more comparable to the unit production manager or assistant director.

If the film company knows it will self-distribute its project or will possibly do so if it does not receive a sufficiently attractive distribution offer, then the company may include provisions in the media and community engagement director's contract to shift this person into the leadership for the distribution phase of the production cycle. This might entail an increase in the revenue participation and a paragraph specifying the duties to coordinate the ongoing marketing efforts, to work with the various online platforms and other distribution outlets, and to coordinate continuing efforts to promote exhibitions at live venues along with marketing support to improve the streaming rates and online rentals and sales. (See chapter 20, pp. 374–382.)

E. The Production Team

1. Jobs of the Unit Production Manager and First Assistant Director

The team of unit production manager (UPM) and first assistant director (AD) fill out the senior management of the film production. The UPM implements the decisions of the producer, and the first AD implements those of the director.

The UPM oversees the logistical details of the production, working through the budget, scheduling, finance, travel, and myriad additional issues that affect the film. The UPM will negotiate many of the agreements for the production and arrange (and rearrange) the production schedule. On union productions, the Directors Guild governs UPM positions despite their budgetary role.

A related position to the UPM is that of *line producer*. On an independent film, there is likely to be a line producer or a UPM, but not both. In a larger production, the UPM may be a permanent employee of the producer who moves from one film project to the next, serving each project exclusively while the producer provides nonexclusive services to a number of films at various stages of development. In this situation, the film company may also hire a line producer who has on-set operational responsibility for the film's expenses.

The first assistant director runs the set, ensuring that each day's schedule is ready for the director—that the call times for shooting, costuming, and makeup are coordinated so each cast member can be costumed and ready in time for the first scheduled appearance. The first AD works with the cast and serves as an intermediary between cast and crew whenever necessary.

Any significant changes made by the UPM or line producer must be filtered through the first AD so that the production can continue to operate smoothly. Like the relationship between producer and director, the relationship between UPM and first AD must be one of respect and constant communication, to set the tone for everyone else.

Although the two team members' tasks are interrelated, they are not interchangeable. The first AD must monitor and participate in the ongoing production and coordinate each day of the shoot. The UPM, in contrast, will often be working on what comes next, adjusting production schedules to account for weather or other uncontrollable variables, revising the budgets as expenses come due, and preparing for the design and logistics issues that come up throughout the production.

Even on the smallest of films, both of these roles must be filled continuously. To reduce the number of participants on a film project, the filmmaker is more likely to succeed by merging of the roles of producer and UPM, or the roles of director and first AD, than by collapsing the UPM and first AD into a single role.

2. How to Select

The primary criteria producers consider when they choose the UPM or line producer and that directors consider when they choose the first AD are the qualities of trust, respect, and confidence in the relationship. More than any other positions, these two roles are extensions of the needs of their supervisors. A personal rapport is essential, so wide latitude should be given to individual preference in the selection process.

If someone is to be hired who has not worked with either the director or producer before, the key is to look for a track record of organization, efficiency, initiative, attention to detail, and experience on film sets. These two roles serve as the engine of the project, propelling the cast and crew late at night, early in the morning, and into long weekends when exhaustion is setting in. They are also the face of the production, because the producer and director do not spend as much time among the rank-and-file production personnel as they do. Their capacity for tact, respect, and professionalism—or lack thereof—reflects directly on the director, producer, and production company. The employer should be concerned about these attributes as well.

Often, production assistants move up through the ranks to become second ADs and eventually first ADs. Others may follow a similar track to become line producers or UPMs. By identifying these climbers early in their career, even a low-budget project may be able to employ someone with strong potential and a reasonable amount of experience.

3. Deals for the Production Team

Both the first assistant director and the unit production manager are covered by the DGA. For a union shoot, the DGA-BA provides the minimum compensation and credit obligations. As with the director, a side letter agreement may be used to reduce the costs to employ union talent in these roles. The side letter may also allow for limited nonunion personnel in these areas, particularly if an experienced director or producer can use the opportunity to train and promote someone who has worked on prior union productions.

F. Cast

1. The Actor

The actors portray the characters in the film. More formally, acting may be defined as "the performing art in which movement, gesture, and intonation are used to realize a fictional character for the stage, for motion pictures, or for television."[3] The task is as simple as that, but it remains perhaps the most difficult role in the creative arts. Some film roles may be portrayed by experienced professionals with years of training to project their emotions on film. Others are portrayed by untrained individuals who simply appear onscreen in the manner sought by the director of the film. Casting choices are often the most fundamental to the success of the entire project.

As mentioned earlier, the independent filmmaker may be a cast member rather than one of the other participants in the film. When an actor has achieved some degree of fame, an independent film may provide an opportunity to both star in and direct the project, as Ed Harris did so successfully with *Pollock*, Denzel Washington with *Fences*, or Bradley Cooper with *A Star Is Born*. For less well-known actors, an independent film may be a chance to star in a role that no other producer would offer. Particularly for minorities and women, independent films offer the ability to create opportunities rather than to wait for Hollywood to offer them. Many independent films may be fueled, at least in part, by the desire of actors to play these hard-to-find parts.

a. Casting Directors

Except on productions with the most modest of budgets, filmmakers rely on casting directors to provide them with information and advice on the actors to be sought, based on suggestions made by the producer and director and *breakdowns* of the script—brief synopses of each character in the film. An experienced casting director has access to talent agents representing union talent, a database and personal knowledge of potential cast members' experience, and some insight into their income histories and box office appeal. By analyzing information about the actors' prior film contracts, the casting director can help negotiate reasonable salaries for the cast and avoid unnecessary delays or unrealistic choices.

For many independent films, the producer and line producer or UPM fill the role of casting director, soliciting the talent agents of potential cast members. To the extent that the producer and director have personal working relationships with any of the preferred cast members, these relationships may serve better than any formal process to interest the actors in the project.

b. Breakdown Services

To inform actors and their agents of the roles to be filled, casting directors rely heavily on script breakdowns. For over 30 years, Breakdown Services Ltd.[4] has been the leading provider of these character synopses, which are available free to casting directors and producers. Breakdown Services' staff writers read and analyze approximately 30 scripts daily, writing the casting information that talent agents download directly from the Breakdown Services website. Based on the breakdowns, agents may submit cast members for the production. In some situations, with the producer's approval, Breakdown Services also allows the actors themselves to access the breakdowns directly. The growth of the Internet and rapid changes in Internet business have expanded how casting information is distributed, with additional tools for filmmakers and actors alike.

Breakdown Services provides an efficient method of providing cast information to the talent community at little cost or trouble to the producer. The true work comes next: sorting through the potentially thousands of submissions to narrow the field and begin the process of auditioning.

2. Talent Agents and Managers

For union projects, the primary official contact flows between the casting director or producer and the agents for the talent. Talent agencies will receive the breakdowns of the script, and, at the same time, the casting director will contact the agents for the star talent that the filmmaker has in mind for the key roles. Occasionally, the agent will be interested in the project. More often, filmmakers pursue stars that prove to be outside the budget for the project, unavailable for the scheduled production period, or simply uninterested in working on an independent film. With tremendous perseverance, however, the production will begin to generate interest from actors whom the filmmaker might wish to cast.

The talent agent's obligation is to maximize a client's income and professional opportunities—which coincides with the agent's own financial interests; typically, the talent agent is entitled to 10 percent of the client's revenue. Occasionally, an independent film script will be powerful enough to convince an agent that the role could transform the client's career. More often, however, the agent will regard a client's participation in an independent film as the loss of the opportunity to work on a higher-paying, higher-profile project. As a result, talent agents are generally a hurdle rather than an aid to independent film production.

An agent will typically suggest a number of other, less-established clients who may be appropriate for the roles identified in the breakdown sheets. Among these less-known performers may be some stellar talent. One of the true benefits of the independent film process is that it provides opportunities to undiscovered talent both behind and in front of the camera.

To attract strong, well-recognized talent, however, the filmmaker should use all available resources to contact potential cast members through informal means. This is where personal and professional relationships make the largest difference. On a low-budget project, a single known star may guarantee at least a streaming distribution agreement. Such a "bankable" star will encourage financing, improve press coverage, and lend credibility to the project. Once an actor becomes interested in the project, the negotiations will still be conducted by the talent agent. It is important, therefore, that the filmmaker work to keep the talent agent somewhat positive toward the project so the agent does not convince the actor to avoid the role.

Some actors also have personal managers. For nonunion actors, a personal manager may be the only professional willing to assist them. If an independent film role might expose an actor to a broader range of opportunities or reinvigorate a stagnant career, the manager may see long-term value in such a relationship. Managers, therefore, are a useful avenue for the filmmaker to attract talent. However, managers should not negotiate contracts or actively pursue job opportunities; that is the exclusive domain of talent agents. Filmmakers should be leery of any manager acting as an agent, particularly in California. Such a manager is likely violating California regulations, various union rules, and other contractual limitations. Particularly in states that regulate talent agencies, such activity is inappropriate and may lead to complications if any dispute arises involving the talent agreements. The filmmaker should therefore always work directly with the actor or through the agent, if represented.

3. Advertisements

In addition to the formal casting processes, using casting directors and breakdown services, a myriad of online databases have developed that allow actors to submit their pictures and resumes for review. Unless the film requires someone of truly unique talent (such as a 4'9" soprano or a sword-swallowing juggler), these databases may be of limited value. On the other hand, some of these sites allow the filmmaker to post casting requirements or breakdowns directly. For nonunion shoots, this may greatly expand the range of possible talent available.

One of the premier traditional casting resources now boasts not only a magazine presence but also Internet resources. *Backstage*, formerly the *Back*

Stage East and *Back Stage West* newspapers, publishes short cast descriptions for both union and nonunion productions. These listings are free and widely read (see http://www.backstage.com). For many independent projects, most of the cast members come through either personal relationships or these advertisements.

4. Auditions and Casting

For motion pictures, casting can take one of three general forms. For well-known performers, no true audition is required. Instead, a meeting or interview will be held between the actor and director to discuss the part and give both parties a chance to get acquainted. While there will be some discussion of the character and the vision of the director, the actor will not be expected to perform the part. This meeting may include some readings from the script, but they are not necessarily required.

For less high-profile actors, a more formal audition may be held. In this setting, the director, casting director, and perhaps the producer or line producer/UPM will observe as an individual actor presents a scene from the production, often together with another actor who has already been cast. If, for example, the film is to star a particular female lead, she may be willing to read the part with a few different actors in the role of the male lead so the director can better judge the chemistry between the actors.

At the other extreme is the *cattle call*. This invariably humiliating experience allows the producers and director to observe potentially hundreds of unknown actors reading for roles in the production. Actors with any modicum of success will not participate in cattle calls, but for unknown actors, cattle calls represent an opportunity (admittedly much like a lottery ticket) to land a smaller part on a production. Casting directors who submit breakdowns through Breakdown Services Ltd. may not then use a cattle call to review the talent submitted. It should really only be used as an alternative to a request that actors submit resumes directly. Also, since the process is painful for both the actors and the producers, cattle calls should not be used unless the production seriously plans to cast from the process. As a backup plan, it is far too time-consuming and disrespectful of the actors. Where it will result in actual casting, however, many, many actors are willing to endure the indignity.

5. The Role of the Union

SAG-AFTRA, which represents both film actors and extras, not only provides for minimum salaries, pension, and health care benefits for its members but also governs work conditions on productions. Regardless of whether a union contract is signed, the independent filmmaker should abide by the SAG-AFTRA requirements designed to provide a safe working environment. Almost every major film accident occurs because work schedules were violated or safety rules ignored. Most independent films do not have the resources to survive even a modest accident, and no film is worth risking the lives of cast or crew.

Under a SAG-AFTRA agreement, the minimum salary for actors depends on the production budget, the amount of time the performer will be in principal photography, and the specific contract signed with the union. SAG-AFTRA provides a range of agreements, ranging from major studio production contracts to contracts designed for student films shot for academic credit. Because of the number of different contracts available—and because they are constantly fluctuating—the filmmaker should contact the closest SAG-AFTRA office early in the preproduction process to determine whether a union agreement can be arranged. The obvious benefit of shooting under a SAG-AFTRA agreement is the ability to cast professional actors. If even one of the preferred cast members is a member of SAG, then the production must enter into a SAG-AFTRA agreement.

Perhaps the biggest drawback to a SAG-AFTRA production manifests itself if the film is to be made outside of a traditional SAG-AFTRA market. SAG-AFTRA operates approximately two dozen regional offices, each covering a carefully mapped geographic zone. Shooting outside those zones can increase the costs under the SAG-AFTRA agreement considerably, so locations should be selected with this in mind. Alternatively, if a particular out-of-zone location is central to the film, the filmmaker may instead opt against using union talent.

The union has created an outreach for independent productions under SAGindie, which "promotes the working relationship between professional actors and passionate independent filmmakers."[5] The department promotes the use of SAG-AFTRA talent in independent production. The ultra-low-budget agreement for projects budgeted under $300,000 allows for both union and nonunion talent.

6. Extras or Background Performers

SAG-AFTRA now provides for union representation of extras, having merged the former Screen Extras Guild into the union. The union agreement requires that a specified number of union extras be hired before nonunion extras can be employed. The particular number depends on both the contract under which the production is authorized and the location of the shoot. For contracts involving low-budget projects, this requirement is often waived.

7. Deals for the Actors

In addition to the primary issues of compensation and credit, cast members are generally concerned about their obligations to the production, mostly regarding the production schedule. The filmmaker usually will be required to accommodate the schedules of the key cast members, particularly if they are working below their normal salaries to participate in the film. In addition to the dates of principal photography, the contract must provide that the actors will be available for any necessary reshoots and for postproduction looping, or redubbing. The contract will typically include a minimum number of days of looping and establish a pay scale for any additional days needed.

Financially, the independent filmmaker also needs to take into account the cost of agents and managers. An agent's 10 percent of each client's revenue cannot reduce a SAG-AFTRA actor's pay below the minimums of the collective bargaining agreement, so the film company will be expected to pay union minimum plus 10 percent. Moreover, because the contract between actor and agent requires that the all funds be paid to the agent and then disbursed, the 10 percent is also subject to the health, welfare, and pension obligations of the film company to the union, which run nearly 20 percent of the payment.

Because agents recognize that the payment amounts for union-minimum, low-budget shoots provide little income but important goodwill, many are willing to waive their commission if the actor asks them to do so in advance of the production. As long as this is planned, and the film company has made it clear to the actor that waiver of the commission is a part of the pre-arranged agreement, budget surprises can be avoided.

The talent agreements should also include contractual obligations to promote the film. For stars working below their normal salary, a contractual commitment to promote the film may be difficult to negotiate, but it should be part of the package for other cast members. Even a small amount of promotion may be critical to the success of the film, so the filmmaker should work to encourage participation, contractually or otherwise.

If there is a possibility of generating additional revenue through ancillary products, soundtrack albums, or other merchandise, then the contract should specify that the film company has the right to commercialize the publicity rights of the actors on these products. The provision should limit the use of each actor's publicity rights to products directly associated with the film, and should include a royalty payment to the actor. The royalty typically will be based on a percentage of income paid to the film company for the item or items.

If the company has contracts for product placement, the manufacturers providing those products may hope to use actors to promote the products in television commercials or Internet ads. Any such arrangements are best negotiated directly between the actor and the manufacturer. SAG-AFTRA provisions will govern the use of its members in commercials, so these provisions will need to be added by separate agreement. The film company should be paid for the use of the film footage in any such advertising, which is in addition to the use of the actors. The agreement between the manufacturer and the film company may include these provisions or they may be negotiated later, if the manufacturer decides to expand beyond product placement into commercials.

13

Equipment and Locations

The legal and business choices in this chapter should be secondary to the aesthetic production goals of the filmmaker. The digital revolution has dramatically affected the range of equipment available, and the business practices are slowly adapting to that change. The ability to digitally alter locations during or after the shoot creates an entirely new set palette with which to paint the images. Each choice affects every other choice.

A. Types of Equipment and Contracts

1. Cameras and Lights

The production company will rent a package of camera equipment and lighting equipment, plus stands, electrical generators, and other related equipment for the film production. Digital's lower cost, ease of shooting, low-light capabilities, and instant recording make it the standard for independent filmmaking.

The filmmaker can still choose 35mm film stock, which continues to be produced by Kodak, but over 90 percent of films are now shot digitally. The 35mm film requires significantly more lighting power than any other format, which requires the film company to select lighting equipment that complements that shooting format. The size and weight of the 35mm camera will also require that most moving shots use dollies or similar equipment.

Whichever format is chosen, rental prices will vary significantly from company to company and region to region. Be sure to shop around. In some areas, it may be cheaper to travel considerably to rent equipment than to pay local prices. The rental contract should always be between the production company and the equipment supplier. The filmmaker should avoid accepting personal liability for rental fees or for any damage to the equipment.

Often the fee will include equipment insurance. Be sure to include this and other costs when comparing potential suppliers. If the production company carries adequate insurance already, it may offer to include the rental company as an additional insured on its own policy rather than paying for an additional policy. Flexibility on this point will vary from company to company.

Finally, some suppliers have weekly rates that offer significant savings over the base cost of daily rentals. They may apply a weekly rental fee equivalent to three or four days of rental. Careful planning is necessary, however, because most contracts do not allow for extensions to convert a daily rental into a weekly rental. It may more be cost-effective to rent for a full week rather than for two days, in case the production schedule proves to be overly ambitious.

2. Firearms and Other Weapons

Filmmakers often wish to use real weapons in the creation of certain scenes. While this is commonly done, independent films that intend to use fewer personnel and guerrilla filming techniques should nonetheless be ready to comply with detailed, time-consuming regulations and supervision. A handgun or rifle is subject to licensing and permit requirements even if it is not operable on the set. While temporarily disabling the weapon is a good idea for safety purposes, it will not change most licensing requirements. If it has been permanently disabled—the interior components rendered unworkable—then it may not be subject to licensing requirements, but even that will vary from jurisdiction to jurisdiction. Swords and other weapons may not have the same licensing requirements, but they may still create a public disturbance if brandished on the street.

In most jurisdictions, even if no film permit is required for the production under the local rules, the production company must still have a film permit if a firearm will be used. And not without reason: In one instance, a shot was fired as part of a lawful, independent shoot on a private farm. The police were called to the scene of the "shooting," the production was shut down, and the production company was assessed substantial fines for the false alarm. Had the production obtained a permit, the police would have had a record of the planned use of gunfire on the set, and the production could have continued.

State and federal laws govern both real weapons and look-alikes. These laws require the production companies to plan ahead when using weapons on sets. If firearms or other weapons are part of a scene, filmmakers should contact the film office in the jurisdiction where the filming is scheduled well in advance of the scheduled shoot. Filmmakers may wish to take advantage of services licensed to provide weapons and pyrotechnics rather than try to borrow props for the filming.

3. Stunts and Special Effects

Stunts and on-set special effects both involve specialized activities with significant degrees of risk. Stunts typically include fight scenes, falls, or other highly choreographed movement. Special effects typically involve pyrotechnics—explosives or fireworks—that in most jurisdictions require state licenses and local permits, even on private property. Both should be conducted under the supervision of experienced professionals, no matter what the production budget.

Attempts to create homemade pyrotechnics can result in serious injury. Unlicensed attempts may void the production's insurance coverage and will certainly make the participants in any accidents personally liable for the losses. If injuries or expenses related to an unlicensed accident disrupt the production budget, the filmmaker might conceivably be personally liable to the investors as well, because the filmmaker's personal negligence cost the production its opportunity to be completed. Needless to say, unlicensed pyrotechnics should be avoided.

Even relatively simple stunts should be done only under the careful supervision of a stunt coordinator. Of course, the line between action and a stunt is not always clear. Common sense should serve as a guide. If the action, done improperly, could result in one of the actors being seriously hurt, then it should be treated as a stunt and conducted only after it has been well rehearsed and all risks have been minimized.

4. "Renting a Crew Member"

Just as stunt coordinators and special effects experts are employed for specific tasks, so are specialized technicians such as the *gaffer* (electrical expert) or *key grip* (individual in charge of the movement of lighting and camera). For nonunion projects, these professional trade union positions may be unnecessary. Particularly on small, digital productions, the filmmaker may reduce the need for such specialists by using handheld cameras and limited professional lighting.

In certain situations, however, a gaffer or key grip may be required. Rather than hiring the person for the entire project, it may be possible to enter into a special arrangement that covers only the particular scenes needed. However, this would not necessarily be compliant with the expert's union obligations. Asking a professional union member to work on a nonunion project runs the risk that the person could be forced to leave the set if requested by a union representative or if the person has a change of heart. This risk can be minimized if the person is hired for a short duration to assist with particular segments of the film.

Alternatively, the producer may determine that the project is complicated enough to require a union crew. The International Alliance of Theatrical Stage Employees (IATSE, or IA) provides locals for all below-the-line production personnel. The IATSE low-budget agreements have three tiers, with Tier-1 for productions no more than $6 million, Tier-2 for productions above $6 million and not more than $10 million, and Tier-3 for productions above $10 million and not above $14.2 million. For productions substantially below the Tier-1 level, the costs may still be prohibitive.

Other professionals, notably the director of photography and the sound mixer, are often package rentals along with their own equipment. If the production rents the equipment, the operator is supplied. Producers should be sure, however, that the production requires the professional services in addition to the equipment. The producer will have far less control over these packages than by renting the equipment from a rental house and employing the professional separately. On occasion, this can limit the producer's discretion over the quality of either equipment or personnel. The producer must carefully scrutinize the references of anyone offering a package. On the other hand, rental equipment does not always perform perfectly, and the professional's familiarity with the equipment may save time and money. Experienced sound mixers and directors of photography provide welcome efficiency and cost-effectiveness for the independent filmmaker.

B. Selecting Locations

In a visual medium, location choices convey much of the story. Each location should be treated as one of the characters in the script. Independent filmmakers often choose to blur the locations represented in the film or otherwise render them unrecognizable, but this denies the filmmaker one of the film's chief assets. Instead, effective use of the film permit process and solid legwork will allow the filmmaker tremendous flexibility in the locations represented in the picture.

1. Use of the Soundstage

The Hollywood of the 1930s built tremendous soundstages where controlled environments could be used to create any set imaginable. The obvious benefit to such spaces is control. Soundstages are enclosed, providing for excellent sound and allowing the production company to reproduce exactly the settings envisioned by the filmmaker. In addition, small portions of rooms or areas can be constructed, allowing even a 35mm camera to move into spaces that it could never enter in the real world. Soundstages also provide certain efficiencies because all the production facilities center on a single location.

The film industry has witnessed another transformation as the soundstage of the 1930s has been augmented by non-Hollywood locations such as the Long Beach geodesic dome (former home to Howard Hughes's *Spruce Goose*) and other major facilities in which film locales can be built. This trend blurs the distinction between soundstage and location shooting. These spaces are not owned by the studios and exist outside of Hollywood. They are typically rented on a long-term basis so that multiple sets can be constructed in the space.

Dedicated soundstages, however, may be too expensive for all but the largest of independent films. The independent filmmaker may instead create a temporary soundstage, by using a larger space as a one-stop location for multiple sets. In a shuttered warehouse, a school building during summer break, or a similar structure, the filmmaker may enter into a single lease that provides a range of environments that can be adapted to various scenes needed throughout the film. Legally, the issues are the same as with any location shoot (see the following discussion).

2. On-Location Shooting

The modern trend for filmmaking—both independent and studio pictures—has been to move out of the studio and into natural locations. Location filming adds realism to movies and expands the range of tools available to set designers even when the designer modifies the location to represent other spaces (such as using futuristic architecture to represent science fiction settings). Location shooting necessarily includes a certain amount of set decoration. If a filmmaker is shooting a film set in the 1950s and selects a neighborhood because of its period houses, then modern attributes must be hidden or removed. A period film cannot retain visual credibility if the featured exterior has a satellite antenna.

Location shooting agreements enable the production company to use the property for the purposes of filming, to portray it in the film, and to alter its name or image in any manner. The film company generally will pay for the right to use the property. Any planned alterations to the property should be specified very carefully in the agreement. Usually, the film company will agree to restore the property to its original condition. When appropriate, however, the film company can agree to make modifications to the property that the owner is permitted to keep, such as repairs to the exterior, repainting, etc. The filmmaker should identify the property owner and the tenants (if different) and add each one to the film company insurance as an additional insured, regardless of whether the party is included in the contract.

In New York and Los Angeles, property owners are very sophisticated about the use of their properties, while in other parts of the country, even the smallest of feature films is a rarity. In any event, the filmmaker should be prepared to discuss other details of the shoot. The property usage agreement may need to specify the use of electricity, telephone, water, or other utility services, provide for late-night access that could entail asking the residents of a residential property to stay at a hotel, and detail the parking requirements. Filmmakers should also be prepared to negotiate with commercial property owners regarding business loss during the period of production. If a filmmaker proposes to shut down a retail business during filming, the business owner will want to be compensated for the lost revenue. Even if the film's eventual release will result in improved traffic to the store, most shop owners will insist on current payments.

Although property owners have very limited rights to stop the use of photographs taken of their property, the same location agreement should also grant the film company the right to make photographs and films of the location. Additionally, a paragraph should be included that acts as a general release of all claims against the film company for use of the images (such as defamation or rights of privacy or publicity)—just in case.

Famous buildings require slightly different agreements. Although an owner may have no right to the copyright in a publicly visible building, if it serves as a visible symbol of a corporation, it may enjoy trademark protection. In addition, the building may have ornamentation—sculpture or murals—that are protected by copyright. In such cases, express permission from the copyright and trademark holders is highly recommended. The First Amendment may serve as a valid defense to any claims for a documentary filmmaker, but for a feature film, there is ample opportunity to secure the shooting rights. Finally, it should be noted that the copyright and trademark rights holder in this situation might not be the same as the tenant of the building who has the exclusive right to grant access. Instead, the building owner must be contacted (usually through the property management company), and perhaps the original artist as well, to gain full permission for the filming.

3. Permits and Requirements

In New York, California, and major metropolitan areas throughout the United States, a filmmaker must obtain a film permit in order to conduct any commercial filming. This often does not apply to news filming and may be inapplicable to documentary filmmakers under either the terms of the particular film ordinance or the First Amendment. As a general rule, film permit requirements are designed to protect the community from the disruptions caused by large productions, and a small digital camera is an advantage, as it will generally go unnoticed on a city street.

Whether a film permit is necessary from a practical standpoint, the permit process in most major areas has become increasingly simple, and the filmmaker may find that the local film commission provides significant assistance in the making of a film. Most film offices have libraries of available locations for shooting. They may also have experience with various locations throughout the area, and they can work with the filmmaker to minimize any disruption to areas in which the filming takes place.

There are very few requirements for obtaining a film permit. The nature of the production must be specified, with particular attention to the number of trucks and amount of parking the shoot will require. Any weapons or pyrotechnics must be detailed, and their use processed through the fire marshal or other specified authority. Finally, there will be a minimum insurance requirement. If the filming will take place on city, county, or state property, then the film office will also require that fees are paid for the use of the property, that usage restrictions are met, and that the jurisdiction is named as an additional insured on the film company insurance.

As cities and states have begun to recognize the enormous economic value filmmaking offers to local communities, most film offices have streamlined the permitting process and provide very helpful resources fully available to the independent filmmaker. Film offices—particularly that of the Office of the Mayor of New York City, the California Film Commission, and FilmLA, the L.A. film office—all provide tremendous resources for independent filmmakers. Other city and state film offices, attempting to compete with Los Angeles and New York, have also grown in scope and resources. Independent filmmakers should take advantage of these resources to the greatest extent possible to reduce costs and improve the quality of the production.

C. Tax Incentives for Location Shooting

As states and cities recognize the value to local incomes from the payments made by film companies and the long-term benefits for tourism by having films use locations for filming, more and more states provide tax incentives to film companies as a way to lure them into the jurisdiction to film or keep them from leaving for Canada or overseas. These reimbursements vary greatly from state to state, but because they can be considerable, filmmakers should take them seriously when deciding where to film.

These incentive programs tie tax benefits to production costs spent in the state or employment opportunities offered to state residents or both. Some programs require the film company to maintain offices in that jurisdiction, while others focus more heavily on itinerant productions. Incentives range from exemption from paying sales taxes or hotel taxes to significant tax credits. Tax credits provide the film company with an offset of its production expenses that can be applied to its future earnings. Some states have tax credits as high as 50 percent of the production budget—which would allow half of the production expenses to be paid from tax credits in years of future revenue. Other states even allow for the credits to be sold to other companies, providing an asset that can be used to finance the film.

The programs in each jurisdiction vary significantly from each other, and states modify the terms almost annually. The local film office provides the best resources for understanding how to maximize the potential tax benefits, and every program is available on the website of the film office or office of economic development.

As discussed in chapter 7 (pp. 149–150), tax credit opportunities should be considered early in production planning, when deciding in what locations to shoot the film. However, because these programs limit eligibility based on whether payments are made within or outside the state and may set similar limits for the employment of personnel, their benefit must be weighed against the project's overall location and personnel needs. If these needs are not harmed by the limitations of the incentive program, then the use of tax credits to finance the film creates some very nice opportunities.

(14)

Shooting the Film

A well-organized production should anticipate most legal and practical issues before arriving on location. To accomplish this, the film company must practice good planning and professional organization. Typically, these responsibilities fall to the location manager, working in conjunction with the line producer, UPM, or producer.

A. Scheduling

Filmmakers rarely have the luxury of filming the script in chronological order. They must schedule the film around those resources that cannot be controlled. First, stars often have only limited dates available to shoot—particularly for the low-paying independent filmmaker. Their availability will set the start and end dates of the shooting schedule. Second, if certain locations are only available during a particular week, then other locations must not be scheduled during that window. Third, weather cannot be controlled, but it can be prepared for. Indoor shooting days should be left until the end of the production so that if inclement weather prevents a scheduled outdoor shoot, those indoor days can be moved up and production will not be shut down waiting for the weather to change. Fourth, budget constraints must be considered. There is no reason to pay people who are not working, so, typically, the larger production days are grouped first and cast and crew are slowly let go as the shooting schedule calls for fewer and fewer people.

Because weather constantly changes, as does the availability of cast and crew members, even the most rigid schedule is likely to be changed throughout the production process. Proposed changes must be evaluated against the other constraints of locations, cast, and budget, and the UPM must be sure that everyone involved in the production is kept constantly aware of the changing schedule. Contracts for locations and equipment should specify target dates but allow the filmmaker to adjust those dates as the production requires.

Each day, the production will prepare a *call sheet* specifying who will be working the following day. The call sheet will provide information about weather conditions and the preparations needed to deal with the weather; information about parking and logistics; and the precise scenes that will be filmed so that the corrects sets, costumes, and props are prepared for the day's work. Since films are rarely shot in sequence, the call sheet provides the critical information confirming the work to come on the following day.

B. Preparing Locations

Well in advance of the day of filming, the location manager must provide the property owner with a contract that specifies exactly what changes are to be made to the location and how they are to be made. Typically, all modifications to the property will be temporary, so the contract should provide a schedule that includes preparation time, a period of filming, and a period for striking the set and returning the location to its original condition.

1. Working the Neighborhood

If the changes are significant or the filming will otherwise affect neighbors, then the location manager should contact them as well to let them know what is happening and, to the extent possible, enlist their support. This is particularly important if the production will shut down streets to traffic, even for short periods. Even a guerrilla filmmaker working with a single handheld camera will need neighborhood support, and a modestly sized independent film project can be quite an intrusion into a neighborhood. Trucks carrying lighting, electrical generators, film equipment, sets, and costumes, and the cars of cast and crew, add up to a logistical invasion larger than most construction projects. The need to remove cars from street parking for exterior shots can become quite a complex task, particularly if the individuals refuse to move their cars voluntarily and the film company requires the city to close the street to parking.

To minimize disruptions, the filmmaker must communicate closely with those who may be inconvenienced by the filming. At least two weeks prior to the scheduled shoot, the location manager should contact the owners of all the properties that may be affected. The location manager should inform the property owners and occupants of the dates of the proposed shooting, the scheduled starting time and approximate end time, the nature of the film and that it is an independent feature (it may be helpful to include some promotional information), the particulars of the shoot (if it involves exteriors, interiors, moving vehicles, etc.), and the needs of the company. If sound matters, then the notice should request that no lawnmowers be used. If a historical period is being recreated, modern cars may need to be removed.

The production company must provide the name, telephone number, and email address of the film company's contact person—and respond immediately to any request. A follow-up should be made the day before the shoot. For most locations, the neighbors typically will be quite helpful.

Business owners will be concerned about interference with their customer traffic. Filmmakers must be prepared to avoid disruption or to work with affected store owners. In some cases, this may include negotiating with a local chamber of commerce on behalf of a large number of retailers. Here, timing becomes critical: interrupting business is much more expensive in December than in January.

2. Closing Streets

If an exterior shot using closed streets is planned, then the city and the police department must be involved. The film company will be most successful if it can minimize the disruption. Given the start-and-stop nature of filming, the filmmaker should consider using intermittent traffic stops. Rather than closing the street, production could stop traffic only while the cameras are running. For many films, intermittent traffic stops are all that will be needed to capture the necessary shots.

If a street must be closed for any significant period of time, the film company must work closely with all the regular users of that street. To close a street, a local film permit is absolutely required, unless the jurisdiction does not issue such permits. The permit is typically conditioned on the film company providing alternative parking, patrolling the intersections to control traffic (or hiring off-duty law enforcement personnel to do so), and gaining the permission of the affected residents or businesses. To get such permission, payment is sometimes necessary, but a tactful request, permission to observe the filming, or an offer to provide pastries or cold drinks often suffices.

C. Daily Production Requirements

Independent filmmakers should utilize the community surrounding their locations to the greatest extent possible. By working with local vendors, the film company may reduce its expenses and improve its relationships—particularly important if the location in question will be used for an extended period. The area Lowe's or Home Depot often benefits tremendously from location shooting. Film companies may also opt to provide cast and crew with prepaid vouchers from local restaurants in lieu of craft service, if it can be arranged in a cost-efficient manner.

1. Set Preparation: Utilities Basics

All but the smallest sets require significant electricity, water, and sewage capability, and the ability to control sound. Unfortunately, these needs are not necessarily compatible. Each of these elements must be planned in advance with careful attention to local regulations.

Electrical power may be obtained through portable generators, temporary *power drops* attached to utility poles (provided by the local electrical utility), or the existing electrical service of the location. The choice of electrical source will depend on the size of the production, the resources available, and the duration of the shoot. If an agreement has been made in advance, a small guerrilla shoot should be able to plug lights directly into the location's power service. A large production will need to bring its own generators, unless it plans to use the location for a significant length of time. In that case, arranging a power drop with the local utility will become more cost-effective. A second advantage of using a temporary power drop is the avoidance of the noise and fuel consumption of portable generators.

If portable generators are selected, the location must be carefully mapped to park the generators sufficiently far from the shooting that their noise does not interfere with the production sound. Large power lines will snake from the generators to the lights and production equipment. The scale of this equipment increases the complexity of location shooting considerably, and adds to the size of the crew.

Water and sewage are also important considerations with any location filming. Water availability varies dramatically from area to area. In urban areas, water hookups are often provided by the location, because the cost to the landowner is not significant. Where well water is used (and in areas facing drought conditions), access to water may be costly and difficult to obtain. If the location will not provide water, then the local utility must be contacted to connect a hose to a fire hydrant, if available, or to provide other suggestions for temporary connections.

The same approach applies to toilets and sewage. The scale of the production will dictate the size of the facility necessary. If the location has facilities, arrange to use them. If that cannot be done, or if the size of the production makes it impractical, then the company will need to rent a *honey wagon*—a trailer with built-in dressing room and bathroom facilities. Most honey wagons will need water and sewage hookups, although honey wagons with storage tanks are also available. In addition, portable toilets that do not use local water may also be rented if no other alternative is available. These options are all more expensive and cumbersome than making arrangements with the location, so the contract with the property owner should be negotiated with these needs and expenses in mind.

2. Parking

Often overlooked, crew parking is a significant logistical component of location shooting in some areas. Even a small production may require extended parking for 10 to 20 vehicles. Larger productions should include a "campsite" area with enough space for individual cars; cast trailers (mobile homes starting at 35 feet in length); a honey wagon ranging from 35 to 65 feet in length; a 35-foot trailer for wardrobe, makeup, and the grip truck; and a much larger truck for lighting and electrical production equipment. Add the portable generators and the parking area can grow to the size of a small college. Locations must be selected that can provide support for these needs. If necessary, the automobile parking can be moved to a remote location and the production can use a van or car as a shuttle between the parking and the rest of the camp.

D. Staying in Control

To keep the location operating smoothly, the location manager must work closely with the line producer or UPM and first assistant director to ensure that the location is used as efficiently, productively, and legally as possible. Efficient use comes from coordinating the shooting schedule and the activities of the cast and crew on the set. Productive use comes from maximizing the amount of usable film shot—by creating multiple scenes at each location so some areas can be prepped while others are being used for filming. Legal use includes compliance with the location permit and its restrictions and with any location agreements.

1. Logistical Planning

Coordination is the key to controlling logistics on the set. When dealing with rental of equipment for the film location, scheduling and availability of equipment is critical. In areas familiar with the motion picture industry, equipment rental companies have a great deal of expertise. In other areas, however, local vendors may not be familiar with the production company's needs. The UPM must be sure to negotiate with these companies and put the dates and times for each piece of equipment into the contract. The location owner must be fully apprised of the equipment that will accompany the shoot so that there are no surprises the morning of filming when the trailers and equipment roll up.

To be cost-effective, timing each piece of equipment is also critical. It may be more affordable to rent a location for an extra day, allowing the set designers and crew more time to prepare the set before the grips and electrical are scheduled to arrive. The honey wagon might not appear on location until the third day. By staggering the activities, costs can be controlled, but the UPM must truly understand the activities occurring on the set at any given moment. Scheduling should take place on an hour-by-hour basis rather than day-by-day.

2. People Planning

Hour-by-hour scheduling is also essential for effective management of locations and personnel. Idle cast and crew reduce efficiency, while a missing cast member can bring the entire production to a halt. Since the UPM manages the crew and the first AD manages the cast, the two must carefully coordinate call times and the day's schedule to be sure that the right people are always available and planning to work on the same scenes.

Independent productions are generally less structured than larger-budget studio films, and crew members may be willing to pitch in to help with needs outside their primary responsibilities. If crew members are given the ability to work on both today's and tomorrow's shooting schedule, they can be kept involved more effectively than in traditional shoots.

3. Budgeting and Cost Control

The original budget for the film should be treated as a historical document, retained in its original form as a tool for comparison. Actual expenditures will begin to deviate from that document before filming even begins. As a result, the budget will need to be updated constantly to reflect the actual expenditures and to project additional expenses necessary to complete the film. For example, if the screenplay requires an additional, unbudgeted polish, the money for it must come out of some other area or the total cost of the film must be increased. Most independent films cannot afford to increase the budget, so something else must go. If the choice is to eliminate a location and its associated costs, the set budget must reflect this change, or the elimination of one location will merely allow the set designer to spend more on other locations. Both the budget and the schedule must reflect every change, and interim budgets should be kept on file.

The need to account for actual expenses becomes most pronounced during location filming. In the heat of the shoot, crew members are often sent out to buy necessary but forgotten items. These last-minute expenses can add up. For a small independent film, such expenses can overwhelm the budget. Receipts should be turned in within minutes of the expenditure and must be turned in by the end of each day. Even on the largest studio shoots, every dollar spent must be accounted for with a receipt, and every receipt must reflect a particular budget item.

The filmmaker must look at expenditures daily to ensure that the production remains on time and on budget. If either the schedule or the budget starts to go awry, the filmmaker should make adjustments. The earlier adjustments are made, the smaller they generally need to be. Careful management can keep problems to a minimum.

4. Costumes and Props

Movies with any significant budget will provide that all costumes be purchased by the production company and can be worn only on the set. To ensure that a film sequence is not ruined by the destruction of a costume, every significant character's costume will have a backup. Even if the perfect pants for a major character can be purchased for $5 at the Salvation Army, the film company may still have to spend hundreds of dollars to reproduce an exact copy by hand. If a costume is used in scenes involving dirty, out-door activity—running through thick woods or climbing rough mountain terrain—the production should probably have three or four duplicates so that the filming can continue quickly if a costume is torn or heavily soiled.

Not all costume damage comes from the scenes being shot. When the cast helps out on the set, it adds another risk to the maintenance of costumes. Clothing can get very dirty from someone helping with lights or moving equipment. Great care must be taken to protect the clothes used for filming.

Properties or *props* also require great attention and care. These are the nonfixed items on set that are handled by the film's characters. If a photograph rests on a mantel, it is set decoration. If that photograph is picked up for a moment by one of the characters, it becomes a prop. Actors take a strong, proprietary view of the props they use and may become very particular about the nature of the props. Like costumes, any props subject to wear and tear need to be backed up by identical copies to ensure that filming will not be held up if something happens to the item.

Managing the props can take a lot of time and energy, far more than first-time filmmakers may expect. Every item needs to be cataloged and carefully noted when it is checked out to the set, so that all the props are returned every night. Some props are only on loan to the film company and need to be returned to their owners once they are no longer required. Failure to return these props can create a significant additional expense for the film company.

Finally, film shoots generate a lot of interest in souvenirs. When members of the public watch filming, they may want to pick up props as small mementos. Cast members and extras often want personal souvenirs, and the props they used are available and important to them. If people are allowed to steal these items, the film company loses all control. If scenes need to be reshot, or if sequences are shot out of order, the missing props may be needed later in the production.

Even the cast and crew may not realize the importance of keeping all props available, so film companies may want to manage their expectations by allowing them to request props to take as souvenirs at the end of production. Keeping a log of requests for those items the producer is willing to give away will let the cast and crew know that there is an acceptable way to earn a memento and will help discourage the casual pilfering that can become very costly on some productions.

E. Managing the Content in the Frame

Although film is an expressive art form, it is also an increasingly international and highly commercial business. Filmmakers should therefore be very selective regarding choices to use a third party's property—copyrighted works, trademarks, readily identified individual names or corporate names—without express permission. Permission is not always difficult to come by. Without the express permission, the errors and omissions insurance (see chapter 11, pp. 223–224) may be drafted to exclude any liability for the use of such content, and the lack of coverage may discourage distributors or exhibitors from buying or showing the work.

The issues regarding clearance become more difficult in the context of international film distribution. Different countries have very different approaches to censorship and to the kinds of content deemed inappropriate. In some cases, this relates to third-party ownership rights, and in other cases it relates to the action being filmed. In the United States, filmmakers risk changes to their MPAA ratings for depictions of smoking. In countries where alcohol is banned, the exhibition of drinking may be discouraged or banned as well. In some cultures, religious images may not be photographed. For example, images of the prophet Muhammad are banned from exhibition in some countries. And depictions of nudity are treated very differently from country to country and from medium to medium.

1. Script Clearance

When a shooting script is prepared, it should be sent for *clearance review*, to ensure that the filmmaker has acquired all the rights necessary to film it. The resulting script clearance identifies all the script elements that may give rise to third-party ownership claims. It will identify the potential legal issues and will instruct the film company to consult with the production attorney to resolve those issues. Many of the topics of the report are discussed elsewhere throughout this book: acquisition of literary rights, purchase of life-story rights for fictional works and documentaries, acquisition of music, and location agreements. The report should be reviewed carefully by the film company and its lawyer to identify the rights that must be acquired and the situations that can be avoided.

Script clearance should be undertaken well before principal photography begins. This provides the production company with sufficient time to make any script changes necessary and to acquire permission for all items to be included in the film. If some of the permissions are not forthcoming, it is helpful to have enough time to seek permission from alternative sources.

Documentaries have a very different set of demands for clearance. Because a documentary filmmaker generally does not artificially create the content of shots, a documentary production may rely much more heavily on the fair use privilege, which allows the incidental inclusion of copyrighted material. Nonetheless, documentary films should also be subject to a clearance process, and documentary filmmakers should minimize conflict with other rights holders when practical. The unique considerations and processes are dealt with in chapter 15 (p. 276).

2. Coverage Shots

Whenever a scene may involve content that is owned by a third party or that may include content banned in various markets, the filmmaker's best strategy is to also shoot an alternative version of the scene that omits the questionable material. Scenes involving nudity can be shot with total nudity, then again with suggestive costumes. If the director wishes to shoot a scene that includes a billboard in the background, the director should also shoot a version of the scene that removes the billboard from the frame.

By shooting coverage shots, the filmmaker gives the film company choices to address clearance problems or censorship. This is far preferable to making the inclusion or exclusion of a scene an all-or-nothing battle. With good coverage footage, any objections can be addressed with relatively inexpensive editing rather than the much costlier reshooting.

3. Location Names

Script clearance reports will identify any overlap with identifiable locations. For example, a fictional locale may coincide with the uncommon name of a real city or region, and the institutions in that location may be unintentionally named in the film. If a script is set in the fictional town of Garonsburg and there happens to be one or two such towns in the United States, then references to Garonsburg High School, Garonsburg General Hospital, and the Garonsburg Police Department may all identify real institutions even though the screenwriter had never heard of them.

The film company does not necessarily have to revise the script to change such conflicting names. As explained in chapter 5 (pp 78–86), the use of an identifiable name will only interfere with the rights of another party if it defames that party or invades that party's privacy rights. A casual

reference that a character attended a high school or was born at a particular hospital is unlikely to defame any person or business. At the same
time, however, film companies should try to avoid exclusions to their errors
and omissions insurance coverage. Even an unfounded lawsuit can be very
expensive. If the fictional location can be changed to a city with a common
name, the fictional name will less likely be identified with one particular
city. Within the fictional locale, the choice of institutional names should
similarly be reviewed to avoid direct references, unless such references are
intentional and important to the film.

4. Background Copyright and Unlicensed Art

For feature films, copyrighted materials should only be used with the
express permission of the copyright owner. The claim that a filmmaker has
a fair use privilege to show another party's copyrighted work generally has
little support if the work is being used as background or foreground decoration on a feature film or television show. Since there is a ready market
for licensing images, the courts are quite reluctant to allow unauthorized
copying of copyrighted works. Moreover, copyright owners tend to be very
protective of their content, so the likelihood of litigation is high even in
those situations in which the merits of the case would favor the filmmaker.

Obvious copyrighted materials may include stock footage, playback
footage on television or in films, images that the set designer would use to
decorate the set (artwork, posters, computer software screenshots), and pictures on T-shirts, jackets, or other costumes. Less obvious materials include
the artwork on product packaging and billboards or public artwork that is
visible on the street where one is filming.

There are exceptions to this general prohibition. For example, if the
filmmaker is shooting cars driving on public freeways and incidentally captures the images of billboards, the film will generally be protected by fair
use, provided that their screen time is brief and the copyrighted materials
are only in the background. Some copyright owners are much more aggressive than others, however, so there is always a risk of litigation. Even with
the background billboards, the errors and omissions insurance coverage
may put an exclusion into the coverage for copyrighted images that are not
cleared, or licensed.

A great deal of public domain content is free to use. In addition to
seeking out artwork from professional and volunteer artists, the production
company can incorporate images and advertising that is no longer protected

by copyright as a way to add verisimilitude to the work without paying unreasonable rates.

5. Consumer Products and Identifiable Brands

Consumer products may be subject to strong third-party ownership rights. The names of goods are often trademarked, and their packages often feature copyrighted images. Scenes showing children playing games or characters eating prepackaged food will typically incorporate both copyrighted works and trademarks.

The best strategy is to seek express written permission to depict the product protected by copyright. The second-best strategy is to show the product itself but not its packaging. Once a soda has been poured into a glass, Coca-Cola no longer has any trademark or copyright ownership of the caramel-colored beverage. The actual product will be given far less legal protection and lend itself to much stronger claims of a fair use privilege than the depiction of the packaging.

Tobacco companies do not provide product placement permission, so film companies are strongly encouraged never to show the brands or use brand names in dialogue. Depending on the jurisdiction, the tobacco companies may be barred by legislation or court orders from providing their products to filmmakers in this fashion, and may even be required to defend against such use. Filmmakers should avoid brand references to tobacco products to the greatest extent possible, and use such content only after weighing the risks against the importance of the scene.

In contrast to copyrighted works, filmmakers may rely on fair use to depict trademarked products or to use the name of such products and services in dialogue. A trademark owner cannot automatically stop a film company from showing its brand name in a scene. If the trademark is said or depicted accurately, the use in the film will not give rise to a successful legal action. Using trademarks without authorization will raise concerns for the insurance company, however, and could make eventual distribution more difficult.

6. Misuse of Products in the Scene

Most independent productions cannot afford the costs of litigating against an aggressive trademark owner, even where the trademark owner is wrong, so caution is warranted. Particular care must be exercised when a trademarked product is used in a dangerous or offensive manner. Manufacturers may feel compelled to take legal action to show their displeasure and send a message to the public that such use is unauthorized, even if there is only a weak legal basis for the action.

For example, in a 2006 episode of the NBC drama *Heroes*, a character mangled her hand in a garbage disposal on which the InSinkErator brand name could be seen lightly etched into the metal. InSinkErator claimed that the scene "casts the disposer in an unsavory light, irreparably tarnishing the product,"[1] when in fact such a dangerous act would injure any person. NBC ultimately chose to digitally alter the shot to remove the trademark rather than face litigation. While NBC had done nothing legally wrong and would very probably have won the resulting lawsuit, the costs required to defend the suit would have been higher than the costs of editing the episode prior to rebroadcast or DVD sales.

7. Nonproblematic Trademark References

The clearance review will respond to any trademark referenced in the script. Clearance reports often include a number of "false positives" if the writer has used a brand name in an action paragraph to describe the use of a product that will appear onscreen. Thus, if a character grabs a facial tissue but the script says the actor grabs a Kleenex, the clearance report will identify a potential conflict with Kleenex. Depicting the product is not the same as using the brand, so these descriptions in the script do not raise issues for the film.

8. Character Names

Unless a work depicts a true story, all screenplays should use only fictional character names. If the script uses a real, living person's name but fictionalizes certain elements of the character, that only increases the likelihood that that the person can claim the use is defamatory, since the fictionalization means the use is knowingly wrong. To avoid liability for characters not intended to represent living persons, the script must not use a living person's name, particularly in cases where

- The name is taken from real persons known to the writers, director, producer, or other senior members of the film company;
- The name relates to the locations or situations in the film; or
- The name is sufficiently unique that the person named can reasonably believe the film relates to that person without any other direct relationship

When a first or last name is used alone, it is much harder to associate it with a particular person than when first and last names are used together. Clearance companies suggest that a full name should not be used unless at least five individuals can quickly be identified as having that name. A quick Internet search is a helpful tool to identify common names.

If real persons' stories are used, then additional reviews and releases are required. The character names should be authorized, particularly if there is an attempt to depict real persons. Finally, names of performers in any of the unions to which the production company is or will become a signatory should not be used.

F. When Things Go Wrong

Even if the filmmaker makes the best possible choices and works as carefully as possible, the complexity of a motion picture almost guarantees that things will go wrong. Locations that have been contractually secured suddenly become unavailable, cast members get sick, sets that looked perfect as scale models do not allow the action to take place properly, the weather will not cooperate . . . the list of possible problems is endless.

Financial contingencies can be anticipated. The budget should include a contingency amount—typically 10 percent of the budget—that cannot be used unless a true emergency develops. Solutions to other possible problems should be prepared in advance by the filmmaker. Backup locations should be identified for all the major locations selected, so that there is someplace to go when things go wrong. The filmmaker should also identify simple scenes that can be shot in readily accessible locations if a day's scheduled scenes fall through entirely.

Other circumstances benefit less from advance planning. If a key cast member becomes unavailable, a double can be used and the dialogue later dubbed in, but this solution has limited effectiveness. Often, it is better to adjust the script than to try to hide the missing cast member.

The most important aspect of crisis management is quick communication throughout the production team. The filmmaker and key personnel must agree upon a strategy to solve the problem as quickly as is reasonable. All those key personnel must understand the final decision made and must communicate it to the cast, crew, and vendors affected by the change. Today, email and web pages can be used to give everyone a place to look for the latest information, call sheets, and changes. If a web page is used, it must be kept up to date. Confirming telephone calls should be made to the cast and crew so that no members of the production are left unaware.

If the communication works effectively, even significant changes can be made with a minimum of intrusion. Things will go wrong, but good producers and filmmakers count on these moments of change to energize the creative muscles of the production. If the practical and legal needs are met, then the creativity can be unleashed most effectively.

15

Special Considerations for Documentaries and Films Based on True Life Stories

In the current media market, documentaries have become a powerful force in both the artistic and commercial worlds. Films like *I Am Not Your Negro, Searching for Sugar Man, Athlete A, Won't You Be My Neighbor, Fahrenheit 9/11, March of the Penguins,* and *An Inconvenient Truth* all garnered critical and commercial success. Streaming services and the decline in traditional journalism have created a strong demand for both short- and long-form documentary filmmaking.

Since documentaries only rarely receive national theatrical distribution, audiences do not treat nontheatrical distribution as an aesthetic judgment against the film. They expect to find relevant documentaries through Netflix, Amazon Prime Video, or PBS. In addition, crafting short-form documentaries is becoming part of the core competence for journalism majors, since the ability to write the story, film the content, edit the narrative, and publish the work reflects the fundamentals of multimedia journalism today.

Documentary films hover closer to the news media business than narrative theatrical motion pictures do, which suggests that documentary filmmakers may wish to consider using traditional and nontraditional news publishers to obtain credentials and gain access to some of the content they wish to cover. Having press privileges may be quite helpful for certain documentaries, and producing shorter news pieces alongside the full documentary may be a way to promote the eventual release of the film and improve access for the camera crew.

Finally, it is important to remember that United States law provides all speakers and writers, including the press and documentary filmmakers, much greater legal protection to publish material than the protections afforded by most other nations. Particularly if the individuals identified in the documentary are residents of Europe, the Middle East, or Asia, the filmmakers should at least be aware of the significantly different laws regarding standards for defamation, invasion of privacy, content with religious overtones, and content that may be considered political advocacy. The information in this chapter does not extend to the challenges faced by filmmakers producing content that may be deemed scurrilous or denigrating—and may even be banned outright—under the laws or standards of other countries or cultures.

A. United States Documentary Film Clearance

The filmmaker has significantly less need for licenses and approvals to shoot a documentary than to create a feature film. The documentary filmmaker relies upon the truthfulness and accuracy of the film presented as much as permission for the legal rights to film the locations, people, and other elements that make up the story.

1. Accuracy in Storytelling: Overcoming Defamation

The greatest legal protection for a documentary filmmaker is the truthfulness and accuracy of the film presented. The primary concerns raised come from complaints regarding defamatory presentations or invasions of privacy by individuals or companies. Under United States law, a party claiming defamation must prove the falsehood of the information. This is much more protective than a rule establishing that truth is a defense, because it puts the burden on the plaintiff to prove that the statements are falsehoods. In so many situations, proof of truth or falsity is extremely difficult to establish. Moreover, if the documentary features individuals who are public officials or public figures, then the filmmaker would only be legally liable if the production knowingly used false material or was reckless in the choice of material presented. Even if the featured individuals are private figures, the filmmaker would have to be at least negligent in the use of the false material to be liable for defamation.

Since litigation is expensive, however, most distributors want to know that they can win any lawsuit without going to trial. Therefore, documentary filmmakers must be able to demonstrate readily that they were not negligent in the making of their film or in its depiction of any persons or companies. This is a higher threshold than the law requires, but it reflects a degree of caution on the part of the distributors not to be caught in expensive and drawn-out legal battles.

To assist in establishing the accuracy of the filmmaking process, documentary filmmakers should take careful notes regarding all sources and record all statements made by sources as faithfully as possible. When videotaping or audio recording sources, the filmmakers should be sure to obtain consent for recording each session on the recording itself. To establish the filmmakers are not negligent, they should verify the facts upon which they rely to the fullest extent possible, keeping logs of the verification.

If one party makes serious allegations against another in the telling of a story, the documentary filmmaker will need to investigate and corroborate those allegations. Often, the lawyers for the distributor will ask for evidence of corroboration, just as they would expect it from network news crews. And unlike the nightly news or newspapers, documentary filmmakers are assumed to have had sufficient time to investigate leads and corroborate information. For example, if a filmmaker is given a story about dangerous working conditions at a slaughterhouse, the filmmaker should find out enough about the source to know if the person was recently denied employment at that plant, fired from that plant, or otherwise had a personal grudge that could color the accuracy of the complaints. This does not make the information inaccurate, but it does highlight the need for corroboration by multiple sources. A whistle-blower may very well have been complicit with the alleged misconduct before going public. The whistle-blower's motivations and behavior must be carefully investigated to show that the filmmaker has taken reasonable care in researching the story. The whistle-blower's conduct may not undermine the story, but it could provide essential context for the audience.

By maintaining logs, writing down the sources of leads, capturing interviews on tape and retaining them, and confirming times, dates, and locations of all the major events, the filmmaker can show appropriate care in researching the story and presenting each detail so that there can be no claim of defamation.

2. Avoiding Invasions of Privacy

Perhaps nowhere does the law protecting the rights of the filmmaker differ more greatly from the industry practice than in the area of invasion of privacy. Under the law, if the information is newsworthy or of public interest, then there can be no invasion of privacy for accurately depicting the story. Minors may be afforded slightly greater protection, but as long as information is public and of public concern, the news reporter and documentary filmmaker are free to use that information. Despite the law, by practice, some distributors demand a signed release proving permission from every person depicted on the screen. Documentary filmmakers must balance the need for documentation and caution with the need to capture the footage necessary to tell their story.

Privacy laws are discussed in greater detail in chapter 5 (p. 66), but several of them are of special concern to documentary filmmakers. In most states, the laws include (1) false light, (2) publicity rights, (3) intrusion into seclusion, and (4) publicity given to matters of private concern. Statements that put persons into a false light are legally very similar to defamatory statements. The false statements need not be as contemptuous as those required for defamation, but the statements must still highly offend an ordinary person. In some states, the rights of publicity are also included as a form of privacy, but publicity rights have increasingly been treated separately as a commercial interest and are discussed elsewhere throughout the book.

Protections against intrusion into seclusion primarily protect against physical intrusion, such as trespassing and planting hidden cameras or microphones in the home of a subject. The use of a high-powered lens used to view through windows might qualify in some jurisdictions, and voyeurs' use of electronic equipment to see under women's skirts or peek into bathroom stalls has extended notions of physical intrusion into public venues. These are obvious invasions of personal space, and such offensive techniques simply should never be used.

The most important and challenging privacy consideration for documentary filmmakers is the protection against publicizing matters of only private concern. A filmmaker should not publicize a private fact if that information is not of legitimate public concern and the publication of that fact would be deemed highly offensive to the ordinary person.

There is little clarity regarding the legal point at which a matter becomes a matter of public concern. Criminal activity is generally considered public, and almost any activity by elected officials and entertainers is fair game. Stories that disclose misconduct or highlight important matters of public policy are all likely to qualify as being of legitimate public concern. On the other hand, a newspaper's casual reference to a student-body officer's previous sex reassignment surgery was deemed not a matter of public concern since it was unrelated to the news story.[1]

Similarly, if a 12-year-old is competing in a spelling bee not open to the public, such a private endeavor, despite the inherent drama, does not become a matter of public concern. On the other hand, if the spelling bee is a public event that anyone can attend, then there can be little claim that taping the competition itself violates the privacy of the participants. This would not, however, extend to the private areas of the competition, such as the green room or the rooms in which the students were waiting along with their parents. A filmmaker does not get to publicize a personal story merely because it makes for good drama.

Fortunately, public concern is not the only test. For the private facts disclosed to be actionable, they also must be highly offensive to a reasonable person, not merely to the particular person who was the subject of the documentary footage. Graphic film footage of accident victims may fall into this category, if the accident was not a matter of public concern and the victims' bloody bodies, personal agony, and vulnerable state were such that a reasonable person would find the broadcast highly offensive. If the rescue is newsworthy, however, then the filmmaker has much greater leeway.[2]

Simply put, filmmakers should pay attention to the privacy rights of the people in their documentaries, being careful to ensure that if individuals depicted have not consented to be in the documentary, they are involved in matters of public concern or their depictions are not highly offensive.

3. Using Consent Agreements to Acquire Rights

Since privacy laws are so ambiguous, the overwhelming practice is to seek permission to film individuals or at least to inform them that filming will be taking place. An actual permission agreement is the most effective tool available to the filmmaker and distributor to eliminate the potential for lawsuits. If the distributor can remind all offended individuals that they signed releases, that will end the complaints. Amazingly, most people will sign such releases.

The release used can be very vague or extremely detailed. The release used by the makers of the mock-documentary *Borat: Cultural Learnings of America for Make Benefit Glorious Nation of Kazakhstan* was very specific. In this highly controversial film, individuals who were unaware that the movie was a parody were included in scenes that were turned into grotesque situations. The release they signed gave the film company clear and unambiguous rights and withstood a number of legal challenges from participants who objected to being the unwitting butt of star Sacha Baron Cohen's jokes:

1. The Participant agrees to be filmed and audiotaped by the Producer for a documentary-style film (the "Film"). It is understood that the Producer hopes to reach a young adult audience by using entertaining content and formats.

2. The Participant agrees that any rights that the Participant may have in the Film or the Participant's contribution to the Film are hereby assigned to the Producer, and that the Producer shall be exclusively entitled to use, or to assign or license to others the right to use, the Film and any recorded material that includes the Participant without restriction in any media throughout the universe in perpetuity and without liability to the Participant, and the Participant hereby grants any consents required for those purposes. The Participant also agrees to allow the Producer, and any of its assignees or licensees, to use the Participant's contribution, photograph, film footage, and biographical material in connection not only with the Film, but also in any advertising, marketing, or publicity for the Film and in connection with any ancillary products associated with the Film.

. . .

4. The Participant specifically, but without limitation, waives and agrees not to bring at any time in the future, any claims against the Producer or against any of its assignees or licensees, or anyone associated with the Film, that includes assertions of (a) infringement of rights of publicity or misappropriation (such as any allegedly improper or unauthorized use of the Participant's name or likeness or image) . . . (d) intrusion (such as any allegedly offensive behavior or questioning or any invasion of privacy), (e) false light (such as any allegedly false or misleading portrayal of Participant), (f) infliction of emotional distress (whether allegedly intentional or negligent), . . . (k) defamation (such as allegedly false statements made on the Film). . . .[3]

The *Borat* film producers were accused of burying the waivers in voluminous boilerplate, including much less likely defenses to claims for an "act of God" and damages from "terrorism or war," but only those two waivers were unrelated to the crass conduct Sacha Baron Cohen had planned for the unwitting participants in the film. Although the original waiver paragraph used on *Borat* included waivers for items not listed here, this slightly shortened list is a useful and appropriate example of the waivers that can be used by documentary filmmakers.

4. Acquiring Location Permits

Although some jurisdictions exempt news companies from the need to acquire location permits, film permit offices and other local authorities generally consider documentary filmmakers to have an obligation to obtain film permits just like feature filmmakers, reality television producers, and commercial still photographers.

In practice, film permit obligations are not that onerous. If a documentary filmmaker plans to interview dozens of individuals in a public park or municipal parking lot, then the activities of the filmmaker have the potential to interfere with the ordinary operation of that venue and will likely attract the attention of the police or the municipality. Having taken the steps to acquire a film permit will protect the filmmaker from interference at the location.

At times, however, the documentary filmmaker operates more like a news crew. In a film such as *Hoop Dreams*, for example, the filmmaker follows the regular activities of its subject. If the subject of the film is meeting friends in a public park or hanging out in a municipal parking lot, it would be unreasonable to demand that the filmmaker avoid the location until a film permit has been arranged. To a certain extent, the filmmaker will rely on good luck to avoid police interference. In most situations, however, the police will accept that the film crew is doing a "news story" in the form of a documentary and allow the filming to proceed.

When the subject of the film is expected to sporadically but often visit a location that would require a film permit for a prearranged shoot, the documentary film company should try to work with the local film office to obtain some form of permit waiver. For example, if the documentary is following an attorney in a high-visibility trial, the film company may be much more successful gaining access to the inside of the courthouse if it has the support of the film office to sit beside the members of the media waving their press credentials. Alternately, the filmmaker may increase access to the story by offering to provide footage to a press outlet, thereby gaining press credentials.

B. Ethical Considerations for the Documentary Film

New media platforms and openness to productions of all lengths have increased the audience for documentary films and brought them to the forefront of public education and engagement. The change in media has simultaneously resulted in the decrease in local newspapers and a significant decline in the overall investment in reporting and professional journalism, shifting the entire US culture away from investigative reporting and toward personal storytelling. In this new context, filmmakers should recognize important ethical considerations when making documentary films and even narrative films that claim to be accurate portrayals of true events.

Along with the growing importance of documentary productions to provide a source of sound investigative reporting for the public, there is the concern that digital editing tools have given filmmakers the ability to create realistic-looking footage to fill any gaps wanted. The use of "deep fakes" has become ubiquitous, enabling the producer to create images of politicians and celebrities saying and doing virtually everything. The ability to easily generate entirely fictional content creates challenges for a filmmaker who might be tempted to recreate a moment that occurred off camera. *Zelig* was a fictional comedy, but today a filmmaker can insert or remove anyone and anything without the audience being able to see the fictionality of the re-creation.

There is no established and universally adopted ethical code for documentary filmmakers. Documentary filmmaking is not journalism, and the power to tell personal stories that have their focus on the "truth" as understood from the unique perspective of the storyteller, rather than any objective truth, is a legitimate role for documentary filmmaking, just as it is for the memoirist. Nonetheless, the public is harmed by practices that devalue truthfulness and create intentional deceptions. A filmmaker may get away with shading the truth on a particular project, but that filmmaker may well find that the distrust engendered by such choices will have career-ending consequences. As a result, a documentary filmmaker should carefully consider adopting an explicit code of conduct that can be part of the assurances given to cast and crew, financing partners, and audiences.

1. Ethical Basics for Documentary Filmmakers

In 2009, the Center for Media & Social Impact at American University attempted to develop an approach to ethics in documentary filmmaking with its study entitled *Honest Truths: Documentary Filmmakers on Ethical Challenges in Their Work.* The study interviewed documentary filmmakers, who focused on the ethical relationships with the subjects interviewed when making documentary films and the relationship with viewers.

The challenge posed in creating an ethical code for documentary film is that every decision made during the production process will shape the narrative. The choice of framing a shot in a particular manner means including certain subject matter in the shot while excluding other content. The need to build relationships and access to the subjects of the documentary will invariably change the filmmaker's understanding about the subject and the content, sometimes expressly but oftentimes subliminally. Promises made by the filmmaker as a condition of gaining access to the subject must be honored to be ethical, but those promises may also compromise the accuracy and honesty of the story being told.

The Center for Media & Social Impact uncovered three simple, general principles to guide ethical filmmaking that focus on the relationships at the heart of the storytelling process, and that reflect the common principles espoused by the documentary filmmakers interviewed throughout the process to "do no harm," "protect the vulnerable," and "honor the viewer's trust."[4]

- Honor your (vulnerable) subjects. Protect them from attack and don't leave them worse off than when you met them.
- Honor your viewers. Make sure that what they understand to be true and real wouldn't be betrayed if you told them where and how you got that image.
- Honor your production partners. Do what you contracted to do, even if you made that bargain with yourself.[5]

The study noted how documentary filmmakers sometimes rely on the standards and practices of new services.

> Where institutional standards and practices exist, as in the news divisions of some broadcast and cablecast networks, filmmakers felt helpfully guided by them. . . . They typically assert that an independent media is a bulwark of democracy, and that the trust—of both audience and

subject—is essential. They eschew conflict of interest. To achieve those goals, standards uphold accuracy, fairness, and obeying of law, including privacy law. Furthermore, producers, who were held responsible for the standards, are typically forbidden to offer subjects the right of review or to restage events; they are required to ensure that image and sound properly represent reality, and that music and special effects are used sparingly. Furthermore, noncommercial public TV news programs explicitly placed journalistic standards above commercial mandates.[6]

Conversely, the report noted that "even filmmakers who work with television organizations with standards and practices may not benefit from them because the programs are executed through the entertainment divisions."[7] Still, broadcast standards value accuracy much more consistently than other media. But broadcast is losing ground to streaming and downloading, and with this change, the organizations that had their roots in journalism are disappearing.

2. Minimums of Ethical Consideration

Implicit in the statement to *honor your viewers*, is the core ethical consideration that may frame the myriad of unique situations faced by documentary filmmakers. At a minimum, the documentary filmmaker must be honest with the audience regarding the nature of the project and the choices being made. Certain information can be included directly in the end roll or crawl concluding the film. In addition, today's filmmaking environment enables the filmmaker to use websites, blogs, and other resources to make the choices regarding the production explicit.

In most cases, sharing foundational filmmaker choices occurs quite naturally. In a film about police misconduct, the filmmakers are clearly approaching the subject from the point of view of the victims of that misconduct. Some scenes may give opportunities for other points of view, but the framing of the story makes the approach clear. In other documentaries or series, however, the commitments made by the filmmaker to the subjects in the film may obscure the actual agenda for the filmmakers.

Filmmakers often grapple with decisions to give the right of review or even approval to the subjects of their films. If the filmmaker is struggling with the consequences of that choice, then perhaps the audience should know that the story that could be told had to be reviewed by the subject first. Moreover, if the filmmaker would not want that information to be made public, then perhaps it was not wise or ethical decision to grant the rights.

Documentary filmmakers should not use digital editing to restage or recreate content without acknowledging that the scenes are augmented or recreated. Defrauding the viewer by staging content undermines the commitment to accuracy and truth that the label *documentary* evokes. A filmmaker may create an entirely fictional work using documentary techniques, but that movie is not a documentary. If recreations or revisions to actual footage are necessary, it should be only be done with full disclosure to the audience.

3. Journalism Code of Ethics

The code of ethics required of journalists is different than the expectations for documentary filmmakers. Nonetheless, many freelance documentary filmmakers take on the "objective" storytelling persona of journalists. When the filmmaker adopts such a position, then the production should adhere to a journalistic code of ethics. This is another way of honoring the commitment to the audience to hold oneself accountable for the public role the production is assuming. Whereas documentary filmmaking has no agreed upon ethical code, the world of journalism has hundreds from which to choose. For these purposes, the Society of Professional Journalists has a simple but clear code of ethics. Documentary filmmakers who undertake objective storytelling would be well served to follow its guidelines.

The preamble for the Society's code serves many documentary filmmakers very well by stressing that "public enlightenment is the forerunner of justice and the foundation of democracy" and "ethical journalism strives to ensure the free exchange of information that is accurate, fair and thorough."[8] The code is organized along four key principles:

Seek Truth and Report It

Ethical journalism should be accurate and fair. Journalists should be honest and courageous in gathering, reporting and interpreting information. . . .

Minimize Harm

Ethical journalism treats sources, subjects, colleagues and members of the public as human beings deserving of respect. . . .

Act Independently

The highest and primary obligation of ethical journalism is to serve the public. . . .

Be Accountable and Transparent

Ethical journalism means taking responsibility for one's work and explaining one's decisions to the public.[9]

Each of these for principles is explained with additional detail. For example, the admonition to *seek truth* includes a number of additional imperatives, several of which apply very well for documentary filmmakers. Journalists should

- Take responsibility for the accuracy of their work. Verify information before releasing it. . . .
- Provide context. Take special care not to misrepresent or oversimplify in promoting, previewing or summarizing a story. . . .
- Be cautious when making promises, but keep the promises they make.
- Identify sources clearly. The public is entitled to as much information as possible to judge the reliability and motivations of sources.
- Consider sources' motives before promising anonymity. Reserve anonymity for sources who may face danger, retribution or other harm, and have information that cannot be obtained elsewhere. Explain why anonymity was granted. . . .
- Avoid stereotyping. Journalists should examine the ways their values and experiences may shape their reporting.
- Label advocacy and commentary.
- Never deliberately distort facts or context, including visual information. Clearly label illustrations and re-enactments.
- Never plagiarize. Always attribute.

The need to be accountable and transparent is even more important for the credibility of the documentary filmmaker, who does not have a news organization to offer its prestige and patina of integrity. The Society's code includes that ethical journalists should "explain ethical choices and processes to audiences."[10] In addition, there is an obligation to "respond quickly to questions about accuracy, clarity and fairness" and to "acknowledge mistakes and correct them promptly and prominently."[11]

Documentary filmmakers are not journalists. They tell many stories of many kinds in many voices with myriad purposes. Nonetheless, the public is better served by those filmmakers who adhere to a code of ethics, and investors and viewers expect their business partners to act with integrity regarding their work and subject matter. Over the span of one's career, those who adopt concrete codes of ethics will find the commitment is repaid through the trust and relationships engendered.

C. When Purchasing a Life Story Helps

In certain situations, the documentary filmmaker may wish to have substantially more access to and control over a story than provided under the law or through a simple release. In these situations, the filmmaker may decide to acquire the rights to a subject's life story, which should increase the access to information and provide exclusive control of the story. With the agreement to pay the rights holder may come a perception that the filmmaker is no longer independent, however, so the filmmaker must carefully weigh the benefits and limitations the relationship might entail.

These same considerations are even more important for a filmmaker pursuing a narrative film based upon a person's true story. Fictionalizing the true story will change the nature of some of the characters, regardless of the filmmaker's commitment to accuracy. Narrative films often benefit from the ownership rights that come from an express agreement. Despite this, often a myriad of individuals are depicted in a story, and the production company will necessarily be selective about which life stories are acquired and which are used without express permission in any given project.

1. Access

Purchase of a life story generally requires the subject of the story to do more than simply acquiesce to filming an interview. The filmmaker may need access to private records, to the names of other individuals associated with the subject, and to details not available to the public. The language of the purchase agreement should obligate the person selling the story rights to actively assist the filmmaker in gaining access to records and information under the subject's control.

Where third parties hold confidential information about the subject, it can only be properly disclosed directly to the subject. With the subject's permission, however, it can also be disclosed to the filmmaker, acting as an agent of the subject. The subject's doctors, lawyers, and accountants will only be able to disclose information with the express written authority of their patient or client.

The express permission of the subject of the documentary may also change the manner in which others with knowledge of the story will confide in the filmmaker. If the request to interview friends and family is accompanied by a letter from the subject asking for full cooperation with the filmmaker, their candor will likely improve.

There is always a cost. For some projects, the cooperation of the subject may imply that the subject will approve of the filmmaker's end product, and critics of the subject might be less eager to participate because of the relationship between filmmaker and subject.

2. Exclusivity

Often the most important reason to purchase a person's story is to ensure that the information remains exclusive to the filmmaker. Under an exclusive agreement, the filmmaker becomes the sole individual to whom the subject can provide personal information. The contract should make it clear that this is not merely a confidentiality provision. The contract limits the access to the filmmaker only, affording the filmmaker a preferred position for those stories of significant public interest and multiple film projects.

Exclusive agreements will not prevent any of the filmmaker's potential competitors from accessing public information about the subject. It will merely prevent the subject from assisting those competitors directly. Nonetheless, if a filmmaker is documenting a public event, acquiring the personal stories of the key participants will improve the ability to tell the story and reduce competition. Anyone else covering the event will be forced to rely on public information alone and will not have access to the unique content provided by the exclusive arrangement.

The filmmaker needs to determine the scope of the exclusive rights being acquired. They may be limited to the filming of the documentary or to a particular period, or they may cover a much broader period and range of media. If the filmmaker acquiring the rights sees potential both for a documentary film and for a fictionalized retelling, then the agreement should be drafted to cover the fictionalized use of the story in addition to the documentary.

The contract may provide additional compensation for such use to provide an incentive for the person selling the rights to continue to feel bound by the agreement. Since such contracts may prove hard to enforce, provisions that encourage the seller's compliance, support, and participation may be very useful to ensure the effectiveness of the agreement.

D. Fair Use for Documentaries

For documentary filmmakers to accurately depict their stories, they invariably need to rely on copyright's fair use provisions significantly more than other filmmakers. This is particularly true if the documentary focuses on literary or visual works or incorporates copyrighted materials as background content, although those are not the only two such categories.

1. Fair Use Basics

Fair use represents a limitation on the exclusive rights held by copyright holders. Under certain conditions, it allows third parties to use copyrighted content without the copyright holder's permission. Broadly speaking, fair use is available "for purposes such as criticism, comment, news reporting, teaching, . . . scholarship, or research."[12] In addition to these broad categories, fair use has developed to protect the rights of researchers, such as documentary filmmakers, to make personal copies of entire works for their research archives, to enable owners of copyrighted works to make backup copies of materials, and to allow consumers to temporarily copy music, television, and film for personal enjoyment at a later time or in a different place.

Fair use is a very fact-specific balance between the rights of the copyright owner and the rights of the person seeking to make copies or to use content without permission. Because it is fact specific, the exact limitations of fair use are often subject to conjecture. Moreover, because of the significant cost of lawsuits, there is a tendency to be unnecessarily cautious regarding the interpretation of the law.

Filmmakers, producers, and distributors must manage not only the legal rights involved but also the costs associated with defending those rights, making documentary filmmakers often feel pressured not to use content in ways that lawyers would reasonably expect to be considered fair use. Nevertheless, fair use is not blanket permission to use copyrighted works that are readily available to license. A low production budget is not a basis for fair use.

The statutory provision of fair use emphasizes four factors to help courts determine whether the party copying material has acted legally.

In determining whether the use made of a work in any particular case is a fair use the factors to be considered shall include—

1. the purpose and character of the use, including whether such use is of a commercial nature or is for nonprofit educational purposes;
2. the nature of the copyrighted work;
3. the amount and substantiality of the portion used in relation to the copyrighted work as a whole; and
4. the effect of the use upon the potential market for or value of the copyrighted work.[13]

The four fair use factors are balanced in the context of the fair use provision's goal of providing broad access to public discourse and a statutory tool to ease the tension between the Copyright Clause of the Constitution and the First Amendment. No single factor is determinative.

Broadly speaking, the law favors documentary film's goals of public comment, so the first prong of the four-factor test will generally weigh in the favor of the filmmaker. This does not mean that the documentary must be ponderous or academic to benefit from the clause. Irreverent or polemical, comical or studious, all works improve public knowledge and thereby benefit the public.

However, the first prong also specifies that to be considered fair use, a work's appropriation of copyrighted material must be *transformative* in nature. A transformative use is one that changes the character of the copyrighted material. Quoting dialogue or showing a short clip as part of a critique of the material is transformative. Merely reproducing the content without comment does not transform it. Thus, if the documentary provides insight or criticism through the context in which the copyrighted material is used, it is much more likely to be considered fair use.

The second prong of the test reflects the fact that stronger copyright protection is given to fictional or highly creative works than to factual ones. While ideas, facts, formulas, and processes are not even protected by copyright, the manner in which they are expressed is given modest copyright protection. Fair use offers very wide latitude to make use of such factual expressions, because copyright should never create a monopoly over facts or ideas.

For most documentary filmmakers, the most important aspects of the fair use test are the last two prongs. Under the third prong, the law makes clear that less is more. The smaller the portion of a copyrighted work one uses, the greater the chance it is considered fair use. Short quotes are more likely to be fair use than recitation of extensive passages; 30-second clips are more likely to be fair use than 5-minute sequences.

Similarly, the fourth prong balances the economic interests of the copyright holder with those of the documentary filmmaker or others who seek to use copyrighted works without permission. To the extent that the documentary film serves as a competing product with the copyright holder's own work, it is less likely to be considered fair use. If the documentary filmmaker's work does not threaten to replace the copyright owner's work in the market, the documentary will more likely be considered fair use.

2. Documentaries About Media and Culture

The greatest challenge in the application of fair use provisions relates to documentaries that focus on media and culture. To effectively communicate, these documentaries often make extensive use of materials copyrighted by third parties. To the extent that the documentary filmmaker employs the sources to illustrate the filmmaker's editorial content, such uses generally do not require the copyright holder's permission. However, the documentary must not become a direct competitor for the copyright holder's work. For example, if a Three Stooges short is shown in its entirety, followed by footage of interviews with comics who learned their craft by watching the Three Stooges, the use of the short would not be fair use. Here, the documentary filmmaker's original content would have only a loose relationship to the copyrighted work, and the use of the entire work would turn the documentary into a commercial competitor of the original. If instead the filmmaker interspersed original interviews with brief clips of the Three Stooges directly tied to the content of the new material, and each clip was no longer than was reasonably necessary to illustrate the original content, that would more likely be considered fair use.

Though not a legal standard, a practical standard that applies to other forms of research can also be applied to documentary filmmaking. Students are taught that using a single source is plagiarism but using five sources is research; the same practical rule may apply to the use of film clips. A documentary that takes all its clips from a single source is much more likely to feel the wrath of the copyright holder than a documentary that draws content from a significant number of sources. If the documentary's emphasis is the impact of television comedy on pop culture, focus on a range of modern television comics rather than only on Jerry Seinfeld. If the real subject is

Jerry Seinfeld, use a broader range of material than just his network television series.

3. Background and Incidental Content

Since a documentary filmmaker implicitly represents that the distributed film is accurate and truthful, the production should not digitally alter the content of footage. The filmmaker must avoid falsifying the trademarked goods, copyrighted materials, and other content captured while filming scenes as they unfold. This creates a significant challenge. Billboards, sculptures, posters, television broadcasts, ring tones, T-shirts, and other copyrighted works are ubiquitous. To change these elements in a documentary would essentially falsify the film's content.

At the same time, the filmmaker should take reasonable steps to limit these elements when practical and appropriate. During an interview, for example, the space behind the interviewees in the frame should not include copyrighted works. If the interviews are taking place in the field and the camera operator has the opportunity to stand facing any direction, then the cinematographer should frame the shot to the extent practical to avoid capturing a copyrighted work in the background. The framing to avoid copyrighted works is no different from framing the shot to avoid shadows or control sunlight.

Increasingly, documentary filmmakers blur out copyrighted background images as well as the faces of individuals for which the production has no clearance rights. Unlike digitally switching the copyrighted or trademarked image, a blurred image will not usually falsify the content. Blurring has become so common that it no longer interferes with the storytelling.

Finally, the filmmaker should not select backgrounds in order to incorporate material for which the production did not get clearance—say, by turning on a television in the background or otherwise staging the appearance of copyrighted material. Such staging may be unethical, and the intentional introduction of the copyrighted work would undermine claims of fair use.

4. Documentary Filmmakers' Statement of Best Practices in Fair Use

In 2005, a coalition of lawyers, law schools, and film industry advocates came together to help outline many of these fair use principles. The effort both clarified the practices commonly used by professional documentary filmmakers and helped advocate that those practices meet the legal guidelines for fair use. The result of that project is the *Documentary Filmmakers'*

Statement of Best Practices in Fair Use, a report available from the Center for Media & Social Impact at the American University School of Communication.[14] (The Center for Media & Social Impact also has other projects related to online video and teaching.)

The *Statement of Best Practices in Fair Use* outlines appropriate and inappropriate applications of fair use by documentary filmmakers. Like the advice offered throughout this book, the report's recommendations can only lay out the various choices filmmakers can make. Ultimately, fair use remains rather fact-specific, and filmmakers must decide for themselves when to seek permission and when to risk legal conflict.

Perhaps the most significant impact of the report has been its acceptance within the insurance industry. As a result of the industry acceptance, insurance companies are demonstrating stronger support for including fair use content in documentaries. "The four companies most used by US documentary filmmakers—AIG, MediaPro, ChubbPro and OneBeacon—all announced programs between January and May 2007 to cover fair use claims."[15] Although the companies providing errors and omissions insurance have changed in the time since the statement was first published, the impact remains significant. The adoption of the statement's standards within the insurance industry is a normative change for acceptable practice that provides documentary filmmakers concrete guidance regarding the scope of risk associated with fair use claims.

E. Acquiring Access to Archive Materials

Documentaries often require archival material to illustrate the filmmaker's story. Fortunately, most television networks operate film archives that sell footage to third parties, and other materials may be obtained from commercial film and television archives. The cost for obtaining archival footage usually includes fees for copying the material and separate fees for licensing the material for use. The licensing costs are typically based upon the length of the film clip, the popularity of the clip for licensing, the nature of the film project, the project's production budget, and the anticipated distribution or projected revenue of the film. Each archive sets its own rates and policies.

1. Sources

Fair use applies to archival footage in precisely the same manner it applies to other content. Moreover, to the extent that important historical events are only available from limited archival sources, the basis for fair use might improve. On the other hand, if the only restriction on access to archival footage is a disagreement regarding a reasonable license fee, then a filmmaker should be cautious before deciding to claim fair use instead. The owner of the copyright is not obligated to assure filmmakers that they can meet their budgets.

In addition, the film archive may require that the filmmaker enter into a contract before footage is released. In the contract, the filmmaker may be asked to pay a licensing fee for the usage of any clip and agree to other terms in the license. Depending on the terms of the license, the filmmaker risks waiving the ability to later claim fair use for any of the archive's footage. The archival agreement may also limit the filmmaker's usage of the acquired content in other ways. The filmmaker should review these agreements carefully to ensure that the contract offers sufficient rights to meet the film's distribution needs.

2. Government-Owned Materials and Other Public Domain Resources

Works authored by the United States government are not protected by copyright and are free to be fully utilized by any party. The same is not true, however, for works created by companies or individuals not working for the government, even if the copyright in these works are later transferred to the government. Similarly, the ownership by the US government of a copy of a work does not have any effect on the copyright. United States military film footage is often in the public domain, because it was filmed by the United States government and its employees acting within the scope of their employment. In contrast, military film footage shot by news companies would not be in the public domain, even if the Library of Congress is the owner of the copyright or of the copies of those materials. Depending on the era, however, the new footage copyright may not have been renewed and on that basis fell into the public domain.

Works published in the United States more than 95 years ago are now generally in the public domain. Each year, a treasure trove of material is added to the public domain. Other works, in contrast, were never protected by copyright.

One of the most valuable public domain collections consists of works created by the Works Progress Administration (WPA), a federal agency established during the Great Depression to create gainful employment for individuals in a vast number of professional fields. WPA artists were federal employees, so their murals, plays, films, and other expressive content were all created with the United States government as its owner and without the benefit of any copyright protection. The Library of Congress maintains an extensive archive of WPA materials.

The Library of Congress also maintains a large library of film and television content. This material is not necessarily in the public domain, however, and the library does not provide any licensing services. As a result, the reading room of the Library of Congress's Moving Image Research Center can be used only if the filmmaker has already obtained clearance from the copyright holders for use of the particular clips. With written permission to use the clips, the filmmaker can obtain quality duplicates by paying the Library of Congress's processing fee. An interesting resource is the Universal Newsreel collection, which contains newsreel segments that were produced twice each week from 1929 to 1967. The collection was released into the public domain by Universal City Studios and made available online.[16]

Individual US states and governments outside the United States do not have the same legal limits on their ability to vest copyright in their original works of authorship as does the US federal government. As a result, film footage and most other copyrightable works created by states or foreign governments may have the same copyright protection as those works created by nongovernment authors.

3. Sufficient Rights

Stock footage often refers to existing film or television material that has been cleared for licensing to filmmakers and media companies. In contrast, archival resources include both stock footage and footage that may not be ready for commercial exploitation without additional licenses.

In a narrative or fictional film, for example, an archival shot of an actor's performance would require the license from the copyright holder in the work and from the actors. Assuming the original movie was made pursuant to a SAG-AFTRA collective bargaining agreement, then the SAG-AFTRA members in the archival footage would be entitled to at least the minimum compensation provided under the agreement. For a documentary, the union obligations and publicity rights claims would not apply. The documentary should be able to use the clips without the actors' express permission.

Nonetheless, for a documentary filmmaker seeking specific archival footage, the film company must conduct full copyright research and clearance to use the film footage itself and all the content within the frame of the film. Copyrighted works captured within the archival footage will need separate copyright licenses or a determination that fair use is appropriate for each work. In the same manner, synchronized music associated with the archival footage will require separate clearances. Again, fair use may apply. The fair use analysis, however, must be applied separately to each copyrighted work captured within the archival clip.

F. Partnerships for Financing and Distribution

Documentary films and nonprofit organizations often have a common agenda of trying to educate the public on particular issues and shaping public opinion. *When They See Us* and *The Central Park Five* were both powerful indictments of the New York criminal justice system and its unjustified conviction of young African American men for a rape they did not commit. *An Inconvenient Truth* has had a profound impact on energy and environmental policy throughout the world, while *Sicko* helped push health care reform to the forefront of the presidential campaign that immediately followed its release.

1. Using a Nonprofit Alliance to Fund Projects

In 2004, the *New York Times* extensively covered the relationship between biased journalism and political power. A documentary focusing on this subject by Robert Greenwald entitled *Outfoxed: Rupert Murdoch's War on Journalism* received contributions "in the range of $80,000 from both MoveOn.org and the Center for American Progress."[17]

The film financing strategy also included a significant distribution strategy. Each of the two political organizations used the film as the focal point for events and urged their membership to view or purchase the film. The twin contributions of direct financing and market financing illustrate the very powerful potential of an alliance between documentary filmmakers and political organizations that share the message of their films.

2. Need for Disclosure of Financing Partners

Every documentary filmmaker should ensure that the credits of the film include a list of the financial investors or charitable contributors who may benefit from the claims of the documentary or with whom a conflict of interest over content might exist. Just as journalists mention when a story involves their employer or a company owned by their employer, sound ethical practice requires that this information be made available in the credits of the documentary. In addition to the ethical obligation, there may be a legal obligation under the laws of various jurisdictions, including the rules governing United States television broadcasts.

3. Issues of Partnership Autonomy

In some cases, support from a nonprofit partner can raise more than disclosure issues. A documentary filmmaker oftentimes has the subject of the film in mind but finds that the point of view regarding that subject changes during the filmmaking process. But a nonprofit partner with a particular agenda may not agree with that change. The parties to the agreement need to specify the extent to which the contributing nonprofit has control over the content or tone of the documentary. While documentary filmmakers would prefer that the funds they receive have no strings attached, the organization providing its name and financial support correctly insists that it has an ethical duty to ensure that its contributions are being used in a manner that furthers the mission of the organization.

If the alliance is a distribution strategy, such as a guaranteed minimum purchase of copies of the film or rentals for public exhibition, then the arrangement can be based on approval after seeing a final version of the documentary. The initial agreement can be more specific than that, providing that the "nonprofit can only withdraw from the distribution agreement if the completed documentary varies substantially from the outline of the film attached to the distribution agreement." In this way, the filmmaker does not have to renegotiate the distribution from scratch, while the nonprofit is protected from being forced to fund a project that no longer supports its position.

If the arrangement is a financing strategy, then either the investor must trust the filmmaker to keep to the message based on the filmmaker's track record and passion, or the investor can contribute funds in stages, tying them to opportunities to see a rough cut and a preview copy of the film. Again, the contract should be specific enough that the investor can only withdraw in the event that the documentary substantially deviates from the project proposal in a manner that adversely affects the mission of the nonprofit or its strategy in supporting the documentary. If the nonprofit desires to wait until the film is finished before deciding to financially support it, then the agreement should make that clear and not establish a contractual relationship that cannot, in fact, be enforced.

(16)

Music

Music has become an integral element of the cinematic storytelling process. Music can be used to accentuate the action, evoking the emotional
response sought by the filmmaker. The source of the music can be introduced without any visual cues, the music can come from natural sources
such as an onscreen car radio or record player, or the music can be performed directly by the characters in the film. Each of these different types
of music not only plays a different role in the story but also has a different
legal relationship with the filmmaker. Music performed by the characters
in the film is labeled *foreground music*. In contrast, both the original musical
score composed for the film and any recorded songs played in the film are
considered *background music*. Because acquiring the rights to music for film,
television, and video games has become the most intricate licensing of any
copyrighted works in the law, each type of music must be treated separately.

A. Licensing Prerecorded Music and Published Music

Since *American Graffiti*, the modern film musical has been reinvented as a
greatest hits collection of popular or cutting-edge genre music. But if a filmmaker wishes to use recordings of popular songs, the production company
must enter the byzantine world of music licensing. The filmmaker takes on
the role of a record album producer, assembling the right mix of sounds and
artists—collected from a variety of songwriters, singers, music publishers,

and record labels. Each party has an interest in the copyright of the songs to be used in the film, and each must be represented in the licensing process.

1. Two Different Copyright Holders

The recording of a popular song is protected by two separate copyrights. First, the *composition* (the lyrics and the written music) is protected by a copyright held by the composers. The composers may consist of a song-writing team, such as Lennon and McCartney; a composer and a lyricist, such as Rodgers and Hammerstein; or a single person. Regardless of the number of composers, they jointly hold a single copyright. In most cases, the composers have assigned these rights to the music publisher, so the publisher is the party with which the filmmaker must negotiate to obtain rights to use the music and lyrics in the film.

Second, the *sound recording* of the song is protected through a copyright held by the producer of the song or the record company that manufactured and distributed the song. The performers on the recording have an economic interest in the recording but no control over the copyright. They primarily look to employment contracts with the record company for participation in the song's revenue.

If the filmmaker wishes to use a particular recording of a song, then the rights must be licensed from both the composers (or the music publisher to which the composers have assigned their rights) and the producer (or record company to which the producer has assigned the rights). For instance, Motown Records, a division of Universal Music Group, owns the recording of "Trouble Man," while singer and composer Marvin Gaye owns the composition rights. If the filmmaker wishes to play the Motown version of the song, then both the representatives of Marvin Gaye as composer and Motown as owner of the sound recording will need to grant permission to use the work. In addition, because of a long, strained history, a variety of different rights must be identified and licensed separately. Failure to include any of these discrete rights in the contract can create substantial problems when distributing the film, or it can result in the entire film being unmarketable in some or all markets.

Every film distributor today intends for each film to be shown theatrically and through streaming services, download, premium cable, broadcast television, standard cable television, nonnetwork broadcast television, and home video machines (DVD, Blu-ray, etc.). To exploit these markets worldwide, the distributor must acquire a number of different music rights. Most distributors expect that the acquisition of all these rights has been accomplished or arranged by the filmmaker.

2. Rights from the Music Publisher: Public Performance, Reproduction, and Synchronization

To properly use a piece of music, the filmmaker needs to acquire three specific rights from the composer or music publisher. Typically, all three rights are acquired in the same license agreement. Together, they give the film company the right to make its own recording of the song for use in the film. To use a prerecorded song, the film company needs these rights from the composer or music publisher plus rights to reproduce the prerecorded song from the record label.

a. Public Performance

In music, the public performance right protects the copyright holder for the composition from any unauthorized performance of the composition in public. Performances of the songs in the movie theater, on television, or streaming over the Internet constitute public performances, so the filmmaker must acquire this right before the movie can be played in such venues. Historically, this right was reserved only for the composers in the song, not the record company in the sound recording. Recently, however, digital sound recordings were granted a limited public performance right. Composers typically assign their rights to a publishing company. The publishing company markets the composition for use in commercials, films, and television, and promotes the song to recording artists. The publishing company will also manage the collection of royalties and payments for the artist from public performances, including performances on streaming services, radio, and television.

For the theatrical distribution of motion pictures, the public performance right must be obtained directly from the copyright holder, typically the music publisher. For other public performances of music, the rights may also be obtained through a license with a performing rights society, such as ASCAP, BMI, or SESAC. Netflix generally seeks to use "buyouts" to purchase all needed music licensing rights for a single, one-time fee. Approaches among the growing number of streamers is continuing to evolve.

b. Reproduction of the Composition

Because the film will be licensed to sell copies via digital downloads and on physical media, the music and score also need to be licensed to allow the film distributor to make multiple copies of the composition. The license to reproduce the song is also known as the *mechanical license.*

c. Synchronization

In addition to the statute-based rights of public performance and reproduction, copyright also recognizes a distinct right to associate a song with a particular audiovisual image. Whether a song is used in films, television, video games, or other multimedia works, the right to synchronize the pictures with the sound is a distinct legal right that must be separately protected. The synchronization or *synch rights* are also provided by the publisher (or the composer, if there is no publisher).

3. Rights from the Record Label: Master Use License

The right of reproduction protects not only the composers but also the recording companies from unauthorized creation of copies of a sound recording in any medium. Most consumers view this as the rule against taping radio broadcasts or ripping CDs, but in a commercial context, it applies to duplicating songs and sound recordings in each print of a film and, more important, in every download of the program or copy of the DVD.

To use a particular prerecorded version of a song, the film company will need to acquire the rights to that particular performance from the record label that owns the copyright in the master recording. If the filmmaker contemplates a soundtrack album, then the reproduction right must extend to use in that format as well.

B. Utilizing Noncommercial Music

Every Hollywood studio has a team of lawyers and paralegals who focus exclusively on the music licensing issues for their productions. The independent filmmaker must find a way to accomplish this same task. Through creative planning, a film company can bring the same artistic vision and entrepreneurial approach to the film's music as it has with every other element of the film.

1. Music Production Library

If the filmmaker is willing to use more generic music, a music production library will be a helpful source of musical content in a wide array of styles, instrumentations, and arrangements. These production libraries own both the composition and the sound recording copyrights, so they provide one-stop shopping for the musical needs of the production.

An alternative to the music bureau is the music clearinghouse. These companies do not own any rights in the music, but they serve to locate the rights requested, help establish the pricing, and ensure that the appropriate rights are identified.

2. Royalty-Free Music

Consumers are sometimes surprised that royalty-free does not mean free. Many royalty-free music services provide compositions and sound recordings for a fixed fee rather than for ongoing royalties. In exchange for the one-time payment, the filmmaker receives the right to use that music.

Not all royalty-free services convey the full suite of rights necessary for feature films. Filmmakers must be careful to acquire the rights to use both the song (music and lyrics) and the prerecorded version of that song. They must also ensure that the royalty-free license includes theatrical distribution of the film, synchronization with the motion picture, and rights to reproduce the song and the particular recorded version of the song in all media. If all these rights are included, then this will be the easiest way to provide songs for the film.

3. Public Domain Music

The independent filmmaker will often choose to avoid licensing songs altogether. The costs and administration simply outweigh the benefits to the story and film. Such a choice will not prevent the use of music; it will only change its source. One alternative is to exploit songs no longer protected by copyright because the work is in the public domain.

As noted elsewhere, all songs and other works published in the United States more than 95 years ago are in the public domain. Many other songs are also in the public domain because the publishers did not renew the copyright during the decades when renewal was required.

Recent changes to copyright law have eliminated many of the loopholes that previously allowed filmmakers and others to treat sound recordings issued before 1972 as if they were in the public domain. After years of confusion surrounding the issue, Congress amended the Copyright Act to provide more consistent protection to sound recordings published within the past 95 years. Though the law still has many nuances, the general rule—that works less than 95 years are likely to be protected by copyright—is now true for sound recordings as well.

Finally, filmmakers must treat the public domain status of the music and the sound recording as separate. A copyrighted sound recording of a public domain composition cannot be used without a license from the sound recording copyright holder. The public domain status of the composition does not strip the sound recording of its copyright protection. To sidestep this difficulty, the filmmaker may choose to record a new version of the public domain music using film company employees.

4. Other Alternatives

Filmmakers may also create original songs for the movie or purchase the copyright to the music outright. In these cases, filmmakers commonly choose to record the music specifically for the motion picture. Regardless of the source of the song, original recordings greatly reduce the scope of rights to be licensed.

Independent films can achieve both artistic and commercial success by identifying bands that are not yet signed to recording contracts. Their songs are not available as commercially licensed music, but the rights can easily be acquired directly from the composers and the band. By featuring their songs, the film may help launch successful careers for new talent and greatly reduce the cost and complexity of acquiring the music necessary for the film.

C. Commercially Licensed Music

Industry tradition has developed a byzantine series of contracts for each of the types of rights, rights holders, and media. The practice has created an absurd number of separate contracts and confusion regarding the use of the music over the life of the film. For some of these choices, the costs may be prohibitive, and the filmmaker must choose to either do without the desired song or risk buying music without all the rights needed to exploit the work in all markets.

For example, as described in chapter 9 (pp. 173–174), the use of a festival license creates significant risk that the film company will not be able to secure ongoing rights to some or all of the songs important to the sale of the film. At a minimum, the filmmaker should note which songs have not been acquired, so that there is no contractual obligation to deliver the rights to particular songs to the distributor of the film. The distributor should provide the filmmaker some leeway to acquire the songs used in the festival release version of the film or mutually agreeable alternatives.

For non-festival contracts, the following are the key provisions of the music license.

1. Term

The rights should last in perpetuity. Although some contracts provide for five-year terms, this means that future sales of the film rights can be frustrated by the inability to acquire (or even identify) the music rights. At a minimum, the contract should include renewal provisions that guarantee the right to renew and specify the renewal fee. Otherwise, too much can go wrong—for example, a new owner of the music rights (say, a company that purchases the music library in a bankruptcy sale) could demand exorbitant fees for the new grant of rights.

Of course, if the movie is never released or has only a short run, then the cost savings of the shorter term will be worthwhile. Since this is generally not the bet being made by independent filmmakers, a short music license term is probably the wrong place to save unless the savings are truly dramatic.

2. Territory

The territory should specify "the universe" rather than any particular region or even "the world." Given the growth of the International Space Station and the increasing length of copyright, which could well extend to over a century, the universe may be the more appropriate territory. There is no reason to license anything less than worldwide, because even short delays in licensing the soundtrack at the time of foreign distribution may frustrate the distribution agreements.

3. Media Covered by License

Standard contracts will typically require a list of media. Given the rapid development of technology and the fact that technological growth is highly unpredictable, the media should be "all media now known or hereafter developed." This should prevent future conflicts regarding various forms of distribution over the Internet and whatever will come after.

Older contracts may list theatrical exhibition, television (be sure to include free and pay or further identify the various tiers of broadcast, satellite, and cable television), foreign distribution, and specialty markets (16mm prints, airplane cuts) but will often omit some of the home distribution technologies, which include streaming, downloading, DVD, Blu-ray, etc. The list of media for both the public performance category and the home use category is evolving, and both should be defined broadly.

4. Public Performance Rights

Most music license agreements are drafted very narrowly. As a result, traditional contracts recognized that the public performance rights were only necessary in those media that were screened publicly. The license of a song in a film extended public performance rights only to theatrical exhibition and television broadcasts. Home presentation of a DVD does not involve a public performance, so many contracts do not give any public performance rights for DVDs or similar products. Nonetheless, videos are often shown in schools, community centers, and other smaller public venues. Without the public performance rights in DVDs and the like, the filmmaker cannot authorize any such performances. For some independent films, the guerrilla marketing strategy could be frustrated by the failure to secure public performance rights across all media.

In addition, the need for public performance rights in digital sound recordings continues to evolve. Recent changes to copyright law have expanded these rights, adding works that had previously not been able to claim digital public performance royalties. Anticipating the ongoing changes that will inevitably occur, filmmakers should acquire digital performance rights in all sound recordings as well as all compositions.

5. Reproduction or Mechanical Rights

The right to reproduce a song is often limited to the home media market (downloads, DVD, Blu-ray, etc.). Nonetheless, each print of the film also includes a mechanical reproduction of the sound recording and the composers' song, so this mechanical license should include all media. The mechanical license applies to both the composer and the record company if the record company's original recording is to be used.

6. Synchronization Rights

The right to use the song in conjunction with the visual image is an aspect of the public performance right. As such, this provision is essential in the composers' agreement, but because of the new digital performing rights, it is advisable that it be included in the license from the record company as well.

7. Scope of Usage

The contracts will narrowly limit the way in which a song may be used. First, the song may not be altered (although it typically can be used in part rather than in its entirety). This means that the lyrics cannot be changed. If a song is to be featured in the foreground as a parody sung by a character, or if it will otherwise be changed for dramatic effect, then this particular usage must be separately negotiated, and such permission will not be granted lightly.

Second, the song can only be used in the film as a whole. Permission to use a song in the film's commercials or trailers must be negotiated separately. The use of the song as part of a music video based on the film must also be separately negotiated.

Third, the filmmaker must provide credits for the composers, publisher, performing artists, and record company from which the rights were licensed. They generally appear in the end credits.

Finally, the filmmaker's rights will be nonexclusive, allowing the copyright holders to license the song to other films as well.

8. Fees

The range of fees can vary greatly, depending on the popularity of the song, the budget of the film, whether the music is used in the foreground or background, whether the music is featured in the story, and what other songs are being licensed. Typically, the United States theatrical and television broadcast rights are contracted on a flat-fee basis. Outside the United States, theatrical performances are covered by licenses provided by performing rights societies. The mechanical rights are increasingly based on a royalty fee tied to the number of units manufactured or sold. To get a general idea of the range of licensing fees and structures, the filmmaker or the production company attorney may wish to consult *Kohn on Music Licensing* by Al and Bob Kohn (see bibliography, p. 452), which provides a list of licensing ranges for the various types of licenses needed.

D. Composers and the Film Score

The original film score is the background music written specifically for the motion picture. Composers such as Elmer Bernstein, John Williams, and Danny Elfman have created intricate orchestral works for film that rival the great opera scores and symphonies of past centuries. Generally, after a series of meetings between the filmmaker and the composer regarding the goals for the music both overall and for each scene, the filmmaker provides the composer with a rough cut of the edited film. The composer creates the score, which is then modified and refined until the musical beats within each measure align perfectly with each frame of the picture. Arrangements are made—either for a live orchestra or for an electronically created performance—and the music is recorded as the finished cut of the film is played. Like Foley artists (see chapter 17, p. 321), the musicians carefully play to match the timing of the action on the screen, accompanying the film as an orchestra would accompany a ballet or opera.

Low-budget filmmakers should consider hiring composers who can not only write the music but also arrange and play the music on digital equipment. There may be as many untried film composers finishing music school as directors finishing film school. The musical triple threat—composer/arranger/performer—can significantly enhance the overall production at a far lower cost than any other solution.

The musical track is recorded separately so that it may be incorporated into the final prints of the film. For foreign distribution, the sound and dialogue tracks are delivered separately so that the original dialogue can be replaced with a dubbed soundtrack.

The filmmaker must also consider the legal status of the film score. It should be created as a work-for-hire, or its copyright should be completely assigned to the film company.

1. Work-for-Hire Productions

Under copyright law, certain types of works vest their copyright in the employer rather than the employee. (See chapter 6, pp. 93–95.) The first of these two situations occurs when an employee creates a work in the regular scope of employment. So, for example, if the film company were to employ the composer for a reasonable length of time for the purpose of writing compositions for the motion picture or pictures created by the film company, then the film company, rather than the composer, may be considered the copyright holder of those compositions.

Courts look at the nature of the employment relationship, with heavy emphasis on tax status, withholdings, and insurance; the ability to control the work; the actual control of the work; and the ability to add additional projects without additional pay. It would not be good planning to rely exclusively on the employment relationship to define a composition as a work-for-hire. At a minimum, the employee should have an employment agreement that carefully specifies that the compositions are created on behalf of the employer and are intended to be treated as work-for-hire.

The second category of work-for-hire provides greater certainty. The filmmaker can specially commission the film score as a work-for-hire. For nine categories of work, a party can specially commission works from non-employees. Among the nine categories are contributions to motion pictures and other audiovisual works. This is very important, because most other musical commissions are excluded from using a contract to establish a work-for-hire relationship. The agreement must be in writing and signed by both parties. The best practice is that the agreement should be signed before the work is begun, but certainly the earlier the better.

2. Assignment of Copyright

If the film receives worldwide success, the score's work-for-hire agreements may create additional difficulties. Some countries do not recognize the work-for-hire concept, rendering any such arrangement unenforceable. To protect against this problem, the employment agreement or agreement for the special commission should include a paragraph stating that any rights not granted as a work-for-hire are irrevocably assigned by the composer to the film company in perpetuity. This means the composer cannot reclaim the rights, and the grant will last forever. (A reversionary right in United States copyright law makes this contractual promise limited to approximately half the life of the copyright. This is why work-for-hire provisions are more useful in the United States, while copyright assignment is more effective abroad.)

The composer may insist on a third alternative: licensing the score for the motion picture but retaining all other rights. In this situation, the rights of the score's composer would be the same as those of the composers of any single featured in the film. If the film company plans to release a soundtrack album, then it should retain at least a nonexclusive right to release the music separately from the film.

In addition, however, the filmmaker should be sure to provide the composer with the ability to use the score on record albums and to distribute the music. The film company can retain all rights to the synchronization of the score but provide a license back to the composer to use the score for other purposes.

E. Performers

In the United States the singers and musicians performing on a song generally have no copyright interests. Thus, no particular language in the performer's contract is necessary to protect the filmmaker's copyright in the work. Despite this, however, performers may protect themselves from bootleg recordings and other unauthorized uses of their performances. The film company should therefore be sure that every singer and musician has signed a contract that specifically authorizes the film company to record the performance and assigns any copyright interest to the film company.

As an added precaution, the language should also include work-for-hire and copyright assignment statements in the form suggested for the composer's contract. The assignment language may help avoid problems involving the interpretation of the contract in foreign jurisdictions, and the work-for-hire provisions may negate any additional changes to the legal status of possible copyright holders.

F. Soundtrack Albums

One of the most common additional revenue sources for filmmakers comes from sales of soundtrack albums. If the movie uses a significant amount of music, particularly popular songs, then a collection of that music as performed in the film may be quite marketable.

Like the movie itself, a soundtrack album requires the licensing of many different rights. They include the rights to the songs (music and lyrics) and the particular recordings of the songs that appear on the album. The license to use the music and lyrics is known as the *mechanical recording right*, which can be acquired by paying the statutory rate to the United States Copyright Office or by licensing it through the Harry Fox Agency (see appendix C, p. 445). The right to use the particular recording of the song is another provision of the master use license, and it should be negotiated at the same time that the rights to use the recording in the film are acquired.

If the recording was made by the film company during production under a license from the music publisher or other composition rights holder, then the film company already owns the recording rights. If the film company recorded the music itself, then it must also comply with any union obligations regarding royalty payments to the musicians for additional uses of their work on the soundtrack album.

The soundtrack album may include original music composed exclusively for the film. This copyright may be owned by the film company or may have been retained by the composer, and in the latter case a mechanical license must be obtained to produce the albums from the film soundtrack or new recordings of the score.

Negotiating the licenses to produce a soundtrack album is much simpler when done at the time the music is originally selected for the film. All of the same parties must give permission to use the music in the movie, so little additional effort is required to license the soundtrack album as well. To avoid increasing the cost of the film, these licenses should be based on a royalty paid on the number of soundtrack albums sold. In this way, the filmmaker avoids any costs until there is revenue.

Postproduction

With a tremendous amount of coordination, communication, and concerted effort—not to mention a little bit of luck—filming has been completed, and postproduction can begin. Realistically, however, some of the postproduction work often begins even while principal photography continues.

A. Editing

Editing is an artistic process. The proliferation of "director's cut" editions of popular films illustrates that many different choices can legitimately be made within the editing process. It also shows that directors often continue to think about the editorial choices they made on their films. In any case, the process of editing allows the director to find the horse hidden in the marble, cutting out all the footage that does not help tell the story.

1. Timing the Editing Process

During principal photography, the director often identifies particular shots and begins assembling a very preliminary cut of the film. Particularly for tightly budgeted independent films, compiling a preliminary edit will allow the filmmaker the opportunity to determine when there is sufficient footage to tell the story. Many compelling scenes never make the final cut of a film, and independent filmmakers simply do not have the luxury of wasting time and money on anything that will not ultimately appear onscreen. If the script has a scene that is interesting but not essential, the producer should slot it later in the production schedule. That will allow the shot to be eliminated if time and funds require hard choices.

Once principal photography ends, the real editorial work begins. Following the wrap of principal photography, the director should take a short break to recover some physical strength after the rigors of filming and gain some perspective on the material shot. The director and editor must look at the footage as fresh observers rather than responding to the conditions of the filming. If there is a separate film editor working on the project, the director should begin to work early, but only once the filmmaker can treat the film with renewed enthusiasm and new objectivity.

2. The Editor's Role

The role of the editor will vary dramatically, depending on the budget of the film project. In larger productions involving International Alliance of Theatrical Stage Employees (IATSE) union crews, the editor (or editors) must also be a member of the union. At the other extreme, many independent films are edited by the filmmaker. When a professional editor is employed, the director and editor will typically work closely throughout filming so that the director can identify the preferred scenes from the dailies and explain the nature of the shots. As this process continues, the editor can work to compile the film as the director focuses on shooting it, allowing the first cut to be completed within days following the end of principal photography.

3. The Director's First Cut

If the filmmaker is not the director, then the role of the director must be carefully determined when the director is hired. Directors Guild of America (DGA) union rules obligate the producer to allow the director to deliver a cut of the film. Even if the production is not governed by union requirements, this obligation provides a useful minimum standard. The director should have the best ideas about the film that's been shot, and the story being told. As such, the director should be expected to provide the primary structure to the final film. If the producer and filmmaker do not like what they receive, then they are free to change it.

4. Rough Cuts

Once the director and editor have viewed the first cut, the real work of sculpting the film begins. Scenes are deleted, reordered, and tightened. The running time starts dropping dramatically. Ultimately, the final rough cut must be made to meet all contractual requirements. To conform to distributor demands, for example, the length of the film may need to be adjusted, and the content may need to be trimmed to achieve a particular MPAA rating (such as R or PG-13).

The editing process should anticipate the need for multiple versions of the film. Alternate shots should be identified for the broadcast television version of R movies, airplane edits, and foreign jurisdictions where censorship rules may vary considerably. Identifying the coverage shots as part of the original editing process may save significant time and effort—if not sanity—when the distributor calls.

Whether to open the editing process to others remains a highly individual choice. Producers will wish to see the film early in the process, but it may be more dangerous to share an uncompleted film than even the screenplay. Relatively few observers have the experience to judge a film that still needs minor adjustments and lacks a score and sound effects.

B. Digital Production

Digital filmmaking has reshaped the process of filmmaking. The ability to see the actual footage replayed in real time has changed the way content is shot on the set. The ability to compile footage every night allows filmmakers to do far more than watch the dailies produced from the prior day. Technology has also dropped the price barrier for equipment and techniques once only available to big budget, Hollywood productions. Much more is now possible. The largest cost for technological wizardry, however, is not the equipment but the labor. Some special effects require thousands of hours of careful, manual digital editing as each frame is redrawn by hand. Independent films rarely have access to such a workforce.

The editing process has been further complicated by the evolution of digital editing technology. Traditionally, directors relied on scratched work prints to show off rough cuts, and they created a particular image that was quite distinct from that of a final film. But a digital file will look perfect, even if the edit is unfinished. As a result, digital viewing may be even more misleading than the scratched print once relied on.

1. VFX—Visual Effects, Including Painting, Rotoscoping, and Compositing

Rotoscoping is the digital technique that separates the foreground images from the background. This allows an actor to be filmed in one location and placed on a different set. Improvements in rotoscoping and related visual effects have shifted the need for location shooting and reinvigorated the importance of sound stage productions. The level of detail that can be achieved with rotoscoping techniques has improved significantly in recent years, allowing the technique to help with costuming challenges and edit facial characteristics rather than be limited to large objects.

Rotoscoping is made much more efficient through the use of bluescreen or greenscreen mattes that are not captured by the camera. Since neither blue nor green is present in human skin tones, these colors can be removed from a shot using a process called *chroma-key*. The camera does not capture the selected color. When two different shots are composited, or layered on top of each other, the content in the bluescreen or greenscreen is not present, making the compositing very efficient.

The use of the blue screen or green screen is called *keying*; it enables a different image to be placed where the screen had been. Both blue and green are used because each has desirable properties for particular lighting conditions. On film, blue channel had a smaller grain, resulting in a cleaner edge for the mattes. On digital, that benefit is less pronounced. Green has a much brighter luminescence than blue, making it the preferred tool for digital compositing. Green is less commonly worn by the subjects of shoots, making it better for costumes. Green's luminescence reflects more green light back on the objects being isolated, so the control of the lighting sources is important, and in some situations, the blue will be preferred.

The backgrounds are generally digitally rendered paintings, an evolution from the matte paintings created by hand on large sheets of glass and used throughout the 20th century. The painted backdrops allow the green-screened foreground action to integrate seamlessly. On some of the most sophisticated projects, the matte is used to extend the breadth of the set on which the actors appear. The tractor-beam set on *Star Wars: Episode IV—A New Hope* used a matte painting to extend nearly to infinity the platform on which the characters stood. Today, the same background would be rendered digitally.

One of the most important types of visual elements that can be added is *computer-generated imagery* (CGI), which allows digital creatures, characters, and other elements to be added to any scene. The quality of CGI and the ability to achieve fluid movement of 3D rendered images has essentially eliminated the separation between live action and animated productions.

Stop-motion filming techniques had a very clear movement style that rendered the animated objects artificial. Visual effects pioneer Ray Harryhausen used these techniques for many successful films, including the Academy Award–winning *Mighty Joe Young* (1949) and his last film, *Clash of the Titans* (1981). Directors such as Tim Burton, George Lucas, James Cameron, and Guillermo del Toro have used these techniques to great advantage as elements in certain films.

Nonetheless, stop motion is slow, expensive, and not naturalistic. CGI can also be expensive and sometimes slow, but it can achieve levels of realism that make it indistinguishable from live-action photography. The *Jurassic Park* movie series was given life through breakthroughs in CGI technology. Chris Sanders's *The Call of the Wild* overcame the production risks of dog-wrangling by using CGI instead of a living dog. CGI is often thought of as essential for science fiction and fantasy films, but it is used to some extent on almost all Hollywood films and an increasingly large percentage of independent films.

The composite work combines the filmed footage with rendered elements from various sources into a completed scene. The compositing of the finished film may come months after the principal photography has ended, depending on the complexity of the CGI and other elements. If reshoots are needed, the production company's ability to have retained costumes, props, locations, and cast will be put to the test.

2. Title Design

Digital filmmaking has also transformed the use of photographed card animated opening credits into creating opening title designs to help establish the mood of the production. Opening credits are sometime left until the end of the picture so that the movie begins with the very first frame of the action. Other movies use the opening titles to introduce the story in addition to providing the contractual credit information to the audience.

Digital editing can blend the title design into any component of the story. Some filmmakers, notably Alfred Hitchcock, developed a signature style in his films that helped establish that a production was under his direction. Most tie the title design into the particular project. Titles can be made very simply or they can become elaborate sequences that take weeks to produce. The filmmaker must be sure that the timing of complex titles does not interfere with delivery of the film and must therefore begin production of the titles early enough to have them ready in time.

3. Color Correction and Color Grading

The palette of a motion picture creates an important, but often subliminal, message and ambiance. All color is comprised of hue, saturation, and brightness, which combine to create the color experienced by the eye. Bright colors tend to signify positive images, while dark tones carry darkness with them. Early Technicolor films had a vibrancy of tone that often contrasted and fought against the realism sought by epic filmmakers.

Digital technology makes the efforts to establish a color palette and correct the color much less challenging than with the color timing process for 35mm films. Assuming the initial white balances were made at the time of shooting, the color can be adjusted during postproduction.

Color correction is first used to bring the oversaturated color from digital recording into a more natural spectrum. This is the spectrum of film stock and may be a perception based on the familiarity with the different norms of image production. A second aspect of color correction is balancing shots in the same scene and integrating scenes into the completed film. For example, if two cameras were used to capture a scene and the images are being intercut, it will be important that the edits between cameras are color-matched so the difference in equipment and point of view does not jar the viewer. By color correcting between the shots, the same person will retain the same coloring throughout the scene. Different scenes may have very different saturations depending on the time of day depicted or the location, but generally filmmakers strive for a unifying tone to the color.

Color grading helps provide that unifying tone to the movie. Color grading creates additional visual depth to the work by highlighting particular elements or scenes or pushing the entire work into a color spectrum that is somewhat different from what the color-corrected film used. Often the terms *color correction* and *color grading* are used interchangeably, but technically the grading is a special effect.

Color is often an afterthought, but poor color balance and inconsistent colors identify a shoot as amateurish. Investing the time and funds for high-quality color will make an important difference in the final project. Filmmakers may consider returning to the color correction after the film has been sold for distribution, to use the new revenue to improve the color an additional time before delivering the final product for distribution.

C. Final Cut: Control of the Final Picture

When the director has finished the film and incorporated some or all of the requested adjustments suggested by the producer, the director delivers a final version of the film. At this point, the producer has the ability to make additional changes to the film without the permission of the director. In rare situations, the director negotiates for final cut, which affords the director rather than the producer the power to control the theatrical version of the film. This is the ultimate power in the production hierarchy, and it is granted only rarely to the most powerful of directors.

1. Initial Control

The filmmaker may retain final cut for an independent film in a number of situations. If the filmmaker is the director and has financed the film without entering into a negative pick-up or distribution agreement, then no other party can usurp the editorial control of the film. The filmmaker should not relinquish such control to a producer unless it is to an entrepreneurial producer who has negotiated that right at the outset. That allows the filmmaker to decide whether to sell the final cut at the outset of the financial relationship.

2. Contractual Control

Depending on the contractual arrangement, the director's influence over the final project will vary. The most successful or most influential directors negotiate the final approval rights over the content of their films, but even these rights are not absolute. The director must meet all contractual preconditions to exercise such control. Typically, this means that the film must be edited to an agreed-upon length (typically somewhere between 93 and 120 minutes), conform to an agreed-upon MPAA rating (most likely PG-13), come within budget (including all preapproved overages), and substantially contain the same scenes and dialogue as provided in the final shooting script.

Steven Spielberg exercised such a degree of control over the final cut of *Schindler's List* that he retained the right to personally supervise the film's adaptation into every foreign language and every foreign censorship edit. Because disputes over final cut are covered by the Directors Guild collective bargaining agreement, these cases are not typically reported.

3. Changes in Control of Final Cut

The most significant benefit to directing an independently financed film is the autonomy it affords. Because there is no distributor financing, there rarely is the type of editorial pressure on the filmmaker that occurs with studio pictures. Nonetheless, distributors will sometimes insist on changes to films as a condition of purchasing them for distribution. So the director is never completely free from outside influences.

When the filmmaker is the producer, the contracts should specify that the producer retains control over the director. As producer, the filmmaker must let the director deliver an initial cut. If possible, the filmmaker/producer should consult with the director when preparing the final cut. This should result in a film that is closer to the filmmaker's vision and will reduce the additional work to resolve differences between producer and director. The parties should work to achieve consensus as much as possible. A common consensus in support of the film becomes critical when the time comes to market and promote the film.

Nonetheless, the contracts must be explicit regarding who retains the ultimate control of the film. Only one person can have final cut. Absent any contractual language to the contrary, that person is the producer of the film, the CEO of the production company that owns the copyright in the final motion picture. If any variations are required, they must be spelled out very carefully in the employment contracts.

Even control of final cut will not end all editing of the film. Censorship needs will differ in various media and markets. Certain words cannot be spoken or images shown on broadcast television or in many countries. The distributors will demand control over the editing to make the film salable in those markets.

D. Sound

Music, dialogue, and sound effects combine to create a critical part of any film. Each of these three different audio elements plays a separate role. Music, as discussed in the previous chapter, can dramatically alter the emotional impact of a scene. Sound effects can emphasize action, turn small visual effects into overwhelming events, or even add characters to the scene. The off-screen cry of a baby, for instance, changes any moment, whether a romantic tryst or an attempted carjacking. The audio quality of the dialogue should remain natural and balanced throughout—the bare minimum for a competent production.

1. Separation of Soundtracks

Each of the three audio elements—music, dialogue, and effects—must be kept separate to allow the sound editor to shape the project and the production company to deliver the film to international distributors. Occasionally individual segments of dialogue must be changed—either for effect or to meet censorship obligations. In other situations, the entire dialogue track must be replaced with rerecorded dialogue in Spanish, Mandarin, or another foreign language. Choices of music may need to be changed for either artistic or legal reasons. As a result, most distributors will insist on receiving the three separate tracks for dialogue, music, and effects. Each of the three tracks should be recorded in stereo or some proprietary enhanced stereo system, such as Dolby, if available.

Although it may seem somewhat counterintuitive, part of the sound editor's job is to separate out some of the recorded sound into the separate tracks. Dialogue is typically further separated into separate tracks by character.

2. Source Music

Given the need for separate soundtracks, source music—music recorded live as part of filming—can create difficulties for the later mixing of the film. For very low-budget productions, recording source music may make sense because the filmmaker uses ambient sound, and one benefit to recording music on location is that it is easier to match the sound with the location's background environment—the ambient noise that exists in every location. For most productions, however, studio recording may be preferable.

To synchronize a studio recording to the performance of the musicians on the set, a previously recorded studio session will be mixed and played during filming. The performers will play along to that reference track, matching their physical movements to the earlier recording. The reference track will be replaced with the studio recording in the final mix.

3. Score

The musical score cannot be finalized until the cut is locked—until all edits have been made so that the timing of the music can be exact. The traditional process involved matching the score to a print of the film. Today, the composer can time the score directly to the digital file playing on a computer.

4. Cue Sheets

If the film includes a traditional score, the composer must provide different musical notations for that score. First, the composer will develop musical timing sheets that provide descriptions of the scenes and the associated music associated with each beat. More important, the composer will refine these notations into musical cue sheets, which track each musical moment.

Cue sheets also include the cues for the score, effects, and dialogue. Each cue is tied directly to the edited film by footage or frame number. The musical cue sheets are part of the written sound description and will be required by most distributors. The cue sheets are critical for foreign distributors to be able to dub the dialogue without disrupting the remainder of the film.

5. Sound Effects and Foley

The original on-set recording may include many of the sounds necessary to make the film feel realistic—or stylistic—as required by the filmmaker: footsteps, doors opening and closing, glass breaking, etc. Nonetheless, a good many of these sounds need to be enhanced by the effects editor. The choices for sounds dramatically shape the impression of each scene and the overall film.

Foley is a particular type of sound effect created by working in a sound-proof stage. The Foley artist works with a variety of props and floor surfaces to create the sounds to match the action on the screen. The Foley artist acts out the sound effects, synchronizing them to the film.

6. Looping

Often, filming conditions simply do not provide for good on-set sound recording. An actor dangling from a building buffeted by wind may be difficult to mike. Even without stunts, background noise like car traffic can obscure the audio. In such situations, the sound editor will use looping, or ADR (automatic dialogue replacement or additional dialogue recording), to loop, or rerecord, the missing dialogue. In other situations, ADR may be needed to correct mistakes in the dialogue or make other necessary changes.

If significant ADR is anticipated, the production schedule should be organized to ensure that the cast members are available for the duty.

Matching dialogue is difficult enough without losing the cast to other projects and delaying the sound editing. For smaller films, scheduling may make ADR a difficult choice. To the extent possible, the filmmaker should rely on good location sound over ADR. Spending a small amount of additional production time to make sure the sound is recorded effectively during the filming can save the filmmaker substantial time and money.

7. Background Sound

Equally important, the sound editor needs to record ambient sound for every set. The background sounds of a silent set create the baseline for later dialogue editing and whatever looping is required. The investment in capturing these 60 seconds of audio can save significant money in the long run and should never be neglected.

E. Testing the Picture

Film directors often feel that audience testing exemplifies the worst excesses of corporate Hollywood, giving a kid with a response card veto power over their vision and integrity. While this perspective overstates the importance of particular response cards, test audiences play a highly controversial role in the completion of a film.

An audience test involves screening a nearly completed film for an audience demographically selected to fit the film's target age and gender. (Studios also select geographically, which refers both to regions and, unfortunately, to race or ethnicity.) These representatives of the target audience view the film and comment on what they have seen on small response cards. The audience is also carefully watched to gauge its reaction.

If the audience is representative and the questions on the cards are appropriate, the filmmaker can learn a great deal about whether the choices made have the desired effect on the audience. If the audience is not representative or the wrong questions are asked, the process can lead to a frustrating round of counterproductive edits and reshoots. Unfortunately, there is no way to know whether the test audience is right or wrong.

In the studio system, the greatest problem directors face with test audiences is that the producer controls the process and the outcome. Directors often invite their own preview audiences—friends, colleagues, and others—to watch the early edits of the film and provide comments. These previews are not significantly different from test screenings—except that the director is able to accept or reject each criticism.

Similarly, since the primary benefit of working on an independent film is the control it provides the filmmaker, the filmmaker should control the testing process as well. That does not necessarily mean rejecting a test screening if the distributor offers to provide one, but the filmmaker should retain control over what will be done with the information the test audience provides.

F. The Ratings System

The acquisition of an MPAA rating is a voluntary step for the production company. The rating is a designation provided by the MPAA Classification and Rating Administration (CARA) that suggests the appropriate audience for the film based on whether and how it depicts sexuality, violence, mature subject matter, tobacco use, etc. Each rating designation (other than X) is an MPAA trademark. No filmmaker can designate a film as having achieved a particular rating without the certification of the MPAA.

Although obtaining a rating is voluntary, the ratings system has tremendous influence on the marketing and sale of films in the United States. Exhibitors treat the ratings as legal obligations and will generally not allow minors under 17 years of age to attend movies rated R without adult accompaniment or to attend movies rated NC-17 at all. At one time, the rating system controlled motion picture distribution. Most newspapers and broadcast television outlets will not accept advertising for NC-17 or X-rated films.

While the motion picture rating system is influential, the absolute power it once carried has lessened. Many marketing strategies ignore newspapers and rely much less heavily on broadcast television. Social media platforms do not have the same restrictions on adult content or contractual relationships that require adherence to the CARA rating system. As a result, unrated movies are much easier to market than they were in prior eras. Nonetheless, because of the need for a CARA rating for mass distribution, many distribution sales agreements still require that the film be rated and receive the particular rating listed in the contract.

To obtain a rating, the filmmaker applies to CARA and pays a relatively modest fee. If the rating is higher than that sought, the rating can be appealed. Appeals are difficult to win, however, requiring a two-thirds vote of the CARA Appeals Board to overturn the initial rating. More frequently, the filmmaker makes small changes to the language or to the length of offending scenes and resubmits the film, satisfying the ratings board's concerns and allowing a lower rating to be applied.

Independent filmmakers should be able to require the domestic distributor to shoulder the cost and administration of the ratings process. There is no value to rating a film until it is ready for commercial promotion, so any expenditure before this is premature. By the time a rating is necessary, the distributor is better equipped to initiate the process.

Increasingly, filmmakers choose not to rate a film. If the use of violence, nudity, or language will result in a rating that will strongly discourage the attendance of the film's intended audience, then the filmmaker may choose not to apply for one. This will make it much more difficult for the film to be shown in previews or on television, but may still be better than, for example, having to sell an R-rated film as a literary work to high schools. Had the R-rated *Schindler's List* been distributed as an independent film, the distributor of this powerful Holocaust film may have chosen not to rate it rather than lose the ability to promote it to schools.

G. Finalizing Credits: Contractual Obligations and WGA Assent

As part of the postproduction process, the final credits for the film should also be locked and repeatedly checked. Misspelled names or omission of earned credits can be very costly to fix. The credits should be reviewed by the production attorney to be sure all contractual obligations are met.

If the film company is a WGA signatory, then it has an obligation to send the tentative writing credits to the union immediately after principal photography is complete. If there is no conflict regarding writing credit, then this process is merely a formality. If multiple writers have been employed on the project, however, and several of them are seeking credit, then the WGA will require a cut of the film and copies of the various writers' drafts of the script so it can determine which of them have the right to be listed in the credits.

H. Delivery Elements

Independent filmmakers face a difficult choice when selecting a medium for delivering the final film, because certain distributors will insist on a full panoply of traditional delivery requirements. Digital film has dramatically changed the expenses of creating the production elements for 35mm films.

The list of elements to be delivered to the distributor must be at the forefront of the film company's attention. If the company does not have the material available, it cannot meet its contractual obligation to the distributor. This would allow a distributor to claim the film company was in breach of the distribution agreement and cancel the arrangement, possibly resulting in the film not being distributed at all. Different distributors will vary these demands to a greater or lesser degree, but the following is a general guide applicable for most distributors.

Filmmakers should not agree to deliver elements that they do not need to create and do not have the money to make. Since the number of prints needed for an independent film is often very small, the additional expenses are unnecessary.

1. The Film

The final cut of the film should be prepared in its original aspect ratio as well as a 16:9 version. The file will likely be stored with a motion picture production lab just as the negative of a 35mm print was stored with a lab. This assures quality control and safekeeping in the event of malware attacks and natural disasters. The lab will provide the process to write the Digital Cinema Distribution Master to be used in the Digital Cinema Package, or DCP. DCP represents a standard format for the various files that together allow the film to be shown in a digitally equipped cinema. The Digital Cinema Distribution Master is just one of the files. The wrapper file or index and the audio file are separate files included in the DCP.

The DCP files consume a significant amount of storage space, so often the easiest method to distribute the files is to write them to a removable hard drive and deliver the hard drive. The CRU drive is preferred because it has become the standard in the industry and can be inserted directly into the projection equipment. The files can theoretically be compressed into a .zip format, but the size of the files makes it even more difficult to ensure that the files do not become corrupted. In addition, all compression involves some level of data loss, so keeping these files uncompressed is the standard practice.

There are film editing tools that will export into the formats needed for the DCP, and these may be useful for festival submissions. Nonetheless, brand-name products such as Adobe Premiere Pro have been reported to have compatibility issues. Instead, film labs will provide the service. Filmmakers may try to use the available tools initially, knowing that the cost of the lab's files will be necessary if the lower-cost alternatives do not create universally operational file sets.

2. For the 35mm Production

For those continuing to work in 35mm, most critical delivery item is the original negative of the cut, finished film and the accompanying optical soundtrack. In addition, distributors typically request an *internegative*—another copy of the negative that is used to strike prints and protect the original negative. Some distribution agreements will also call for an *interpositive*—a print of the film used to make the internegative. If the film is shot on 16mm, the filmmaker must first transfer the film to 35mm before creating the other elements. The internegative and interpositive apply only to celluloid film, whether shot on 16mm or 35mm.

3. Sound and Music

The delivery of sound is a critical component of the final delivery requirements. As described earlier, the typical distributor will require sound separated for dialogue, music, and effects. The distributor may additionally request a stereo or Dolby version, resulting in a six-track mix that must be encoded to work in the DCP package.

In addition to the recorded sound, the written materials necessary to create the sound mix must be delivered. They include copies of the music cue sheets with the necessary timing, the title of each composition, and copyright clearance information, such as copyright owner and publisher.

Distributors will also require the actual music license agreements for each licensed composition used in the film. Every song used, regardless of length, will require an accompanying license from the music publisher and, if the film uses a prerecorded version of the song, from the record label.

4. Titles and Credits

Just as the distributor demands various formats of the print, it will also typically require that the titles be made available both in the final film and as a separate file. Of course, the filmmaker's list of contractual credits must also be complete and supplied to the distributor in writing to assure the distributor that the filmmaker has met all legal obligations.

5. Lab Access Letters

Many of the production elements are stored in a film laboratory rather than with the filmmaker. This facilitates production and distribution. The labs act as an escrow agent, holding the negatives and other elements of the film so that the distributor or distributors can gain access without gaining ownership. To grant the distributor access to a lab's stored materials, the filmmaker signs a simple letter to that effect. The letter grants the lab permission to produce whatever versions of the material are necessary for the distributor and requires that nothing will be removed from the lab without both the filmmaker and the distributor being notified. In this way, neither can disrupt the business of the other.

6. Closed Captions

For many distributors, the film company must also provide closed caption files to enable the project to meet legal requirements under the Americans with Disabilities Act. In some cases, the distributor will advance the cost of these additional materials, but they will eventually be required. The closed caption files will also be a delivery requirement for Amazon's various distribution options and many other direct-to-market services.

7. Promotional Material

The independent filmmaker typically has little ability to help with the promotional requirements of the distributors. Although most distributors will cut their own trailers, they will expect that the filmmaker has cleared the music for such use. They will also seek a variety of photographs of the cast and the shoot to be used in the promotion. Typical requests include color images of the film; additional photographs of the production; color and black-and-white shots of the cast and key production employees; and press books or press kits, if any exist. The filmmaker should remember to shoot still photographs regularly during the course of production so that marketing materials are available. If the film company has engaged in a social media campaign during the production, then these elements were being created and consumed daily throughout the production process. At least a few elements should be held back from the social media campaign to provide the distributor with additional fresh content that has not already been exposed in the marketplace.

The filmmaker may be requested to provide the artwork and materials for the one-sheet poster of the film; both are more important than production photographs. Although the distributor may wish to control all the marketing, the filmmaker should try to meet this demand as a way to control the style and tone of the promotional materials. On the crass assumption that people are generally lazy, the filmmaker may be able to control substantially more of the marketing campaign if the film company voluntarily creates the initial materials as part of the distribution package.

8. Documentation

The required range of documentation will vary considerably from distributor to distributor. The filmmaker should be prepared to provide a certificate of copyright and a statement certifying that the distributor has exclusive rights in the territories granted under the agreement. The transfer of exclusive rights to the territories should be filed with the US Copyright Office, and copies should be made available to the distributor upon request. Distributors will also require a copy of the final screenplay and shooting script.

If the distribution agreement provides that the film will or will not receive a particular rating or ratings (e.g., G or NC-17), then the film company must provide documentation from the MPAA. For independent films, the filmmaker should try to negotiate the distribution agreement to require the distributor attend to this obligation.

The distribution agreement will often establish which party is obligated to obtain errors and omissions insurance. The film company will be required either to submit a copy of the insurance policy or the documentation necessary for the distributor to purchase the insurance. In addition, the film company must provide documentation relating to the filmmaker's valid ownership of the film and its constituent elements. Because the specific documentation requirements will vary greatly, they should be treated as subject to negotiation.

I. Storage and Delivery

The designated film lab should serve as the repository for the DCP or original negative of the film, the final soundtracks, and the alternate scenes and other footage that could conceivably be used in the distribution of the film. Digital films should also have an off-site backup at a secure data warehouse facility.

Everything else will reside with the film company—or more likely in the garage of the filmmaker. If the film is shot on 35mm, then hundreds of hours of undeveloped film stock may be stored there (at high risk of damage and decay). Similar hours of images will be stored on removable hard disks or other digital storage media. Material that may be necessary for distributors in additional markets or territories should be included in the lab storage, while the remainder can be kept at home.

The lab access letter serves as the primary vehicle for delivery. Rather than providing physical copies of most materials required by distributors, the filmmaker can simply authorize access to them. By limiting the ability of both the distributor and the filmmaker to remove the film without notice or permission, the lab helps protect against any unscrupulousness by either party.

The filmmaker must assume that the distributor could go bankrupt or fail to make payments at any point. Although this most likely will not happen, the mere possibility that the original negative could be handed to the distributor and lost or destroyed invokes a filmmaker's nightmare that no amount of money could rectify. The filmmaker must be careful to give only copies of film elements and documents rather than the originals. The originals should always stay in the lab. If the distributor breaches its contract, the filmmaker must be in a position to grant the rights in the film to a new party. If the first distributor has physical custody of the film, the filmmaker is at its mercy. If the original materials are in the lab, the filmmaker can move on.

Finally, the production budget should include the cost of a long-term lease of a storage facility for the documents, film, and other materials. Film must also be archived with particular attention to temperature and humidity, so the types of storage must be carefully selected. The good news is that most independent films will succeed or fail rapidly after their release, and the extra storage can be either justified or eliminated shortly after the film comes out.

Selling the Movie: Distribution and Marketing

18

Promoting the Production— From Script to Screen

The Marketing and Community Engagement Director for the production sits atop an entire division of the production company dedicated to making the film a public event rather than a private experience. When done successfully, the film or series will develop its audience as it grows through preproduction and principal photography, creating a hunger and demand for the work or works of the production company.

A. Marketing Begins Before Principal Photography

Given the importance of social networking and the likelihood that a project's best revenue will come through a streaming platform, the marketing for a movie now begins well before principal photography. Film companies must spend considerable time and effort cultivating an audience that will be receptive to a film's release. While the filmmaker does not necessarily need to become a marketing specialist any more than the filmmaker needs to become a corporate securities expert, someone in the production's leadership must be committed to the long-term strategies to build anticipation for the project and champion its release.

Audiences are drawn to films because of subject matter, writers, directors, and cast, and because of affinities based on geographic community, age, race, ethnicity, religion, hobbies, and vocation. The independent film producer should work with the writers and director to identify which of these elements will be emphasized in the marketing of the film, and the corresponding audience communities must be courted as soon as the film company has confidence in its message. For example, San Diego's Comic-Con has become a critical stop for the launch of genre films such as *Star Trek* and *The Dark Knight* and series like *Stranger Things*. Religious conventions and communities may be an essential launching pad for films of interest to those groups. Mel Gibson's *The Passion of the Christ* broke new marketing territory by courting religious communities well before the film was finished, encouraging group sales, advance home video purchases, and written praise of the project.

1. Start with the Distribution Strategy in Sight

Virtually every production of every size has some presence to engage with its potential audience as soon the title is announced. IMDb lists productions in their earliest preproduction stage, enabling the industry and the fans of particular actors, writers, directors, and series to follow the progress being made.

For online series and web content, the nature of the production work is much like traditional broadcast series work. There is a demand to feed the beast, providing the audience new material on a regular schedule, often weekly or less. Netflix changed television consumption with its decision to begin producing short series of 6–13 episodes as a series rather than a broadcast series of 22 episodes. But the tradeoff for the shorter number of episodes in a season has been the practice of dropping the entire season at once. Essentially, Netflix has merely increased the viewing length of feature films from three to ten hours.

Maintaining a YouTube, Twitch, or Facebook channel requires a significant amount of content being produced on a very regular basis. The terms of service for these competitors change regularly as Google, Amazon, and Facebook—the three owners of these services—jockey to maximize revenue and market share.

A feature film can opt to be much more circumspect about the content it produces and distributes during preproduction and principal photography. While it has the option to engage less actively, the production company can also choose to be very vigorous and engaged. If the project is a feature film using a crowdfunding or crowd financing campaign, then it will need nearly as much content as an online series as a way to engage the donors or investors.

2. Essential and Optional Material

Film companies tend to get caught up in the details of making the movie, but marketing is about reinforcing the reasons to attend the finished film. Rather than providing a weekly update on principal photography, the update should focus on reminding the core audience why the forthcoming movie will benefit their community and be worth the wait. Since the film will be available almost everywhere eventually, the investment in this audience will be very helpful.

Every film or series needs a trailer to tell enough about the work to entice the audience while avoiding the elements of the story that give away the ending or serve as a substitute for the film. Unfortunately, many two-hour films can be edited down to a three-minute trailer. Particularly if the story is a one-joke premise, the trailer will do untold damage to the marketability. Filmmakers should learn from this. Even assuming the trailer does not give away a film's ending, if a trailer can capture the entire story, chances are that the story needs to be reimagined.

In contrast, productions have been funded because the public fell in love with a short film. The short introduced the characters and conflict, helping finance the feature-length version of the story. The constant return to remakes and sequels demonstrates that an audience is more than willing to engage in a fresh retelling of a story the audience already knows. For these films, the trailer and the collateral material must capture what is fresh about the production. Typically, this is a new cast, and may also include the locations and modern production techniques.

Beyond the trailer, a great deal of content can be used to capture the attention of the public online. The type of content should relate to the core audience. If the project is driven by its cast or its director, then the social media and website should lean into those members of the company to engage the public. If the film is targeting an audience, then those elements of the storytelling become the most important. For example, if the film is religious in nature, then the material should include short segments that reinforce why the religious audience needs to support this message. Endorsements from religious leaders, on-camera interviews, targeted social media, and similar techniques can be used to create a community.

If the story is based on a book, comic book, or video game, then short articles regarding the translation to the big screen generally promote interest. If the story is closely based on a true life story, then material that provides information on that connection is also helpful. The reason for choosing to tell a story based on preexisting material is to connect with its existing audience. Online engagement offers the time to begin that relationship.

If the film is a science fiction project, then the engagement team should take advantage of science fiction and comic book conventions to meet potential audience members both in person and online. There may be the potential to collaborate with other storytellers by finding a freelance graphic artist to come on board and create a comic book version of the film for use in a crowdfunding campaign or marketing campaign. Like the filmmaker, the comic book artist may find the collaboration a positive endeavor. Science fiction films have a strong affinity with video games, so the video game streaming platform Twitch might serve as a useful tool.

The point of social media marketing is that the audience does the work. The public are the broadcasters as well as the audience, creating a many-to-many network that can embrace a project and drive recognition, or it can ignore even a highly funded campaign and cause that project to fade into oblivion. For direct marketing, the engagement team should focus on constant online engagement, starting with the most connected audience—the followers of everyone involved in the production—and moving outward to the people inside the followers' networks—and so on, and so on.

3. What Not to Sell

For the independent filmmaker, the primary benefit of a prerelease campaign is the control it provides over the nature of the message. The film *Innerspace* was a broad comedy initially sold as a science fiction thriller. The audience reaction to the movie as a science fiction film was utter disinterest. The film was so unanimously ignored that the distributor actually rereleased the movie with a new campaign focused on its comedic aspect, and the movie finally gained some revenue and credibility.

Prerelease materials must be balanced between revealing so little that they annoy audiences and so much that they make the movie feel old when it is finally released. "Teaser" campaigns that reveal nothing about the film have very short shelf lives, so they should only be used in the days leading to the film's release. Similarly, footage from the shoot should be provided very selectively. Without color correction and special effects, the scenes may present a far less professional image than that hoped for by the film company, and it would be very expensive to polish the footage sufficiently.

Clips of documentary films may be more effective than clips from narrative films at attracting an audience. Documentaries rarely have surprise endings anyway, so clips reflecting aspects of the movie being developed may encourage the audience and perhaps even improve access to individuals who have content relevant to the film. For many documentaries, there is less postproduction work than for narrative films, so the cost of readying clips should also be less.

4. Informational Websites

The Internet is home to a great number of websites that talk about films. Many of these allow the public to provide information about specific movies. The film company should take advantage of this and actively post information about its own movie. In particular, the company should be sure the film is properly listed on IMDb, a powerful search engine that provides detailed cast and crew information. If nothing else, IMDb enables the cast and crew to move on to their next productions, and part of the filmmaker's duty is to help continue the careers of all those individuals who invested time in the production.

All postings about the film should include links back to the film company's website and provide a hub for the social network outreach on each platform utilized by the production company. SEO (search engine optimization) and links back to the film company's own website both continue to improve native search rankings, so maximizing the search links remains a beneficial aspect of the marketing. If sharable content is posted directly from the company website and the tools make it easy for the fans of the cast and crew and the supporters of the crowdfunding campaign to post and reshare content, then the network will expand.

The two most significant tools are the ratings system of Netflix and the commentary system on IMDb, an Amazon company. In both cases, strong ratings and positive comments on the film will make it more visible to others. The filmmaker should encourage everyone who has seen the movie at festivals, in previews, and during the initial release to promote the film as positively as they are willing. Following this same strategy, the film company should use its website and other platforms to let interested viewers know when the film is available for preorders. Often, the number of reviews is very small, so a few passionate fans can have a powerful impact on the ratings— and sales—of the films in prerelease.

5. Social Networking

Social networking has become a powerful online tool, connecting professionals on sites such as LinkedIn or friends on sites like Facebook. The film company should create accounts on each of the major social networks to help encourage interest in the film and build an email list of potential viewers. The ability to let the production be followed and to engage with the audience directly will be very helpful, particularly for nontheatrical releases.

Filmmakers cannot afford to be shy. Ask audience members to remember to provide reviews. App developers and product manufacturers are constantly reminding customers to rate their products, and the ratings for films mean even more in terms of placement on the streaming and downloading service platforms. Provide easy links in all media and engage consistently.

6. Return of the Cliff-Hanger: Webisodes

The Internet has reshaped the music industry and will do the same to both television and motion pictures. In recognition that much of the content on the Internet is transmitted in shorter segments of two to six minutes, television companies have already begun producing webisodes of this length to distribute over the web. These webisodes complement existing programming and increasingly will replace it. For example, animated webisodes have been released to maintain interest in the Iron Man comics franchise, and Star Wars animated shorts were released between feature films.

Webisodes are reintroducing an old dramatic form. During the 1940s and 1950s, cliff-hangers were the very popular shorts presented before feature films. Saturday-morning audiences would come to see their favorite characters struggle through chases, crashes, and other life-threatening situations—but each short would end in the middle of just such a crisis. The open-ended conclusion kept the kids wanting to come back the following week. Eventually, however, these shorts lost ground to the weekly television episode and were dropped from theatrical bills.

Webisodes return to the cliff-hanger formula and may constitute an alternate manner for a filmmaker to tell a story. In some cases, a previously completed film can appropriately be edited into a series of 20 six-minute episodes. At the end of each episode, the filmmaker appends the web address for the film and a short ad encouraging the viewer to buy the DVD. Webisodes may also be an opportunity to further develop the story of the film, providing additional content that explores the backstory of the main characters, side stories relating to minor characters, or mini-sequels that keep the characters and central themes of the movie in front of the audience.

Webisodes may begin to replace independent filmmaking. Shooting a two- to six-minute movie requires far less time and effort than a feature-length film. That said, telling a complete and fulfilling story in six minutes is more challenging than doing so in two hours. The short will not generate significant revenue, but a series of such shorts can provide filmmakers with a sample reel to help open doors.

A webisode is a different art form from a feature-length film. But, hopefully, each medium will help improve the other.

B. Marketing Through Traditional Distribution Channels

For the production company in search of an eventual theatrical release, the most important audience is the small world of film distributors who purchase films to sell. The film distributors market the films using the traditional windows of theatrical, home rental/sale, pay-per-view, premium cable, broadcast, and basic cable, with sales to Netflix, YouTube Premium, and Amazon Prime Video generally in the home rental window, though sometimes they are delayed until the pay-per-view window.

Distributors generally work by playing the odds. A distributor will "buy" a number of movies and then support only the movie that proves easiest to sell. The only cost to the distributor is the advance, and often distributors buy films with little or no advance. If the distributor has not committed to a significant advance or a contractual obligation to spend money on a title, then that film may sit in the distributor's catalog without any marketing effort. The distributor will focus most of its attention on those films in which it has a large investment and those films that begin to gather market interest on their own. If a title becomes hot, the distributor will usually take advantage of the momentum.

To build the momentum, the film company must help promote the film. This may duplicate a small distributor's job, but realistically it will help the film to stand out from the rest of the distributor's catalog. A side benefit is that promotion often promotes the filmmaker and the rest of the cast and crew as much as the particular film, an angle that is far more valuable to the production team than to the distributor. On the other hand, the time spent in active promotion pulls the filmmaker away from developing the next motion picture and can easily sidetrack a career.

The good news is that the efforts to create a positive word of mouth for the acquisition or motivation of a distributor complement the efforts to engage directly with the film audience described in the previous section. The production company should employ a two-pronged effort, engaging the audience and the market makers on the festival circuit and in the media.

1. Festivals and Critics

Perhaps the easiest step in the filmmaker's own campaign is garnering positive reviews for the film. If the project is successful when screened, the film will be much more likely to become a commercial success. If the film does not play well, then the marketing efforts will do little to change opinions. The good news is that some people like brussels sprouts. No matter how quirky or idiosyncratic the film, as long as it is not a technical disaster, some critic out there will rave about it.

The hardest thing about working as a filmmaker is that the corollary is also true. No matter how brilliant the film, some critics will find it repugnant and many will find it old hat. Criticism goes with the territory.

To get good reviews, the film company simply needs to screen the film where critics will see it and wait for some of those critics to write strong, laudatory articles about the film. Since critics come to film festivals, the film needs to be shown through the festival circuit. To manage the criticism, the filmmaker should be selective. The most famous of film festivals will propel the project to a national stage. At the same time, investing all the time and effort to be largely ignored at one of the most prestigious festivals will tend to close doors.

Regional film festivals will often generate a good deal of press hoping to boost the films on exhibit. If a filmmaker can take advantage of favorable hometown support, then the filmmaker should build this into the distribution strategy. Hometown support will also help with the filmmaker's access to financing on the next project and the filmmaker's general sense of well-being and success. A filmmaker who is not yet famous in New York or Los Angeles can still be something of a celebrity in a smaller market with fewer local heroes. The film is unlikely to be seen by a distributor at these festivals, but the positive reviews will be helpful for later negotiations.

2. Hometown Press

If the film is to be shown in a one-newspaper town, which is the vast majority of communities today, then the paper's film critic must be invited to the opening. Often critics' reputations for the types of movies they like and dislike are well known, but an unsympathetic critic cannot be avoided. The critic is likely to show up anyway—just with a grudge. If the local critic truly has a vendetta against the filmmaker or a public hatred for the genre, then open the film elsewhere.

The local film critic will not be the only journalist to write a story. When a local resident makes good, that makes local news. Often the stories are very kind, designed to make everyone feel good about their neighbors. This is very helpful press. Local television, radio, online magazines, and even blogs all need local content. Every bandwagon has to start somewhere, and the lightest piece of hometown fluff will still pad the publicity package. If the article compliments the film itself, then so much the better.

3. Specialty Markets

Independent films often tell stories that speak to small communities rather than the mainstream. Although Spike Lee's *Do the Right Thing* and Steven Spielberg's *Schindler's List* were nationally recognized films, most niche projects fizzle at the box office and as a result do not receive studio financing. Still, independent filmmakers create these movies as powerful testaments to their heritage and culture. Having made such a film, a filmmaker should turn to these communities for its first audience.

This strategy involves both the institutions of a community and the community itself. First, within each self-identified community are organizations that serve as the focus of that community's public outreach. Enthusiastic support from the leadership of these organizations may open doors to mainstream distribution and will certainly enhance media attention. These organizations are typically part of national and international coalitions of similar organizations that share common interests. Letters of introduction from local leadership may expand the potential to reach national boards.

Second, these community organizations may be able to deliver interested audiences for the filmmaker. Particularly for a film in a small platform or four-wall release (when a filmmaker rents the theater, discussed in chapter 19, p. 363), a strong, positive endorsement by the local community newsletter or paper will do far more to sell tickets than any paid ad. The filmmaker may even consider encouraging the community group to four-wall the film directly for only a modest fee. Let the local church underwrite the costs of the evening and keep the proceeds (less the fee) as a fundraiser. The filmmaker will have made a modest profit and generate substantial word of mouth regarding the film.

The collaboration with these special interest groups can occur both before and after the official release of the project. Organizations love to get in on the ground floor. Offering "prerelease" screenings to help recoup costs and gain word of mouth can significantly improve the buzz and enthusiasm for the film and provide some income that does not have to be shared with distributors. As noted in the discussion on revenue distributions, a direct payment for showing the film will earn the production company more than twice the revenue as the same payment made by the public to an exhibitor. A savvy production company can spend months in prerelease sales to community organizations.

4. Distribute Advance Copies

Nothing tells the story better than the story itself. No one sells the film better than those who believe in it. The filmmaker can combine these two truisms into a powerful marketing tool. Every member of the cast and crew has acquaintances who will be interested in seeing the project. Some of them may be helpful in finding a distributor or soliciting a positive review. The combined contacts of cast and crew may create a powerful base of people willing to screen the film and promote it to their friends and contacts. Add the investors to this group, and the list begins to have some potential as a marketing tool.

Rather than distributing DVDs without introduction, the contact person from the cast and crew should draft a letter that explains why the person is receiving the film and by whom the mailing was initiated. Follow-up information should also be included so that interested recipients can get additional information. At worst, this technique serves as a nice community-building tool within the film company. At best, it may open doors the filmmaker never knew existed.

C. Contractual Commits in Marketing

Negotiations with the film's stars and key personnel may also give rise to contractual obligations regarding the film's marketing efforts. At a minimum, both the filmmaker and any distributors must respect the obligations regarding credit size and placement granted to particular cast and crew members. Additionally, some cast members may have negotiated for picture placement in the marketing campaign. In that case, the filmmaker and distributor must use the photograph of the particular cast member in the posters and marketing material.

If other cast members negotiated "favored nations" provisions in their employment agreements, then they also are entitled to the photo placement. These contracts can severely limit the flexibility of the marketing campaign. If the distributor creates a great campaign that would violate the contractual rights of an actor, then the filmmaker must seek that actor's permission to waive the contractual obligation and use the campaign.

The original contracts for the cast and crew members should have included a provision granting the filmmaker the right to use the person's publicity rights, including name, likeness, voice, and signature, as part of the marketing and packaging of the film. If written permission was not provided, then it should be obtained prior to using any person in the marketing of the film.

In the agreement between the filmmaker and any distributor, these contractual obligations should be incorporated to become a contractual obligation on the part of the distributor. In the case of the production company's website and social media campaigns, the production company must be mindful of its contractual obligations regarding the use of the publicity rights granted by the cast and crew as well as any limitations that have been placed on it.

There may have been other contractual obligations, such as the commitment to acknowledge film offices, provide thank-you credits to investors, and similar duties. While the website is technically not the same as the end credits in the film, it is a useful tool to promote the people and organizations that helped get the project completed. It is good practice, if not a legal requirement, to provide these credits when practical.

D. Marketing Other Elements of the Project

For films that have been successfully distributed, whether through theatrical release, download and streaming, or online platforms, additional revenue opportunities may present themselves. For all additional sources, the filmmaker must be sure to have secured the legal rights to the film's marketing materials for such uses. This means signing contracts with the creators of those materials to cover not only the film in every media but also all products related to the film. If the distributor of the film created the marketing materials, then the distribution agreement should include a license to use those materials in distribution markets not controlled by that distributor—and in all potential product markets.

1. Novelizations

While many films derive from novels or short stories, the story told in the film often makes for good reading as well. Therefore, films are increasingly the source for new novels. Assuming the film company properly purchased all the elements of the story, no additional contracts are necessary to create the novel of the film. Many screenwriters view the novelization as an opportunity to maintain control of the story, and they may seek the right to be the writer of the novel if they so choose. (This is referred to as a *right of first refusal;* the filmmaker is obligated to ask the screenwriter before asking anyone else.)

One compromise on the awarding of the right of first refusal to the screenwriter is to condition the grant on the screenwriter receiving sole screen credit, pursuant to the film's credit dispute policy. So a single screenwriter who truly wrote and controlled the story will receive that same opportunity with regard to the novel, while screenwriters who may have contributed to the story in a less exclusive way can be politely told no. Of course, the filmmaker can still offer the opportunity to write the novel to one of the screenwriters who received shared credit, but there would no longer be a contractual obligation to do so.

The novelization rights will be sold to a publishing house, which will typically distribute the novel only in a mass-market paperback or trade paperback edition. If the film is an original story, and a particularly compelling one literarily speaking, the filmmaker may seek to use the novel to promote a theatrical distribution deal.

2. Merchandizing and Licensing

Perhaps the biggest windfall for motion pictures today is the merchandise tie-in. *Star Wars* (perhaps the largest-budget independent film ever created) spawned an empire of toys, games, dolls, and paraphernalia that now spans four decades. Like the creation of the soundtrack album, the key to merchandizing is control of the necessary elements. First, the filmmaker must control the marketing rights to the title, artwork, and photographs used to promote the movie. Second, the filmmaker or the product manufacturer must license the publicity rights of the actors.

An action figure cannot be created using the likeness of an actor without that actor's express permission. While these publicity rights are typically assigned to the film company for the ability to make and market the film, that contract would not cover dolls or games. These items must be separately licensed, and the actors will generally receive a small royalty or profit participation from these agreements.

Even a small film is likely to develop posters and T-shirts. These items are certainly popular among the cast and crew, but they might develop some market interest. The popularity of these items has as much to do with the cast or the artwork as it does with the film, so it should be treated as a slightly different business opportunity from the film itself. The sale of these items is not covered by the actors' publicity rights provisions in their employment agreement, so additional permission will be required.

3. Story Rights

Finally, the filmmaker may sell the story itself. It is no longer uncommon for Hollywood to remake movies that are still available on video and played often on television. *Planet of the Apes* and *Rambo* illustrate this temptation. In addition, filmmakers are often haunted by the difficult choices imposed by very low-budget filmmaking and may wish to revisit the material later in their careers.

Story rights may include simple remakes or provide for the expansion of the original story through sequels, prequels, and spin-offs. Sequels are not limited to action stories like *Star Wars* or characters like James Bond. Children's characters naturally lend themselves to multiple adventures. Character-driven stories such as *Terms of Endearment*, *The Godfather*, and *Chinatown* opened the door for continuing sagas.

The ability to exploit the story rights in new projects brings the legal analysis full circle to the beginning of the book: the ability to create new works will depend on what rights were initially purchased, which entities own the rights, and how the financing was structured. The filmmaker should have made these original choices with an eye toward the film being produced and the future stories yet to be told. By acquiring sufficient rights, the filmmaker can increase the opportunities to participate in the lives of the characters as they develop from individual films into franchises.

19

Theatrical Distribution

The distribution of audiovisual works is far different in the Internet age than it was during the time of the major studios and major broadcast networks. Before the streaming explosion and the use of mobile devices to make viewing ubiquitous, a filmmaker would engage a sales agent to help land a theatrical distributor. If the film achieved United States theatrical distribution, that would open the door for a series of agreements involving international theatrical distribution and the distribution windows of home video, pay-per-view, premium cable, broadcast, cable, and specialty markets. Without the theatrical distribution, the title would generally be sold to home video and premium cable without the option for pay-per-view or broadcast. Though this model generally held true, each genre had a slightly unique distribution profile, and many individual films overperformed or underperformed the sales based on its cast and its critical reception.

The time-based structure of the distribution windows has been eroding with the growth in importance of Netflix, Amazon Prime Video, YouTube Premium, and Hulu. The addition of major streaming services, such as Disney+ and Apple TV+, and the move to online distribution by the broadcast conglomerates began to challenge this model. The closure of the movie theaters in 2020 due to the novel coronavirus has accelerated the deconstruction of this model. Streaming services have supplanted premium cable, and they have become the second most significant market for independent film, after theatrical distribution.

In addition, although the number of theatrical releases has always been a fraction of the films commercially released, there is also the ability to distribute directly through the Internet on YouTube, Vimeo, iTunes, MUBI, Festival Scope, Shudder, Docsville, IndieFlix, and many others. These different platforms offer many options for the filmmaker.

As a result of the fragmentation in the market, filmmakers face many more choices than in prior eras. This chapter focuses on how best to address the preparation needed to distribute the film and grow an audience.

Theatrical distribution remains the ultimate success for all films. The hope of being discovered through a showing at Sundance Film Festival or South by Southwest (known simply as "South By" to insiders and written as SXSW) remains a real but challenging goal. New Yorkers will gravitate to the Tribeca Film Festival. The good news is that for a few films every year, the hope turns into reality.

A. Distribution Economics

The rental of films from distributors to theatrical exhibitors is a complex transaction, defined by historical relationships and years of legal conflict during the 1930s through the 1950s that continue to shape the transactional practices today.

The challenge is that Sundance, for example, receives approximately 4,000 features for the 120 presentation slots. SXSW receives over 7,000 submissions, but that likely includes shorts as well as feature-length projects.

The number of theatrical releases has risen, topping the levels that had been achieved before the 2009 recession. In 2018, there were 873 theatrical releases, a modern record. That number dropped to 792 in 2019. Only 87 of the films theatrically released in 2019 were from major Hollywood studios. This makes room for independently created films to fill the remaining holes. Despite the financial dominance of the major studios, the market of 2019 still created many opportunities for independent films to have theatrical releases. Theatrical releases in 2019 accounted for only 31 percent of the overall motion picture market, with 56 percent shifting to the digital market, and the physical market of DVDs and Blu-rays declining to 13 percent. In addition, 73 percent of the market is foreign, with only 27 percent representing the US and Canadian market. The collapse of the theatrical market in 2020 due to the coronavirus pandemic will likely be reversed in years to come, but the explosive increase in streaming will result in a long-term decline in theatrical distribution, hasten the end of the physical market, shrink the cable markets, and further extend the dominance of the digital market.

Even before 2020, the numbers painted a picture of a theatrical market that is driven by blockbusters and internationally focused titles. Many movies do all their business in a two- to four-week period, with tremendous drop-offs in sales after the opening weekend. For an independent film that needs word of mouth to build, there is no longer the patience in the marketplace for a slow opening and build. It can still happen, but the data demonstrates that most small releases end with little revenue or impact.

The other takeaway is that for most independent production companies, the best strategy involves self-distribution based on a strong investment in time and effort to build an audience in anticipation of the film's release. The film will be shown in festivals and in hometown exhibition and then sold exclusively on Vimeo for a one- or two-month exclusive window before being pushed to every conceivable online platform. But most filmmakers still think in terms of theatrical distribution, so this chapter follows the traditional distribution approach, and chapter 20 (p. 366) provides the strategies for nontheatrical distribution.

B. Money Flows and Returns to the Production Company

The money earned at the box office is shared among many parties. As noted in chapter 9 (pp. 167–176) on budgeting, collecting the funds at the bottom of the waterfall comes only after all the other parties in the revenue streams have received their returns.

1. Exhibitors' Participation in Revenues

The average film provides very roughly half of its box office revenue to the exhibitor with the other half returning to the distributor—but this is not how the contracts are structured. Instead, the theater is guaranteed a *nut*, or minimum revenue for showing the film, and the distributor is guaranteed a *floor*, or minimum revenue of the next monies earned above the nut. Assuming the film has done well enough to fulfill both guarantees, both the distributor and the exhibitor split the revenue from ticket sales on a sliding scale.

In the first week the percentages may range such as 70:30 in favor of the distributor. As the weeks continue, the percentage begins to become more balanced toward the exhibitor, creating an increasing financial incentive for the exhibitor to keep a film longer. The distributor, in contrast, is encouraged to spend aggressively on marketing to maximize the ticket sales in the first week or two of distribution. Increasingly, marketing efforts have devoted greater and greater emphasis on attendance on a film's opening weekend.

The exhibitor enjoys higher attendance and other benefits from the front-loading of the audience into fewer weeks. The overhead for running a theater includes the movies' projectionists, ticket takers, popcorn sellers, and cleaning crew. These employee expenses over a given period of time remain largely the same regardless of a film's popularity during that period. Since the overhead is inelastic, the greater the revenue, the lower the overhead as a percentage of gross income, resulting in a greater profit. Movie theaters also have a very high profitability on their concession items, and the distributors do not receive any percentage of this income. So movie theaters earn higher revenue from the greater attendance generated by a succession of big openings and short runs than the modest attendance generated by a single film's extended run.

2. Change in Audience Expectations

Audience behavior has both followed and encouraged this trend. With the large number of screens for a national release and the decrease in time for films to stay in theaters, theatergoers feel increased social pressure to attend a film when it first opens. In addition, publication of reviews, blogs, clips, and spoilers has driven audiences to see a film in the opening week or to wait for it online.

3. Relationship to the Independent Film

A broad, national distribution strategy is only one way to sell a movie. There remain theater chains dedicated to independent and foreign films and other movies that benefit from more niche marketing. Unfortunately, the high cost of marketing does not favor these theaters, which rely on much smaller but loyal audiences and marketing through websites, newsletters, and word of mouth. These exhibitors continue to struggle to remain solvent.

Theatrical distribution continues to provide important marketing support for streaming, downloads, sales, and broadcast, which will occur later in the film's distribution life, so these alternative distribution channels remain extremely important for the independent film industry. Whether they are a critical part of a particular film's strategy depends on the costs of production, the advertising budget, and the expectations of the filmmaker and distributor.

C. How to Entice and Select a Distributor

For most theatrical distribution, the film company must enter into an agreement with a film distributor that will promote the film and negotiate with theaters in each of the exhibition markets. The distributor will be responsible for shaping the marketing and publicity strategy, paying for marketing, striking prints of the film, and promoting the film in each market in which it is shown.

If the filmmaker is highly adept at writing, directing, or editing films, then the filmmaker may prefer to avoid investing years learning how to sell them as well. The filmmaker and the film are both better served if the filmmaker works to create movies and allows the distributor to perform its obligations to promote and market its films.

The duty of the filmmaker is simply to create the best possible market opportunities for the distributor. This requires that the filmmaker take certain strategic steps to prepare the film for sale to the distributor and to ensure that the distributor can meet its obligations. Each of the following steps helps to increase the odds that the film will be sold to an enthusiastic and experienced distributor.

1. Show Only Final Product

The filmmaker should show only the completed film unless there is no feasible alternative. Few people have the ability to watch a film with the sound incomplete, the color not balanced, or cuts missing, without judging the overall quality of the film based on its missing elements. Worse, distributors will not recognize their lack of that ability. Many subtle techniques that polish the final version operate below the audience's consciousness. If the techniques were noticeable, they would detract from the film. Thus, the more polished the final film, the more misleading the unfinished preview.

If the filmmaker cannot afford to finish the film, the production company would be better advised to present an extended trailer of the film, along with a one-sheet poster and production stills. The distributor needs a good trailer and promotional material to sell the film; the quality of the film itself is secondary. For the filmmaker faced with the hardest decisions regarding the last few dollars in the production budget, the trailer and promotional materials should be the priority unless the film can be completely finished—not just rough cut.

2. Sell the Biggest Markets First

Distribution costs for a studio film often exceed the total costs of independent films. Each 35mm print of the film may cost $3,000 to $5,000, so a wide distribution of 3,000 screens can run as much as $1 million in print costs alone. DCP is cheaper, but not significantly so. If a film is to open nationally, advertising costs often run between $20 million and $200 million, depending on the size of the release and the intensity of the campaign.

Although independent films are rarely treated to this level of marketing, the filmmaker should not ignore the long-term impact of any substantial market investment. A strong advertising campaign does not automatically result in theatrical ticket sales, but it is not uncommon for a film to bomb at the box office but later soar to the top of the video sales or streaming popularity with almost no additional marketing. A distributor who controls both theatrical and video distribution should be much more willing to invest in promotion than a distributor that owns only one of those markets. The combined budget of the two markets distributed separately will invariably be less than what a single distributor would spend on them.

The filmmaker should incorporate this marketing reality into the sales strategy. Early in the selling cycle, the filmmaker should insist that the United States market be sold only to distributors who can exploit all or most of the domestic markets. The goal is to sell all United States rights to maximize the value of the sale. Selling small pieces of the domestic market will frustrate the ability to finalize deals with companies that exploit rights across all markets.

3. Know the Film

Perhaps the hardest job of the filmmaker is to realistically assess the value of the film. The filmmaker knows intimately what the film cost to make but has little idea how many people would be willing to pay full price to see it at the movie theater. In order to have realistic conversations with film distributors, the filmmaker must develop some perspective on the film. A lack of perspective can cut both ways: Early in the sales process, the filmmaker may believe that the film should win all the Oscars. After a few months of distributor rejections, the filmmaker may think that the film should not be allowed on public access television, even at 2:00 AM.

Realism helps build credibility with the distributor, assists in properly positioning the film within the distributor's catalog of films, and creates a solid basis for the contract negotiations. Without these attributes, even the most marketable film may go unseen.

Knowing the film is most critical when the filmmaker has choices regarding the distributor. If the filmmaker receives multiple distribution offers, this knowledge will match the film to the strengths and successes of the distributor.

4. Enter Film Festivals Selectively

The independent film marketplace is something of a community. For filmmakers who consistently create independent work, the premier film festivals are the professional equivalent of the Academy Awards—an opportunity to move among peers as leaders in the industry. New filmmakers can learn a great deal about the realities of the industry by participating and seeking out mentors.

Participating in film festivals serves as an efficient way to get the filmmaker's work in front of potential distributors and a paying audience. Most films are made to be viewed in social settings. Comedies, for example, are always funnier to a viewer laughing along with a live audience. Film festivals provide a powerful marketing opportunity and a chance to display the film to a distributor in a far superior setting than on a television in an office.

The filmmaker must still be careful. Not all festivals are alike. Some are stellar events; others are of less value. Filmmakers must be selective or the submission fees and time commitments may undermine any value of attending the festivals. The filmmaker should learn what films have previously come out of each festival, whether the festival is a true marketplace for distribution deals, and in what regard a festival is held by the independent film community. Local festivals in the filmmaker's hometown may be given special consideration. They can create opportunities for press coverage, and travel fees are eliminated.

The more prestigious North American festivals include the Sundance Film Festival, the New York Film Festival, the Toronto International Film Festival, the Montreal World Film Festival, the South by Southwest (SXSW) festival, and the Telluride Film Festival. These festivals are highly competitive, but the exposure should help improve the chances of distribution for most films. That is not to suggest that getting into one of these festivals will guarantee a distribution deal. The New York Film Festival shows approximately 50 films annually, and the Sundance Film Festival screens approximately 120. Only a small percentage of the films shown even at these festivals go on to theatrical distribution.

Even if the percentages seem hopeless, there is a silver lining. Film festivals put the filmmaker in a room with thousands of other filmmakers, producers, distributors, and others with the same profession and passion. Even if the film does not end up in theatrical release, it may impress producers looking for talent on other projects or actors willing to take a risk on new material. The opportunities are real.

5. Go Where the Buyers Are: Attend Film Markets

In addition to the competitive film festivals, many films debut at film markets such as the American Film Market, held every November in Santa Monica, or the Cannes Film Market, held in conjunction with the Cannes Film Festival. Typically, film markets are huge, weeklong affairs with thousands of participants. While there may be some panels, mixers, and other secondary activities, the primary goal is to screen films for sales agents and distributors seeking to purchase content. These markets are likely to be more financially rewarding than film festivals, since the former are geared to film buyers more than the general public.

Filmmakers may try to be strategic about participation in film markets as part of an overall distribution strategy. The filmmaker may reduce the film's marketing guarantee if the film is sold at a film market prior to winning a significant festival award. On the other hand, the distributor may anticipate a better response from competitions than what ultimately occurs, so that the guarantee advanced would be higher. Ultimately, such timing is a matter of serendipity.

D. Knowing the Distributors

Distributors tend to specialize in a particular strategy they use for distribution. Major studios specialize in the distribution of nationally released and heavily marketed films. They do not regularly use the tools that drive smaller marketing campaigns, so they are less familiar with such campaigns and less competent at carrying them out. Small distribution companies, on the other hand, do not have the staff or experience to handle the distribution of over 5,000 prints, a simultaneous worldwide release, and a $50 million advertising buy. When seeking distributors, rather than focusing on the size of the distribution company, the filmmaker should consider whether its distribution strategy will help the film find an audience.

The filmmaker should know who the significant distributors are so that when one expresses an interest, the filmmaker can quickly assess the credibility of its enthusiasm. The filmmaker should look carefully at films that have a similar audience demographic to the movie and identify those projects that were effectively released by their distributor. Both the filmmaker and the potential distributor will be more successful if they share a common vision on how the film can best be marketed and supported.

1. The Majors

Each major motion picture producer operates as a major motion picture distributor as well. The vast majority of films produced in the United States are released domestically by these companies. They are vertically integrated telecommunication giants that own production and distribution companies along with many other media resources.

Although the corporate ownership has varied considerably over the past century, the roster of film studios has changed only slightly since the early days of the MPAA. There are now five majors: Warner Bros. (WarnerMedia), Universal Studios (NBCUniversal), Sony Pictures Entertainment (formerly Columbia Pictures Entertainment), Paramount Pictures (ViacomCBS), and the Walt Disney Company, which recently acquired 20th Century Fox. MGM was the seventh original member of the MPAA and has emerged as a mini-major with a healthy film library and limited production slate. In 2019, Disney dominated the box office with 38 percent of all revenue. The launch of Disney+ has been the fastest rollout of any streaming platform, becoming the service with the third largest audience behind Netflix and Amazon Prime Video.

2. The Mini-Majors

All the majors also own smaller film production companies. Although each company is operated in its own idiosyncratic fashion, these smaller, wholly owned companies often make their own purchasing decisions. The changes in media have led to multiple reorganizations within the studios. Many of the studio-owned companies have been consolidated, transforming these companies into in-house brands of their parent studios, without separate purchasing staff or distribution strategies. Other companies with large production slates in film, scripted television, and other media include Lionsgate, MGM Studios, Miramax (no longer associated with the Weinsteins), Open Road Films, IFC Films, and STX Entertainment.

3. The Streaming Platforms

More important than the next tier of film distributors are the streamers who produce original content for streaming and downloading, often with the occasional, limited theatrical release for prestige films. Netflix leads all other companies in working to transform the distribution model for narrative films, documentaries, and series. Amazon Prime Video has emerged as the other leader in online content production and distribution. Disney+ had planned to build its subscriber base to 50 million viewers by 2022, but instead surpassed 73 million in its first year.

Apple has entered the market with a similar business model labeled Apple TV+. CBS launched Paramount+, NBC created Peacock, and the Discovery Channel created Discovery+. Every traditional broadcast company is looking to deliver its content online and to create additional content produced for nonbroadcast markets. These online formats are rapidly subsuming the role of the subscription cable services Showtime and HBO, which are likely to decline in importance as the market turns to the streaming services at the expense of cable. Although each of the streaming services is a distribution platform, most are also producing original content and buying independent projects directly. In consequence, a transaction with a major streaming service replaces both the distribution and exhibition deals for traditional film sales. Except in rare instances, the acquisition by one of these services will result in a nontheatrical release. Chapter 20 (pp. 368–369) provides details on these transactions.

4. Everyone Else

There are hundreds of independent film distributors working in the United States, but few of the remaining distributors have significant impact on the theatrical market. Even though most independent filmmakers do not have the opportunity to distribute their films theatrically, the possibility should not be conceded without a fight. If no experienced theatrical distributor offers a contract, the filmmaker should begin to work with the remaining distributors on how best to maximize the impact of the film.

E. The Importance of International Distribution

Throughout the filmmaking industry, the larger growths in revenue have come from Asia and Central America, with some modest growth coming from Europe as well. Filmmakers who fail to distribute in these markets may easily forgo half the film's potential revenue. At the same time, independent filmmakers have few resources to carefully monitor distribution activities across the globe, so it is critically important that they work with companies that have established track records.

If a film is successful in attracting the interest of a large distribution company, that company is likely to seek worldwide distribution rights. Assuming the company has an established record for selling its films overseas, this one-stop shopping arrangement is likely to provide the filmmaker with the greatest opportunity to earn international revenue and to return to producing new works. Moreover, a single distributor is likely to craft domestic and foreign marketing strategies that complement each other.

As an alternative, the filmmaker should seek out an international sales agent, which can work to sell the film in the various unsold territories. As with every other distributor, the key to selecting the international sales agent is the track record it has had with sales of similar films.

In addition to providing access to foreign markets, the international sales agent should guide the filmmaker regarding the distribution requirements and censorship standards in each market or territory. The filmmaker should be able to rely on the international sales agent to know how the movie will fit into these standards and practices.

Whether negotiated directly with the distributor or through an international sales agent, the distribution agreement should specify that any modifications to the film must be approved by the film company, rather than being made unilaterally by the foreign distributor, and it should provide the film company with the authority to withhold the film from any market that would require unacceptable changes to the content of the film.

F. The Distribution Deal

Every distribution agreement, large or small, covers the same fundamental issues. The distributor must promote the film in various media, collect payments, and share those payments with the film company. In addition to the filmmaker's delivery obligations, discussed in chapter 17 (pp. 324–328), additional concerns should also be addressed.

1. Media and Territory

The territory of the film includes both the media markets and the geographic area in which the distributor is acquiring the right to show the work. The United States and Canada are usually sold as a single territory, referred to as North America (which may or may not also include Mexico, depending on the definitions in the agreement).

Unless the agreement provides for worldwide distribution in all media, this provision must very clearly spell out what countries and what media markets are covered by the agreement so that additional contracts can be negotiated with other distributors to build up the worldwide distribution of the movie. For example, the provision for domestic television should include pay-per-view, pay cable, network, syndication, free cable, satellite, and any and all forms of television transmission now or hereafter existing. The section should specifically include or exclude streaming and download-ing. It should also specifically include or exclude interactive services such as YouTube on consumer devices other than television, including mobile phones, tablets, and computers.

2. Term

The term of the distribution agreement will vary depending on the range of markets covered by the agreement. If the agreement is limited to domestic theatrical distribution, then there should not be significant activity more than one year after distribution begins. Recognizing that the distributor may need some flexibility regarding the start of the campaign, the term in such a situation should be limited to from two to five years.

Further, the filmmaker may wish to insist that the distribution rights terminate if the film has not been released in any of the listed markets within 18 months of delivery of the finished film to the distributor. This short drop-dead provision may be somewhat difficult to negotiate, but it provides significant protection for the filmmaker properly concerned about the film being left in the back of the distributor's catalog.

3. Advances and Payments

With significant debts generated throughout film production, the film-maker may be most concerned about the up-front payments to be made by the distributor, which are advances against the future income generated by the film. As income flows in from the various markets, the distributor will withhold any additional payment to the filmmaker until the filmmaker has earned an amount equal to the advance. An advance is a minimum payment, because the filmmaker will be entitled to keep the entire amount without regard to the total income generated by the distribution.

If the filmmaker does recoup the advance, the production company will then be paid a percentage of the revenue generated by the film. Payment will be determined based on the total gross income generated. The distributor will keep 20 to 30 percent of the theatrical and video income, and 40 to 50 percent of the income from other markets. After the distributor deducts this fee, it deducts its expenses for the marketing and promotion of the film, often including its costs in attending national marketing conventions and other general overhead costs. The remainder of the net proceeds is then paid to the filmmaker.

Because of distributors' ability to manipulate the reporting of gross income and expenses, the filmmaker should focus primarily on the advance. Industry practices reduce the net proceeds paid to the filmmaker to a relatively small portion of income generated.

4. Distributor's Guarantees of Marketing Expenses and Marketing Commitments

Almost as important as the advance is the distributor's guarantee regarding the size of the marketing campaign. Even though the costs of the marketing campaign ultimately come from the filmmaker's portion of the revenue, the larger the campaign, the more likely the film will be viewed. The filmmaker can always ask the distributor to cut back on the campaign if the expenditures are no longer needed, but invariably filmmakers want larger campaigns than distributors are willing to provide. Without a contractual obligation from the beginning, the filmmaker is at the mercy of the distributor.

The distributor and filmmaker should also agree to a written plan for the distribution of the film prior to signing the distribution agreement. Although it would be unreasonable to make such a plan part of the contract, it should serve as the basis for discussion. The marketing plan must be highly opportunistic and therefore quite flexible, but the fundamentals should be explicit. Like any battle plan, the distribution plan will need regular updating as markets outperform or underperform expectations and the strategies are refined. A written plan provides an excellent communications tool for the filmmaker, the cast and crew who have an interest in the film's success, and the investors who are waiting for their returns.

5. Audits

Given the importance of the advance, payments of guarantees, and accounting of the marketing expenses, the filmmaker must be able to monitor or audit the books of the distributor. More specifically, the filmmaker must have the right to have the books made available to the film company's designated accountant. Often a distributor will seek to limit access or limit the amount of time the filmmaker has to conduct an audit or bring action on one, but the filmmaker should resist limiting this legal protection.

6. Foreign Sublicensing

If a distributor does not have the ability to fully exploit some markets or territories, it will often sublicense them to other companies. This sublicensing arrangement can be an efficient substitute for the filmmaker's own attempts to track down those markets and cover them with different distributors. Often, however, the sublicensee is actually a company owned by the distributor itself, meaning that the distributor is making the profit as the sublicensee and charging the filmmaker a premium for its own licensing fee. Unless the total fees are capped, an unscrupulous distributor can claim twice the revenue by sublicensing to its own subsidiary. Filmmakers should be careful to cap the sublicensing fees to limit the revenue that can be lost to this practice.

In addition, to the extent possible, the filmmaker should seek advances for each territory exploited, because foreign royalties may be difficult to negotiate. Beyond theatrical distribution, the ways in which foreign markets are exploited may be mandated by the laws of the country in question. In many countries, for example, if a film is broadcast on terrestrial television—over the airwaves—then cable operators are allowed to carry that broadcast simultaneously on local cable systems in exchange for paying into a national fund. The owner of the film is then eligible to receive a portion of those funds.

Each country may have its own revenue sources for such a national fund, including cable retransmissions royalties, surcharges on physical media, rental royalties, educational royalties, theatrical box office levies, public performance royalties for video and streaming, and many others. Typically, the money is collected by a national rights society similar to American Society of Composers, Authors and Publishers (ASCAP) and divided among the registered content owners. This means the filmmaker must register with dozens of collection societies in hundreds of counties.

Fortunately, the Independent Film & Television Alliance (IFTA) provides a collection service that acts as both registration agent and collection agent for these funds. Registration is far simpler when handled by the IFTA, and filmmakers are much more likely to receive royalties through the collective powers and efforts of IFTA than through a distributor or sales agent in a particular country.

G. Rights to Withhold from the Distributor

The distribution agreement should be quite explicit regarding limitations on the distributor. No rights should be granted unless the distributor can exploit those rights and the filmmaker can be assured that there will be a return. In addition, distributors often request certain legal controls, but these requests should be carefully limited or refused.

1. Copyright and Ownership

The distributor may need the right to edit the film for certain markets, particularly foreign markets. Nonetheless, the distribution agreement should not be an assignment of copyright and should not grant the distributor the right to remake the film or create new projects out of the story or related rights. The editing rights must be limited to those changes required by local censorship laws or changes for accommodating foreign languages. These accommodations may also include translating the title in either a literal or a conceptual fashion. Except for these specific changes, the distributor should have no power to modify the film. This limitation may not apply if the film project is purchased outright by a major studio's distribution arm, but for all other purchasers, the copyright and ownership in the story should be retained by the filmmaker.

2. Marketing Materials

Unless the distribution agreement provides contractual rights to the filmmaker, the filmmaker is likely to have no consultative rights or approvals in the distributor's marketing campaign. Even if the filmmaker initially supplied the one-sheet, production stills, and other tools of the marketing campaign, the distributor may still have absolute control.

The marketing campaign often defines the film in the public's mind, but as mentioned earlier, the distributor is typically the party that creates this campaign. In deals involving small distributors, the filmmaker can negotiate to have significant participation in, and ownership of, the marketing.

Particularly in a situation in which multiple distributors will distribute the film in various markets and media, each distributor must agree that the filmmaker will own any marketing materials. This way, the materials from the theatrical campaign can be used to promote the video sales of the film, even if the two markets are licensed to different distributors. This arrangement is also helpful if the distribution agreements expire and later interest in the film requires the filmmaker to promote the picture again. In addition to legal ownership, the agreement should provide that at the end of the contract term any remaining materials be given to the filmmaker or destroyed, at the filmmaker's discretion.

H. Staging the Domestic Theatrical Distribution

Distributing the film requires tremendous coordination and a good deal of cooperation on the part of the exhibitors. Exhibitors are entitled to bid on each film separately and may choose not to show a particular film. In addition, theater chains buy films for each screen (or at least each theater complex) rather than for the chain as a whole. These rules have developed over the years to protect independent theaters and small chains from the larger chain competitors.

1. National Release

Studios generally release their films nationally, meaning in each major market in the United States and Canada on the same date. This allows them to maximize the impact of paid advertising and drown out negative reviews with a well-financed campaign. Studios have increasingly distributed internationally on the same day-and-date as the North American release as well, to reduce the window of opportunity for video piracy. The opening in one region may occur a week or two earlier to allow for the stars to appear at premieres, with the Asian dates often preceding the North American dates. Although the exhibitors negotiate individually, a large national campaign tends to announce an official release date, which forces exhibitors to participate or be left behind. A small theater chain wishing to be part of the release of *Star Wars XXII* must be willing to stop showing whatever film it otherwise would play on that date to make room for the blockbuster release. Independent film distribution strategies must carefully consider the national release dates of major studio pictures, lest the independent film be forced out of theaters to make room.

2. Markets Sold in the Presale Agreement

Depending on the financing techniques employed, some distribution choices may already be settled. For example, if the presale agreements (see chapter 7, p. 126) call for exhibition in certain territories at specified times, these terms will dictate all other agreements. Presale agreements may allow some flexibility regarding the scheduling of actual release dates. A small film's release in overseas territories should not have a material impact on its domestic release, and good international reviews can even be exploited as part of the domestic marketing effort.

Once a film has been released theatrically in its first market, the order of the subsequent markets does not really matter. There is no need to hold up the distribution in India while awaiting Europe, or to make sure Japan has the film before Korea. Audiences do not travel to see films abroad, the problems of piracy are not diminished, and distributors are generally not sufficiently sophisticated to create any meaningful strategy for international release dates.

If a portion of the presale agreement comes from online sales or other markets, the filmmaker should be able to delay the release in that medium for a specified period of up to one year so that the film company can take every opportunity to release the film theatrically first.

3. Platform Release

The best-known strategy for distributing an independent film is known as a platform release. The film opens in one city (often New York, Chicago, or Los Angeles) selected for the size of the market, the influence of the critics, and the opportunity for word of mouth to spread to other areas. Assuming positive reviews and good word of mouth, audiences for the film should grow, and its per-screen revenue may well equal or exceed that of the top blockbusters playing at the same time. Exhibitors are far more interested in the per-screen revenue than the national grosses, because per-screen revenue translates into ticket sales and concession traffic.

After two to four weeks, press and audience reaction may generate interest sufficient to move to additional markets. If the campaign is highly successful, new cities will continue to be added. In this way, a movie may play 5 to 10 major markets. If the film is doing well in 10 markets, then the distributor may choose to expand still further, adding an additional 10 markets, and so on, until national distribution has been accomplished. More likely, the expansion stops being an efficient strategy well before the first 100 markets have been hit, but the film will still have had a very successful theatrical run and will be positioned well for post-theatrical distribution.

The timing and geography of the platform release is highly dynamic, reacting not only to the success of the film in question but also to other film openings throughout the country. This allows exhibitors to gain confidence in the film and gives them the flexibility to add it to their schedule when the blockbusters begin to fizzle.

4. Four-Walling

A filmmaker without any other options may still buy the opportunity to have a film shown in a commercial theater. In a four-wall arrangement, the distributor or filmmaker rents the theater, rather than licensing the picture to the theater. Typically, only a filmmaker who could not otherwise attract a distributor would do this. The filmmaker pays a rental fee for the theater for a specified period and receives all income from ticket sales; the concession income may be either kept by the theater or apportioned, depending on the cost of the rental and the agreement between the parties.

Four-walling may seem like an act of vanity, but it can be much more than that. Sometimes the limited run will be enough to get a local critic to see the film and elicit a positive review. It may result in generating some interest among potential distributors.

Four-walling may even be profitable, particularly if the film is uniquely attractive to a specific local audience. For example, four-walling may do very well when a film is promoted exclusively within a geographic region, to a concentrated religious community, to the local gay and lesbian community, or on a college campus. Other exhibitors will not be able to promote within those communities nearly as effectively as a filmmaker who has created a work geared to that particular audience.

I. Protecting Academy Award Eligibility

Filmmakers may wish to protect their eligibility for the Academy Awards. It could happen. The Academy of Motion Picture Arts and Sciences requires that to be eligible for the prestigious Oscar, a movie must be a feature film of more than 40 minutes in length, publicly exhibited exclusively for at least seven days for paid admission in a commercial theater in Los Angeles County from a print that meets the 35/70mm or DCP digital technology standards. The rules are very clear about activities that will make a film ineligible for consideration:

> Films that, in any version, receive their first public exhibition or distribution in any manner other than as a theatrical motion picture release will not be eligible for Academy Awards in any category. Nontheatrical public exhibition or distribution includes but is not limited to:
>
> - Broadcast and cable television
> - PPV/VOD
> - DVD distribution
> - Inflight airline distribution
> - Internet transmission
>
> Motion pictures released in such nontheatrical media **on or after the first day of their Los Angeles County theatrical qualifying run remain eligible**. Also, ten minutes or ten percent of the running time of a film, whichever is shorter, may be shown in a nontheatrical medium prior to the film's qualifying run.[1]

Additional rules regarding theatrical exhibition inside the United States state that previews and festivals do not affect eligibility. Film companies should be very careful regarding the development of their marketing materials to be sure that any clips posted from the film do not exceed the 10 percent or 10 minute rule. And if the film has an opportunity to play theatrically in Los Angeles, then the Academy Award rules may have an impact on the timing of the nontheatrical distribution strategy.

Four-walling a picture will not make it eligible for the Oscars and neither will a platform release that does not have a week's paid run in Los Angeles. If this matters to the film, based on its content and reception, then the distribution strategy will need to take an exhibition in Los Angeles into account.

Award eligibility for the 93rd Academy Awards were modified to reflect the closure of most movie theaters due to the coronavirus pandemic. The changes allowed films intended for theatrical release but instead "initially made available through commercial streaming, VOD service or other broadcast" to qualify if they otherwise met the eligibility conditions.[2]

The modification of the eligibility rules also provides that filmmakers can earn eligibility by opening in a theater in any of six metropolitan areas, rather than just Los Angeles. The cities creating eligibility are "Los Angeles County; City of New York [Five Boroughs]; the Bay Area [counties of San Francisco, Marin, Alameda, San Mateo and Contra Costa]; Chicago [Cook County, Illinois]; Miami [Miami-Dade County, Florida]; and Atlanta [Fulton County, Georgia]."[3] The rules changes are written for the 93rd Academy Awards only, and it remains to be seen whether any of these modifications will create longer-term change.

(20)

Nontheatrical Distribution

This chapter highlights the most important strategies for distribution of those projects that do not start with a theatrical release, and outlines particular uses of new technologies that help to maximize a low-budget or self-directed distribution plan. Even if an indie distributor is working to distribute and promote the film, many of these steps will help the campaign and give the filmmaker an important role in the process.

For most filmmakers, nontheatrical distribution means using the new digital platforms as the release windows. *Transactional video on demand*, or TVOD, represents rentals and sales from iTunes, Google Play, Redbox (which still has DVD rentals), and other platforms offering a single title for the transaction. *Subscription video on demand*, or SVOD, covers the streaming services from Netflix, Amazon Prime Video, YouTube Premium, iTunes, and the major studios, including Disney+ and Paramount+. There is also *advertising video on demand*, or AVOD, which includes advertiser-based streaming content that competes with or complements basic cable, including Hulu, Acorn TV, BritBox, Pluto TV, and many other services.

The business models continue to shift as broadcast and cable channels expand to Internet-based distribution under the industry term *over-the-top TV* (OTT). OTT had been disrupting cable and even broadcast content delivery as early as 2018. The 2020 coronavirus pandemic disrupted media production and consumption just as it disrupted all other aspects of public life, and its changes to viewing habits and production resources will be felt for years.

A. Video on Demand Markets

The global marketplace is much larger than the portion of the market mediated by theatrical film releases. For many projects, the lack of a theatrical release means selling the movie directly to the next window for the release, including the TVOD downloads on iTunes, Amazon, and Google Play; DVDs and streaming on Redbox; and SVOD streaming on Netflix, YouTube Premium, and Amazon Prime Video.

1. Continuing Role for the Film Distributor

If the film was acquired by a film distributor, then the film distributor will likely have the rights to distribute the film through the remaining distribution windows even without a theatrical release. A production company can try to negotiate an arrangement that terminates the agreement with the distributor unless the distributor sells the film in theatrical markets, but generally the filmmaker pursuing a theatrical distribution strategy rather than an online YouTube channel wants to have the distributor generate as much money from as many markets as possible.

As described in chapter 19 (pp. 356–360), a healthy distribution agreement is likely to include some key milestone obligations for guaranteed promotion on the part of the distributor. As with every contract, the language in the agreement means little unless those obligations are followed by the parties. The contract should be clear on what happens in the event that there is no sale for theatrical distribution. Since the percentages dictate that a film will be released nontheatrically, it is important to have carefully considered those provisions of the distributor agreement.

The most important role for the distributor in the nontheatrical distribution is to promote the premium placement of the product. Audiences shop for films much as they shop for groceries. In the grocery aisles, customers notice the goods on the endcaps much more than they do on the regular shelves. Food distributors pay for the right to place their goods on the endcaps in order to promote demand for their product. Similarly, the placement at the top of the marketing window for the films on a TVOD or SVOD service will significantly increase the sales and viewership. If a film can only be found through an active search by the viewer, it will be missed by most of the public. A film without distribution is much less likely to receive any visibility than a film represented by a respected distributor that has a successful catalog of films.

2. Global Streaming on Demand Distribution

Companies like Netflix that provide subscription video on demand (SVOD) generally work directly with the film distributor. All the steps needed to make a successful theatrical campaign are the same for Netflix. Netflix will often require worldwide distribution rights, and it purchases the rights for its content outright. This means that Netflix will pay a single lump sum payment to acquire all rights necessary to distribute the work in perpetuity. To the greatest extent possible, Netflix will also seek to purchase outright any underlying rights and all music rights. This is a significant change from modern filmmaking, reflecting a business model much more like the old Hollywood studio productions from the 1920s through the 1960s.

Because of the growth of Netflix's own productions, it directly purchases a much smaller amount of independent content than it once did. It continues, however, to purchase from film distributors and film aggregators (which are essentially distributors that do not even pretend to provide marketing services). The payments for these films are generally quite low. Netflix has reportedly dropped its acquisition fees for independent films from the low five figures to transactions often below $10,000. It also licenses the catalogs of distributors on a nonexclusive arrangement, paying even less per picture.

Netflix does continue to make occasional, high-priced purchases at the major movie festivals. It also fosters new talent through relationships with established filmmakers. In 2019, for example, Netflix offered nineteen features created by first-time directors through these various avenues.[1] This is a small fraction of Netflix's overall content, but it makes Netflix a significant distributor of independent film.

In contrast, Amazon Prime Video is fully integrated into the Amazon e-commerce platform. As such, it provides strategies for both self-distribution and distributor distribution. Amazon Studios operates in much the same way as does Netflix. Amazon Studios is primarily a content producer, but it also acquires both studio and independent works to keep the Amazon Prime Video service competitive with Netflix and the other streaming services.

Amazon Studios launched in 2015 with a strong emphasis on independent film, starting off with Spike Lee's *Chi-Raq*. In recent years, however, it has significantly revised its content focus to purchase films that are much more aligned with its streaming audience. Again, like Netflix, Amazon is focused on fueling the high rate of consumption among its streaming audience with content that reinforces the viewership interests of that audience.

Amazon's streaming series hit, *The Marvelous Mrs. Maisel*, and its predecessor, *Mozart in the Jungle*, featured romantic dramedy that skewed toward an older demographic. Recent film purchases *Late Night* and *Brittany Runs a Marathon* were box office duds that fit the Amazon Prime Video demographic well and are quite successful as part of the streaming strategy. *The Aeronauts* also fits the demographic, but with better box office success. The theatrical release for films such as these is little more than a marketing teaser. The revenue splits actually incentivize Amazon to keep the theatrical distribution small and short so that the primary audience will belong to Prime Video.[2]

Amazon can be expected to continue to purchase a small number of independent films and give a few of those short theatrical releases. Amazon and Netflix have largely commandeered the independent film market, which further distances independent film from theatrical distribution. At the same time, the resources of Netflix and Amazon are fueling projects and supporting audiences.

Although streaming on Amazon and Netflix will create great opportunities to be seen by large audiences, Netflix will pay only a few hundred dollars for nonexclusive streaming rights. Amazon uses a per-minute approach to measure the total viewership. Unfortunately, the rate Amazon pays decreased substantially in 2018 from 15 cents per hour viewed to 6 cents per hour. For films with between 100,000 and 999,999 hours, there are improved payment rates, then it drops back to the 6-cent rate. These are very small numbers and parallel the rather low payments paid by streamers in the music industry.

Competition for viewers remains very fierce among the glut of providers. Apple TV+ and Roku are both aggressively acquiring content to compete with the leading services. This may develop a market for independent films, but it has not yet done so. There are also many other streaming services, but all of these are much smaller with even fewer financial benefits for filmmakers.

3. Digital Downloads through iTunes, Google Play, and Amazon

In terms of production revenue, sales generate significantly more return than views. Although the public is rapidly moving toward a streaming model in its consumption of video just as it has done for music, the market for sales continues to be important for film and series. More important, this market will continue be much more profitable than streaming for the filmmaker. iTunes and Google Play, for example, give the distributor 70 percent of the funds earned on videos sold. Amazon on Demand is 50 percent. Each $9.99 download generates between $5 and $7 for the production company, less the amounts due to the distributor or aggregator. Rental rates are subject to the agreement between the distributor and the platform but are likely to be similar to the rates for sales.

Theoretically, a production company can work directly with iTunes to place a film on its site. iTunes, however, encourages filmmakers to work with an aggregator. The aggregator helps iTunes curate the content and ensures that all the production elements are ready and available for the upload. Although aggregators are not nearly as discriminating as distributors, they still play quality-control and customer-support roles that iTunes does not want to provide. In addition, an aggregator makes payments easier for iTunes because the funds go from iTunes to the aggregator, which is then responsible for paying the monies owed to the filmmaker. Having an extra step before payment, however, is generally not beneficial for the filmmaker.

Even if the production company chooses to sell directly rather than through a distributor or aggregator, it cannot work directly with iTunes. Instead, iTunes requires that the necessary materials be encoded to iTunes specifications through an approved encoding house.

The Google Play store is very similar to iTunes in every imaginable way. Given Google's ownership of YouTube, it has little interest in smaller titles being part of the Google Play portion of the business. As a result, it only accepts submissions through aggregators.

4. Digital Placement Aggregators

The aggregators are really content-encoding services much more than true film distributors. They do not provide marketing services. Instead, they simplify the process of getting onto the digital download and streaming services. Aggregators provide certain technological benefits, primarily around encoding the files to meet the delivery requirements of each online platform. They also may be able to provide the encoding for the creation of closed captions. Aggregators may have preferred placement with Amazon and other video platforms, helping make a title more readily discoverable for the consumer. An aggregator is not needed for Amazon's Prime Video Direct, but it may still help with placement.

Technically, an aggregator is not needed for iTunes, but a production company must have at least five films available before iTunes will work with it directly. For the first-time filmmaker, an aggregator is a requirement. The iTunes list of approved aggregators is a good starting point, even if the film company does not ultimately place any product on iTunes. At the time of this writing, there were 20 aggregators that supported movies and television content with the "preferred plus" designation by Apple.

On the other hand, as a middleman between the download and streaming services and the film companies, the aggregators provide a useful service but also pose a business risk. The very popular aggregator Distribber, for example, went bankrupt in late 2019, leaving its clients as unsecured creditors hoping to get months and even years of back royalties out of the court proceedings.

Late payments are a huge red flag for any distributor or aggregator. The terms of the cash flow are specified in the contract. Since everything is automated, quarterly payments are the longest any payment periods should be. If a payment is missed, the production company should assume the company is in trouble and move to a more secure platform.

B. Cable and Television Markets

1. Tightening Theatrical and SVOD Release Windows

The traditional cycle of film distribution starts with domestic theatrical distribution; approximately three months later, the film is released on DVD, the digital platforms, and pay-per-view; then six months following that it is released on premiere cable channels such as HBO or Showtime. After that, the largest films get network broadcast premieres, then free cable screenings. This cycle releases the film in the most expensive markets first. Since theater tickets are the most expensive option for the audience, common wisdom holds that once a film has been made available on HBO the chance for a theatrical release is over. While the logic may be generally sound, for independent films there are opportunities to schedule against the model.

DVDs and Blu-ray discs of a film are sold to Redbox, which offer movies to consumers based on a per-disc rental. There is also still a modest DVD market through national discounters such as Target, Walmart, Amazon, Costco, and Sam's Club. Children's titles and holiday films do particularly well in the direct-sales market, because they are well-priced gifts and are often purchased on impulse. Blockbusters also have success in this category. This market, however, is rapidly disappearing under the financial pressure of the streaming services.

Films with small platform releases or four-wall theatrical releases have very modest marketing budgets. The paid advertising and positive film reviews will remain in the audiences' minds for only a short time. Filmmakers utilizing these sorts of theatrical releases are very likely to benefit from shortening the theatrical exclusivity from three months to a few weeks. This is precisely what Netflix has been doing with its own prestige pictures, and Amazon is occasionally following suit. For a filmmaker working with a distributor, shortening the modest theatrical window should improve the bounce from theatrical to SVOD and the other markets.

2. Cable Premiere as Catalyst

Short distribution windows can create a momentum of their own. Disney regularly cycles its classic animated films on and off television and in and out of stores, so that every showing is a new premiere. (Because these films are directed at younger viewers, a large part of the audience changes every five years, and the youngest viewers have never before been exposed to the work.) Similarly, a short "premiere" on HBO or Showtime creates tremendous exposure, but that exposure may not destroy the film's marketability in smaller art house theaters around the country.

Less than half the potential audience will be exposed to the film if it premieres on a single premium cable channel. Therefore, a significant number of viewers may be willing to pay theater prices to see the film; they would have been exposed to considerably more marketing as a result of the film's brief television appearance than if it had gone directly into limited theatrical release. Of course, such a distribution scheme requires the consent of the television network and the theatrical exhibitors that primarily show new releases, but for the right movie, it is a viable alternative. The marketing impact of a premiere cable network should also boost audience if the film later moves to the digital streaming and downloading platforms. The order of the release windows is designed around blockbusters and may not affect viewership for independent films.

One unfortunate consequence of opening through a cable channel is that the film would lose its eligibility for Academy Award consideration, as mentioned earlier in the chapter.

3. PBS

Like the premium cable networks, Public Broadcasting Service stations show movies unedited and uninterrupted. Each public television station purchases its contents individually, however, which creates two separate PBS markets for the filmmaker. First, the filmmaker may be able to sell the film to the production companies that create or buy content for use on PBS programs. The PBS series *Independent Lens*, for example, "is the largest showcase for independent documentaries anywhere on U.S. television, premiering 22 new films each season. The series is curated jointly by ITVS and PBS." It "has presented more than 380 films to public television audiences" since 2003.[3] The filmmaker's work may be appropriate as content packaged for such series—particularly if it is a documentary. Second, the filmmaker may license the work to any particular PBS station. This creates hundreds of possible sales, and the PBS stations can work like the premium cable stations to promote the film and expose it to a potential theatrical audience.

4. Director's Cut and Unrated Versions

As a marketing method for DVD and Blu-ray sales and rentals, distributors have taken to rereleasing films as unrated versions, extended editions, or so-called director's cuts. In some cases, these are significantly different movies with dramatically longer running time or additional adult content. In many situations, however, these are modestly edited versions intended merely to add NEW AND IMPROVED to a product's label.

The strategy works. Director's cuts sometimes generate additional reviews or new-release press coverage, helping to publicize the film's availability and boost sales. "Uncensored" versions of risqué movies tend to sell well and promote both versions of the film.

Contractually, the alternate cuts should not be treated as new films and should not require new payments to the various parties involved in the project. Instead, they count toward any royalty or residual obligations. Some care should be taken, however, to ensure that the film company has control over the distributor's use of this technique and that any marketing is accurate. If the distributor wishes to release a director's cut, the version released should have been prepared by the director or, at a minimum, have the approval of the director. If an unrated version featuring nudity is released, the filmmaker either must have had nudity releases from the cast members involved or must obtain such clearances before the film is rereleased.

C. Self-Distribution

Just as technology has transformed self-published literature from the world of vanity press into a viable commercial alternative, it has turned self-distribution into a legitimate and potentially preferred commercial choice independent filmmakers should consider seriously. As the filmmaker shops the film to distributors, the filmmaker must weigh these companies' offers against the potential to achieve nearly the same results through direct marketing and sales.

1. When to Self-Distribute

The benefits of self-distributing are improved compensation, concentration, and control. The filmmaker who chooses this option does not have to give a substantial percentage of gross revenue to a distributor that invests little time or personal effort on the film. Finally, the filmmaker can avoid having to compromise with the distributor regarding the distribution strategies or messages of the film. These advantages should be weighed against the broader distribution and greater gross revenue that are possible with a distributor.

Self-distribution is a very practical strategy, particularly if the budget of the project was small and the film or series does not have the type of A-list talent or strong reviews from a national festival needed to promote the film.

Some productions make this choice from the outset and build it into all their business plans. Other companies pursue the theatrical distribution dream but realize that the decisions made regarding casting, the inability to sell the film at Sundance—or even be invited to Sundance—and the lack of prestigious awards from the film festival circuit mean that any deal with a distributor will be so one-sided as to kill any chance at financial return.

From a psychological standpoint, the filmmaker that pursues a self-distribution strategy from the beginning will be far more satisfied with the distribution outcome of the film than the filmmaker who lapses into self-distribution out of desperation following a failed pursuit of a sales agent and distributor. Nonetheless, when self-distribution is the only option, the filmmaker owes it to the cast, crew, investors, and audience to shake off any sense of disappointment and pursue self-distribution as the best remaining outcome.

One way the production company can navigate these challenges is to empower the media and community engagement director to take over the lead role at this point in the film company's life cycle. If the company has engaged the right person, then that person, who's most involved with the media and marketing strategy, can manage the self-distribution, freeing the filmmaker to move on to the next project.

2. Initial Steps for the Self-Distributor

One of the harder aspects of self-distribution is the obligation to undertake the distribution effort as if the film being distributed is someone else's work. The filmmaker cannot return to the film to tinker with the editing or music. During the distribution cycle, everything must be done as if the film is owned by a third party.

The steps for self-distribution are essentially the same as those the film company would expect from an outside distributor:

1. Prepare cover art that will be the visual element to sell the film on digital platforms. Just as producers sometimes sold their movies based on the posters, eye-catching cover art makes a tremendous impact on the public as they scroll through the online streaming and rental choices. A great cover image might even improve the chance at distributor interest, so this is not an expense to avoid.

2. Prepare a strong press kit with a brief log line and longer synopsis, photographs, and background information on the story and the writers, director, and cast; include any positive reviews; and have video clips available.

3. Prepare the digital files, including the closed caption files, stereo sound, and high-quality video that can be replayed at HD or better. The film company has essentially the same delivery requirements for self-distribution as it would have through a distributor.

4. Prepare a digital release strategy that utilizes aggregators, if appropriate, for iTunes and Google Play, Amazon Prime Video Direct, Vimeo Pro, and other platforms, prioritizing those platforms that have the best financial return.

5. Engage the online audience through Facebook, the production company website, and various social media platforms to plan for a virtual launch party.

6. Contact theaters and chains that specialize in independent films to explore a theatrical release. Concentrate on theaters in the filmmaker's hometown and theaters located in communities

particularly interested in the film—urban communities for an urban film, San Francisco or Minneapolis/St. Paul for gay and lesbian films, New York and Los Angeles for Jewish or Israeli films, etc.

7. Consider running a four-wall theatrical opening if the production can guarantee some press attendance and a hometown or supportive local audience that will ensure the event at least breaks even. This official opening will help considerably with the investors, cast, crew, and supporters, who can see their hard work on the silver screen in front of a paying audience. Particularly off-season, such openings should be relatively inexpensive and can be quite a boost to the film.

8. Consider selling a package to the crowdfunding audience, friends, family, and the friends, family, and supporters of the cast and crew. Particularly if the project involves a message or strong commitment to a particular social agenda, offering a DVD/download, hat or T-shirt, and other mementos can offer a value that people will pay be willing to purchase. No one really wants to buy a $20 DVD, but people might be willing to buy a one-time $30 package that includes the shirt, DVD, digital art for their phone and laptop, and small poster. The net revenue on the package is much higher than on just the rental of the film. Selling the package as part of the film's premiere or some other special event will add a buzz and immediacy for the audience to get involved in the mini-campaign. This premium can be distributed using a crowdfunding platform as a thank-you for getting the film distributed.

9. Assess the potential of a paid marketing strategy using Facebook or similar social media marketing. While generally a money-loser, audience-mapping advertising will be very effective for films focused on dedicated, focused communities and social issues, both for narrative film and documentaries.

10. Develop a strategy for packaging the DVD, including the artwork and credits on the front and back of the DVD package. Unless there is an obligation to provide a significant number of DVDs through a crowdfunding campaign, these will likely be made through Amazon's Media on Demand feature so the production company will not be stuck with boxes of unsold DVDs.

11. Continue to work the film markets to meet with international sales agents. If the film company is having no luck with paid

distribution, then selling foreign markets in any media will bolster the potential for the film to grow in the marketplace and encourage later United States sales.

These steps may prove time-consuming, but they represent the essential steps for preparing the film for market. Most of the revenue from self-distribution, however, will come not from a limited theatrical run but from the new opportunities for self-promotion described as follows.

3. Creating an Online Presence in Vimeo

Very few websites pay filmmakers for streaming content. As noted earlier, Netflix will pay a small payment for nonexclusive rights to nontheatrically distributed films. Amazon Prime Video pays 6 cents per hour of viewership. Vimeo and YouTube are the two most important distribution channels not yet described as part of the distributor marketing. Neither need a third party to assist with their use, so they are the primary tools for self-distributing filmmakers. Of course, the self-distributing filmmaker should also use the tools to directly engage Amazon. If the costs to purchase the services of an aggregator are worth the additional investment, then placing the film in iTunes and Google Play should not be difficult. Having the film made available on these platforms might help investor relations even if the total revenue does not cover the cost of aggregator fees.

Vimeo is a true filmmaker video sharing platform. Others are available as well, but Vimeo seems to be the strongest from among the dozens that launched over the past two decades. Vimeo allows filmmakers and others to upload videos to the platform and control the viewership of the video. The service has approximately 170 million members, a fraction of YouTube but only slightly smaller than Netflix, making it a very healthy community.

Vimeo has a monthly charge for all but the most basic of services. For the active window of distribution, most production companies would start at the Vimeo Pro level of service. This allows for 1 TB of storage each year and 20 GB per week. The web player can be customized and the media embedded onto other social platforms. The video can be uploaded in "private mode" for collaborations during the production process and for special events prior to the film's release.

Once in public mode, the video can be viewed by members of the Vimeo community. The filmmaker can rent, sell, or set subscription rates on its channel. The best news is that Vimeo charges only 10 percent, allowing the production company to retain 90 percent of this revenue. For a project that will largely be consumed by the dedicated audience who has followed the production along on social media and on its website throughout the preproduction and principal photography phases of the work, hosting the film on Vimeo and retaining 90 percent of the revenue seems like a very fine option.

In contrast to YouTube, Vimeo provides the videos in an ad-free environment, making it a preferable user experience to that on YouTube. It does have monthly fees, but if there is a sustainable audience, the ad-free environment should improve the viewer's enthusiasm for the film.

Self-distributed filmmakers should consider Vimeo as a premiere window before moving to the less generous and more difficult streaming and downloading services. Vimeo does not have the prestige of iTunes, but it puts the filmmaker in charge and allows the filmmaker to recoup costs from the loyal audience.

Vimeo complements Amazon Prime Video very nicely. The revenue split makes it a better partner for the filmmaker, suggesting that it should be launched in advance of any Amazon Prime Video account. Vimeo also has content review features that inform the production company about the audience and the viewer behavior. If the audience drops out before the film is finished, then the filmmaker can see approximately how far into the feature the audience begins its decline. There are additional features and higher price points, but the services of Vimeo Pro give filmmakers a great deal of control over the initial, online release of their projects, making it an excellent initial resource.

4. Building an Online Revenue Business on YouTube

If Vimeo is the HBO or Showtime of the Internet, YouTube is its basic cable. It boasts over 1 billion users. YouTube does not pay for user-supplied content. Google has separated the content sold through its YouTube Premium SVOD service, its Google Play rentals and sales, and its user-generated content on YouTube into very discrete markets. There are many other video platforms as well, such as Instagram TV and Snapchat, though they tend to launch and fail. As audience-building tools, each of these platforms plays a useful role for the film company, but YouTube remains the dominant online advertising platform. If the goal is to pursue funds through advertising, it is the essential first step.

The option to monetize YouTube opens through the YouTube Partner Program, which has a threshold of 1,000 subscribers and 4,000 hours of content having been watched over the past year. If the lessons of chapter 18 regarding the promotion of the film from the beginning of the preproduction phase have been followed, the production company will have hit these minimums in the run up to the theatrical release of the project. The minimums are much harder for a production company that produces a single feature than for a company developing series content.

The best way to think about YouTube is as an advertising platform for the film. Enticing trailers, behind-the-scenes interviews, conversations and interviews with the people in the film and those related to the story in the film, and other ancillary content will drive viewers. If the content is engaging, it will start to trigger a revenue stream.

Ad revenue on YouTube is based on ad viewership rather than the production viewership. YouTube monetizes the advertising rather than the time spent consuming the video. This has a perversely negative effect on long-form feature content. The more absorbing and effective the content, the more likely the audience has been able to tune out the advertisements. Without the advertisement engagement, there will be no money for the filmmaker. For this reason, among others, YouTube is better suited to short series than to feature-length projects.

The shift from a feature to a series of shorter segments may sometimes be done as a simple postproduction decision. If the feature film is produced with segmentable scenes, then the YouTube version of the film—which will typically be the last window for distribution—can consist of 10 to 15 segments. Each segment will create a new opportunity for the viewer to return to the content and see the production.

The segmentation actually adds a certain convenience for the audience as well, making it easier to consume the content on a mobile device. Such a strategy is not ideal for every feature film, but it provides yet another option for a filmmaker struggling to pay off credit cards and loans.

The YouTube channel also works very well to engage the audience with clips about the project and issues related to the topics involved in the project. If the project is an ongoing series, then the regularly scheduled drops of new content will help drive viewership and interest. Even for a feature-length film, however, there are ways to produce content that relates to the subject matter of the films.

As a primary revenue driver, there are two keys to unlocking Google revenue: audience engagement and SEO. The first key to YouTube success is engagement with a very focused audience interested the content provided by the filmmaker. Next, the successful YouTube producer will emphasize search engine optimization to maximize the ability of the filmmaker's content to be found through YouTube and Google searches and to be prioritized on the YouTube algorithm so the material is shown higher in an organic search.

Although content of almost every conceivable type is available on YouTube (adult content is barred), it is not primarily geared toward long-form, narrative feature films. Still, the time spent on YouTube has increased to an average of 40 minutes per session. Creating series can be successful in this platform.

In addition, YouTube provides an excellent platform to market merchandise related to the project. Today's audience does not like to pay for content, but it does pay for experiences and branded affiliation. T-shirts, mugs, hats, lunchboxes, phone cases, and other items can be branded through the film's artwork and the imagery captured during production. Through third-party production companies and drop-shipped goods distribution, the company can essentially license its intellectual property and market the goods for on-demand production to the audience. Each item sold has approximately the same revenue as the rental or sale of the film, so these efforts can make a significant difference.

For filmmakers who undertake their production with these elements in mind, the opportunity exists to incorporate product-oriented elements. Baby Yoda became an instant success for Disney's *The Mandalorian*. Netflix's *Stranger Things* utilized many iconic products and logos from the 1980s but also introduced its own logo and other elements into a line of merchandise. Through on-demand production, there is little risk to adding these items in hopes of strengthening the audience relationship. YouTube is about advertising and merchandising. On a free platform without any quality control, "you get what you pay for." For filmmakers uncomfortable with maximizing crass commercialization of their production, it is not a good fit.

5. Selling Physical Copies Along with Digital Services on Amazon

Since most of the download strategies do not pay significant revenues at present, the best solution for self-distribution is for the film company to sell the film itself. Once a film is released on DVD, the film company's website should always have it available for purchase. The company can choose whether to refer the purchaser to a commercial website like Amazon.com or incorporate an online store function directly into the film site's software.

This section outlines the logistics involved in these and other online sales opportunities.

The DVD sale is not dead, but the decline is precipitous. DVD sales reached their peak of $16.3 billion in 2006. A combination of a recession and changing technology has dropped that revenue by over 86 percent to $2.2 billion in 2018. Still, a $2 billion market is worth considering. The market has been replaced with free content from YouTube and other mobile platforms as well as subscription services from Netflix, Amazon Prime Video, and a myriad of other services. Home sales seem to be concentrated on children's titles and holiday films. For filmmakers in these and other specialty markets with similar characteristics, the DVD direct sale should be included in the strategy. For other filmmakers, however, this market may no longer be worth the investment.

A fulfillment service provides a range of services, from pressing discs and printing packaging to full-service order control and customer shipping. Larger companies such as Technicolor and Deluxe have the capacity to handle millions of units of a particular movie. Other companies are much smaller but can provide the back-end framework of the film company's online store, which allows consumers to purchase the DVD directly from the website for the movie.

In today's digital environment, producers of books, software, CDs, and movies can provide small-volume print-on-demand services for cost-per-unit prices that historically would have been available only for print runs of at least 1,000 copies. For digital media, a print-on-demand order may consist of the burning of a DVD just as it would be burned using a computer hard drive. The disc then has a label printed on the other side to complete the process. In contrast, large-volume orders are pressed rather than burned. A pressing places the content of the media in the mechanical process as one of the physical elements, along with the plastic, aluminum, and lacquer of the disc. The aluminum image is formed with the content etched into it from the beginning rather than being modified through a laser burning process.

Amazon continues to attempt to corner the market on online sales and physical distribution. The company's growth strategy provides an impressive opportunity for self-distributing filmmakers. Through its print-on-demand service Media on Demand, the successor to CreateSpace, Amazon provides full DVD duplication services, packaging services, and UPC bar code labeling at costs that compare quite favorably to other DVD fulfillment houses.

Amazon also provides for web sales of the products. The DVDs will be sold directly through Amazon, and the film company can also sell them through an online store. Whether the film company chooses to sell through Amazon or through a DVD fulfillment house, the direct revenue it earns through these ventures is likely to be considerably higher than the traditionally small sales the company would have earned had the DVDs been sold through a small nontheatrical distributor. If the production company has retained the rights to DVD sales, there is no reason not to use Media on Demand or a similar service to give the public the option to purchase copies of the film.

Additional Considerations for Ultra-Low-Budget Projects

For today's aspiring filmmakers, the low cost of television-quality digital production equipment and improved access to distribution channels makes the appeal of unfinanced filmmaking stronger than ever. An ultra-low budget, unfinanced film may provide novice filmmakers with a demo reel to show off their abilities, a trailer to help fund feature projects, or simply an outlet for the filmmaker's creative ambitions. These projects can develop into very successful online channels and develop in both quality and quantity over time.

The approach to the story should be crafted to fit the resources of the filmmaker. The budget constrains and challenges the filmmaker, and the film must be made within those limitations if it is to be completed. The film must also meet the filmmaker's goals to tell the story and attract an audience. By keeping both filmmaking goals and the constraints of the production in mind, today's unfinanced filmmakers have the opportunity to tell a broader range of stories than they would ever have been able to tell before.

A. Differences Between Unfinanced and Conventional Independent Filmmaking

Unfinanced filmmaking is truly a subset of independent filmmaking. Every aspect of planning, budgeting, principal photography, and postproduction discussed in previous chapters is just as applicable to the unfinanced film. Nevertheless, there are unique concerns for filmmakers who have such little financial support.

Unfinanced filmmakers are under greater pressure than other independent filmmakers to plan carefully, rehearse diligently, and film efficiently. Unfinanced films have little or no money set aside to fix mistakes in postproduction or to reshoot sequences. As a result, the filmmaker must be more vigilant when preparing each scene.

In contrast to typical studio projects and even other independent productions, the cast and crew of an unfinanced film are likely to be local and willing to spend time together to rehearse scenes, develop the script, learn which props are essential, and walk onto the set ready to capture the film. This sense of solidarity is the reason theatrical casts can move so readily from a community theater onto a movie set. Similarly, this is why cast and crew can come together to create such effective horror movies. Unfinanced filmmakers should capitalize on this camaraderie to enhance the filmmaking process.

While the motivations behind making an unfinanced film may seem self-indulgent, the practice of such filmmaking must be highly disciplined. Whether filming on weekends in locations that can be carefully controlled for continuity or filming very quickly, the filmmaker must plan ahead for each shot and keep experimentation to a minimum. The reliance on volunteers, the lack of backups for costumes and props, and the limited ability to fix things financially should propel the unfinanced filmmaker to move quickly from scene to scene, capturing as much footage as possible each day.

By starting with detailed planning and working with quick, exacting deliberation, the unfinanced filmmaker will gain the confidence of the cast, crew, and supporters. The successful completion of the project will then serve as professional proof that the filmmaker and the entire production team can be trusted with funding for increasingly larger projects.

B. Contingent Professional Assistance

One option for unfinanced filmmakers is to find less experienced attorneys, accountants, and other professionals who are willing to work on contingency. Early in their career, many professionals are willing to invest their time and effort to learn the movie business by accepting deferrals for their pay. Filmmakers may identify volunteer attorneys through the Volunteer Lawyers for the Arts network of legal referral services (http://www .vlany.org). While these professionals may not have the depth of experience of seasoned veterans, the price is right, and the services will make a tremendous difference to the filmmaker.

An expanded strategy would include hiring as an executive director someone with a strong legal background who could review the work of the young attorney. On occasion, experienced professionals in the film industry are willing to work on contingency in exchange for screen credit and revenue participation. Of course, such a negotiation begins with the script and requires confidence on the part of the experienced professional in the talent, vision, and resourcefulness of the filmmaker.

C. Financial Essentials

The business of filmmaking involves minimizing professional risks while maximizing distribution opportunities and revenue streams. These goals may appear at odds with guerrilla and unfinanced filmmaking, but they remain goals to keep in mind when shooting an unfinanced film.

Even unfinanced filmmaking costs money. The purchase or rental of a camera involves some expense. If the shoot lasts three or four weeks, the cost to provide drinks and food on the set can add up. The key to reducing the costs is to cut out any nonessential expenses, combine expenses with other activities, and set realistic goals for the project.

1. Risk Management

Filmmakers face direct financial risk that the funds invested in the film will not result in any financial return, or worse, will not result in a completed film project. If the filmmaker commits to spending up to $15,000 of the filmmaker's own money on food, equipment, insurance, rights, and music, and then the money runs out before the project is completed, the entire investment is lost. On the other hand, if the filmmaker can accomplish the same tasks by using an investor's $15,000 capital investment, then there is no personal financial risk.

The second form of risk stems from liabilities that occur while filming. The filmmaker or film company will be responsible for any contractual obligations or liabilities for accidents such as property damage or personal injury. This form of risk is minimized through the purchase of insurance (see chapter 9, p. 177) and the creation of a formal business structure (see chapter 2, p. 18).

Business planning can reduce risk, but it cannot eliminate it. If a filmmaker creates a corporation with no assets, the courts will ignore that corporate entity and continue to hold the owner of the company personally responsible for the contractual and tort liabilities of the company. In the case of an unfinanced film, the use of a corporate structure or LLC to create limited liability will only have limited effect.

Purchase of general liability insurance, therefore, becomes the most significant single purchase an unfinanced filmmaker can make. It protects both the filmmaker and the parties who might become injured. The filmmaker must also be prepared not only to pay for the goods and services ordered by contract but also to purchase insurance on the cameras or other more expensive items.

2. Loans and Investors

Because of complex federal and state securities laws, the cost to properly document even the simplest of investor agreements can greatly exceed the budget for many unfinanced films. On the other hand, seeking investors in violation of state and federal securities laws hardly seems to be an appropriate approach. As a result, unfinanced filmmakers often struggle with their financing. The recommendations for nonprofit fiscal sponsorship and receipt of gifts discussed in chapter 7 (pp. 139–142) are particularly helpful for unfinanced productions.

Instead of seeking investors, very small budgets can be raised either through gifts or loans. A loan document can be drafted in extremely simple language. As discussed in *The Entrepreneur's Intellectual Property & Business Handbook*,[1] a simple loan can provide the funding necessary to pay for the costs to start a business—here the film company—without significant documentation.

Personal loans are not uncommon for start-up businesses or for first-time filmmakers. Generally, they are nothing more than oral agreements in which the parents of the filmmaker provide some money in exchange for vague promises that "I'll repay this as soon as I can." With family, these are often considered "gifts" that the lender expects never to be repaid.

Formalizing these relations may be more trouble than it is worth. At a minimum, however, the filmmaker should specify the expectations of the loan with some written document. While a contract or note would be preferable, even a receipt letter would go a long way to avoid the problem of disputes. For example, one such letter could include the following:

[Date] [Name] [Address]

Dear Mom,

Thank you very much for the nonrecourse loan of $5,000 last night, which I plan to use for the production of my film project entitled [Title]. This letter will confirm the terms of that loan as we discussed them. As I said last night, all the money will be used for the film. Among other things, your loan will help me rent equipment and cover some of the operational costs.

Just as I explained when you provided me the loan, I intend to repay you the entire amount of the loan plus 5 percent interest. I hope to repay you over the next three years—beginning the first payment a year from now, but if you need the money earlier, I will repay it within a month of your asking. I also appreciate that you will only ask for the money from the money I make through the film.

If I misunderstood any of the terms of the loan, please let me know immediately. Your confidence in me and in the film means a great deal to me. Thank you for your generosity and your faith.

Love, [Signature]
[Signature]
Received and Agreed by [Mom's name]

Admittedly, this letter leaves much to be desired. Still, it clarifies the financial transaction and will serve as a clear reminder of the actual terms long after the exact memories of the offered loan are forgotten. As such, it will discourage disputes more than resolve them—an extremely important part of managing a business.

To be effective, the letter should be dated and signed by the filmmaker, and, even better, it should be countersigned by the friend or family member making the loan. As this example does, the letter should state that it reflects the oral understanding between the parties. It should be sent very soon after the loan is offered (or received) so that it is contemporary with the funds, rather than drafted months or years later, once the parties are in the middle of a dispute. The letter may seem awkward, an unduly formal way to speak to one's mother (or aunt or friend), but the letter achieves a number of very important goals.

First, the letter clarifies that the funds were not a gift or an equity investment. It binds the recipient to understand the loan obligations, and it clarifies to the lender that no ownership interest in the company is conveyed as a result of the loan.

Second, the letter identifies the exact amount of the loan, the interest payment due and the payment schedule. These are the same terms any commercial loan would require. The purpose again is to set the rules of the relationship in place. Because the letter allows the lender to call the loan on thirty days' notice, it is drafted as a demand loan. By omitting the phrase "but if you need the money earlier I will repay it within a month of your asking" the demand nature of the loan can be removed.

Third, the letter establishes the loan is a nonrecourse loan both because it describes the loan as nonrecourse in the first sentence and because it explains the term with the phrase "you will only ask for the money from the money I make through the film."

The letter is not intended to serve as a legal contract, though if countersigned it should stand up as one. More important, it is evidence of an oral conversation and contemporary understanding of the parties. It captures the essential terms of a loan agreement in three simple paragraphs rather than the two pages of formal text used by banks and commercial lenders. Any of these key terms can be adjusted, though each should be addressed in such a letter.

In managing a start-up business, a little goes a long way. A simple letter like this provides much of the same protection as a properly drafted and complex loan agreement. Although having a lawyer draft the loan agreements would be better, the letter sent by the entrepreneur achieves many of the same goals at little cost. For family and close friends, this may be enough. As the complexity of the transaction increases, however, or the relationship moves beyond family, more formal documents are increasingly important to protect the parties from misunderstandings.

Using nonrecourse loans instead of investments makes a good deal of sense in the context of unfinanced and low-budget filmmaking. The dollar amounts invested are very small, and the chances of repayment are quite low. Most contributors in this situation are acting for the benefit of the filmmaker rather than for their own financial gain, so this approach will generally meet their needs.

3. Values of Unfinanced Filmmaking

Since unfinanced filmmaking does not provide meaningful financial compensation for its participants, the filmmaker must take particular care to provide a positive experience for everyone involved in the filmmaking process. As film attorney and producer Dan Satorius put it, "no-budget filmmaking depends on the goodwill of others. You do yourself a favor and you will do a service to those low-budget filmmakers who follow you by treating people fairly."[2]

Among the practices important for unfinanced filmmakers, the most critical include following through on all promises made to cast, crew, investors, location owners, and others; picking up after the film company at all locations; treating everyone with respect and appreciation; being generous with credits; and always remembering that the success of the film relies on the kindness of strangers.

4. Food and Copies

Most beginning actors and crew members are ready to apprentice themselves for free. This is the reality in Hollywood and in most other locations throughout the country. It is the reason the professional unions protect jobs so aggressively. There is no end to the number of people who will accept less than minimum wage, if given the chance to work in the movies.

The new filmmaker must appreciate that if the production cannot afford to provide any payment to cast and crew, the filmmaker must make every effort to provide some benefits to the people for working on the production. At an absolute minimum, the set should always have ample food and refreshments for everyone. The filmmaker is also responsible for maintaining a positive, energetic, and supportive environment on the set for all the cast and crew.

If the film company can find a few more dollars, then T-shirts, hats, or some other item of memorabilia can provide a value to the cast and crew that vastly exceeds its actual cost. Given the choice between a $25 payment or a T-shirt available exclusively to those people who worked on the film, most members of the cast and crew will take the shirt over the check. And all will remember the shirt long after the money has been forgotten.

Finally, a thank-you note and copy of the film should be given to everyone credited on the film or in any other way responsible for the film's completion. This is a sign of courtesy and respect to those who worked on the project. The DVD also provides a positive sign to supporters of the film-maker that the movie resulted in a tangible success. Even if the movie did not return any financial reward, the existence of the DVD greatly increases the chance that the cast, crew, and financial supporters will be ready to work with the filmmaker on the next project. This is one example where a digital download does not substitute for a tangible object. If DVDs are unavailable, a download and production poster will help provide some tangible memorabilia.

D. Personnel Agreements

An unfinanced film company remains responsible for meeting its legal obligations regarding minimum wage, tax withholding, and other hour and wage laws. If the film company does not have the resources to abide by these obligations, then at a minimum the company should use a formal business structure to make the company's best-faith efforts to meet its obligations.

1. General Partnerships

A general partnership provides an obvious business structure for the unfinanced production company, and in fact will be formed by operation of law if the filmmaker takes no additional steps. Participants working closely with the filmmaker could be treated as general partners unless they are clearly identified as employees, independent contractors, or volunteers (see chapter 2, pp. 24–27). In a general partnership, all the parties are jointly responsible for the business and share equally in the potential for its losses.

The general partnership model automatically provides every general partner with equal authority and ownership, but the authority and ownership interests can be varied by written agreement. As general partners in the business, the participants are owners rather than employees. The partnership agreement should specify the rights and responsibilities of each partner, including the structure for allocation of profits, which of the partners have decision-making authority, and which partners have primary responsibility for debts.

The same agreement should also set forth the partners' ability to enter into the agreement, confirm their availability during the shoot, and provide that the partners grant to the partnership the rights to use their name and likeness in association with the film and its marketing, as well as all other key employment provisions.

In the absence of a written agreement specifying the rights and interests of the parties, a general partnership provides shared ownership of all interests and risks among all the parties. For the filmmaker, this may result in parting with a great deal of ownership and control of the project in exchange for relatively small contributions from the other members of the film company. This may be a very high cost, given the filmmaker's own hard work, and thus a general partnership should be undertaken with caution. The use of a written agreement can provide some significant protections.

2. Independent Contractors

Since a general partnership exposes the partners to unlimited liability for the obligations of the company, many cast and crew members will be unwilling to become general partners. Bona fide independent contractors hired by the film company need not become general partners, provided the filmmaker documents the independent contractor agreement as described in chapter 6 (pp. 93–94). For cast members and many of the crew, however, acting as an independent contractor will not work. State employment laws and federal tax laws provide detailed rules regarding the characterization of workers as employees or independent contractors, and the film company has little power to vary these classifications. However, unfinanced films shot on an intermittent schedule may require little full-time commitment by the participants. Under these conditions, more of the participants may qualify as independent contractors.

3. Nested LLCs and Joint Ventures

Unfinanced film companies may consider a variation of the nested-LLC model described in chapter 3 (pp. 46–48). Under this variation, the filmmaker forms an LLC for the purpose of making films. The LLC enters into a joint venture with a general partnership composed of the cast and crew, under which the LLC is responsible for all financing and budget while the general partnership is responsible for all personal services. In this way, all contracts will be executed by the LLC rather than the general partnership, and the LLC will be primarily responsible for all obligations. Along with sufficient insurance, this structure should minimize the potential for personal liability among the cast and crew.

E. Genres Well Suited to the Unfinanced Film

The no-budget film has been around since the Edison Trust acquired Woodville Latham's patent on the shutter gate and started the motion picture business. But modern ultra-low-budget productions owe their paternity to filmmakers like Edward D. Wood Jr. and Roger Corman. As an art form, the unfinanced film may be considered a genre unto itself, but this is misleading. Several different genres are particularly well suited to small-budget productions.

1. Horror and Suspense

In the 1970s, the homemade films *Halloween* and *The Texas Chainsaw Massacre* redefined the horror and suspense genre. The genre was reenergized in the late 1990s by the success of the low-budget *The Blair Witch Project*, and it continues to provide a potentially large financial return on very small investments. In unfinanced horror films, the lack of polish only adds to their subconscious believability. Moreover, the pressure is on the characters, not sophisticated special effects, to convey the tension in the films. For beginning filmmakers, horror and suspense movies continue to be excellent training vehicles. These are also a source of excellent content for online series. Horror and suspense shorts, a bit like the cliffhangers of an earlier age, work very well for YouTube channels.

2. Documentaries

Documentaries are particularly well suited to shooting with small budgets. Since they do not require sets, costumes, or paid actors, documentaries can eliminate many of the expenses of the filmmaking process. Most documentaries are not released theatrically, so a first-time documentary filmmaker may choose to shoot with less expensive equipment, making the size of the crew and the cost of the equipment rental much lower. In addition, unless the filmmaker stages reenactments or asks the film's subjects to perform on behalf of the film, the documentary filmmaker is not responsible for the activities of those individuals being filmed, so the production can film high-risk activities such as motocross or hang gliding without incurring liability. As soon as the film company begins to stage events, however, it takes on the same obligations as with a narrative film project.

The documentary filmmaker is in the best position to hire the limited and often intermittent crew as independent contractors, to serve from time to time when the production is on location. Even if the documentary film has a few full-time employees, the film company can likely use a payroll service and meet its obligations readily even on a low budget.

3. Cinematic Nonunion Theater

Nonprofessional theater continues to be a mainstay of art and culture throughout the world. More than a source of endless productions of *Our Town* or *Grease*, many small, nonunion theaters provide the first opportunity for new playwrights to develop their craft. Most of these productions run for a few weekends and are never seen again.

Unfinanced filmmaking can provide an extremely useful opportunity for these playwrights and their directors, producers, and casts. By working with a small theater to film original plays and musicals, the filmmaker can capture a version of the production for posterity. These productions can be shot either on stage or on more realistic sets, and they can range from filmed stage performances to full movie adaptations. They usually land somewhere in between.

While members of the Actors' Equity Association actors' union will generally not agree to such productions, most other performers would jump at the chance to participate in the film version of the show. Similarly, original plays and musicals produced under union-approved Broadway agreements generally preclude this technique, but many original productions would benefit from the opportunity unfinanced filmmaking provides to increase their audience.

Contractually, the rights in the play and the script need to be clarified. Often the theatrical director is also the filmmaker, combining the projects into a single activity and using the same actor and crew contracts. These contracts need to provide for both live and filmed versions of the production. The playwright will generally not consider the unfinanced movie to be the definitive motion picture version, so the contract will likely allow the film company to produce only this one version of the motion picture. The writer will retain all other rights, such as the rights to create sequels or remakes. In this way, the playwright may use the unfinanced version as a demo reel for promoting the sale of the play and eventually a more professional film version.

F. Building on Film School

New filmmakers often create their first feature as part of their graduation from an undergraduate or masters of fine arts film program. While tuition costs a considerable amount, the value of an education extends well past the technical skills developed in one's field—it represents a transformative experience for every graduate. As such, the investment in film school may be a very strategic method for financing one's first film.

Moreover, for the unfinanced filmmaker, great value may be found in the video and digital filmmaking programs of community colleges. For the cost of a few thousand dollars, the filmmaker will receive access to equipment, insurance, cast and crew, locations, editing equipment, professional discounts, and a host of other resources. A person seeking to break into documentary or feature film production would benefit tremendously from utilizing the resources of these low-cost community college programs. Oftentimes the availability of community college resources will not be limited to the particular courses offered. This means that by signing up for the program, the filmmaker may gain immediate access to many of the resources necessary to begin production on projects chosen by the filmmaker rather than selected as part of course requirements.

Conclusion

The world of independent filmmaking is changing rapidly. The viewer-ship—or consumption—of audiovisual content has reached all-time highs. Audiences watch content in IMAX movie theaters, using 3D glasses, with VR headsets, on televisions, computer screens, six-inch phone screens and 1.5-inch digital watches. Epic series can be told over the course of dozens of episodes released during a span of multiple years, or presented in short videos lasting only seconds.

Increased interactivity enables the viewers to comment on the episodes and provide feedback in nearly real-time to the creators. Other technologies are blending the concept of a video with that of a video game, as the audience becomes increasingly involved in the storytelling.

Despite these many changes, the business basics, artistic essentials, and craft that underlies great visual storytelling remains the same. Compelling stories featuring universal ideas and emotionally connected characters drive the audience to want more. This book serves as a something of a blueprint, providing bumper guards for the artists, storytellers, and supporters of the craft of filmmaking.

Hopefully, the suggestions and lessons provided in this book have made the filmmaking process more understandable, less distracting, and easier to manage. The goal, after all, is to help simplify the moviemaking, allowing the filmmaker to focus on the work captured in the frame. Whatever the format and regardless of budget, great stories are waiting to be told, and an

army of actors, writers, directors, cinematographers, designers, and producers are waiting to pitch in.

Roger Ebert and Gene Siskel understood the audience well when they closed their television episodes with "See you at the movies," but an earlier age may have captured it even better. To quote Judy Garland and Mickey Rooney, "Hey kids, let's put on a show."

PART

Appendixes

APPENDIX

Sample Agreements

The sample agreements are for guidance only. Reference should be made to the most current terms of any referenced collective bargaining agreement and current laws. Each contract should be dated and signed by all parties in their corporate capacity (not personally); however, the signature blocks are not reproduced in the samples.

1. Author Agreement (for WGA Members, Modified Low-Budget Agreement)

When countersigned below, the following will constitute the terms and conditions of the agreement ("Agreement") between Productions LLC ("Company") and the writer identified below ("Author") in respect to the motion picture tentatively known as "The Picture" ("Picture").

1. **Employment and Services.** Company hereby employs Author in connection with the development of the Picture pursuant to the terms and conditions hereof, and Author hereby accepts such employment.

    1.1   Author will render the writing services set forth in this Agreement on behalf of Company or such other parties as may be designated by Company and in accordance with Company's instructions.

    1.2   Author shall render all services as are customarily rendered by writers of first-class feature-length theatrical motion pictures in the motion picture industry, as, when, and where required by Company, and shall comply with all reasonable directions, requests, rules, and regulations of Company in connection therewith, whether or not the same involve matters of artistic taste or judgment, and will incorporate into Author's written material the changes, revisions, deletions, or additions as may be required by Company or any representative designated by Company.

2. **WGA Low-Budget Agreement.** Company shall undertake to become a signatory to the Writers Guild of America Minimum Basic Agreement (MBA), and shall produce the Picture as a low-budget picture at $1,200,000 or less. Provided Company becomes a signatory to the WGA, all provisions of the then-applicable MBA as modified by the Low-Budget Agreement shall be incorporated by reference and shall take precedence over any conflicting provisions of this Agreement.

3. **Compensation.** Upon the conditions that Author fully performs all services and obligations required hereunder and that Author is not in default or material breach of any obligation due to Company, Company shall pay Author as full and complete consideration for such services and for all rights granted hereunder, the following sums at the following times:

   3.1   Company shall pay Author a purchase price of $_____.

   3.2   Company and Author have agreed to defer payment of one hundred percent (100%) of the screenplay purchase price owed to Author. It is presently anticipated that the budget shall remain at or below $500,000. If, however, the budget exceeds $500,000 (while remaining below $1,200,000 upon commencement of principal photography) Company shall pay $10,000 to Author and apply this against any deferred monies owing on the screenplay purchase price.

   3.3   Company shall offer Author the opportunity to perform any rewrites or polishes on the script requested in writing by Company, which shall be compensated at the MBA minimum.

   3.4   Company shall pay Author a script publication fee of $5,000, which is due thirty (30) days after final determination of the writing credits on the Picture. If the Picture budget remains at or less than $500,000, then Author agrees to request the publication fee be deferred along with the screenplay purchase and/or first rewrite compensation.

4. **Term.** The term of this Agreement shall commence on the date hereof and shall continue thereafter until Company has fully completed all services required hereunder, unless sooner terminated or abandoned in accordance with the provisions of this Agreement.

5. **Credit.** Provided Author completes all services required hereunder and the Picture is completed by Company, then Author shall receive credit on the screen, in motion picture trailers, and in paid print advertising issued by Company and under Company's control which is at least 10 inches or larger.

    5.1   The credit shall be "_____" or such other credit as determined exclusively by the WGA.

    5.2   No casual or inadvertent failure to comply with the provisions of this clause shall be deemed to be a breach of this Agreement by Company. Author shall notify Company of any breach of this paragraph, after which Company shall take reasonable steps to correct all new prints, copies, and advertising on a prospective basis, but Company shall not be required to recall or alter any prints, copies, or advertisements in production or distribution. No monetary damages are available for breach of Company's duties under this paragraph.

6. **Work-for-Hire and Assignment of Rights.** Author acknowledges that all of the results and proceeds of Author's services in connection with the Picture, the Material (as such term is herein defined), is created by Author as a "work made for hire" specially ordered or commissioned by Company with Company being deemed the sole author of all the results and proceeds. To the extent such Material is not treated as work-for-hire, it is hereby assigned, granted, licensed, and conveyed to Company for all purposes in perpetuity. For purposes hereof, the "Material" shall include, without limitation, Author's Screenplay, any drafts thereof, characters, plots, names, locations, themes, trademarks, or other literary or intellectual property associated with the Picture or relating to the Picture that have been created or written by Author at any time prior to the date of the Agreement or during the term of this Agreement.

    6.1   Without limiting the foregoing, Author acknowledges that Company is and will be the sole and exclusive owner of the Material, including all rights of every kind and nature in, to, and with respect to Author's services in connection with the Material, the Picture, and the results and proceeds of the Picture, and that Company will have the right to use, refrain from using, change, modify, add to, subtract from, and exploit, advertise, exhibit, and otherwise turn to account any or all of the foregoing in any manner whatsoever and in any and all media whether now known or hereafter devised throughout the universe. These rights include, without limitation, remakes, prequels and sequels, trailers, making-of specials, featurettes, websites, promotional material, Author interviews, all forms of television, radio, stage, home viewing devices, portable viewing or listening devices, phonograph and sound recordings, print and electronic publications, and game rights in all languages, as Company in its sole discretion will determine.

6.2 Author waives any and all "droit moral" or "moral rights of authors" or any similar rights or principles of law of authors to the greatest extent allowed by applicable law that Author may now or later enjoy in the Material. It is agreed that Author's consideration for the Material is included in the compensation to be paid pursuant to the Agreement.

6.3 In addition to all other right granted herein, to the extent necessary, Author irrevocably assigns, licenses, and grants to Company throughout the universe, in perpetuity, the rights, if any, of Author to authorize, prohibit, or control the renting, lending, fixation, reproduction, distribution, exhibition, display, or other exploitation of the Picture by any media and means now known or hereafter devised as may be conferred upon Author under applicable laws, regulations, or directives, including, without limitation, any rental and lending rights pursuant to any European Union ("EU") directives or enabling or implementing legislation, laws, or regulations enacted by the member nations of the EU.

7. **Name and Likeness.** Author grants to Company the right, in perpetuity and throughout the universe, to use Author's name, likeness, activities, attributes, or biography in connection with the production, exhibition, advertising, publicizing, and other exploitation of the Picture and all subsidiary and ancillary rights therein; provided, however, that in no event will Author be depicted as using or endorsing any product, commodity, or service without Author's prior written consent. Notwithstanding the foregoing, Company's use of Author's name in a billing block on any item of merchandise or other material will constitute an approved use of Author's name that will not require Author's further consent.

8. **Representations and Warranties.** The Author hereby represents and warrants as follows:

8.1 The Material has been and will at all times be written solely by and is original with Author; no element of the Material infringes upon any other literary property.

8.2   The Material is wholly fictional, no portion of the Material has been taken from any other source (other than the public domain), and the Material does not constitute defamation against any person or violate any rights in any person, including, without limitation, rights of privacy, publicity, copyright (whether common law or statutory, throughout the universe), trademark, publication or performance rights, or rights in any other property, and any rights to consultation regarding the Material or any element thereof.

8.3   In addition to the foregoing, all representations and warranties and indemnities of the parties set forth in the Author's Certificate of Authorship pertaining to the Picture are incorporated in full in this Agreement by reference.

8.4   Author has full right and power to enter into this Agreement and perform all obligations hereunder, including, without limitation, all rights necessary to convey each and every right granted herein.

9.   **Indemnification.** If any claim, action, suit, or proceeding is brought or threatened alleging facts that, if true, would constitute a breach of Author's representations, warranties, and covenants under the Agreement or the Certificate of Authorship, Author shall immediately notify Company and Company's legal counsel thereof in writing. Company will have the sole right to control the legal defense against such claims or litigation, including the right to select counsel of its choice and to compromise or settle any such claim, demand, or litigation. Author shall indemnify and hold harmless Company, the members and corporations comprising Company, and its and their respective employees, officers, agents, assigns, and licensees from and against any and all liabilities, claims, costs, damages, and expenses (including reasonable attorneys' fees and court costs) arising out of or in connection with a breach or alleged breach of the foregoing covenants, warranties, and representations. Company agrees to immediately notify Author of any claims alleging facts that, if true, would constitute a breach by Author of any representations, warranties, or covenants under the Agreement or the Certificate of Authorship and to indemnify and hold Author harmless from and against any and all liabilities, claims, costs, damages, and expenses (including reasonable attorney fees and court costs) arising out of any claim or legal action with respect to content added to the Material by Company and in connection with claims arising from the production, distribution, and exploitation of the Picture (except for matters covered by Author's representations and warranties under this Agreement

or any other agreements relating to Author's grant of rights to, or rendition of services for, Company).

10. **Insurance Coverage.** Author will be covered as an additional insured under Company's policies of errors and omissions and general liability insurance, if Company procures these policies, subject to the policies' terms, conditions, and exclusions.

11. **Reimbursements.** Author shall be reimbursed for all reasonable advances or expenses incurred by him in the capacity as screenwriter pursuant to this Agreement with respect to the production of the Picture, such as for location travel, housing, and the like, provided such expenses have been approved by Company in advance and Author provides adequate documentation and receipts of the expense.

12. **Unique Services.** It is hereby agreed and understood that Author's services to be furnished hereunder are special, extraordinary, unique, and not replaceable, and that there is no adequate remedy at law for breach of this contract by Author.

    12.1 Company shall be entitled to both legal and equitable remedies as may be available, including both injunctive relief and damages. Company may elect not to submit arbitration for the purpose of seeking emergency, preliminary, or temporary injunctive relief.

    12.2 Author's services shall be in such time, place, and manner as Company may reasonably direct in accordance with customary motion picture industry practice. Such services shall be rendered in an artistic, conscientious, efficient, and punctual manner to the best of Author's ability to adhere to the budget and shooting schedule.

13. **Resolution of Disputes.**

    13.1 The MBA sets forth the grievance and arbitration procedures relating to all matters under the jurisdiction of the WGA.

    13.2 Any disputes not subject to the MBA shall be resolved by arbitration in accordance with the then rules of the American Arbitration Association ("AAA"). Any party hereto electing to commence an action shall give written notice to the other party hereto.

    13.3 The arbitrator or the referee shall diligently pursue determination of any Arbitration under consideration and shall render a decision within one hundred twenty (120) days after the arbitrator or referee is selected. The determination of the arbitrator on all matters referred to it hereunder shall be final and binding on the parties hereto; provided, however, that except as specified in Section 12, above, the arbitrator shall be bound by the terms of the Agreement and the Certificate of Authorship so that all awards shall be for monetary award exclusively and no injunctive relief or specific performance can be brought against the parties.

13.4 The award of such arbitrator may be confirmed or enforced in any court of competent jurisdiction. The referee, arbitrator, or its designee shall have full access to such records and physical facilities of the parties hereto as may be required. The costs and expenses of the referee or arbitrator, and the attorneys' fees and costs of each of the parties incurred in such, shall be apportioned between the parties by such arbitrator, as the case may be, based upon such arbitrator's determination of the merits of their respective positions.

14. **Confidentiality; Publicity.** Company shall have the exclusive right to issue and to license others to issue advertising, press information, and publicity with respect to the Picture, and Author shall not circulate, publish, or otherwise disseminate any such advertising or publicity without Company's prior written consent. Author shall treat and hold all budgeting, financial information, and nonpublic production information in confidence and shall not disclose such information to any third party without the prior written approval of Company.

15. **Assignment.** Author agrees that Company shall have the right to assign, license, delegate, lend, or otherwise transfer all or any part of its rights or duties under this Agreement at any time to any person. Author acknowledges that the personal services to be rendered by Author hereunder are of the essence of this Agreement and agrees that Author shall not assign this Agreement, in whole or in part, to any person, and that any purported assignment or delegation of duties by Author shall be null and void and of no force and effect whatsoever. This Agreement shall inure to the benefit of Company's successors, assigns, licensees, grantees, and associated, affiliated, and subsidiary companies.

15.1 **No Obligation.** Company agrees to use all reasonable efforts to cause the Picture to be produced, however, the parties recognize that the production of an independent motion picture is an inherently difficult undertaking. Company is under no obligation to produce the Picture hereunder. In the event Company abandons production of the Picture hereunder, Author is entitled to such fixed compensation as had previously accrued and is not entitled to any additional compensation, damage, or loss as a result of such failure to undertake or complete the Picture.

15. 2 **Assurances.** Each party shall execute all documents and certificates and perform all acts deemed appropriate by the Company or required by this Agreement in connection with this Agreement and the production of the Picture.

15.3 **Complete Agreement; Merger.** This Agreement together with the Certificate of Authorship constitutes the complete and exclusive statement of the agreement among the parties with respect to the matters discussed herein and therein and they supersede all prior written or oral statements among the parties, including any prior statement, warranty, or representation.

15.4 **Section Headings.** The section headings that appear throughout this Agreement are provided for convenience only and are not intended to define or limit the scope of this Agreement or the intent or subject matter of its provisions.

15.5 **Applicable Law.** Each party agrees that all disputes arising under or in connection with this Agreement and any transactions contemplated by this Agreement shall be governed by the internal law, and not the law of conflicts, of the State of _____.

15.6 **Amendments; Notices.** Any amendments, modifications, or alterations to this Agreement must be in writing and signed by all of the parties hereto. Any notice or other writing to be served upon either party in connection with this Agreement shall be in writing and shall be deemed completed when delivered to the address listed above.

15.7 **Severability.** Each provision of this Agreement is severable from the other provisions. If, for any reason, any provision of this Agreement is declared invalid or contrary to existing law, the inoperability of that provision shall have no effect on the remaining provisions of the Agreement, and all remaining provisions shall continue in full force and effect.

15.8 **Counterparts.** This Agreement may be executed in counterparts, each of which shall be deemed an original and all of which shall, when taken together, constitute a single document.

IN WITNESS WHEREOF, the parties hereto have executed and delivered this agreement as of the date written below.

. . .

2. Certificate of Authorship

I, _____, an individual, certify that, pursuant to an agreement ("Agreement") between Productions LLC ("Company") and me in connection with a motion picture photoplay tentatively entitled "The Picture" ("Picture"), all literary material of whatever kind or nature, written or to be written, furnished or to be furnished, by me, and all of the results and proceeds of my services in connection with the Picture (all such literary material and all such results and proceeds being referred to collectively herein as the "Material") was or will be solely created by me as a "work made for hire" specially ordered or commissioned by Company for use as part of the Picture, with Company being deemed the sole author of the Material and the owner of all rights of every kind or nature, whether now known or hereafter devised (including, but not limited to, all copyrights and all extensions and renewals of copyrights) in and to the Material, with the right to make all uses of the Material throughout the universe and all changes in the Material as Company deems necessary or desirable. The Material will also include, without limitation, any and all ideas, characters, stories, trademarks, treatments, screenplays, and other material, of whatever kind or nature, in connection with or relating to the Picture, created or written by me at any time prior to the date of the Agreement (collectively, the "Preexisting Material"), and I irrevocably grant, assign, and vest Company with all rights of every kind and nature, whether now known or hereafter devised (including, but not limited to, all copyrights and all extensions and renewals of copyrights) in and to the Material and the Preexisting Material, and the Preexisting Material will constitute part of the Material for all intents and purposes under this Certificate of Authorship.

Without limiting the foregoing, I irrevocably assign, license, and grant to Company, throughout the universe, in perpetuity, any and all of my rights to authorize, prohibit, or control the renting, lending, fixation, reproduction, or other exploitation of the Picture by any media and means now known or hereafter devised as may be conferred upon me under applicable laws, regulations, or directives, in any jurisdiction throughout the world, including, without limitation, any rental and lending rights pursuant to any European Union ("EU") directives or enabling or implementing legislation, laws, or regulations enacted by the member nations of the EU.

I waive all rights of "droit moral" or "moral rights of authors" or any similar rights or principles of law that I may now or later have in the Material. It is agreed that my consideration for the Material is included in the compensation to be paid pursuant to the Agreement.

I warrant and represent that: (a) I have the right to execute this document; (b) except to the extent that it is based on material assigned to me by Company to be used as the basis therefor, the Material is or will be original with me; (c) the Material does not and will not defame or disparage any person or entity or infringe upon or violate the rights of privacy, publicity, or any other rights of any kind or nature whatsoever of any person or entity; (d) the Material is not the subject of any litigation or of any claim that might give rise to litigation; (e) I have not done, nor will I do, any act or thing that diminishes, impairs, or otherwise derogates from the full enjoyment by Company of all of Company's rights in and to the Material; and (f) I have not heretofore assigned, conveyed, encumbered, or otherwise disposed of or impaired any rights in and to the Material. If any claim, action, suit, or proceeding is brought or threatened alleging facts that, if true, would constitute a breach by me of my representations, warranties, and covenants under the Agreement or this Certificate of Authorship, I will immediately notify Company and Company's legal counsel thereof in writing. I agree that Company will have the sole right to control the legal defense against such claims or litigation, including the right to select counsel of its choice and to compromise or settle any such claim, demand, or litigation. I will indemnify and hold harmless Company, the members and the corporations comprising Company, and its and their respective employees, officers, agents, assigns, and licensees from and against any and all liabilities, claims, costs, damages, and expenses (including reasonable attorneys' fees and court costs) arising out of or in connection with a breach or alleged breach of the foregoing covenants, warranties, and representations; and Company agrees to immediately notify me of any claims alleging facts that, if true, would constitute a breach by me of my representations, warranties, or covenants under the Agreement or this Certificate of Authorship and to indemnify and hold me harmless from and against any and all liabilities, claims, costs, damages, and expenses (including reasonable attorney fees and court costs) arising out of any claim or legal action with respect to material added to the Material by Company and in connection with claims arising from the production, distribution, and exploitation of the Picture (except for matters covered by my representations and warranties under this Agreement or any other agreements relating to my grant of rights to, or rendition of services for, Company).

I agree to execute any documents and do any other acts as may be required by Company or its assignees or licensees to further evidence or effectuate

Company's rights as set forth in this Certificate of Authorship or the Agreement. On my failure promptly to do so within five (5) business days following Company's request and delivery to me of the applicable documents or within five (5) business days following Company's request for such other acts, I hereby appoint Company as my attorney-in-fact for such purposes (it being acknowledged that such appointment is irrevocable and coupled with an interest) with full power of substitution and delegation.

I further acknowledge that: (a) in the event of any breach of the Agreement by Company, I will be limited to my remedy at law for damages, if any, and I will not have the right to terminate or rescind this Certificate or to restrain, enjoin, or otherwise impair the production, distribution, advertising, publicizing, or exploitation of the Picture or any rights in the Picture, and (b) nothing herein will obligate Company to use my services or the results or proceeds thereof in the Picture or to produce, advertise, or distribute the Picture.

I agree that Company's rights with respect to the Material or my services may be freely assigned and licensed, and in the event of an assignment or license, this Agreement will remain binding on me and inure to the benefit of any assignee or licensee; provided, however, that on an assignment by Company, Company will remain secondarily liable for its obligations under the Agreement unless such assignment is to: (a) a "major" or "mini-major" (as customarily understood in the motion picture industry) motion picture company or to a United States free or pay television network or other financially responsible party that assumes in writing all of Company's obligations under this Agreement; (b) an entity into which Company merges or is consolidated; (c) an entity that acquires all or substantially all of Company's business and assets; or (d) a person or entity that is controlled by, under common control with, or controls Company; in which event Company will be relieved of its obligations under Author's Agreement. I agree that except as provided in the Author's Agreement, I will not have the right to assign this Certificate of Authorship or delegate the performance of my obligations to any person or entity and any purported assignment or delegation will be void.

I have caused this document to be executed as of _____ [date].

. . .

3. Producer Agreement

This Agreement is made and entered into as of the date first ascribed below, by and between XYZ Film Company LLC, 1234 Main Street, Hollywood, California 90210 ("Company") and John Doe, an individual, 5678 W. 46th St., New York, NY 10021 ("Producer"), with reference to the following facts:

Company is a wholly owned limited liability company owned by Jane Roe ("Writer/Director").

Company has or will acquire rights to a screenplay to be written and directed by Writer/Director and desires to make such screenplay into a motion picture (the "Picture"); and

Producer has extensive professional experiences as a line producer and producer of feature motion pictures.

Now Therefore, in consideration of the mutual covenants, conditions, and undertakings hereinafter set forth, the parties hereto agree as follows:

1. **Services Provided.** Company hereby employs the services of Producer, and Producer hereby accepts such employment, for the purpose of serving as producer and line producer of the Picture, for the period of [three (3)] weeks of preproduction, [five (5)] weeks of principal photography on an exclusive basis, and such postproduction as is reasonably necessary for completion of the Picture on a nonexclusive but first-priority basis. Each week shall include six working days. The Producer will provide such services as are generally performed by producers, including the coordination of all creative, financial, technological, and administrative processes throughout the term of this agreement, subject to the direction and control of Company and such other contracts as Company shall enter with other parties.

2. **Term.** The term of this Agreement shall commence on the date hereof and shall continue thereafter until Producer has fully completed all services required hereunder, unless sooner terminated in accordance with the provisions of this Agreement.

3. **Credit.** Provided Producer completes all services required hereunder and the Picture is completed by Company, then Producer shall receive credit on the screen, in motion picture trailers, and in paid print advertising issued by Company and under Company's control which is at least 10 inches or larger. The credit shall be "Produced by John Doe." On the screen such credit shall be displayed above or before the title of the Picture in a size of type not less than *fifty percent* (50%) of the size of type used to display the

title of the Picture. At its sole discretion, Company may assign "Produced by" credit to one or more additional persons in addition to Producer in the event Company determines such other person or persons provided substantial producer services in addition to Producer. No casual or inadvertent failure to comply with the provisions of this clause shall be deemed to be a breach of this Agreement by Company. Producer shall notify Company of any breach of this paragraph, after which Company shall take reasonable steps to correct all new prints, copies, and advertising on a prospective basis, but Company shall not be required to recall or alter any prints, copies, or advertisements in production or distribution. No monetary damages are available for breach of Company's duties under this paragraph.

4. **Consideration.** In consideration for Producer's services hereunder and provided Producer is not in default hereunder, Company shall pay Producer as follows:

(a) Fixed Consideration. Producer shall receive a stipend of [$100.00] per day actually worked during preproduction and principal photography, not to exceed [Forty-Eight Hundred ($4,800.00)] Dollars. The payment shall be paid on a weekly basis.

(b) Net Profits. If Company produces the Picture, Producer shall receive an amount equal to [ten percent (10%)] of one hundred percent (100%) of Net Profits in the Gross Receipts of the Company in the Picture or [One Hundred Thousand ($100,000)] Dollars, whichever is lower.

(i) Gross Receipts means all income, if any, actually received by Company from the sale, exhibition, or distribution of the Picture in theaters, video/DVD or similar format, broadcast television, satellite, cable exhibition, or any other method of exhibition, display, or performance now known or hereafter created. Gross Receipts does not include income from any other source related to the Picture, including, without limitation, income derived from sale of sequel, prequel, or remake rights, publishing interests such as novelizations, comic books, etc., sales of the screenplay, "making of" or other related projects, or any other spin-offs or related Company projects or activities.

(ii) The term Net Profits shall mean the Gross Receipts, less the deductions of all Company expenses of every kind related to the Picture. Without limiting the foregoing, the deductions shall include all costs, charges, and expenses paid or incurred in connection with the preparation, production, completion, and delivery of the Picture, deferred compensation, charges for any services, union or trade obligations, interest expenses, obligations to any completion guarantor, legal and accounting charges, the cost of all material, services, facilities, labor, insurance, taxes (other than income, franchise, and like taxes), copyright royalties attributable to the Picture for music, artwork, script, or other, judgments, marketing and promotional expenses, distribution fees, recoveries, settlements, losses, costs, and expenses, including reasonable attorneys' fees, sustained or incurred by Company in connection with the Picture or anything used therein and in connection with the production thereof. Company shall pay Producer twice annually all amounts due hereunder for all monies accrued during the preceding six-month period, not later than forty-five (45) days following the end of each such period.

(c)   Reimbursements. Producer shall be reimbursed for all reasonable advances or expenses incurred in the production of the Picture, such as for location scouting, equipment rental, and the like, provided such expenses have been approved by Company in advance and Producer provides adequate documentation and receipts of the expense.

5.   **Authority.** Company shall coordinate with Producer throughout the production to the greatest extent practicable throughout production; provided, however, Company reserves final approval of all essential production elements including, without limitation, script, budget, casting, locations, and film editing. Subject to direction of Company, Producer shall comply with all contractual and union and guild obligations and Company requirements.

6.   **Termination.**

(a)   This Agreement may be terminated by Company at any time, with or without cause. If Company elects to terminate this Agreement and Producer is not in default hereunder, Company shall pay Producer all accrued fixed compensation and a pro rata proportion of the contingent compensation. (By way of example, if Producer is terminated after 12 days, Producer will receive 12/48 of the contingent compensation, equal to 25% of 10%, meaning 2.5% of the Net Profits.) The costs of additional producer(s) shall be added to the cost of production. In the event Company determines Producer has materially breached any obligations hereunder, no contingent compensation shall be paid.

(b)   This Agreement may be terminated by Producer upon seven days' advanced written notice. Unless otherwise agreed in writing by the parties, in the event Producer terminates this Agreement, Producer shall receive only the accrued fixed compensation but shall not be eligible for any contingent compensation.

7.   **Work Made for Hire.** Company shall own the copyright in the Picture without any claim by Producer. Producer is employed as on a work made for hire as a specially commissioned audiovisual or motion picture work and acknowledges that the copyright in the Picture shall vest exclusively in Company as author.

(a)   The Picture shall be registered for copyright in Company's name both in the United States and elsewhere.

(b)   To the extent Producer has created any copyrighted elements incorporated into the Picture and such work-made-for-hire provision is not recognized by the jurisdiction, Producer hereby assigns all rights or the maximum rights allowed under that jurisdiction's laws to Company, including, without limitation, Rental Lending Rights if recognized, rights to enforce any claim of attribution and integrity, or rights to exploit any interest in the Picture in any media now known or hereafter developed.

8.   **Unique Services.** It is hereby agreed and understood that Producer's services to be furnished hereunder are special, extraordinary, unique, and not replaceable, and that there is no adequate remedy at law for breach of this contract by Producer.

(a)   Company shall be entitled to both legal and equitable remedies as may be available, including both injunctive relief and damages. Company may elect not to submit to arbitration for the purpose of seeking emergency, preliminary, or temporary injunctive relief.

(b)   Producer's services shall be in such time, place, and manner as Company may reasonably direct in accordance with customary motion picture industry practice. Such services shall be rendered in an artistic, conscientious, efficient, and punctual manner to the best of Producer's ability to adhere to the budget and shooting schedule.

(c)   Producer grants to Company the perpetual nonexclusive right to use and license others to use Producer's name, biography, and reproductions of Producer's physical likeness and voice in connection with the production, exhibition, advertising, promotion, or other exploitation of the Picture and all subsidiary and ancillary rights therein and thereto; provided, however, Company shall not use or authorize the use of Producer's name or likeness as a direct endorsement of any product or service without Producer's prior consent.

9. **Resolution of Disputes.** ANY AND ALL DISPUTES HEREUNDER SHALL BE RESOLVED BY ARBITRATION OR REFERENCE. ANY PARTY HERETO ELECTING TO COMMENCE AN ACTION SHALL GIVE WRITTEN NOTICE TO THE OTHER PARTY HERETO. THEREUPON, IF ARBITRATION IS SELECTED BY THE PARTY COMMENCING THE ACTION, THE CLAIM ("ARBITRATION MATTER") SHALL BE SETTLED BY ARBITRATION IN ACCORDANCE WITH THE THEN RULES OF THE AMERICAN ARBITRATION ASSOCIATION ("AAA"). The arbitrator or the referee shall diligently pursue determination of any Arbitration under consideration and shall render a decision within one hundred twenty (120) days after the arbitrator or referee is selected. The determination of the arbitrator on all matters referred to it hereunder shall be final and binding on the parties hereto. The award of such arbitrator may be confirmed or enforced in any court of competent jurisdiction. The referee, arbitrator, or its designee shall have full access to such records and physical facilities of the parties hereto as may be required. The costs and expenses of the referee or arbitrator, and the attorneys' fees and costs of each of the parties incurred in such, may be apportioned between the parties by such arbitrator, as the case may be, based upon such arbitrator's determination of the merits of their respective positions.

10. **Confidentiality; Publicity.** Company shall have the exclusive right to issue and to license others to issue advertising and publicity with respect to the Picture, and Producer shall not circulate, publish, or otherwise disseminate any such advertising or publicity without Company's prior written consent.

11. **Assignment.** Producer agrees that Company shall have the right to assign, license, delegate, lend, or otherwise transfer all or any part of its rights or duties under this Agreement at any time to any person. Producer acknowledges that the personal services to be rendered by Producer hereunder are of the essence of this Agreement and agrees that Producer shall not assign this Agreement, in whole or in part, to any person, and that any purported assignment or delegation of duties by Producer shall be null and void and of no force and effect whatsoever. This Agreement shall inure to the benefit

of Company's successors, assigns, licensees, grantees, and associated, affiliated, and subsidiary companies.

12. **No Obligation.** Company agrees to uses all reasonable efforts to cause the Picture to be produced, however, the parties recognize that the production of an independent motion picture is an inherently difficult undertaking. Company is under no obligation to produce the Picture hereunder. In the event Company abandons production of the Picture hereunder, Producer is entitled to such fixed compensation as had previously accrued and is not entitled to any additional compensation, damage, or loss as a result of such failure to undertake or complete the Picture.

13. **Assurances.** Each party shall execute all documents and certificates and perform all acts deemed appropriate by the Company or required by this Agreement in connection with this Agreement and the production of the Picture.

14. **Complete Agreement.** This Agreement constitutes the complete and exclusive statement of the agreement among the parties with respect to the matters discussed herein, and it supersedes all prior written or oral statements among the parties, including any prior statement, warranty, or representation.

15. **Section Headings.** The section headings that appear throughout this Agreement are provided for convenience only and are not intended to define or limit the scope of this Agreement or the intent or subject matter of its provisions.

16. **Attorneys' Fees.** In the event any action or arbitration proceeding be instituted by a party to enforce any of the terms or conditions contained herein, the prevailing party in such action shall be entitled to such reasonable attorneys' fees, costs, and expenses as may be fixed by the court or arbitrator.

17. **Applicable Law.** Each party agrees that all disputes arising under or in connection with this Agreement and any transactions contemplated by this Agreement shall be governed by the internal law, and not the law of conflicts, of the State of _____.

18. **Notices.** Any notice or other writing to be served upon either party in connection with this Agreement shall be in writing and shall be deemed completed when delivered to the address listed above.

19. **Amendments.** Any amendments, modifications, or alterations to this Agreement must be in writing and signed by all of the parties hereto.

20. **Severability.** Each provision of this Agreement is severable from the other

provisions. If, for any reason, any provision of this Agreement is declared invalid or contrary to existing law, the inoperability of that provision shall have no effect on the remaining provisions of the Agreement, and all remaining provisions shall continue in full force and effect.

21. **Counterparts.** This Agreement may be executed in counterparts, each of which shall be deemed an original and all of which shall, when taken together, constitute a single document.

. . .

4. Actor Employment Agreement (for SAG-AFTRA Modified Low-Budget Agreement)

When countersigned below, the following will constitute the terms and conditions of the agreement ("Agreement") between Productions LLC ("Company"), and the artist identified below ("Artist") in respect to the motion picture tentatively known as "The Picture" ("Picture").

1. The Parties anticipate that the Picture shall be directed and produced as follows:

   DIRECTOR:

   COMPANY EXECUTIVE:

   PRODUCTION COMPANY:

   CASTING DIRECTOR:

   LOCATIONS:

2. The Artist's name and contact information is as follows:

   NAME OF ARTIST:

   NAME OF ARTIST FOR CREDIT (IF DIFFERENT):

   ROLE: ROLE #:

   ADDRESS:

   RESIDENCY/CITIZENSHIP:

   TELEPHONE:

   CELL OR PAGER:

   SOCIAL SEC#:

   CORP: FED ID#:

   GUILD MEMBERSHIP: STATION 12 CHECKED: _____

   [Station 12 is the SAG-AFTRA member eligibility clearance, a requirement for all SAG-AFTRA productions.]

   ARTIST'S AGENCY/AGENT:

   AGENT'S ADDRESS:

   AGENT PHONE / FAX:

   MANAGER:

   MANAGER ADDRESS:

   MANAGER PHONE / FAX: (p) / (f)

3. **Accommodations.** Artist will be provided the following accommodations:

   Dressing Facilities. One room in a double banger or equivalent space.

   Travel. To be determined (coming from _____).

   Hotel. First-class accommodations (otherwise known as Bed/Breakfast with private bath) in _____.

Transportation. Nonexclusive transportation with top-tier cast to and from set.

4. **Start Date.** The anticipated start date is on or about _____. Employment shall continue from and after the starting date for the period necessary to complete all continuous services required by Company from Artist, but for not less than said guaranteed period.

5. **Consideration.** In consideration for Artist's services hereunder and provided Artist is not in default hereunder, Company shall pay Artist as follows:

   (a) SAG-AFTRA Agreement. Company and Artist are each subject to the Screen Actors Guild Modified Low-Budget Production Contract, (SAG-AFTRA Agreement), which terms are hereby incorporated into this Agreement by reference. Unless otherwise provided in the SAG-AFTRA Agreement, the fixed compensation shall be paid as follows:

       (i) Salary. As a portion of consideration for Artist's services hereunder, Artist shall receive a salary of $933.00 per five-day week (Salary).

       (ii) Guarantee. Once the Picture commences principal photography, the Artist will receive compensation for not less than one (1) weeks of production.

       (iii) Postproduction. Any postproduction compensation will be paid at the minimum SAG-AFTRA Agreement scale.

       (iv) Per Diem. Artist shall receive an additional $__.00 per day worked as a per diem to cover the costs associated with food, travel, and related out-of-pocket expenses.

   (b) All compensation payable hereunder on a weekly basis shall be payable not later than Thursday of each week for the period ending on the preceding Saturday. Payments for any period of less than a week shall be at a daily rate determined by prorating the weekly rate on the basis of the number of days in the five-day workweek at the time and place involved, subject to the SAG-AFTRA Agreement. No additional payments shall be required in respect of services rendered at night or on Sundays, Saturdays, or holidays or for meal delays, hazardous work, violation of rest periods, or otherwise, or for exhibitions of the Picture on television or in supplemental markets, except to the minimum extent, if any, specifically required by the SAG-AFTRA Agreement.

[For above-the-line talent only, include (c) and (d)]

(c)   Payment Schedule. Company shall pay Artist four times annually all amounts due hereunder for all accrued Net Profits during the preceding period for the first three years following the theatrical release of the Picture and twice annually thereafter. Such payments shall be due sixty (60) days following the completion of the prior accrual period.

(d)   Net Profits. If Company produces the Picture, Artist shall receive an amount equal to [two percent (2%)] of one hundred percent (100%) of Net Profits in the Gross Receipts of the Managers of the Company in the Picture. Gross Receipts means all income, if any, actually received by Company from the sale, exhibition, or distribution of the Picture in theaters, video/DVD or similar format, broadcast television, satellite, cable exhibition, or any other method of exhibition, display, or performance now known or hereafter created. Gross Receipts does not include income from any other source related to the Picture, including, without limitation, income derived from sale of sequel, prequel, or remake rights, publishing interests such as novelizations, comic books, etc., sales of the screenplay, "making of" or other related projects, or any other spin-offs or related Company projects or activities.

The term Net Profits shall mean the Gross Receipts to Managers of the Company, less the deductions of all Company expenses of every kind related to the Picture. Without limiting the foregoing, the deductions shall include all costs, charges, and expenses paid or incurred in connection with the preparation, production, completion, and delivery of the Picture, deferred compensation, charges for any services, union or trade obligations, interest expenses, obligations to any completion guarantor, legal and accounting charges, the cost of all material, services, facilities, labor, insurance, taxes (other than income, franchise, and like taxes), copyright royalties attributable to the Picture for music, artwork, script, or other, judgments, marketing and promotional expenses, distribution fees, recoveries, settlements, losses, costs, and expenses, including reasonable attorneys' fees, sustained or incurred by Company in connection with the Picture or anything used therein and in connection with the production thereof.

6.   **Services Provided.** Artist will render services, whenever and wherever Company may require, in a competent, conscientious, and professional

manner, having due regard for the production of the Picture within the budget, and as instructed by Company in all matters, including those involving artistic taste and judgment; but there shall be no obligation on Company to actually utilize Artist's services, or to include any of Artist's work in the Picture, or to produce, release, or continue the distribution of the Picture. If, after the expiration or termination hereof, Company should require further services of Artist in the making of retakes, added scenes, looping, post-synching, publicity interviews, personal appearances, stills, and similar matters, Artist shall render such services on a daily basis, subject to Artist's availability with compensation at the SAG-AFTRA Agreement minimum, except that no compensation shall be payable for looping or postsynching, or for publicity interviews, personal appearances, and stills, and if Artist completes all continuous services required by Company from Artist before the expiration of said guaranteed period, and is dismissed by Company, no compensation shall be payable for the number of days equivalent to the number of working days between such dismissal and the expiration of said guaranteed period.

7. **Premieres/Film Festivals.** Should Artist render all services required herein and appear substantially in the film, Producer shall use its best efforts to obtain invitations to premieres/film festivals, with such invitations extended on a favored nations basis with other cast members.

8. **Term.** The term of this Agreement shall commence on the date hereof and shall continue thereafter until Artist has fully completed all services required hereunder, unless sooner terminated in accordance with the provisions of this Agreement.

9. **Credit.** Provided Artist completes all services required herein and appears recognizably in the Picture as released, then Artist shall receive credit on the screen. The screen credit shall use the Name of Artist for Credit listed above. No casual or inadvertent failure to comply with the provisions of this clause shall be deemed to be a breach of this Agreement by Company. Artist shall notify Company of any breach of this paragraph, after which Company shall take reasonable steps to correct all new prints, copies, and advertising on a prospective basis, but Company shall not be required to recall or alter any prints, copies, or advertisements in production or distribution. No monetary damages are available for breach of Company's duties under this paragraph. If Artist is to receive credit in paid advertisements, said obligations shall apply only to the billing portion (excluding artwork and advertising copy) of advertisements issued by Company or under its

direct control relating primarily to the theatrical exhibition of the Picture and which are issued prior to the date five (5) years after the release of the Picture. Billing requirements shall not apply at any time to teasers, trailers, radio and television advertising, group, list, or special advertisements, commercial tie-ups or by-products, or any advertisements of eight column inches or less.

[For above-the-line talent only, include (a) and (b)]

(a) Screen Credit. Company shall give Artist an onscreen credit in the main title sequence of the motion picture on a single card and in all listings of cast.

(b) Paid Advertising. Should Artist render all services required herein and appear recognizably in the Picture as released, Company shall provide Artist credit in the billing block in paid print advertising issued by Company which is at least 10 inches or larger and where the billing block appears. Position in the paid ads will be the same as on the main title cast credits at the same size of type and prominence as other actors accorded credit in the billing block. Paid ads will also be accorded in the same manner on all posters and one-sheets when a billing block is included.

10. **Work Made for Hire and Transfer of Rights.** All results and proceeds of Artist's services hereunder (including, but not limited to (i) all acts, poses, plays, and appearances of Artist, (ii) all literary, dramatic, and musical material written, supplied, or improvised by Artist whether or not in writing, (iii) all designs and inventions of Artist hereunder, and (iv) all photographs, drawings, plans, specifications, and sound recordings containing all or any part of any of the foregoing) shall constitute works prepared by Artist as an Artist of Company within the scope of Artist's employment hereunder, and accordingly, the parties agree that all of the foregoing are and shall be considered "works made for hire" for Company; and that Company is and shall be considered the author thereof for all purposes and the owner throughout the world of all of the rights comprised in the copyright thereof, and of any and all patents, trademarks, and other rights thereto. Artist will, upon request, execute, acknowledge, and deliver to Company such additional documents as Company may deem necessary to evidence and effectuate Company's rights hereunder, and hereby grants to Company the right as Artist's attorney-in-fact to execute, acknowledge, deliver, and record in the United States Copyright Office or elsewhere any and all such documents.

(a) To the extent any Rights are not transferred to Company as a work made for hire, Artist hereby exclusively and irrevocably transfers such Rights to Company.

(b) To the extent Artist has created any copyrighted elements incorporated into the Picture and such work-made-for-hire provision is not recognized by the jurisdiction, Artist hereby assigns all rights or the maximum rights allowed under that jurisdiction's laws to Company, including, without limitation, Rental Lending Rights if recognized, rights to enforce any claim of attribution and integrity, or rights to exploit any interest in the Picture in any media now known or hereafter developed.

11. **Additional Services of Artist.**

(a) Dubbing. Company shall have the right to use a double to represent Artist's physical appearance and to dub or simulate Artist's voice and other sound effects, in whole or in part, in English and all other languages; provided, however, that Company will not dub Artist's voice in the English language, except as follows: (i) when necessary to expeditiously meet the requirements of foreign exhibition; (ii) when necessary to expeditiously meet censorship requirements, both foreign and domestic; (iii) when Artist shall fail and refuse to render the required services, or when Artist is not readily available when and where Artist's services are required hereunder; and (iv) when, in Company's opinion, Artist's voice, accent, or other performance hereunder, including singing and rendition of instrumental music, does not meet Company's requirements in connection with the role.

(b) Soundtrack recordings. Company and its successors, assigns, and licensees shall have the right to use the name, voice, and likeness of Artist in connection with phonograph records, CDs, or any other media now known or hereafter created, produced, or reproduced from the soundtrack of the Picture or any part thereof without additional compensation to Artist.

(c) Related services. Artist shall (i) render services prior to the starting date without compensation in connection with wardrobe preparation, fittings, tests, auditions, rehearsals, prerecordings, consultations, publicity interviews, and similar matters, subject to Artist's availability; (ii) act, pose, sing, speak, play such musical instruments as Artist is capable of playing, and otherwise appear and perform in said role; and (iii) render services in connection with promotional films, trailers, and electrical transcriptions produced in connection with the advertising and exploitation of the Picture. Such services shall be rendered either during or after the term hereof, but if after the term hereof, subject to Artist's availability. Behind-the-scenes footage and clips from the Picture and (subject to clearance from the owners thereof) from other motion pictures in which Artist has appeared may be utilized in connection with such promotional films and trailers. No additional compensation for the services referred to in this subdivision (c) or for the use of such clips or such footage shall be payable.

12. **Wardrobe.** Artist shall provide such modern wardrobe for said role as Artist may possess and all other wardrobe and clothing which is not visible on the screen. Company shall provide all visible character and period wardrobe for said role, if any. Any wardrobe which Artist is required to furnish hereunder shall be suitable, in Company's opinion, for said role. All wardrobe furnished or paid for by Company shall be and remain its property and shall be returned promptly to Company. If any wardrobe furnished by Artist is damaged without Artist's fault while being used in connection with Artist's employment hereunder, Company will be responsible for such damage.

13. **Unique Services.** It is hereby agreed and understood that Artist's services to be furnished hereunder are special, extraordinary, unique, and not replaceable, and that there is no adequate remedy at law for breach of this contract by Artist.

(a) Company shall be entitled to both legal and equitable remedies as may be available, including both injunctive relief and damages. Company may elect not to submit arbitration for the purpose of seeking emergency, preliminary, or temporary injunctive relief.

(b) Artist's services shall be in such time, place, and manner as Company may reasonably direct in accordance with customary motion picture industry practice. Such services shall be rendered in an artistic, conscientious, efficient, and punctual manner to the best of Artist's ability to adhere to the budget and shooting schedule.

(c) Artist grants to Company the perpetual nonexclusive right to use and license others to use Artist's name, biography, and reproductions of Artist's physical likeness and voice in connection with the production, exhibition, advertising, promotion, or other exploitation of the Picture and all subsidiary and ancillary rights therein and thereto; provided, however, Company shall not use or authorize the use of Artist's name or likeness as a direct endorsement of any product or service without Artist's prior consent.

14. **Representations and Warranties.**

   (a) Company warrants and represents that it has the full right, power, and authority to enter into this Agreement and to grant all rights granted herein, that it is not under, nor will it be under, any disability, restriction, or prohibition with respect to its rights to fully perform in accordance with the terms and conditions of this Agreement, and that there shall be no liens, claims, or other interests which may interfere with, impair, or be in derogation of the rights granted herein.

   (b) Artist warrants and represents that Artist is free to enter into this agreement and not subject to any conflicting obligations or any disability which will or might prevent Artist from or interfere with Artist's execution and performance of this agreement; that all literary, dramatic, and musical material, designs, and inventions of Artist hereunder will be original with Artist or in the public domain throughout the world, and shall not infringe upon or violate any copyright of, or the right of privacy or any other right of, any person, and that Artist is a member in good standing of such labor organization as may have jurisdiction, to the extent required by law and applicable collective bargaining agreements.

15. **Indemnifications.**

   (a) Company hereby agrees to indemnify Artist from and against any damages, liabilities, costs, and expenses, including reasonable attorneys' fees actually incurred, arising out of or in any way connected with any claim, demand, or action inconsistent with the Picture, its obligations under this Agreement, or any warranty, representation, or agreement made by Artist herein.

   (b) Artist hereby agrees to indemnify Company, Company's successors, licensees, distributors, subdistributors, and assigns, and the respective officers, directors, agents, and Artists of each of the foregoing, from and against any damages, liabilities, costs, and expenses, including reasonable attorneys' fees actually incurred, arising out of or in any way connected with any claim, demand, or action inconsistent with its obligations under this Agreement, the Rights, or any warranty, representation, or agreement made by Artist herein.

   (c) The warranties and representations of this paragraph shall survive the termination of this Agreement.

16. **Resolution of Disputes.** The provisions of the Screen Actors Guild Codified Basic Agreement for Independent Producers with respect to the arbi-

tration of disputes shall be applicable to Artist's employment. Any dispute not subject to arbitration by the Screen Actors Guild shall be subject to arbitration by the American Arbitration Association.

17. **Employment.** All payments made for services under this Agreement will be treated as wages for the purpose of all taxing authorities, including United States federal, state, and local income-related and employment-related taxes. Company will deduct all taxes as may be required by any lawful authority.

18. **Confidentiality; Publicity.** Company shall have the exclusive right to issue and to license others to issue advertising and publicity with respect to the Picture, and Artist shall not circulate, publish, or otherwise disseminate any such advertising or publicity without Company's prior written consent. Artist hereby grants to Company the right to issue and authorize publicity concerning Artist, and to use Artist's name, voice, and likeness and biographical data in connection with the distribution, exhibition, advertising, and exploitation of the Picture. Without limiting the generality of the foregoing, Company may use Artist's name, voice, and likeness, provided reference is made to the Picture or the literary property or screenplay upon which the Picture is based, or any part thereof, or to Artist's employment hereunder, and provided Artist is not represented as using or endorsing any product or service.

19. **Assignment.** Artist agrees that Company shall have the right to assign, license, delegate, lend, or otherwise transfer all or any part of its rights or duties under this Agreement at any time to any person including, without limitation, Artist's name, likeness, and biographical data, and all representations and warranties hereunder. Artist acknowledges that the personal services to be rendered by Artist hereunder are of the essence of this Agreement and agrees that Artist shall not assign this Agreement, in whole or in part, to any person, and that any purported assignment or delegation of duties by Artist shall be null and void and of no force and effect whatsoever. This Agreement shall inure to the benefit of Company's successors, assigns, licensees, grantees, and associated, affiliated, and subsidiary companies.

20. **No Obligation.** Company agrees to use all reasonable efforts to cause the Picture to be produced, however, the parties recognize that the production of an independent motion picture is an inherently difficult undertaking. Company is under no obligation to produce the Picture hereunder. In the event Company abandons production of the Picture hereunder, Artist is entitled to such fixed compensation as had previously accrued and is not

entitled to any additional compensation, damage, or loss as a result of such failure to undertake or complete the Picture.

21. **Contingencies.**

    (a)   Artist's services and the accrual of compensation hereunder, and the running of any periods herein provided for, shall be suspended without notice during all periods (i) that Artist does not render services hereunder because of illness, incapacity, default, or similar matters beyond Company's control; (ii) that production of the Picture is prevented or interrupted because of force majeure events (i.e., any labor dispute, fire, war, governmental action, or any other unexpected or disruptive event sufficient to excuse performance of this agreement as a matter of law), or the death, illness, or incapacity of the director or a principal member of the cast. All dates herein set forth or provided for shall be postponed for a period equivalent to the period of such event. If any matter referred to in (i), other than default, shall exist for five business days or more, or if any matter referred to in (ii) shall exist for eight weeks or more, or in the event of any refusal to perform or other default on the part of Artist, Company may terminate Artist's engagement hereunder. Notwithstanding anything herein contained, if any suspension under (ii) shall continue for two weeks or more, Artist may render services for others during the continuance of such suspension, subject to immediate recall on the termination of such suspension.

    (b)   Company may secure life, health, accident, cast, or other insurance covering Artist, or Artist and others, and Artist shall have no right, title, or interest in or to such insurance. Artist will submit to usual and customary medical examinations for Company's insurance purposes (including self-insurance) and will sign such applications or other documents as may be reasonably required in the premises. Artist may have Artist's own physician present at any such examination at Artist's own expense. Company has the right to terminate this Agreement in the event that Artist fails to pass such medical examination or does not provide the necessary documentation to allow for an insurance policy to be written.

22. **Assurances.** Each party shall execute all documents and certificates and perform all acts deemed appropriate by the Company or required by this Agreement in connection with this Agreement and the production of the Picture.

23. **Complete Agreement.** This Agreement constitutes the complete and exclusive statement of the agreement among the parties with respect to the matters discussed herein and it supersedes all prior written or oral statements among the parties, including any prior statement, warranty, or representation. Except as herein expressly provided, this agreement cancels and supersedes all prior negotiations and understandings relating to the Picture and contains all of the terms, conditions, representations, and warranties of the parties hereto in the premises. Nothing herein contained shall be construed so as to require the commission of any act contrary to law and wherever there is any conflict between any provision of this agreement and any present or future statute, law, ordinance, or regulation, the latter shall prevail, but in such event the provision of this agreement affected shall be curtailed and limited only to the extent necessary to bring it within legal requirements.

24. **Section Headings.** The section headings which appear throughout this Agreement are provided for convenience only and are not intended to define or limit the scope of this Agreement or the intent or subject matter of its provisions.

25. **Applicable Law.** Each party agrees that all disputes arising under or in connection with this Agreement and any transactions contemplated by this Agreement shall be governed by the internal law, and not the law of conflicts, of the State of _____.

26. **Notices.** Any notice or other writing to be served upon either party in connection with this Agreement shall be in writing and shall be deemed completed when delivered to the address listed above.

27. **Amendments.** Any amendments, modifications, or alterations to this Agreement must be in writing and signed by all of the parties hereto.

28. **Severability.** Each provision of this Agreement is severable from the other provisions. If, for any reason, any provision of this Agreement is declared invalid or contrary to existing law, the inoperability of that provision shall have no effect on the remaining provisions of the Agreement, and all remaining provisions shall continue in full force and effect.

29. **Counterparts.** This Agreement may be executed in counterparts, each of which shall be deemed an original and all of which shall, when taken together, constitute a single document.

IN WITNESS WHEREOF, the parties hereto have executed and delivered this agreement as of the date written below.

. . .

5. Actor Nudity Rider

When countersigned below, the following will constitute the terms and conditions of the nudity rider agreement ("Rider Agreement") between Productions LLC ("Company"), and the artist identified below ("Artist") in respect to the motion picture tentatively known as "The Picture" ("Picture").

The parties hereto acknowledge that the Picture has "nude scenes" that will require the Artist to render services in the nude. The Artist has read the screenplay for the Picture prior to receipt of this agreement and hereby consents to rendition of such services in the nude as may be required.

The Artist [shall/shall not] be in any scenes requiring below-the-belt frontal nudity.

Specifically, the nude scenes included in the Picture permit filming of [description of scenes, genitalia depicted, and contact such as simulated sex, rape, etc.]

Company shall not add additional actions (e.g., depiction of genitalia or simulated acts not listed above) without the express written consent of Artist, who shall be provided not less than 24 hours advance notice. Nothing shall prohibit the addition or alteration of scenes without additional consent for the nudity described above, provided all new scenes are fully disclosed in the preceding paragraph.

Producer hereby agrees that during any phase of production involving nudity, the set shall be closed to all persons having no business purpose in connection with the production. Producer further agrees that there shall be no still photography of nudity and all provisions of the Screen Actors Guild Basic Agreement relating to the filming of nudity shall apply.

Except as provided herein, all terms related to the parties shall remain those set forth in the Actor Employment Agreement.

IN WITNESS WHEREOF, the parties hereto have executed and delivered this agreement as of the date written below.

. . .

6. Talent and Appearance Release

This release is appropriate for extras and for individuals shown in background photographs.

For valuable consideration, receipt of which is hereby acknowledged, I hereby give Productions LLC, including its assignees or licensees, or anyone associated with the Picture (collectively "Company"), the absolute, irrevocable right and permission, forever and throughout the world, in connection with the motion picture tentatively entitled "The Picture" (the "Picture"), the following:

1. The perpetual and universal right to photograph and rephotograph me (still and moving) and to record and rerecord, double, and dub my voice and performances, by any methods or means, and to use and authorize others to use my name, voice, and likeness for and in connection with the Picture. Copyright for all such work shall vest exclusively in Company as a work made for hire of an audiovisual work. If such vesting of copyright is deemed invalid, then I hereby assign any copyright to Company.

2. I hereby approve the use of my name, voice, and image by Company in any manner related to the Picture and forever release and discharge Company from any and all claims, actions, and demands arising out of such use.

3. [This paragraph is the *Borat*-style long-form release, to be used when "any and all claims" in paragraph 2 is likely to be challenged.] I agree to waive any and all claims against the Company or against any of its assignees or licensees, or anyone associated with the Picture, that include assertions of (a) infringement of rights of publicity or misappropriation (such as any allegedly improper or unauthorized use of my name or likeness or image) (b) intrusion (such as any allegedly offensive behavior or questioning or any invasion of privacy), (c) false light (such as any allegedly false or misleading portrayal of Participant), (d) infliction of emotional distress (whether allegedly intentional or negligent), (e) defamation (such as allegedly false statements made on the Picture), or (f) intellectual property rights (such as copyright, trademark, unfair competition, trade secrets, patents, Lanham Act, or other state or federally protected interests).

4. For purposes hereof, the Picture shall include audiovisual works of any kind now known or hereafter created (including, without limitation, motion pictures, episodic productions, sequels, or prequels), soundtracks (including soundtrack albums), trailers, and documentary and/or "making of" pictures, advertising, and packaging for any or all such materials.

5. Company is under no obligation to produce the Picture hereunder. This Agreement shall inure to the benefit of Company's successors, assigns, licensees, grantees, and associated, affiliated, and subsidiary companies.

6. This Agreement shall constitute our full understanding unless amended to the contrary in writing and signed by both parties. I acknowledge and agree that in entering into this agreement I have not relied upon or been induced by any promise or representation (express or implied, oral or written) of Company or any person acting for Company, which is not contained in this Agreement. This Agreement shall be governed by and construed in accordance with the laws of the State of _____ applicable to contracts entered into and fully performed therein.

Date: _____ ACCEPTED AND AGREED

. . .

For Talent under 18 years of Age: I [printed name], represent I am the parent or guardian of [Minor's Name], the above-named Talent. For value received, I hereby consent to this Agreement in his or her behalf.

. . .

7. Location Release Form

I hereby give Productions LLC, its employees, agents, independent contractors, parents, subsidiaries, affiliates, licensees, successors, and assigns (collectively "Company") for good and valuable consideration, receipt of which is hereby acknowledged, permission to access, enter upon, and use the property identified below and the contents thereof and the appurtenances thereto (the "Property") for the purpose of photographing and recording images, audiovisual works, and sound recordings at this location (the "Material") in connection with a motion picture ("Picture") on or about the shooting date(s) listed below.

1. Company may place all necessary facilities and equipment on the Property and agrees to remove same after completion of work and leave the property in as good of condition as when received. Company will use reasonable care to prevent damage to said Property. Company shall provide me certificate of insurance naming the Property owner as additional insured.

2. I irrevocably grant to Company all rights of every kind in and to the Material including, without limitation, the right to exploit the Material throughout the world, in any and all languages, an unlimited number of times, in perpetuity in any and all media, now known or hereafter invented, in and in connection with the Picture, and for advertising and promotional purposes in connection therewith, and all rights, including copyright in the Material, shall be and remain vested in Company. Copyright for all such work shall vest exclusively in Company as a work made for hire of an audiovisual work. If such vesting of copyright is deemed invalid, then I hereby assign any copyright I may have acquired in the Material to Company.

3. I release and discharge Company from any and all claims, actions, and demands arising out of or in connection with the Material, including, without limitation, any and all claims of infringement of copyright, libel and slander, and invasion of privacy. Company shall indemnify the Property owner against any third-party claims of copyright infringement, libel and slander, and invasion of privacy regarding the Material or Picture.

4. For purposes hereof, the Picture shall include audiovisual works of any kind now known or hereafter created (including, without limitation, motion pictures, episodic productions, sequels, or prequels), soundtracks (including soundtrack albums), trailers, and documentary and/or "making of" pictures, advertising, and packaging for any or all such materials. Company is under no obligation to produce the Picture hereunder.

5. I represent that I own or control all rights to grant entry to this location and am authorized to negotiate this release and that I have read and fully understand the contents hereof.

The signature below shall provide the same permission whether permission was authorized before or after the actual filming of the Material.

Location Address/Description: _____

Shoot Dates: _____

Name: _____ Title: _____

Signature _____ Date: _____

. . .

8. Joint Author Agreement—Collaboration Agreement

This Joint Author Agreement is made between [Name, address] and [Name, address], sometimes referred to collectively as "Parties" and individually as "Party." In consideration of the execution of this Agreement, and the undertakings of the Parties as hereinafter set forth, it is agreed as follows.

1. **Copyright Contribution.** Each Party has contributed copyrightable content as well as ideas, themes, plots, live performances, and similar copyrightable and uncopyrightable material to the episodic series and live performance series presently entitled "[title]" (collectively the "Work") with the intention that their contributions be merged into inseparable or interdependent parts of a unitary whole. For purposes hereof, the Work includes both those episodes previously created and those that the Parties shall create on an ongoing basis as part of the episodic series.

2. **Joint Authors.** The Parties agree that the Work will be a joint work of authorship under US Copyright law. The Parties agree that the rights and obligations of each Party shall be determined by US Copyright Law except as provided in this Joint Author Agreement ("Agreement").

3. **Ongoing Collaboration.** Throughout the term of the Agreement, the Parties shall collaborate in the writing of the Work, and upon completion of each episode or copyrightable component thereof shall be the joint authors of the Work or separable portion thereof in equal measure.

4. **Shared Credit.** The Parties shall have shared author credit in all listings, ads, opening credits, end credits, or other locations where the author of the Work is listed or identified, and each Party shall use best efforts to ensure that shared credit is afforded to the other Party. In any registration of copyright in the Work or other distribution of the work for any purpose, each Party shall be listed as coauthor, and the Parties shall use all reasonable care to ensure that both Parties are identified as joint authors on all copies of the work and in all presentations of the work under the Parties' control.

5. **Withdrawal.** If, prior to the completion of the Work, either Party shall voluntarily withdraw from the collaboration, then the other Party shall have the right to complete the Work alone or in conjunction with another collaborator or collaborators, and in such event the percentage of ownership, as hereinbefore provided in paragraph 1, shall be revised by mutual agreement in writing.

6. **Mutual Consent Required.** Neither Party shall exploit the work in any manner without the written consent of the other Party, which consent,

however, shall not be unreasonably withheld. For purposes of this provision, exploitation includes, without limitation, any and all nonexclusive or exclusive licenses to distribute, publicly perform, adapt, sell, license, or otherwise voluntarily dispose of the Work.

7. **Loans, Recoupment, Revenue.** To produce the Work, including live tapings and audiovisual distribution of the work, the Parties may be required to provide funds for the purposes of exploiting the Work. All such payments provided by a Party to produce the Work or any aspect thereof shall be treated as loans by the Parties. The Parties shall keep careful records of all such loans as well as the costs associated with the creation and exploitation of the Work. The compensation earned from exploitation of the Work shall be used (1) to repay the loans on a pro rata basis and then (2) as payments to each Party on an equal basis.

8. **Equal Distribution of Sale Proceeds.** The Parties shall share on an equal basis the proceeds from the sale or any and all other disposition of the Work and the rights and licenses therein and with respect thereto, including but not limited to the following: a. Motion picture rights b. Sequel rights c. Remake rights d. Television film rights e. Television live rights f. Stage rights g. Radio rights h. Publication rights i. Interactive rights j. Merchandising rights.

9. **Future Authorship.** Should the Work be sold or otherwise disposed of and, as an incident thereto, the Parties be employed to revise the Work or adapt it into another medium, the total compensation provided for in such employment agreement shall be shared by them on an equal basis. If either Party shall be unavailable for the purposes of collaborating on such revision or adaptation, then the Party who is available shall be permitted to do such revision or adaptation and shall be entitled to the full amount of compensation in connection therewith, provided, however, the availability of either Party to participate in the revision should not be incorporated into the calculation of the purchase price for the Work.

10. **Representations, Warranties, and Covenants.** As relates to the contributions made by each Party, each Party hereby represents and warrants that he/she is the author of his/her contribution to the Work and owner of all rights granted herein, and that none of the contributions made to the work violate the copyright or other legal rights of any third party. Each Party hereby represents and warrants that he/she has the full legal right, power, and authority to enter into this agreement. Each Party hereby represents, warrants, covenants, and agrees that these provisions shall remain true and correct for him/her throughout the term of this Agreement.

11. **Assignment.** The rights granted herein shall inure to the benefit of the Parties, its licensees, successors, and assigns. In the event the Parties enter into a partnership, corporation, LLC, or other entity and transfer their rights under this agreement to that entity, the terms of this Agreement shall govern that new agreement except to the extent the parties agree to amend these terms in writing signed by both Parties.

12. **No General Partnership.** Nothing in this agreement shall constitute the formation of a general partnership, and neither Party shall have the right to contract or bind the other Party, except as specified herein. Until such time as a corporation or LLC has been formed for the exploitation of the Work, [Name] shall have authority to exploit the Work as a sole proprietor, and [Name] shall assist as an independent contractor. Each Party shall undertake to represent that no general partnership has been formed and to disclaim any authority not specifically provided in this Agreement.

13. **No Obligation.** Neither Party is under any obligation to invest funds in the Work or to participate in the creation of future material to the Work. In the event that either Party wishes to discontinue participation, he/she shall give written notice to the other party. All copyright and interest in the Work created prior to the notice shall remain a joint work. Following the notice by either Party to terminate the joint authorship, neither Party shall have the right to create additional content that exploits the copyright or other intellectual property interests of the Work, except upon the mutual consent of the Parties, which shall not be withheld unreasonably. Either Party may elect to seek arbitration under this Agreement should the consent be unreasonably withheld.

14. **ARBITRATION.** ANY AND ALL DISPUTES HEREUNDER SHALL BE RESOLVED BY ARBITRATION. ANY PARTY HERETO ELECTING TO COMMENCE AN ACTION SHALL GIVE WRITTEN NOTICE TO THE OTHER PARTY HERETO. THEREUPON, IF ARBITRATION IS SELECTED BY THE PARTY COMMENCING THE ACTION, THE CLAIM ("ARBITRATION MATTER") SHALL BE SETTLED BY ARBITRATION IN ACCORDANCE WITH THE THEN RULES OF THE AMERICAN ARBITRATION ASSOCIATION ("AAA"). The arbitrator or the referee shall diligently pursue determination of any Arbitration under consideration and shall render a decision within one hundred twenty (120) days after the arbitrator or referee is selected. The arbitrator may issue awards of compensatory damages, but shall have no authority to award indirect, incidental, consequential, special, exemplary, or punitive damages. The arbitrator shall provide the parties with a

written description of the reasons for any award or decision rendered. The determination of the arbitrator on all matters referred to it hereunder shall be final and binding on the parties hereto. The award of such arbitrator may be confirmed or enforced in any court of competent jurisdiction. The referee, arbitrator, or its designee shall have full access to such records and physical facilities of the parties hereto as may be required. Each party shall pay for its own costs of arbitration.

15. **Additional Provisions.**

15.1 **Further Assurances.** The parties hereto shall execute and deliver any and all additional documents and instruments and shall do any and all acts reasonably necessary to give effect to the provisions of this Agreement and the intent of the parties.

15.2 **No Waiver, Etc.** None of the terms of this Agreement can be waived or modified except by an express agreement in writing signed by all parties. There are no representations, promises, warranties, covenants, or undertakings other than those contained in this Agreement, which represents the entire understanding of the parties. The failure of either party hereto to enforce, or the delay by either party in enforcing, any of its rights under this Agreement shall not be deemed a continuing waiver or a modification thereof, and either party may, within the time provided by applicable law, commence appropriate legal proceedings to enforce any or all of such rights. No person, firm, group, or corporation other than Licensee or Licensor shall be deemed to have acquired any rights by reason of anything contained in this Agreement.

15.3 **Entire Agreement, Amendments.** This Agreement, and the Exhibits attached as a part hereof and incorporated by reference, constitute the entire agreement between the parties hereto with respect to the subject matter hereof and supersede all prior or contemporaneous written or oral agreements between them or any of their affiliates with respect to the subject matter hereof. No change, modification, alteration, amendment, agreement to discharge in whole or in part, abandonment, or waiver of any of the terms and conditions of this Agreement shall be binding upon any party, unless same shall be made by written instrument signed and executed by the proper officers of each party, with the same formality as the execution of this Agreement.

15.4 **Notices.** Any notice or other communication given hereunder shall be in writing sent certified or registered mail, postage-paid return receipt requested, or given in hand sent by a recognized national courier service next-day delivery, to each respective party at its home office, or to such other addresses either party shall have theretofore designated by notice hereunder. Any such notice shall be deemed given one day after its sending, at the address listed on the Statement of Work.

15.5 **Counterparts.** This Agreement may be executed in one or more counterparts, all of which shall be considered one and the same agreement and shall become effective when one or more counterparts have been signed by each party and delivered to the others.

15.6 **Governing Law.** This Agreement shall be governed and construed in accordance with the laws of the State of California applicable to agreements made and to be performed entirely within such State.

15.7 **Severability.** If any provision of this Agreement shall be held or deemed to be or shall, in fact, be inoperative or unenforceable as applied in any particular case because it conflicts with any other provision or provisions hereof or any constitution or statute or rule of public policy, or for any other reason, such circumstances shall not have the effect of rendering the provision in question inoperative or unenforceable in any other case or circumstances, or of rendering any other provision or provisions herein contained invalid, inoperative, or unenforceable to any extent whatever. The invalidity of any one or more phrases, sentences, clauses, sections, or subsections of this Agreement shall not affect the remaining portions of this Agreement.

IN WITNESS WHEREOF, the parties hereto have duly executed this Agreement as of the day and year first written below.

. . .

WGA Writing Credit Definitions

Excerpted from Writers Guild of America West, Screen Credits Manual, *WGA official website, accessed January 27, 2021, https://www.wga.org /contracts/credits/manuals/screen-credits-manual.*

Introduction

A writer's credits play an enormous role in determining our position in the motion picture and television industry. Our professional status depends on the quality and number of screenplays, teleplays, or stories that bear our name. Writing credit is given for authorship of the work the audience sees on screen, including plot, characters, dialogue, scenes and all other elements that comprise our work.

. . .

II. Credit Determination Procedure

A. Notice of Tentative Writing Credits

Theatrical Schedule A of our MBA provides that the Company will concurrently send to the Guild and to each participating writer, or to the current agent of a participating writer if that participant so elects, a Notice of Tentative Writing Credits ("Notice"). The Company also is required to provide each participating writer (or designated agent) a copy of the final shooting script (or if such script is not available, the latest revised script).

. . .

C. Agreement Among Writers

When more than one writer has participated in the writing of a motion picture, then all participating writers have the right to agree unanimously among themselves as to which of them shall receive writing credits on the screen and in what form, provided that the form agreed upon is in accordance with the terms of Theatrical Schedule A of the MBA, and provided the agreement is reached in advance of arbitration. The MBA also provides that the form of such credit shall not be suggested or directed by the Company.

. . .

III. Guild Policy on Credits

A. Rules for Determining Credit

Credit is determined by the material contributed to the final shooing script (as represented on the screen), rather than by the Arbitration Committee's personal preference of one script over another.

1. "Written by"

"Written by" is used when the writer(s) is entitled to both the "Story by" credit and the "Screenplay by" credit.

This credit shall not be granted where there is source material of a story nature. However, biographical, newspaper, and other factual sources may not necessarily deprive the writer of such credit.

"Written by" credit generally will not be shared by more than two writers. In unusual cases, and solely as the result of arbitration, the names of three writers or the names of writers constituting three writing teams may be used. The limitation on the number of writers applies to all feature length photoplays except episodic pictures and revues.

2. "Story by"

The term "story" means all writing covered by the provisions of the MBA representing a contribution "distinct from screenplay and consisting of basic narrative, idea, theme or outline indicating character development and action."

"Distinct from screenplay" means that the contributions considered for story should not be applied to screenplay credit, nor should contributions considered for screenplay credit be applied to story credit.

Even though the Arbitration Committee at times receives only material in screenplay form, a screenplay document often encompasses story contributions distinct from screenplay contributions. It is up to the Arbitration Committee to examine a screenplay carefully with this in mind. A story may be written in story form or may be contained within other literary material, such as a treatment or a screenplay, for purposes of receiving "Story by" credit.

It is appropriate to award a "Story by" credit when: 1) the story was written under employment under Guild jurisdiction; 2) the story was purchased by a signatory company from a professional writer, as defined in the MBA; or 3) when the screenplay is based upon a sequel story written under the Guild's jurisdiction. If the story is based upon source material of a story nature, see "Screen Story" below.

Story credit may not be shared by more than two writers.

Irreducible Shared Story Minimum: In the case of an original screenplay, the first writer shall be entitled to no less than a shared story credit.

3. "Screen Story by"

If the writer is furnished source material of a story nature but takes from it only a springboard, a characterization, an incident, or some equally limited contribution, creating a substantially new and different story from the source material, the writer may receive "Screen Story by" credit, but only as the result of arbitration. In such cases, the author of the source material may be given credit that specifies the form in which such material was acquired—for instance, "From a Play by," "From a Novel by," "From a *Saturday Evening Post* Story by," "From a Series of Articles by," "Based on a Story by," etc. There is no percentage requirement to receive this credit. "Screen Story" credit may not be shared by more than two writers.

4. "Screenplay by"

A screenplay consists of individual scenes and full dialogue, together with such prior treatment, basic adaptation, continuity, scenario, and dialogue as shall be used in, and represent substantial contributions to the final script.

a. Guidelines for the Arbiters in Determining Screenplay Credit

A "Screenplay by" credit is appropriate when there is source material of a story nature (with or without a "Screen Story" credit) or when the writer(s) entitled to "Story by" credit is different from the writer(s) entitled to "Screenplay by" credit.

Screen credit for screenplay will not be shared by more than two writers, except that in unusual cases, and solely as the result of arbitration, the names of three writers or the names of writers constituting three writing teams may be used. The limitation on the number of writers applies to all feature length photoplays except episodic pictures and revues.

i. Original and Non-Original Screenplays

For purposes of determining "Screenplay by" credit, two categories of screenplays are recognized:

1) Original screenplays. In the context of credit determination, "original" does not refer to the unique creative quality of a screenplay, but rather to the absence of assigned source material. Original screenplays are not based on source material. In addition, for a screenplay to be considered original, the screenplay must have been written by the first writer without any intervening literary material by another writer pertaining to the project.

. . .

The first writer on an original screenplay is entitled to no less than shared "Story by" credit.

2) Non-original screenplays. In the context of credit determination, "non-original" does not refer to the unique creative quality of a screenplay, but rather to the presence of assigned source material. All other screenplays not covered in (1) above shall also be considered non-original for the purpose of credit determination.

Sequels and remakes are considered to be non-original screenplays: The classification of a screenplay as original or non-original for credit determination purposes shall be made based solely on the final shooting script for the motion picture.

ii. Percentage Requirements

1) Original screenplay: The first writer on an original screenplay shall be entitled to screenplay credit if such writer's work represents a contribution of more than 33% to the final shooting script. Any subsequent writer or writing team must contribute 50% to the final shooting script. A subsequent writer who is a production executive, or a subsequent writing team that includes a production executive, must contribute more than 50% to the final shooting script.

2) Non-original screenplay: Any writer, including a production executive, whose work represents a contribution of more than 33% to the final shooting script shall be entitled to screenplay credit.

. . .

5. "Adaptation by"

In the interest of avoiding a multiplicity of credits, the Guild is opposed to the general use of the "Adaptation by" credit. However, the Guild recognizes that there are certain unusual cases where credit is due a writer who shapes the direction of screenplay construction without qualifying for "Screenplay by" credit. In those special cases, and only as a result of arbitration, the "Adaptation by" credit may be used.

6. "Narration Written by"

"Narration Written by" credit is appropriate where the major writing contribution to a motion picture is in the form of narration. The term "narration" means material (typically off-camera) to explain or relate sequence or action (excluding promos or trailers).

7. "Based on Characters Created by"

"Based on Characters Created by" is a writing credit given to the writer(s) entitled to separated rights in a theatrical or television motion picture on each theatrical sequel to such theatrical or television motion picture.

Where there **are** no separated rights, "Based on Characters Created by" may be accorded to the author of source material upon which a sequel is based.

8. No Other Credits Approved

Any form of credit not expressly described in this Manual shall be used only upon receipt of a waiver from the Guild. Fewer names and fewer types of credit enhance the value of all credits and the dignity of all writers.

B. Production Executives

The term "production executives" may be misleading to some. As used in the MBA, "production executives" are not specifically studio employees, as the term is often understood, but rather individuals who receive credit either as a producer in any capacity, or as the director. Writers should be aware that receiving any form of producing or directing credit qualifies them as a production executive for the purpose of arbitration. . . .

1. Automatic Arbitration Provisions

Theatrical Schedule A of the MBA provides:

"Unless the story and/or screenplay writing is done entirely without any other writer, no designation of tentative story or screenplay credit to a production executive shall become final or effective unless approved by a credit arbitration as herein provided, in accordance with the Guild rules for determination of such credit."

2. Notice Requirements

If a production executive intends to claim credit as a team on any literary material with a writer(s) who is not a production executive, the production executive must, at the time when such team writing begins, have signified such claim in writing to the Guild and to the writer(s) with whom the production executive claims to have worked as a team. Failure to comply with the above will preclude such production executive from claiming co-authorship of the literary material in question, and such literary material shall be attributed to the other writer.

. . .

D. Withdrawal from Credit

A participating writer may not withdraw from credit on a motion picture on which the writer is the only participating writer.

Prior to the time a credit question has been submitted to arbitration, a writer may withdraw from screenwriting credit for personal cause, such as violation of the writer's principles or mutilation of material the writer has written. If the other writer-contributors do not agree, the question shall be referred to arbitration. The Arbitration Committee in such cases shall base its determination on whether there is such personal cause. After screen credits have been determined by arbitration, a writer may not withdraw from writing credit.

Withdrawal from writing credit will result in loss of any and all rights accruing from receipt of writing credit. Use of a pseudonym rather than withdrawing from credit will not result in such a forfeiture.

Resource Listings

Unions and Associations

Breakdown Services Ltd.
2140 Cotner Avenue
Los Angeles, CA 90025
Los Angeles: (310) 385-6920
New York: (310) 385-6920
Toronto: 416-923-1292
Vancouver: (604) 943-8850
http://www.breakdownservices.com

Directors Guild of America
7920 Sunset Boulevard
Los Angeles, CA 90046
(800) 421-4173
(310) 289-2000
http://www.dga.org

**International Alliance of
Theatrical Stage Employees
(IATSE)**
207 West 25th Street, 4th Floor
New York, NY 10001
(212) 730-1770
http://www.iatse-intl.org

Producers Guild of America
11150 West Olympic Boulevard,
Suite 980
Los Angeles, CA, 90064
(310) 358-9020
http://www.producersguild.org
bryce@producersguild.org

**Screen Actors Guild–American
Federation of Television and
Radio Artists**
5757 Wilshire Boulevard, 7th Floor
Los Angeles, CA 90036
(855) SAG-AFTRA / (855) 724-2387
https://www.sagaftra.org
info@sagaftra.org

Writers Guild of America West
7000 West Third Street
Los Angeles, CA 90048
(800) 548-4532
(323) 951-4000
http://www.wga.org

Script Clearance Services

Act One Script Clearance
230 N. Maryland Avenue, Suite 201
Glendale, CA 91206
(818) 240-2416
Fax: (818) 240-2418
http://www.actonescript.com
info@actonescript.com

Clearance Lab
1875 Century Park East, Suite 700
Los Angeles, CA 90067
(800) 713-8504
https://theclearancelab.com
info@theclearancelab.com

IndieClear Script Clearance
1150 Highland Avenue
Glendale, CA 91202
(818) 956-6049
Fax: (818) 476-5801
http://www.indieclear.com
scriptclearance@indieclear.com

Music Clearance Resources

BZ/Rights & Permissions
145 West 86th Street
New York, NY 10024
(212) 924-3000
Fax: (212) 924-2525
http://www.bzrights.com
info@bzrights.com

Greenlight
Branded Entertainment Network
15250 Ventura Boulevard, Suite 300
Sherman Oaks, CA 91403
(310) 342-1500
http://www.greenlightrights.com
greenlight@bengroup.com

The Harry Fox Agency
601 W. 26th Street
New York, NY 10001
(202) 742-4375
Fax: (202) 742-4377
(212) 834-0100
Fax: (646) 487-6779
www.harryfox.com

**National Music Publishers'
Association (NMPA)**
1900 N Street NW, Suite 500
Washington DC, 20036
(202) 393-6672
http://www.nmpa.org

Insurance Companies

Abacus Insurance Brokers
2512 Wilshire Boulevard
Santa Monica, CA, 90403
(424) 214-3700
https://www.abacus.net
info@abacus.net

Arthur J. Gallagher & Company
2850 Golf Road
Rolling Meadows, IL 60008
(630) 773-3800
https://www.ajg.com

**Chubb Group of Insurance
Companies**
150 Allen Road, Suite 203
Basking Ridge, NJ 07920
(908) 903-2000
Fax: (908) 903-2008

https://www.chubb.com/us-en
/business-insurance/film-producers
.aspx

Hiscox Insurance Company Inc.
520 Madison Avenue, 32nd Floor
New York, NY 10022
(866) 283 7545
https://www.hiscox.com/brokers
/media-liability

**Intact Insurance Specialty
Solutions**
605 Highway 169 North, Suite 800
Plymouth, MN 55441
(800) 662-0156
https://www.intactspecialty.com/en
/index.page?

Payroll Services

Cast & Crew
2300 Empire Avenue, 5th Floor
Burbank, CA 91504
(818) 848.6022
Fax: (818) 848.9556
https://www.castandcrew.com

Entertainment Partners Inc.
2950 North Hollywood Way
Burbank, CA 91505
(818) 955-6000
https://www.ep.com

Entertainment Payroll Companies
ABS Payroll & Production
Accounting
7530 North Glenoaks Boulevard,
Suite 100
Burbank, CA 91504

(818) 848-9200
https://abspayroll.com
Info@abspayroll.net

Media Services
500 S. Sepulveda Boulevard, 4th
Floor
Los Angeles, CA 90049
(310) 440-9600
https://www.mediaservices.com
clientservices@mediaservices.com

Topsheet
2416 West Victory Boulevard, Suite
223
Burbank, CA 91506
(805) 267-9185
https://www.topsheet.io

Financial Services

Comerica Entertainment Group
2000 Avenue of the Stars, Suite 110
Los Angeles, CA 90067
(310) 557-4000
Fax: (310) 557-4010
https://www.comerica.com/business
/industry-solutions/specialized
-industries/entertainment.html

**Independent Film & Television
Alliance**
10850 Wilshire Blvd., 9th Floor
Los Angeles, CA 90024
(310) 446-1000
Fax: (310) 446-1600
http://www.ifta-online.org
info@ifta-online.org

Completion Bond

Barrow Group
110 E. Crogan Street
Lawrenceville, GA 30046
770-338-7392
Fax: (770) 338-5440
https://www.barrowgroup.com

Tokio Marine, HCC Insurance Holdings
13403 Northwest Freeway
Houston, TX 77040
(713) 462-1000
http://www.tmhcc.com/en-us

Sales Agents

Cinetic Media
555 West 25th Street, 4th Floor
New York, NY 10001
(212) 204-7979
Fax: (212) 627-9498
http://www.cineticmedia.com

Creative Artists Agency
2000 Avenue of the Stars
Los Angeles, CA 90067
(424) 288-2000
Fax: (424) 288-2900
https://www.caa.com

The Film Sales Company
515 E 118th Street
New York, NY 10035
(212) 481-5020
Fax: (212) 481-5021
http://www.filmsalescorp.com

Submarine Entertainment
197 Grand Street
New York, NY 10013
(212) 625-1410
http://www.submarine.com

WME (formerly William Morris Agency)
9560 Wilshire Blvd.
Beverly Hills, CA 90210
310-285-9000
https://www.wmeagency.com

Film Commissions

California Film Commission
7080 Hollywood Boulevard, Suite 900
Hollywood, CA 90028
(800) 858-4749
(323) 860-2960
Fax: (323) 860-2972
http://www.film.ca.gov
filmca@film.ca.gov

FilmLA
6255 Sunset Boulevard, 12th Floor
Los Angeles, CA 90028
(213) 977-8600
Fax (main): (213) 977-8610
Fax (permits): (213) 977-8601
https://www.filmla.com
info@filmla.com

Mayor's Office of Film, Theatre & Broadcasting
1697 Broadway, 6th Floor
New York, NY 10019
(212) 489-6710
Fax: (212) 307-6237
https://www1.nyc.gov/site/mome/index.page

Top Film Festivals

South by Southwest Film Festival
PO Box 685289
Austin, TX 78768
(512) 467-7979
https://www.sxsw.com/festivals/film

Sundance Film Festival
5900 Wilshire Boulevard, Suite 800
Los Angeles, CA 90036
(310) 360-1981
Fax: (310) 360-1969
https://www.sundance.org

Tribeca Film Festival
(212) 941-2400
http://www.tribecafilm.com
festival@tribecafilm.com

Theater and Film Bookstores

Concord Theatricals
(Owner of Samuel French and Tams-Witmark catalogs)
235 Park Avenue South, 5th Floor
New York, NY 10003
(866) 979-0447
https://www.concordtheatricals.com

Larry Edmunds Bookshop
6644 Hollywood Boulevard
Los Angeles, CA 90028
(323) 463-3273
http://www.larryedmunds.com
info@larryedmunds.com

Motion Picture Association of America (MPAA)
15301 Ventura Boulevard, Bldg. E
Sherman Oaks, CA 91403
(818) 995-6600
Fax: (818) 285-4403
http://www.mpaa.org

Motion Picture Distributors: The Majors

Paramount Pictures Corporation
5555 Melrose Avenue
Los Angeles, CA 90038
(323) 956-5000
http://www.paramount.com

Sony Pictures Entertainment
10202 West Washington Boulevard
Culver City, CA 90232
(310) 244-6926
http://www.sonypictures.com

Universal Studios
100 Universal City Plaza, Suite 3200
Universal City, CA 91608
http://www.universalpictures.com

Walt Disney Company
500 South Buena Vista Street
Burbank, CA 91521
(818) 560-1000
https://www.disney.com

Warner Bros.
4000 Warner Boulevard
Burbank, CA 91522
(818) 954-6564
https://www.warnerbros.com

Streamers

Amazon
PO Box 81226
Seattle, WA 98108-1226
(888) 280-3321
https://www.amazon.com

Film Movement
237 West 35th Street, Suite 604
New York, NY 10001
(212) 941-7744
https://www.filmmovement.com

IndiePix
31 East 32nd Street, Room 1201
New York, NY 10016-5509
(212) 684-2333
http://www.indiepixfilms.com

MUBI
668 High Street
Palo Alto, CA 94301
(650) 289-0283
https://mubi.com

Netflix
100 Winchester Circle
Los Gatos, CA 95032
(866) 579-7172
http://www.netflix.com

Significant Independent Producers

HBO Independent Films
230 7th Avenue
New York, NY 10011
(212) 876-8000

IFC Films
11 Penn Plaza, 18th Floor
New York, NY 10001
http://www.ifcfilms.com

Lions Gate Entertainment
2700 Colorado Avenue, Suite 200
Santa Monica, CA 90404
(310) 449-9200
https://www.lionsgate.com

Magnolia Pictures
49 West 27th Street, 7th Floor
New York, NY 10001
(212) 924-6701
Fax: (212) 924-6742
https://www.magpictures.com
mail@magnoliapictures.com

Media Asia Entertainment Group
24/F Causeway Bay Plaza II
463–483 Lockhart Road
Causeway Bay, Hong Kong
+852 2314 4288
Fax: +852 2314 4248
http://www.mediaasia.com
wwdist@mediaasia.com

Miramax
1901 Avenue of the Stars, Suite 2000
Los Angeles, CA 90067
(310) 409-4321
https://www.miramax.com

Open Road Films
3003 West Olive Avenue
Burbank, CA 91505
(310) 248-3300
https://www.openroad.la

Palisades Tartan
156 West 56th Street
New York, NY 10019
(212) 265-2323
www.palisadestartan.com
support@palisadestartan.com

Palm Pictures
1460 Broadway
New York, NY 10036
(646) 790-1211
http://www.palmpictures.com

Pathé International
6 Ramillies Street
London W1F 7TY United Kingdom
+44 207 462 4429
Fax: +44 207 631 3568
https://pathe.com/en

RLJ Entertainment
8515 Georgia Avenue, Suite 650
Silver Spring, MD
(301) 608-2115
https://www.rljentertainment.com

Samuel Goldwyn Films
8675 Washington Boulevard, Suite
203
Culver City, CA 90232
(310) 860-3100
Fax: (310) 872-5077
http://www.samuelgoldwynfilms.com

Showtime Networks
1633 Broadway
New York, NY 10019
(212) 708-1600
https://www.sho.com

StudioCanal
1 Place du Spectacle
Espace Eiffel
Issy Les Moulineaux 92130
France
+33 1 7135 3535
https://www.studiocanal.com

STXfilms
3900 West Alameda Avenue, 32nd
Floor
Burbank, CA 91505
(818) 524-7000
https://www.erosstx.com

**Village Roadshow Entertainment
Group**
10100 Santa Monica Boulevard,
Suite 200
Los Angeles, CA 90067
(310) 299-8605
https://vreg.com

Wild Bunch
99 rue de Dunkerque
75009 Paris, France
+33 1 5301 5030
Fax: +33 1 5301 5049
London Office:
Bluelight
25 Powis Terrace
London W11 1JH, United Kingdom
+44 (0)20 7792 9791, ext. 1
Fax: +44 (0)20 7792 9871
http://www.wildbunch.biz

Video

Redbox
1 Tower Lane, Suite 900
Oakbrook Terrace, IL 60181
(866) 733-2693
https://www.redbox.com

Selected Bibliography

Legal Reference Books

Appleton, Dina, and Daniel Yankelevits. *Hollywood Dealmaking: Negotiating Talent Agreements for Film, TV, and Digital Media.* 3rd ed. New York: Allworth Press, 2018.

Baumgarten, Paul A., Donald C. Farber, and Mark Fleischer. *Producing, Financing and Distributing Film: A Comprehensive Legal and Business Guide.* 2nd ed. Pompton Plains, NJ: Limelight, 1992.

Blumenthal, Howard J., and Oliver R. Goodenough. *This Business of Television.* 4th ed. New York: Billboard Books, 2006.

Brabec, Jeff, and Todd Brabec. *Music Money and Success: The Insider's Guide to Making Money in the Music Business.* 8th ed. New York: Schirmer Trade Books, 2018.

Farber, Donald C.. *From Option to Opening: A Guide to Producing Plays Off-Broadway.* New York: Limelight, 1989.

———. *Producing Theatre: A Comprehensive Legal and Business Guide.* 3rd ed. Pompton Plains, NJ: Limelight, 2006.

Farber, Donald C., and Peter A. Cross. *Entertainment Industry Contracts: Negotiating and Drafting Guide.* Newark, NJ: Matthew Bender, 1986.

Garon, Jon M. *Entertainment Law and Practice.* 3rd ed. Durham, NC: Carolina Academic Press, 2020.

————. *The Entrepreneur's Intellectual Property & Business Handbook.* 2nd ed. Fort Lauderdale, FL: Manegiare Publications, 2018.

————. *Pop Culture Business Handbook for Cons and Festivals.* Fort Lauderdale, FL: Manegiare Publications, 2017.

Grippo, Charles. *The Stage Producer's Business and Legal Guide.* New York: Allworth Press, 2002.

Halloran, Mark. *The Musician's Business and Legal Guide.* 5th ed. New York: Routledge, 2017.

Kohn, Al, and Bob Kohn, *Kohn on Music Licensing.* 5th ed. Alphen aan den Rijn, The Netherlands: Wolters Kluwer, 2018.

Lastowka, Greg. *Virtual Justice: The New Laws of Online Worlds.* New Haven, CT: Yale University Press, 2010.

Litwak, Mark. *Contracts for the Film & Television Industry.* 3rd ed. Beverly Hills, CA: Silman-James Press, 2012.

————. *Dealmaking in the Film & Television Industry.* 4th ed. West Hollywood, CA: Silman-James Press, 2016.

Moore, Schuyler M. *The Biz: The Basic Business, Legal and Financial Aspects of the Film Industry in a Digital World.* 5th ed. West Hollywood, CA: Silman-James Press, 2018.

Passman, Donald S. *All You Need to Know About the Music Business.* 10th ed. New York: Simon & Schuster, 2019.

Nonlegal Reference Books

Ascher, Steven, and Edward Pincus. *The Filmmaker's Handbook.* New York: Plume Books, 2013.

Bernard, Sheila Curran. *Documentary Storytelling: Creative Nonfiction on Screen.* 4th ed. New York: Focal Press, 2016.

Cones, John W. *Dictionary of Film Finance and Distribution: A Guide for Independent Filmmakers.* Baltimore: Algora Publishing, 2013.

Donaldson, Michael C., and Lisa A. Callif. *Clearance & Copyright.* 4th ed. West Hollywood, CA: Silman-James Press, 2014.

Erickson, Gunnar, Harris Tulchin, and Mark Halloran. *The Independent Film Producer's Survival Guide: A Business and Legal Sourcebook.* 3rd ed. New York: Schirmer Trade Books, 2011.

Goodell, Gregory. *Independent Feature Film Production.* Rev. ed. New York: St. Martin's Press, 1998.

Herstand, Ari. *How to Make It in the New Music Business: Practical Tips on Building a Loyal Following and Making a Living as a Musician.* 2nd ed. New York: Liveright Publishing, 2019.

Maier, Robert G. *Location Scouting and Management Handbook: Television, Film, Still Photography.* New York: Focal Press, 1994.

Malone, Alicia. *Backwards and in Heels: The Past, Present and Future of Women Working in Film.* Coral Gables, FL: Mango Publishing Group, 2017.

Maschwitz, Stu. *The DV Rebel's Guide: An All-Digital Approach to Making Killer Action Movies on the Cheap.* Berkeley, CA: Peachpit Press, 2007.

Parks, Stacey. *The Insider's Guide to Independent Film Distribution.* 2nd ed. New York: Routledge, 2017.

Rabiger, Michael, and Courtney Hermann. *Directing the Documentary.* 7th ed. New York: Routledge, 2020.

Rodriguez, Robert. *Rebel Without a Crew: Or How a 23-Year-Old Filmmaker with $7,000 Became a Hollywood Player.* New York: Plume Books, 1996.

Rosen, David, and Peter Hamilton. *Off Hollywood: The Making and Marketing of American Specialty Films.* New York: Grove Press, 1990.

Sales, John. *Thinking in Pictures: The Making of the Movie* Matewan. Reprint ed. Cambridge, MA: Da Capo Press, 2003.

Schenk, Sonja, and Ben Long. *The Digital Filmmaking Handbook.* 6th rev. ed. Los Angeles: Foreing Films Publishing, 2017.

Stockman, Steve. *How to Shoot Video That Doesn't Suck: Advice to Make Any Amateur Look Like a Pro.* New York: Workman Publishing, 2011.

Trottier, David. *The Screenwriter's Bible: A Complete Guide to Writing, Formatting, and Selling Your Script.* 7th ed. West Hollywood, CA: Silman-James Press, 2019.

Vogel, Harold L. *Entertainment Industry Economics: A Guide for Financial Analysis.* 10th ed. Cambridge, UK: Cambridge University Press, 2020.

Acknowledgments

In the acknowledgments for this third edition of *The Independent Filmmaker's Law and Business Guide*, I add to the already long list of friends and professionals who assisted me with the book's production. My publications would not be possible without my wife and partner, Stacy Blumberg Garon, who suffers though every edition and every edit of my work as both sounding board and copy editor.

Since writing the earlier editions, I had the pleasure to serve as the chairperson of the New Hampshire Film Commission and to represent some tremendously talented independent filmmakers. For many years, that office was under the direction of the New Hampshire commissioner of cultural resources, Van McLeod, and his passing has left a great loss in the creative community.

Every project teaches me a great deal, but particular recognition goes to the creators behind two of those projects: Buzz McLaughlin and Aaron Wiederspahn for *The Sensation of Sight*, and Derrick Comedy, the brilliant collaboration behind *Mystery Team*. In both these projects and in many others, I have been fortunate to work with an excellent legal team from the law firm of Gallagher, Callahan & Gartrell, including Denis Maloney, Esq., and Dodd Griffith, Esq., sophisticated securities and tax attorneys who have had the fortune—good and bad—to learn independent filmmaking as our needs have grown.

As I explained in the acknowledgments to the first edition, the two people whom I most wish to recognize for the completion of this book were unaware that I had written it, yet they were central to both the need for the book and many of its underlying themes. As a young attorney in Southern California, I had the opportunity to work with two separate clients, Jonny Solomon and Peter Henry Schroeder, on a number of projects. Jonny is a brilliant comic and talented producer. Peter Henry is a gifted writer and electrifying director. Neither is famous, but both are extremely talented and resourceful. Through working with Jonny, Peter Henry, and many other clients early in my legal practice, the most central theme of this book was developed. That theme—*you cannot find opportunities; you must create them*—is central to many of the guiding principles for independent film-makers. The experience I had working on independent film projects with these two individuals was the primary impetus for writing this book and for teaching hundreds of lawyers the art of trying to serve creative, driven individuals.

There are also a great many people I need to acknowledge for the development and completion of this book. I wish to thank many colleagues at Nova Southeastern University, Northern Kentucky University, Hamline University School of Law and Franklin Pierce Law Center. Colleagues Susan Stephan, Dennis Honabach, Debra Moss Vollweiler, and Bob Jarvis are some of the more recent names, in addition to help in the previous editions from Carol Swanson, Anne Johnson, and Barb Gritzmacher. Many of my colleagues at Franklin Pierce, including Susan Richey, Esq.; Sophie Sparrow, Esq.; Mary Sheffer, Esq.; Bill Hennessey, Esq.; and Donna Jakusik, provided helpful advice and ongoing encouragement. Many other friends and colleagues also shared their experience and provided helpful suggestions. Dan Satorius, Esq., motion picture expert at Lommen, Abdo, Cole, King & Stageberg, P.A.; Jeremy Williams, Esq., deputy general counsel for Warner Bros.; Greg Hartmann, Esq.; Wendy Baldinger and Doug Baldinger; Shimona Pratap Singh; Deepak Nambiar; and Lena Abdin each contributed material that helped shape the text and encouraged my completion of it.

I also want to recognize the time and effort of my publishers at Chicago Review Press, including Jerome Pohlen, who gave this book a home, and the editorial assistance of Devon Freeny and Joseph Webb, who helped make the manuscript more accurate and readable.

In the first edition of the book, I acknowledged my sons Avery and Noah and their brother, Alec "Sasha" (z"l), who seldom complained at the time for those nights I rushed through a goodnight song and who knew when to entice me away from the computer and back to the more important things. Their enthusiasm for art and science continues to provide me the motivation I need when my own focus blurs, and to stay connected to the next generation of artists and art forms.

Notes

2. The Film Company

1 "Exempt Purposes—Internal Revenue Code Section 501(c)(3)," IRS official website, accessed January 27, 2021, https://www.irs.gov/charities-non-profits /charitable-organizations/exempt-purposes-internal-revenue-code-section-501c3.
2 26 U.S.C. § 6115 (2021); see "Substantiating Charitable Contributions," IRS official website, accessed April 16, 2021, https://www.irs.gov/charities-non-profits /substantiating-charitable-contributions.
3 "Tax-Exempt Status for Your Organization," IRS official website, February 2021, https://www.irs.gov/publications/p557.

4. Duties of the Film Company

1 29 C.F.R. § 541.302.

5. The Property of the Film Company: The Film Concept

1 Jon M. Garon, *The Pop Culture Business Handbook for Cons and Festivals* (Fort Lauderdale, FL: Manegiare Publications, 2017).
2 17 U.S.C. §§ 101, 106 (2006). In the case of sound recordings, copyright holders also have the exclusive right to perform the work publicly by means of a digital audio transmission.
3 17 U.S.C. § 101.
4 *Stewart v. Abend*, 495 U.S. 207 (1990).
5 *Russell v. Price*, 612 F.2d 1123, 1128 (9th Cir. 1979).
6 17 U.S.C. § 204.
7 17 U.S.C. § 304(b). But note that works for which copyright expired before 1976 remain in the public domain. The rules for each piece of material may vary greatly, so it is vital that the copyright of an older work be reviewed before assuming that it is in the public domain.
8 *Russell v. Price*, 612 F.2d 1124.
9 17 U.S.C. § 102. The law lists eight categories of works subject to copyright protection: (1) literary works; (2) musical works, including any accompanying

words; (3) dramatic works, including accompanying music; (4) pantomimes and choreographic works; (5) pictorial, graphic, and sculptural works; (6) motion pictures and other audiovisual works; (7) sound recordings; and (8) architectural works.

10 US Copyright Office, "Copyright Basics" (circular 1, 2019), https://www.copyright .gov/circs/circ01.pdf.

11 17 U.S.C. § 102(b). ("In no case does copyright protection for an original work of authorship extend to any idea, procedure, process, system, method of operation, concept, principle, or discovery, regardless of the form in which it is described, explained, illustrated, or embodied in such work.")

12 *Restatement (Second) of Torts* § 559 (1977). Under California law, "libel is a false and unprivileged publication by writing . . . which exposes any person to hatred, contempt, ridicule, or obloquy, or which causes him to be shunned or avoided, or which has a tendency to injure him in his occupation." *Cal. Civ. Code* § 45 (West, 1999).

13 *New York Times Co. v. Sullivan*, 376 U.S. 254, 279–280 (1964).

14 *James v. San Jose Mercury News Inc.*, 17 Cal. App. 4th 1, 10 (App. 6th Dist. 1993), quoting *Mosesian v. McClatchy Newspapers*, 205 Cal. App. 3d 597, 608–609 (App. 5th Dist. 1988).

15 *Mosesian v. McClatchy Newspapers*, 233 Cal. App. 3d 1685 (1991).

16 *Gertz v. Robert Welch Inc.*, 418 U.S. 323, 344 (1974).

17 *Davis v. Costa-Gavras*, 654 F. Supp. 653, 655 (S.D.N.Y. 1987).

18 *Masson v. New Yorker Magazine*, 501 U.S. 496, 522 (1991).

19 *Springer v. Viking Press*, 90 A.D.2d 315, 457 N.Y.S.2d 246 (1st Dept. 1982), *aff'd*, 60 N.Y.S.2d 916, 470 N.Y.S.2d 579 (1983).

20 *Restatement (Second) of Torts* § 652E.

21 *Gertz v. Robert Welch Inc.*, 418 U.S. 323 (1974).

22 William Lloyd Prosser, *Handbook of the Law of Torts*, 4th ed. (Saint Paul, MN: West, 1971), 802–804. "The right to withdraw from the public gaze at such times as a person may see fit, when his presence in public is not demanded by any rule of law is also embraced within the right of personal liberty." *Pavesich v. New England Life Ins. Co.*, 122 Ga. 190, 196, 50 S.E. 68, 70 (1905).

23 *Restatement (Second) of Torts* § 625B. ("One who intentionally intrudes, physically or otherwise, upon the solitude or seclusion of another or his private affairs or concerns, is subject to liability to the other for invasion of his privacy, if the intrusion would be highly offensive to a reasonable person.")

24 *Price v. Hal Roach Studios Inc.*, 400 F. Supp. 836, 843 (S.D.N.Y. 1975).

25 Cal. Civ. Code § 3344 (2020).

26 *KNB Enters. v. Matthews*, 78 Cal. App. 4th 362, 368, 92 Cal. Rptr. 2d 713, 718 (2d Dist. 2000), holding use of models' photographs on subscription website constituted actionable violation of *Cal. Civ. Code* § 3344, not preempted by federal copyright laws.

6. Contracts

1 17 U.S.C. § 101 (2021).

2 US Copyright Office, "How to Investigate the Copyright Status of a Work," (circular 22, 2013), https://www.copyright.gov/circs/circ22.pdf.

3 *Id.*

7. Financing the Film Project

1 One specific breakdown is as follows: 20 percent paid weekly during preproduction; 60 percent paid weekly during principal photography; 10 percent paid upon delivery of the rough cut; and 10 percent paid upon delivery of the completed picture. Paul A. Baumgarten, Donald C. Farber, and Mark Fleischer, *Producing, Financing and Distributing Film*, 2nd ed. (Pompton Plains, NJ: Limelight, 1992).

2 *Report to the Commission: Regulation Crowdfunding*, Securities and Exchange Commission, June 18, 2019, available at https://www.crowdfundinsider.com /wp-content/uploads/2019/06/SEC-regulation-crowdfunding-2019_0.pdf.

3 "About the Charity Film Awards," Charity Film Awards official website, accessed January 17, 2021, https://charityfilmawards.com/about-the-charity-film-awards (site discontinued).

4 "Guidelines for Comprehensive Fiscal Sponsorship," National Network of Fiscal Sponsors, accessed April 2, 2021, https://www.fiscalsponsors.org/resources.

5 *Id.*

6 "Tax Credit Overview and Frequently Asked Questions," Ohio Film Office, accessed April 2, 2021, https://development.ohio.gov/filmoffice/Incentives.html.

7 "Topic No. 420 Bartering Income," IRS official website, accessed January 27, 2021, https://www.irs.gov/taxtopics/tc420.

8 Internal Revenue Code §§ 721(a), 707(a)(2).

9 Treasury Regulation § 1.721-1(b)(1); the income should be based on the value of the service at the time provided. *Revenue Procedure* 93-27, 1993-2 C.B. 343; providing nontax treatment for profit participation or partnerships.

10. The Investors' Package

1 *TSC Industries Inc. v. Northway Inc.*, 426 U.S. 438, 449 (1976); *Basic Inc. v. Levinson*, 108 S. Ct. 978 (1988).

2 Securities Act of 1933 § 4 (2), codified at 15 U.S.C. § 77d (2) (2020). *See* "Investor Bulletin: Private Placements Under Regulation D," SEC official website, accessed January 19, 2021, https://www.sec.gov/oiea/investor-alerts-bulletins/ib _privateplacements.html.

3 Securities Act of 1933 § 4 (2), codified at 15 U.S.C. § 77d (2) (2020).

4 Securities Act Regulation D, 17 C.F.R. § 230.501 (2020).

5 Securities Act Regulation D, 17 C.F.R. § 230.506 (2020).

6 17 C.F.R. § 229.105—(Item 105) Risk factors.

11. Assembling the Production Team

1 Annenberg Inclusion Initiative, "The Inclusion Rider: Legal Language for Ending Hollywood's Epidemic of Invisibility," accessed January 15, 2021, https:// annenberg.usc.edu/research/aii#inclusionrider.

2 Annenberg Inclusion Initiative, Inclusion Rider Template, March 2018, http:// assets.uscannenberg.org.s3.amazonaws.com/docs/inclusion-rider-template.pdf.

3 SAG-AFTRA, Moderate Low Budget Project Agreement (for Non-episodic Projects), accessed January 15, 2021, https://www.sagindie.org/media/MPA _SAMPLE2020.pdf.

4 SAG-AFTRA, "Code of Conduct on Sexual Harassment," 2018, https://www .sagaftra.org/files/sag-aftra_code_of_conduct_f2_2.pdf.

12. The Key Members of the Independent Film Company

1 Producers Guild of America, "Frequently Asked Questions," accessed January 15, 2021, https://www.producersguild.org/page/faq (page discontinued).

2 Directors Guild of America, Basic Agreement, 2017, https://www.dga.org /Contracts/Creative-Rights/Basic-Agreement-Article-7.aspx, § 7-101.

3 *Encyclopedia Britannica Online*, s.v. "acting," accessed January 15, 2021, https://www.britannica.com/art/acting.

4 Breakdown Services Ltd. official website, accessed January 15, 2021, https://www.breakdownservices.com/index.cfm.

5 SAGIndie, "Who Are We?," accessed January 15, 2021, https://www.sagindie.org /about/.

14. Shooting the Film

1 Paul R. La Monica, "A Mangled Hand, a 'Heroes' Suit, and NBC," CNN Money, October 17, 2006, https://money.cnn.com/2006/10/17/commentary/mediabiz/.

15. Special Considerations for Documentaries and Films Based on True Life Stories

1 *Diaz v. Oakland Tribune*, 139 Cal. App. 3d 118, 126 (1983).

2 *Shulman v. Group W Prod. Inc.*, 18 Cal.4th 200, 214–242 (1998).

3 Steven E. Helland, "The Standard Consent Agreement That Protects Sacha Baron Cohen," Fredrikson & Byron, July 20, 2018, https://www.fredlaw.com/internet _technology_trademark__advertising_alerts/2018/07/20/1940/the_standard _consent_agreement_that_protects_sacha_baron_cohen/.

4 Patricia Aufderheide, Peter Jaszi, and Mridu Chandra, *Honest Truths: Documentary Filmmakers on Ethical Challenges in Their Work*, Center for Media & Social Impact, September 2009, http://archive.cmsimpact.org/sites/default/files /Honest_Truths_--_Documentary_Filmmakers_on_Ethical_Challenges_in_Their _Work.pdf.

5 Patricia Aufderheide, "Honest Truths: Looking at a Groundbreaking Ethics Report, Five Years Later," April 15, 2015, https://www.documentary.org/feature /honest-truths-looking-groundbreaking-ethics-report-five-years-later.

6 Aufderheide, Jaszi, and Chandra, *Honest Truths*, http://archive.cmsimpact.org /sites/default/files/Honest_Truths_--_Documentary_Filmmakers_on_Ethical _Challenges_in_Their_Work.pdf.

7 *Id.*

8 Society for Professional Journalists, "Code of Ethics," September 6, 2014, https://www.spj.org/ethicscode.asp.

9 *Id.*

10 *Id.*

11 *Id.*

12 17 U.S.C. § 107 (2020).

13 *Id.*

14 Center for Media & Social Impact, *Documentary Filmmakers' Statement of Best Practices in Fair Use*, American University, November 18, 2005, https://cmsimpact .org/code/documentary-filmmakers-statement-of-best-practices-in-fair-use/.

15 Patricia Aufderheide, "Fair Use Put to Good Use: 'Documentary Filmmakers' Statement' Makes Decisive Impact," IDA official website, August 15, 2007, https://www.documentary.org/online-feature/fair-use-put-good-use-documentary -filmmakers-statement-makes-decisive-impact.

16 Internet Archive, "Universal Newsreels," accessed January 15, 2021, www
.archive.org/details/universal_newsreels.

17 Robert S. Boynton, "How to Make a Guerrilla Documentary," July 11, 2004, *New
York Times Magazine*, https://www.nytimes.com/2004/07/11/magazine/how-to
-make-a-guerrilla-documentary.html.

19. Theatrical Distribution

1 Academy of Motion Picture Arts and Sciences, "Rules & Eligibility," accessed
January 15, 2021, https://www.oscars.org/oscars/rules-eligibility.

2 Academy of Motion Picture Arts and Sciences, "Rule Two—Eligibility
Addendum," October 6, 2020, https://www.oscars.org/sites/oscars/files/rule-two
-eligibility-addendum.pdf.

3 *Id.*

20. Nontheatrical Distribution

1 Jen Yamato and Wendy Lee, "Netflix Turns to First-Time Filmmakers for an Edge
in Streaming Wars," *L.A. Times*, January 25, 2020.

2 Chris Lindahl, "Amazon Studios, Once an Indie Haven, Concludes That Films Are
Products," IndieWire, October 9, 2019, https://www.indiewire.com/2019
/10/amazon-studios-shift-focus-theatrical-film-release-streaming-subscribers
-1202180248/.

3 "Independent Lens: Submissions," PBS official website, accessed January 27,
2021, https://www.pbs.org/independentlens/about/submissions/.

21. Additional Considerations for Ultra-Low-Budget Projects

1 Jon M. Garon, *The Entrepreneur's Intellectual Property & Business Handbook*, 2nd.
ed. (Fort Lauderdale, FL: Manegiare Publications, 2018).

2 Daniel M. Satorius, "Other People's Money: Financing the Low Budget
Independent Feature Films with Private Equity Securities Offerings,"
Entertainment and Sports Lawyer 16:3 (Fall 1998).

About the Author

Jon M. Garon is professor of law and director of the Intellectual Property, Cybersecurity, and Technology Law Program at Nova Southeastern University Shepard Broad College of Law. He is a nationally recognized authority on technology law and intellectual property, particularly copyright law, entertainment, and information privacy. A tenured member of the law faculty, Professor Garon teaches Constitutional Law, Information Privacy Law, Cyberspace Law, Copyright Law, Entertainment Law, and related courses. He is the author of six books and more than 50 book chapters and academic articles, and he has presented at more than 200 programs across the United States. A Minnesota native, he received his bachelor's degree from the University of Minnesota in 1985 and his juris doctor degree from Columbia University School of Law in 1988.

Professor Garon served as dean for NSU's Shepard Broad College of Law from 2014 to 2020, providing strategic leadership on programming, curriculum, enrollment management, marketing, and finance. Prior to joining Nova Southeastern University in 2014, Garon was the inaugural director of the Northern Kentucky University Salmon P. Chase College of Law, Law + Informatics Institute from 2011 to 2014. The Law + Informatics Institute integrates specialized programming on technology and information systems as it applies across legal disciplines. He also served as dean and professor of law at Hamline University School of Law in St. Paul, Minnesota, and interim dean of the Graduate School of Management from 2005 to 2006.

Before Hamline, Professor Garon taught Entertainment Law and Copyright at Franklin Pierce Law Center in Concord, New Hampshire, and Western State University College of Law in Orange County, California.

His teaching and scholarship often focus on business innovation and structural change to media, education, and content-based industries. His other books include his debut novel *Burn Rate* (2019) and nonfiction works *The Entrepreneur's Intellectual Property & Business Handbook* (2nd ed., Manegiare Publications, 2018), *Pop Culture Business Handbook for Cons and Festivals* (Manegiare Publications, 2017), and *Entertainment Law & Practice* (3rd ed., Carolina Academic Press, 2020), *A Short and Happy Guide to Privacy and Cybersecurity Law* (West Academic, 2021), and *Law Professor's Desk Reference* (Carolina Academic Press, 2021).

Professor Garon's forthcoming books include *Parenting for the Digital Generation: The Parent's Guide to Digital Education and the Online Environment* (Rowman & Littlefield, 2021), *Intellectual Property Law and Practice: A Contemporary Approach* (West Academic, 2022), and a Chinese-language compilation of his works on entertainment law.

Professor Garon can be reached at Nova Southeastern University Shepard Broad College of Law at garon@nova.edu. He may also be contacted through his law firm, Gallagher, Callahan & Gartrell at (800) 528-1181 or garon@gcglaw.com. You can find more publications and learn more at IMDb, SSRN, and Amazon.com or at his website, http://garondigital.com.